Special Education in Ontario Schools

Special Education in Ontario Schools

SEVENTH EDITION

Sheila Bennett and Don Dworet
with Ken Weber

Highland Press

Published by
Highland Press
Box 496, St. Davids, ON L0S 1P0
Telephone (905) 685-5568
Fax (905) 685-4327
E-mail hldpress@cogeco.ca

Library and Archives Canada Cataloguing in Publication

Bennett, Sheila, 1961-
    Special education in Ontario schools / by Sheila Bennett,
Don Dworet ; with Ken Weber. -- 7th ed.

Includes indexes.
ISBN 978-0-9865873-1-3

    1. Special education--Ontario. I. Dworet, Don, 1950-
II. Weber, K. J. (Kenneth Jerome), 1940- III. Title.

LC3984.2.O5W42 2013   371.909713   C2012-906288-X

Design: Daniel Crack, Kinetics Design www.kdbooks.ca
Editor and Production Editor: Donald G. Bastian, Bastian Publishing Services Ltd.
Indexer: Monica Kanellis

Printed and bound in Canada by Webcom Inc.

1 2 3 4 5   17 16 15 14 13

This book is dedicated to the memory of Don Reilly,
a tireless advocate for students with special needs
throughout the province

Contents

Preface

CLASSROOM practices, administrative procedures, and Ontario government policies in special education are built on the ideal that it is possible to respond to the strengths and needs of every student with an exceptionality. Legislation in the province guarantees access to public education for all students regardless of their needs. Further, it assures that students with exceptionalities will have access to programs and resources to meet their special needs. Individual boards and schools are set up to deliver special education services and support, ranging from simple modification and/or accommodation of a student's program to allocation of complex specialized resources and even to changes in building design. Ministry regulations reinforce ideal professional practices such as the development and monitoring of Individual Education Plans (IEPs).

In recent years, educating students with exceptionalities has received almost as much attention as in 1980 when the province passed legislation requiring all boards to provide programs and services to students with exceptionalities. This more recent attention has led to increases in funding, greater emphasis on parental involvement, refinement of the IEP development process, publication of Ministry of Education Resource documents focusing on inclusion of students with exceptionalities in the regular classroom, and attention to helping students with exceptionalities complete their secondary school graduation requirements. Educators in this relatively new century are not questioning whether students with exceptionalities should be in their classrooms but rather how they may be taught most effectively. This seventh edition of *Special Education in Ontario Schools* continues to emphasize that what is of most importance is not where a student receives a program but that the student receives the best programming possible. The focus for teachers should no longer be on "fixing students" but rather and more importantly on changing instruction in the regular classroom to meet the needs of all students.

On the front lines, so to speak, classroom teachers and educational assistants draw on training in special education, and on their own resources and talents and creativity, to bring everything together for students with special strengths and needs. Ontario educators have long been recognized – not just in their own province, but elsewhere, as well, for their leadership and commitment in matters relating to students with exceptionalities. These qualities are a major reason that special education has been implemented so successfully as a fully functional and vital element in the province's broader system.

Like all systems put together by human beings, special education in Ontario reveals occasional faults. But the system is dynamic. It responds to evolving needs and philosophies; it develops; it adapts; and most of the time it improves. In any case, special education will only be as effective as the people at every level who make it work. Ultimately, special education can succeed as a concept, as a principle, and most importantly as a practice only through the actions of professionals who are committed to the belief that every student has a right to the best that schooling can offer. Ironically, the ideal of special education is to put itself out of business. The goal for which it strives is a system of education in which adaptation and accommodation to meet the needs of every student is automatic, and in which the very idea of special education is unnecessary.

~

We the authors of *Special Education in Ontario Schools* are grateful for advice, assistance, and support on the part of many caring professionals in special education.

Thanks are due particularly to Barry Finlay and his colleagues at the Special Education Policy and Program Branch, Ontario Ministry of Education, as well as Kathryn Archambeault, Marion Bennett, Peggy Blair, Diane Book, Alexandra Dunn, Cheryl Duquette, Jenessa Dworet, Les Galambos, Mary Harrison, Debbie Hayne, Randy Hill, Andrea Jack, Heather MacKenzie, Kimberly Maich, Robert Maich, Tania Mason, Cheryl Missiuna, Susie Palumbo, Laura Reece, Kelly Anne Russell, Tracy Sacco, Rebecca Shultis, Heather Snider, and Elizabeth Starr.

Special Education: Then and Now

DECEMBER 12, 1980, was a landmark day in the history of education in Ontario. On this date, Lieutenant-Governor John Black Aird signed Bill 82, the *Education Amendment Act*, into law. This act dramatically changed how students with exceptionalities would be educated by Ontario's publicly funded school system. With the signing of this document, it was no longer optional for boards of education to accept students with special needs into their schools. Rather, school boards would now be required to provide education to all students regardless of any disability they may have. Disability would no longer be a barrier to entering or participating in the regular school system.

Within a very short time, special education became an integral part of Ontario's system. It did so with such relative ease, it is tempting to believe that Bill 82 was a law just waiting to be passed. Yet the long journey to special education as it is today was anything but simple and smooth. This chapter outlines a few of the bumps.

Dateline 1957 – The Case of Ruthie

IT was not until she was almost eight years old that Ruthie began attending school. To begin with, her parents knew she was, in her father's words, "something behind the other young ones." Then there was the long walk down the concession and across the side road to the one-room school. She'd have to do this walk alone, and everybody knew Ruthie had a habit of wandering off.

Even at age eight, Ruthie's future as a student was uncertain at best.

"We don't have to take this child in if you don't want," the chairman of S.S. #12 School Board had said to the brand new teacher in August. "It's going to be hard enough in your first year without having a retarded child to look after. The regulations are clear. We don't have to take her. It's up to you."

But the teacher welcomed Ruthie and made her feel part of the tiny student body at S.S. #12. Two girls in grade 8 took her outside to the toilet every day just before recess and noon hour. One of the older boys built her an extended desktop so she could more easily enjoy her favourite activity: colouring on the back of discarded rolls of wallpaper. The younger children, a bit perplexed at first because Ruthie didn't speak, soon learned to ignore her strange noises. And every day after lunch, Ruthie crawled happily onto the teacher's lap to hear the next installment of "the afternoon story."

By the end of the school year, Ruthie could recognize her own name in print, understand and follow routines, and count up to ten – and most importantly, in the teacher's view, she no longer wandered away.

She might have shown even more development the next year, but Ruthie got caught in a swirl of events that even her parents couldn't quite follow. S.S. #12 was closed in June, along with all the other one-room schools in the township. Students were now to be bused to a brand new central school. Ruthie's teacher got married that summer and moved to the other end of the province. At "Central," the school inspector told the staff in primary/junior that no one was obligated to take Ruthie, but if anyone volunteered, she could be admitted.

There were no takers. Ruthie never went to school again.

Note: In this chapter and throughout this book, the term "parent" represents parents, guardians, and appropriate caregivers.

Long Ago and Far Away

Just Survival

Until relatively recent times, society's concern for people with special needs was minimal. Even the Greek and Roman cultures, which we generally view as enlightened and sophisticated, did not treat people with disabilities very well. In Athens, under Solon's law, for example, children with disabilities were placed in clay vessels and abandoned. In Rome, children with disabilities were customarily thrown into the Tiber River. And it was not unusual for wealthy families to keep a person who was mentally handicapped for entertainment. No less a personage than the moralist philosopher Seneca reported that his wife kept a "feeble-minded dwarf," ostensibly for that purpose. Even Aristotle, whose writings dominated Western thought for more than a thousand years after his death, described people who were deaf as "incapable of reason, no better than the animals of the forest," and "unteachable."

There were some exceptions to this almost universal attitude. The Talmud offered enlightened instructions regarding people who are blind and deaf, and Hippocrates' investigations into epilepsy and intellectual disability suggested that scientific curiosity about special needs was not entirely absent. However, the impact of these exceptions was very limited.

In the Middle Ages, there were a few bright spots. Saint Nicholas Thaumaturgos, fourth-century bishop of Myra in Lycia (now Turkey), became known as a protector of people who were feeble-minded, but there is little evidence to show what he accomplished. (Saint Nicholas was also the patron saint of sailors and pawnbrokers and the prototype of Santa Claus!) Some monks and other clergy established hospices. However, the superstitions of the day, along with a powerful belief in demonic possession and the sheer demands of mere survival, meant that persons with disabilities were very much on their own.

A few strides were made in Europe in the post-Renaissance era, but they, too, were isolated, short-lived bursts of change: the accomplishments of individuals with will and drive rather than the product of a general amelioration in attitude. When these individuals died, the fruits of their efforts died with them. For example, there is the case of Ponce de Leon (1529–c. 1582), the Spanish monk who taught deaf children to speak and read (often confused with the explorer who visited Florida in 1513). De Leon's methods were apparently very successful, but these techniques are lost and unknown to us largely because there was no general impetus after his death to continue their use.

> "Every child has a claim on the community for the best means of moral and mental cultivation."
> – Harvey Peet, President, New York Institution for the Deaf and Dumb, 1855

Attitudes Begin to Change

Louis Braille (1809–1852) had more lasting success with an alphabet for people who are blind, which he adapted from a cipher system invented by Napoleon Bonaparte's staff. By Braille's time, attitudes had also begun to shift. British philosopher John Locke (1632–1704) had impressed intellectuals in the Western world with his philosophy of "sensationalism," which, among other things, took issue with the long-held view that children are born with innate characteristics imprinted by God, nature, or the devil. Instead, Locke argued, newborns are a tabula rasa, a blank slate waiting to be written upon. Ever so slowly, this idea, given further impetus by writers such as Voltaire, Rousseau, and Goethe, began to chip away at the notion that people with disabilities are the unfortunate product of some Great Plan and therefore should be left alone.

Still, the march toward enlightenment was slow, and innovation was actively discouraged. Jean Marc Itard (1775–1838), who discovered and tried to teach Victor, the wild boy of Aveyron, and Sir Frederick Treves (1853–1923), who rescued John Merrick, better known as the Elephant Man, are among the best recognized of those who broke new ground, but their humanism was too radical for their contemporaries. Inertia, or a general indifference to people with disabilities, was evident well into the mid-twentieth century, particularly in carnival shows, which continued to exhibit physically unique persons like Merrick.

Canada Moves Forward

Though strongly resisted in the United States, there was some progress in education for people who were deaf and/or blind in Canada. In 1831, in Champlain, Québec, Ronald Mcdonald, a former priest, opened a school for people who were deaf, which became Canada's first formal special education project. Similar schools opened in Halifax (1856), Toronto (1858), and Winnipeg (1884). A school for people who were blind opened in Toronto in 1872, and another opened in Halifax a year later. In Ontario, the vigorous work of John Barrett McCann brought about the founding of two residential schools: the Ontario Institution for the Education and Instruction of the Deaf and Dumb, at Belleville, in 1870, and the Ontario Institution for the Education and Instruction of the Blind, at Brantford, in 1872. These schools were followed soon after by the first Canadian residential institution for people who were developmentally disabled, which opened in Orillia in 1876.

These institutions reflected a growing sense of social responsibility in the general population, as well as a developing interest in people with special needs. Although some of the teaching methods used in the institutions seem odd today, and although the language and terminology would make contemporary educators wince, the mere existence of residential schools for people with special needs was a striking development for the time, especially in light of the fact that educating the so-called normal population was still far from universal.

Dateline 1965 – The Case of Leo

No one was more exasperated by Leo's lack of language skills than his mother. A former teacher, she had sent his two older sisters off to grade 1 so well prepared that they both skipped a grade. Not Leo. To be sure, he appeared to be just as bright. Certainly he was charming – so what if he had a few odd speech patterns? That was nothing unusual in a youngster. Yet no matter what she did, Leo's mother just could not teach him to recognize letters.

Not that she pushed him to frustration. She was too wise and experienced a mother and teacher for that. But she'd never seen anything quite like this. Take the letter "A," for example. Leo would willingly trace it, colour it, find all examples of the letter hidden about the kitchen, and sing the "A" song. Yet, though he would then recognize the letter without a prompt for maybe two or three days, after a week on "B" and "C," the letter "A" would be gone. And it would be really gone! That was part of the exasperation. Reintroducing "A" to Leo was not a simple matter of stimulating recall. It was as though he'd never ever seen it before.

Of course, Leo's printing was disastrous, and it didn't improve as he got older. At the end of grade 1, Leo's principal boldly left the "Printing" mark blank on Leo's report card so he could pass into grade 2. But the problem was still there. So was his letter recognition problem and lack of progress in learning to read. Leo's mom's friends tried to console her with the explanation that boys are almost always slower, but Leo just didn't get any better. Nobody could come up with an explanation, although the grade 4 teacher had seen another boy like Leo once before, who had become a real problem because no one seemed able to do anything for him.

Still, the situation was not all bad. As long as Leo was given only one instruction at a time, he worked hard and reliably. Leo's father had him help out on Saturdays at his successful plumbing business. Indeed, it may have been the plumbing business that provided an out for everyone, because by grade 5, Leo's behaviour was changing. He still found reading and writing torture. He had already repeated two grades, and was facing failure again. In grade 5, Leo was no longer getting headaches and stomach pains during language arts, but he was acting out in progressively alarming ways. That was the main reason that Leo's mother reluctantly agreed to an arrangement for him to leave school to work for his dad. Even so, one of her worst fears came true some years later. When Leo's dad retired, he had to sell the business. Even though Leo was willing and handy, he had not learned to read and write well enough to run things.

Some Help but Much More Needed

Despite the operation of the schools mentioned above, much more needed to be done. Due to a combination of economics, geography, and limited concern, comparatively few children with special needs were served, relative to the number of people with disabilities in the population who needed assistance. Resources were aimed at the most overt and visibly obvious exceptionalities. In addition, the curricula for these students were strongly biased toward industrial training. The idea was, in the words of a contemporary, "to make something of the students" so they might find gainful employment. To be fair, that mission very much followed the wishes of the students' own parents and families, who felt that this approach at least offered these students some hope of independence.

Not even this much support was held out to students with exceptionalities whose needs were less obvious and who consequently were harder to understand or even to acknowledge. As a result, students with a learning disability (the term did not even exist until 1963), or those with what we see today as behavioural problems, usually were early dropouts. Right through to the final quarter of the twentieth century, dropouts were regarded – and saw themselves – as poor educational material. Industry absorbed these students into fairly low-level assembly-line employment and reinforced these perceptions.

Even established schools that were designed to serve students with special needs were not always secure, especially if their faculties attempted to be innovative. The Ontario School for Crippled Children (now part of Bloorview MacMillan Children's Rehabilitation Centre in Toronto) had quickly established an international reputation for its programs. As early as 1890, faculty at the Orillia institution had developed advanced school programs for its clientele. Yet both schools had to struggle to keep their programs going in the face of widespread criticism. Students with profound needs were often seen as poor candidates for education, on the premise that educating them served little purpose and offered only a minimal return to society. In light of that hypothesis, it is ironic that societal benefit apparently played no role at all in discussions of special education for students who were especially able. Public education for gifted students was almost unheard of until the 1970s.

Acceptance of Responsibility

For many years before the end of the Second World War, proponents of a philosophy called eugenics believed that society should be protected from genetic contamination by placing "unfortunates" in institutions. In 1918, a coalition of medical doctors, social workers, and influential citizens had formed the Canadian National Committee on Mental Hygiene to pressure the government to expand custodial facilities for people who were feeble-minded and whose spread was the result, in the committee's opinion, of "procreation by unsound stock, the numbers of which were being accelerated by the government's admittance to the Dominion, of degenerate immigrants" [sic].

Framed as a concern for the public good and a seemingly well-intentioned concern for the less able, supporters of eugenics were successful in effecting a policy that not only segregated people with special needs, but also, in practical terms, isolated them.

> "Individuals with disabilities should be served whenever possible in general education classrooms in inclusive neighbourhood schools and community settings."
> – Council for Exceptional Children, 1993

Dateline 1979 – The Case of Peter

ITEM number five on the agenda at the county school board meeting appeared innocuous enough. It read:

Approval of funds to install elevator, renovate main entrance, washroom, fire exits and classroom doorways as outlined in Report 995A.

To Pete and his family, and to three other families with sons and daughters who had severe physical disabilities, item number five was full of implications. Pete had muscular dystrophy. Over his years in elementary school, the condition had developed to a point where he could no longer walk for more than a few metres without risking a serious fall. The walking itself was accomplished with the help of crutches, which Pete used in alternating wide swings. He was spending longer and longer periods in a wheelchair and now required some assistance when using the washroom.

In a few months, Pete would be eligible to attend the secondary school in his community. But he would not be able to get around in this old building, much less get in or out of it, unless some major structural changes were made. In addition, some kind of arrangement would have to be developed to meet his personal hygiene needs. Nothing in either education or civil law obligated the board to do these things, but because Pete and his family were well known and active in their relatively small community, the local trustees agreed to consider the matter.

The motion was defeated, but so narrowly that Pete's family was encouraged to press for another possibility. Since 1974, Ontario's *Education Act* had permitted school boards to provide special education services if they chose to, and by now, some boards in the province were doing that. Some schools had been renovated to accommodate students with physical disabilities. Pete's family, supported by an advocacy group, began urging the local board to arrange for, and bear the cost of, Pete's enrolment at one of these.

The trustees listened carefully and sympathetically, but they approached the proposal cautiously because there were a number of students in a situation similar to Pete's. So cautiously, as it turned out, that the motion kept being tabled. Pete's parents, wary of the outcome, reluctantly sold their home, moved out of the community, and relocated to another part of the province near a school that had been modified for students with special needs like their son's.

However, by the end of the Second World War, what began as a trickle of doubt about eugenics became a flood, largely because of the role of eugenics in Fascism. In the 1960s, the swell of concern for the individual rights of all persons led governments to enshrine these rights in law. Ontario, for example, established its first Human Rights Commission in 1962. By the end of the decade, any notion of racial or cultural superiority, or indeed any kind of exclusive human purity, was anathema. Western culture was ready to consider that every human being has worth.

An Era of Positive Change

In Ontario, special education as we know it today came of age over the past sixty years. As early as 1950, the Hope Commission recommended expansion of special education programs; the point at which the march to Bill 82 got underway, however, was in the 1960s, a decade in which episodic, disconnected attempts to somehow improve the lot of students with exceptionalities shifted to a goal-directed, coherent movement aimed at educating children with special needs according to those needs.

The change occurred around this time for a number of reasons. Throughout the 1960s, the civil rights movement in the United States maintained that all people, regardless of race, creed, or colour, should be treated equally. This mantra was taken up by advocates for people with special needs, who argued successfully that physical, emotional, or cognitive disabilities should not, in themselves, be a barrier to equal treatment. In 1975, the Congress of the United States passed the *Education for All Handicapped Children Act*, Public Law 94-142, which mandated that all students be provided a publicly supported education in the "least restrictive environment." Under this law, children with exceptionalities were given the right to a free and appropriate education, and their parents were given the right to due process and confidentiality. Boards of education were also mandated to provide a range of educational services and were required to provide an individual education plan for each child deemed exceptional (Winzer, 2008).

The Normalization Principle Comes to Canada

Separation of children by ability was still prominent well into the middle of the twentieth century, but by the time Ontario enacted Bill 82, in 1980, the notion was succumbing to the principle of *normalization* developed in Scandinavia by Bengt Nirje and championed in Canada by Wolf Wolfensberger.

In essence, proponents of normalization argue against iinstitutionalization. They contend that persons with special needs should be viewed more for their similarities, not their dissimilarities, to others. In this view, once persons with exceptionalities are integrated into mainstream society, they will take on the behaviours of the norm because they will have had more normal models to follow.

This concept, which suggests unlimited growth and improvement instead of ceilings and limitations, struck a powerful chord, not just in Ontario, but also throughout North America. In only about twenty years, government policies across the U.S. and Canada changed from building and expanding care-based facilities to employing strategies that prompted the closing of these centres and the integration of their residents into the larger community.

Dateline 1989 – The Case of Justin

A flurry of October transfers meant that Justin's grade 3 class acquired a new teacher only a week before his situation was scheduled for special review by an Identification, Placement, and Review Committee (IPRC). The new teacher wisely allowed the full-time educational assistant in grade 3 to work with the school's resource teacher in putting together documentation for Justin's IPRC. The assistant was experienced and held in high regard in the school, and she had worked with Justin for the past two years. More importantly, she was one of the few adults who could understand Justin and manage his behaviour effectively.

Over the past several years, Justin had been variously diagnosed as autistic, AD/HD, learning disabled, cerebrally dysfunctional, and mentally disabled by a variety of clinical psychologists, some of them in private practice and others employed by the school board. While Justin was still in kindergarten, an IPRC took the unusual step, for a student so young, of identifying him as "exceptional: behavioural." Justin's mother signed on to the identification, but only because it would allow the school to bring in extra resources: She served notice that she would appeal any move to take her son out of a regular class, a position that she maintained through reviews in grades 1 and 2 in the face of growing evidence that a regular class environment was not working as it should for him.

The special review in grade 3 was arranged by the principal, who, for everyone's sake, was making one more stab at modifying Justin's class placement. She planned, if that failed, to initiate a rarely used process that could declare him "hard-to-serve" and thereby exclude him from the school. Fortunately, everyone, including the boy's mother, agreed to an adjustment. Justin would begin each day in the grade 3 class and then, with the assistant, join a small resource class. He would, depending on his mood and behaviour, return to the regular class as frequently as possible and for as long as possible. Above all, it was agreed that flexibility would prevail and that both the assistant and the teachers would be free to make ad hoc decisions as necessary.

For Justin – and everyone else involved – the long-term outcome was positive. He spent increasingly more time in the regular grade 3 class, but there was always a friendly, secure home base to go to if the need arose. Perhaps most telling: The annual IPRC review in grade 4 lasted only ten minutes.

Decisions in the Hands of Educators

Before the 1960s, the predominant approach to providing services for students with exceptionalities was a medical one that focused on what was wrong with the student. Educators in the 1960s, and even more so in the 1970s, began to replace this popular view with a wider, more ecological view that incorporated the whole person. The ecological perspective examines the relationship between the child and the learning environment (including personnel, resources, and materials) to allow the child to learn successfully.

At the same time, teachers and paraprofessionals also began to recognize their own strengths and the potential of their own contributions to the education of a student with exceptionalities. Using the medical model, teachers or educational assistants are expected to defer to some greater, outside expertise; using the ecological focus, in contrast, they are encouraged to exercise their considerable intuition, knowledge, and experience. As a result, students with special needs are seen as people who can be educated, not as people who should be in custody, or medical cases for whom intellectual development and learning are secondary to coping with a handicap.

Perhaps more important, ultimately, is this perspective's effect on the way special education

service is delivered. In the medical model, expertise is visited upon the classroom from above and afar. In the ecological model, which requires empiricism, hypothesis, flexibility, and constant program modification, decision-making and the delivery of services are seen to be much more current, not to mention appropriate, by happening on-site. By the time the *Education Amendment Act* was only a decade old, therefore, the trend in Ontario was toward educating students with special needs in the local community school – specifically, in the regular classroom.

Political Advocacy Becomes Prominent

The protest movements of the 1960s were successful not only in improving the social and legal situation for visible minorities, but also in alerting the parents of students with exceptionalities that they could achieve more for their sons and daughters by acting collectively rather than alone. Political activism by parents and other advocacy groups began to have, and continues to have, a powerful effect on governments. The strength and sophistication of lobbying efforts by the Learning Disabilities Association, the Association for Bright Children, and the Association for Community Living, among many others, have been instrumental for decades now in motivating educational jurisdictions to improve the lot of students with exceptionalities. In fact, many participants in the process that eventually gave birth to mandatory legislation in Ontario acknowledge quite candidly that without the activity of advocates, the legislation may not have come about as soon as it did. As an important result of this powerful advocacy, it became accepted – indeed, *required* – practice to involve parents or their representatives in any educational decision-making involving their child.

Bill 82: Major Changes to Ontario's *Education Act*

In December 1980, five years after the passage of U.S. Public Law 94-142, and after Nova Scotia and Saskatchewan had passed similar legislation, the legislature of Ontario passed Bill 82, the *Education Amendment Act*. Once this act was passed, special education became a normal, functioning part of Ontario's education system with remarkable speed. Some teachers still active today can point to a time, before 1980, when the idea of sending students with special needs to a regular school was not even considered by most jurisdictions in the province. Yet by just ten years after 1980, special education was as integral to the system as notebooks and chalk.

Although the legislation itself is extensive, the elements most immediately affecting students and their families, teachers, schools, and boards are these:

- All students resident in the province of Ontario are entitled to a publicly supported education. Every school board in the province is required to provide special education programs and services for students with exceptionalities. If a board cannot provide programs and services, it must pay another board to do so.
- School boards are to establish Identification, Placement, and Review Committees (IPRCs), the chief function of which is to identify whether a student is exceptional and then decide on a placement for him or her. (For more on the IPRC, see chapter 5.)
- Parents of a student with an exceptionality

are to be included in the IPRC process. An appeal process is available if the parents are dissatisfied with identification or placement decisions.
- Every school board is required to establish a Special Education Advisory Committee (SEAC) to advise on matters of special education programs and services.
- A comprehensive special education plan must be developed and maintained by each school board. In this plan, programs and services are outlined for public and Ministry examination. The "Plan" is to be updated and amended as necessary to meet the current needs of exceptional pupils. Currently, discussions are underway to include the special education plan not as a separate document but as a part of the overall school board plan.
- School boards are required to implement procedures for early and ongoing identification of students' learning abilities and needs.

> *"School boards must be held accountable for the academic achievement of all students and for reporting that achievement to parents."*
> – Bennett & Wynne, 2006,
> *Special Education Transformation*

Implementation Occurs

At the Board Office

Even critics of the Ontario legislation agree that the expectations it raised were met, for the most part, in the years that immediately ensued. When the bill was passed, in 1980, the province's school boards were given five years to establish their plans and systems. Yet in the majority of boards, special education policies and practices were fully operational well before the deadline.

More subtle, but certainly crucial to rapid implementation, was the relative ease with which special education became a natural feature in every school board. And it came about in the face of major challenges. Before the legislation, for example, separate school boards did not provide programs and services for what were called, in 1980, "trainable retarded pupils," and thus most of them had to build services from scratch in a very short time. Many smaller school boards, both public and separate, had to develop special education systems with little or no existing base on which to build. Even boards that already had some services before 1980 did not offer the comprehensive systems that could be found almost anywhere in the province only five years later.

All boards have now established offices of special education with a staff to provide consultative and administrative assistance to schools and teachers to help ensure that students with special needs receive appropriate programs and services in whatever classroom they may be placed.

In the Classroom

Still another challenge was finding front-line staff to make the systems work on a daily basis. In 1980, very few teachers in the province undertook special education as a career path. Yet the combination of teachers' inherent skills and readiness to learn on the job and a mass professional development drive by the Ministry and of the province's universities soon caused this vital component to be addressed. Within a decade, provincial authorities were able to point to a large cadre of teachers clearly committed to the field. Today, over *thirty* years after the passage of Bill 82, most, if not all, Ontario teachers willingly accept students with exceptionalities into their classrooms.

Equally urgent was the need for resource and support personnel, especially educational assistants, whose role soon took on even more importance as schools began to deal with a variety of special needs never before encountered in schools. Ontario's colleges were quick to show leadership, developing effective education programs for paraprofessionals; this paid immediate dividends: The graduates quickly proved their value in classrooms. It is important to note that, in spite of some recent progress, teacher education in special education at the preservice level continues to struggle with preparing educators to meet the complexity of today's classrooms.

It is encouraging to note that, in 2012, the Ontario Ministry announced its support for an extended Teacher Education program, recommending that the amount of time for educating future teachers be extended by up to one year. The level of diversity in classrooms is greater than ever before; educators need to have a thorough understanding of assessment and intervention strategies for a wide range of students with varying educational, social, intellectual, physical, and developmental needs.

Special Education Plan

Under Regulation 306, each board of education must establish and maintain a master plan setting out the programs and services it will provide. The plan must be reviewed yearly, and every two years the board must prepare a report for the Ministry of Education. In 2000, the Ministry issued a policy document setting standards for these plans.

At Home and School

Parents can play a crucial role in educating children with exceptionalities, one that is qualitatively and quantitatively different from the one generally required in supporting the education of other children. The idea of parent support for education was hardly a novel one in 1980, but the manner and extent of parental involvement that grew as a result of special education had never been seen before. A few senior administrators found the experience more challenging than they were used to, but for the most part, the outcomes proved to be positive.

Since the passage of Bill 82, the amount of parental participation required in the development of the educational program offered to a student with exceptionalities has gradually increased. Currently, Individual Education Plan (IEP) forms ask parents to indicate that they were involved in the plan's development and to sign off on it. (For more on IEPs, see chapter 5.)

Given that, in grade 2, Onisa regularly brought clippings from the *Globe and Mail* and the *Economist* to show-and-tell, no one in her school was the least bit surprised when, in grade 6, she won a UN-sponsored trip to Geneva, Switzerland, for her essay on the meaning of democracy. Still, during the promotion and placement meetings that were held at the end of the school year, Onisa's regular grade 6 teacher and her "Challenge Program" teacher were uneasy.

Onisa had been identified as "gifted" for some time, and her academic achievements were remarkable, especially during her earlier years at the school. But a standardized achievement test administered just before the end of the year in grade 6 hinted at somewhat more modest abilities. Onisa was still clearly in the superior range, but if the language and general awareness categories were factored out, so only her results in math/science remained, she was actually below the mean for her class. Both of Onisa's teachers were intrigued that this confirmed an unevenness that they had noticed: a contrast between what appeared to be giftedness in language and her quite ordinary ability in math and science.

This presented a dilemma for the teachers, because in their board all students left for new schools after grade 6. For Onisa to continue in the Challenge Program and be able to develop her unique abilities, her identification as gifted would need to be confirmed by the annual IPRC review. However, whereas the Challenge Program from grades 1 to 6 was an individualized, in-the-regular-class, enrichment offering, from grade 7 on, students identified as "gifted" were generally placed in self-contained classes* for an across-the-board enhanced curriculum (including advanced-level math and science).

Happily, the school board's resources and the professionalism of its staff were brought to bear on Onisa's behalf. The head of the gifted program was aware of several other students with a similar math/science versus language imbalance, students who shared Onisa's interests. Accordingly, Onisa and these students were recommended for the same grade 7 class. The class was in a school designated for the specially enhanced curriculum. The educators involved made sure that Onisa and her peers retained their identification so arrangements could be made with a minimum of fuss, if, in the future, it appeared that any of them would be better off with the enhanced curriculum.

In fact, after six months in her new school, Onisa declined to make the switch when it was offered (although one of her peers accepted). After twelve months had passed, she was eligible once again to compete in the UN essay contest. This time her first step in the process was to write and request an appointment with the federal Minister for External Affairs.

---

* At one time, both special educators and advocates freely used "segregated class" (and sometimes "dedicated class") for the special, separated classes created for students with exceptionalities, but the euphemism "self-contained" was soon used in Ministry documents.

Outstanding Issues

The Role of Parents

After many years of establishing the IPRC process, many boards of education found it more effective to work closely with parents in the development of their child's program as soon as concerns for the child's progress were identified. Boards found that these co-operative efforts diminished the need for IPRCs. Though regulatory requirements, such as the appeal process, are still in place, many boards, as a result of the co-operation of parents and professionals in the development of the Individual Education Plan (IEP Resource document, 2004), found IPRCs to be *unnecessary*. Though still in place in a large number of boards, the child's educational program is not dependent on IPRC decisions. It is important to note, however, that a parent cannot appeal an identification and/or placement unless that decision was made by an IPRC. Under the legislation, parents can request an IPRC be held to discuss their child's needs at any time.

In addition to the personal role of parents in their child's program, the Ministry of Education also reinforced the parents' role by first establishing, then strengthening, the Special Education Advisory Committees (SEACs).

SEACs

Every Ontario school board is required to establish a Special Education Advisory Committee, usually with membership taken principally from various parent associations in the community. These groups play a key role in educating the public about special education in general. They have input into decisions about special education finances. They are strongly involved in all aspects of the Special Education Plan, and often are an effective liaison between parents and board in potentially difficult situations.

Some boards in the province were already working with parent and advocacy groups as a matter of course before these committees were officially set up. Still, the fact that this very important role was enshrined in provincial policy suggests that parental involvement is conceived as beneficial in many ways.

In 1997, the Ministry of Education reissued its regulation governing SEACs, Reg. 464,* further strengthening parents' role. In 2003–2004, the Ministry established information and training programs for SEAC members.

---

* The Ministry of Education periodically issues regulations that, essentially, have the force of legislation. These are given a number, with the year of issue following. The regulation dealing with SEACs, for example, is O.Reg.464/97. The Ministry also issues Policy/Program Memoranda that are more explanatory than regulatory but are still considered to have administrative authority. PPM 89/90, for example, describes the role and workings of the province's residential demonstration schools for students with learning disabilities.

The Role of Educational Assistants

With the increasing population of students with exceptionalities came the need for more educational assistants (EAs) in both regular and self-contained classrooms. The Ministry of Education suggested in the Individual Education Plan Resource Document (2004) that the EA's role is to assist the teacher by helping students with their learning activities, monitoring and recording their achievements in these activities, and assisting with providing appropriate activities as described in the IEP. Though principals and teachers have some discretion in how EAs will be used, the IEP document offers some guidelines to the role that EAs can provide in the delivery of educational programs and services to students with exceptionalities.

The Appeal Process

Parents dissatisfied with an IPRC decision can take their case first to an appeal board and then, if matters are unresolved at this level, to a special education tribunal. (As of January 2011, the tribunal became part of Social Justice Tribunals Ontario.) Concerns about the fairness of appeal boards (put together on an ad hoc basis for each appeal) were raised on the premise that the boards were weighted in favour of the school board. Indeed, some school boards did not help matters by frequently appointing representatives who might be seen to lack objectivity. Although an early 1990s study of appeal board hearings showed that the process gives parents a fair and effective hearing, the province subsequently modified this stage of the process to minimize perceptions of unfairness by giving parents a greater voice in choosing members of the appeal board. Parents choose one member of the board (out of three) and participate in choosing the chair.

The tribunal stage, too, weathered a rigorous examination in the 1990s in a legal action that ended up in the Supreme Court of Canada. (See the Eaton Case, pages 12–13.)

The Move to Inclusion

At first it was fairly standard practice, in most jurisdictions, to place students with exceptionalities in self-contained classes according to their particular needs. Sometimes these students were placed in these classes in a school in their neighbourhood; more often, they were placed in schools quite a distance from their home. This service delivery approach of putting students with special needs in self-contained classes within schools was considered not only normal but also beneficial for all concerned. Enrolling students with exceptionalities in their neighbourhood schools was generally known as "mainstreaming" or "integration." This movement toward integration was also influenced by the concept of "least restrictive environment." This term was drawn from U.S. legislation requiring multidisciplinary teams to place students with special needs in an environment as close to a regular classroom in a regular school as possible.

In only a very short time, however, the special education agenda was effectively overwhelmed by pressure from some parents and professionals to place students with exceptionalities in regular classes full time. These parents and professionals pointed out, with the support of powerful empirical evidence, that in many, if not most, cases of mainstreaming, schools hosted two parallel groups, a regular one, and one with students with special needs alongside it looking to get in. Students with exceptionalities were in the school but not really of it.

In response, the Regular Education Initiative emerged in the mid-1980s. This initiative was a metaphor more than a strategy, but one that had considerable impact, supporting a shift in the educational mindset from the subtle parallelism of mainstreaming to a fuller, more natural integration of students with special needs into the school system.

The next, almost simultaneous, step was advocacy in favour of "inclusion" or "inclusionary schooling." In many ways, this approach was also just a shift in vocabulary, but it put even more emphasis on the principle of automatically placing students with exceptionalities in the classrooms that they would normally attend if they did not have a special need. Inclusionary schooling is now the predominant Ontario model of service delivery; it is expected that all students with special needs will be accepted into, and will benefit from, regular classroom placement.

In tandem with the pressure for full inclusion was the shadow cast by legal concerns: whether a school board's decision to place a student in a separate, special class was a violation of his or her equality rights under the *Canadian Charter of Rights and Freedoms*. The 1997 Supreme Court of Canada decision in *Eaton v. Brant County Board of Education* did much to put this issue to rest.

Eaton v. Brant County Board of Education

In 1994, an IPRC review determined that experience and common sense made it clear that, after three years in a regular class, the subject child, an eleven-year-old with extensive special needs, was not benefitting from inclusion and her interests would be best served in a special class. The parents first appealed this decision to the civil court, which directed the situation back to the appeal process established by provincial legislation. The IPRC was then upheld by an appeal board and subsequently by a tribunal. The tribunal decision, in turn, was upheld by a judicial review, but then was overturned by the Ontario Court of Appeal, which held that a placement without consent is discriminatory under Section 15 of the *Charter*.

The Ontario Court's position was emphatically rejected by the Supreme Court of Canada, in a 9–0 ruling. The original decision was restored, making it clear that there is no *Charter* presumption in favour of inclusion. The Supreme Court's decision also had the effect of affirming Ontario's special education legislation. In its written judgment, which quoted large parts of the tribunal decision, the High Court reinforced the notion that placement of children with special needs should be decided on a case-by-case basis, with the principal determinant being the child's best interests. This outcome did much to diminish the litigiousness that had been growing in connection with special education legislation; it also had the effect of motivating parties on all sides to search for compromise and for "on-the-ground" solutions to the needs of exceptional students. This willingness to compromise has led to a greater emphasis on the Individual Education Plan and to program development accomplished through co-operative efforts of school personnel, parents, and, if the student is sixteen years of age or older, the student.

Accommodating Inclusion

Even before the Eaton case began, the provincial government had taken steps toward accommodating the inclusion issue and amalgamating this point of view with other, usually more eclectic, positions taken by many teachers, school boards, and academics. While most people agree on the moral and philosophical merits of full inclusion as an objective, in practice it was not always successful. Perhaps more importantly, results in the classroom sometimes prove ambivalent, at best. The ideal implied by inclusion is that, when placed in the regular class, a student with an exceptionality will learn with their peers. While this is true, in order for that learning to be successful, program individualization and support for both students and teachers are essential. While the notion of inclusion is all students learning together, the reality of successful inclusive practice is the creation of differentiated learning opportunities and environments by which all students in the class can learn and be supported. Although full inclusion remains a fundamental goal of special education, on-the-ground reality is generally more fluid.

Thus, as early as the spring of 1991, the Minister of Education declared to the Ontario legislature that integration of pupils with exceptionalities into local community classrooms would be the norm

wherever possible, but that, inasmuch as an integrated setting may not be appropriate for every child, school boards would be encouraged to offer a full range of alternative educational placements. This position, which at the time seemed reasonable, educationally sound, and politically astute, has been challenged and continues to be adjusted: Inclusive placement is increasingly favoured over alternate placements.

In 2006, the Ontario Ministry of Education issued the report *Special Education Transformation*, which presented the results of discussions of a working group composed of teachers, principals, Ministry officials, students with special needs, advocacy groups (including parents), and members of faculties of education. The report stated that "the first consideration regarding placement would continue to be the regular classroom. A range of options would continue to be available for students whose needs could not be met within the regular classroom. These placements would be duration-specific, intervention-focused and subject to regular reviews" (Bennett & Wynne, *Special Education Transformation*, 2006, p. 8). Currently, the large majority of students with exceptionalities are in neighbourhood schools being educated with their peers, but because inclusion remains an adaptable concept, a minority continues to be accommodated in other ways.

Turning to Mediation

Note that, although appeals and litigation are popular avenues in Ontario, legal struggles have figured into just a very tiny number of situations since the passing of the *Education Amendment Act*. There have been thousands of IPRC decisions since 1980, but only a handful of tribunals; this indicates quite strongly that the process does the job it was designed to do. Another more recent and positive trend, which so far has no basis in the legislation, is the use of mediation to resolve impasses. Both parents and boards are finding this technique to be far less costly and time-consuming than formal appeals and usually minimizes post-adversarial residue. The *Special Education Transformation* report, referred to earlier (Bennett & Wynne, 2006), further promoted mediation as a preferable approach to dealing with special education disagreements between parents and board than appeal board/tribunal avenues.

Dateline 2004 – The Case of Theodor (Teddy)

UNTIL the day in late September when Teddy set fire to the hair of a girl seated in front of him, not one teacher in his new high school had paid attention to the special education department's description, in his case, of reactive attachment disorder (RAD) and what might counter its effects. The fire, however, raised Teddy's profile significantly among staff, not to mention the fact that he vandalized several cars the very next day.

Like most educators, few of Teddy's teachers had ever heard of RAD. Among the paraprofessionals at the school, only one had knowledge of it: She had dealt with a similar situation at an elementary school. Teddy's case, everyone soon learned, was almost a stereotype. He had been born in Romania when perestroika came to that beleaguered country, and had spent his first three years in an ill-kept, underfunded, and grossly understaffed state orphanage. His adoptive parents – Canadians from Ontario – devoted the next three years to helping him overcome the effects of severe malnutrition and a mild but correctable spinal deformity. Yet, by the time Teddy began senior kindergarten, his parents were painfully aware that the boy's problems went far beyond his stomach and his back.

Like many children with this syndrome, Teddy had never felt love or experienced bonding in his early, formative years; indeed, his very survival day-to-day during that time was uncertain. There is little doubt that had he been born in Canada, similar treatment would have been categorized as child abuse. Despite the efforts of the loving and deeply caring couple who adopted him, Teddy's developing years were marked by low self-esteem, profoundly manipulative behaviour, aggression, defiance, and – this being a key element of the syndrome – a pronounced lack of capacity for remorse, or of what our culture sees as moral perspective.

Although Teddy – not to mention his parents and teachers – had barely survived his elementary school experience, his two years of senior public school with the same teacher and under a very watchful and ready-to-intervene principal had been, by comparison, relatively peaceful. But now, in high school, the worst of Teddy's behaviours were front and centre, a fact confirmed in a behavioural checklist that his special education teacher asked staff to complete in advance of an IPRC review. Clearly, steps would have to be taken.

The Current "State" of Special Education

Continual Change and Adaptation

Overall, the education community, students, and parents have adjusted well to the sweeping changes in the educational provisions for students with special needs effected by the *Education Amendment Act* and its related regulations and policy memoranda. Indeed, much of what has been altered was barely noticed except by administrators and by parents with a specific area of interest. Typical of the latter group were parents of children who were developmentally disabled, when, in 1993, the provincial government, in what was known as Bill 4, removed the term "trainable retarded" from the *Education Act*. The same bill removed the "hard-to-serve" section, which comprised a complicated, never-used set of clauses that allowed a board to exclude a pupil.

Significant modifications to official policy and practice were introduced in 1998 when the province reissued the regulation concerning the IPRC process. The new regulation (Reg. 181) expanded the responsibilities of the committee in a variety of ways, required a written Educational Plan for the exceptional student, and generally strengthened the role and rights of parents. In the years immediately following, the written plan, known as the Individual Education Plan (IEP), took on more and more importance, and its development and use for exceptional students was subject to increasingly intense scrutiny, especially by the Ministry.

In 2002, the Ministry made available a voluntary template, thus providing a theoretically ideal format against which individual boards and schools could compare their own. It is important to note that, in the 2009/10 academic year, 14.89 percent of the entire student population received special education programs and services. Of this group, 5.5 percent were not formally identified by an IPRC but received these services as a result of an IEP being developed to meet these students' specific needs. Additionally, 80 percent of elementary and 84 percent of secondary students receiving special education programs and services during this time were placed in regular classrooms for all or part of the school day.

Further developments include the Co-ordinated Services Unit set up in 2001 to establish improved service coordination across several provincial ministries; the *Ontario Disabilities Act, 2002,* which placed specific accessibility obligations on public sector groups such as school boards; and a pilot program in 2003 on standards for autism. The Special Education Project (an ongoing venture) deals with the development and implementation of policies and programs. Other fine-tunings include the amount and quality of support materials now available from the Ontario Ministry of Education.

A good example of the latter is the resource guide *Effective Educational Practices for Students with Autism Spectrum Disorders*, available on the Ontario Ministry of Education website (**www.edu.gov.on.ca**). This work provides extensive programming suggestions to help teachers deliver appropriate programs for, and effective instructional approaches to, teaching students with autism spectrum disorder.

In 2005, the Ministry of Education issued *Education for All: The Report of the Expert Panel on Literacy and Numeracy Instruction for Students with Special Education Needs, Kindergarten to Grade 6* (Ontario Ministry of Education, 2005). This report further emphasized the importance of accepting students with special needs into the regular classroom and provided approaches (Universal Design for Learning and Differentiated Instruction) to help teachers effectively instruct these students along with their classmates. At the time of writing, a new document, in draft form, *Learning for All, K–12*, further expands the approaches found in *Education for All, K–6* to ensure that all students, especially those with exceptionalities, receive an education appropriate to their needs. This document emphasizes the need for teachers to assess all their students and provide programs that help all students close any gap between their ability and what they are currently achieving.

Regardless of the activities outlined above, the fact that there have been relatively few major alterations in Ontario's official special education policy and practice reinforces the impression that the system works well. Experience has demonstrated that, when modifications become necessary, teachers and individual schools and boards, with the support of the Ministry of Education and university and college faculties, are more than competent in bringing them about.

The Situation Today

For Ontario students with special needs, universal access to education is guaranteed. The definite first choice of placement is the regular class. And perhaps most importantly, students with exceptionalities are just that: *students*. In short, special education has become a normal, integral, and functional part of the system. Not that change and development and improvement will no longer be needed; adjustments will always be necessary and will continue to happen. Special education in Ontario is positioned so that changes to it occur in the larger context of all educational development. As education itself adjusts to social change, technology, and general needs, special education will adapt with it. In that context, future developments in special education are likely to be expressed in positive refinements of gains that have already been made.

Dateline 2008 – The Case of Jamie Edwards

JAMIE Edwards has not had a lot of success in school so far. Now in grade 2, he had difficulty both academically and socially in senior kindergarten and grade 1. In both years, teachers brought him to the attention of Ms. Markesh, the school's learning resource teacher, because of his spontaneous outbursts and slow academic achievement.

Ms. Markesh suggested that many of his developmental difficulties may be due to his age (he was the youngest student in the class, having been born on January 2) and that as he matured, his social and academic ability would improve.

His new teacher, Ms. Singh, believes that Jamie's difficulties are more than just a question of maturity – that a change in Jamie's program may be needed for him to be more successful throughout the school day. She has discussed this with Ms. Markesh, and together they have decided it is time for Jamie to be brought to the attention of the In-school Team. In addition, Ms. Singh has met with Jamie's parents to discuss the situation, and they have agreed to permit their son to be assessed.

In the meantime, and with Mr. and Mrs. Edwards' enthusiastic support, Jamie has begun to meet with the learning resource teacher twice a week. During these sessions, he works on his regular class assignments; this gives him some "wiggle room" to complete work as well as time to catch up on some skills identified by both Ms. Singh and Ms. Markesh as in need of development.

Ms. Singh noted that Jamie's outbursts disappeared almost immediately, a fact that pleases both Ms. Singh and his classmates, who are now more willing to work and play with him. Ms. Singh, working collaboratively with Ms. Markesh, is comfortable adjusting her program and taking Jamie's (as well as her other students') strengths and needs into account as she develops her lesson plans for the day. Having become comfortable with universal design for learning and differentiated instruction, professional development topics that she has explored considerably over the past two years, she habitually designs lessons that provide for a variety of learners.

The In-school Team's discussion centred on behavioural and academic skills that have already begun to improve. While there was consensus that Jamie is not currently in need of identification, it was agreed that assessment will still be a useful tool in planning his continued success. Both Ms. Singh and Ms. Markesh have happily accepted the task of deciding on and administering the necessary assessments.

Dateline 2013 – The Case of Jason Masters

JASON is seventeen years old and now in grade 11 at an urban secondary school. He started school at age four when he was placed, along with his friends, in kindergarten. Though Jason has Down syndrome, he has been in regular grade classrooms throughout his school career.

In each grade, his teachers worked closely with the school's Learning Resource teacher, as well as, in most grades, educational assistants, who provided reinforcement of new learning and helped Jason to stay on task. During his primary division years, Jason was an active member of his class and demonstrated a real flair for drama. He even had a lead role as the cowardly lion in the primary division's production of *The Wizard of Oz*. Jason had several friends, participated in all class and school activities, and generally experienced a very successful early school period.

During his junior division some difficulties both academic and behavioural began to develop. Jason continued to improve academically but at a slower rate than his friends. He became frustrated over this and at times just shut down and refused to work. His grade teacher understood Jason's actions, and working closely with the parents, developed materials that Jason could take home so that he could review the work he missed during the day. In grade 5, his new teacher continued this practice but had to regularly modify the curriculum to ensure that Jason would progress academically. Often his friends assisted him and reminded him to stay "on track."

Entering high school, Jason and his parents were excited and encouraged by the transition process that ensured flexible course selection and attention to maintaining social connection through strategic placement. Jason chose an arts-focused program that allowed his acting skill to shine through, but he also participated in many of the same classes and activities as his friends. Like many high school students, Jason drifted away from some of the friends he had made in earlier school years, acquiring other friends who shared similar interests and passions. As his parents noted, "He loves to hang out with his drama crew!"

Now, nearing the end of his grade 11 year, Jason, his parents, and the school staff are working together to plan what will happen as he approaches grade 12 and what will be, for many of his friends, a transition out of school and into post-secondary training of some sort. Jason and his parents are open to having Jason continue at school until the age of twenty-one (as is typical for many students identified with exceptionalities) but have made it clear that the next few years should not look like a continuation of regular school. Fortunately for Jason, the school and the school board agree. They have been, for many years, delivering a program that makes use of job coaches, hired by the board, to help young adults become active members of the working community. Jason has already been given opportunities to volunteer in the local theatre company and will begin next year as a part-time employee in the costume and makeup department.

Jason sees these experiences as transitioning him, after high school, into post-secondary training in theatre and production at the local college or more permanent employment.

Either way, Jason has lots of plans and, like all students his age, lots of dreams. What he also has is a support system that will allow him the opportunity to pursue them.

Readings and Resources

Note: For in-depth detail on provincial legislation, regulations, policy/program memoranda, funding guidelines, and a range of information and services from the Ministry of Education, see *Special Education: A Guide for Educators* (Ontario Ministry of Education, 2001), available from the Ministry's publications branch or for downloading at http://www.edu.gov.on.ca/eng/

Ainscow, M., & Margarida, C. (2006). Inclusive education ten years after Salamanca: Setting the agenda. *European Journal of Psychology of Education, XXI*(3), 231–38.

Bennett, S., & Wynne, K. (2006). *Special education transformation: The report of the co-chairs with the recommendations of the working table on special education*. Ontario Ministry of Education. Toronto: Queen's Printer for Ontario. Retrieved at: http://www.edu.gov.on.ca

Bunch, G., & Valeo, A. (1997). *Inclusion: Recent research*. Toronto: Inclusion Press.

Cantrell, M., Cantrell, R., Valore, T., & Fecser, F. (1999). A revisitation of the ecological perspective on emotional/behavioral disorders: Underlying assumptions and implications for education and treatment. In L. Bullock & R. Gable (Eds.). Monograph published by Council for Children with Behavioral Disorders.

Carrier, J. G. (1986). Sociology and special education: Differentiation and allocation in mass education. *American Journal of Education, 94*, 281–312.

Council of Administrators of Special Education (1997). Position paper on delivery of services to students with disabilities. *Keeping in Touch.*

Eaton v. Brant County. SCC#24668, February 7, 1997.

Foerter, J., et al. (1991). *Special education: Bridging the centuries.* Ontario Teachers' Federation.

Grover, S. (2002). Whatever happened to Canadian children's equality rights? A reconsideration of the Eaton special education case. *Education and the Law, 14*(4), 253–63. doi:10.1080/0953996022000056021

Hutchinson, N. L., & Martin, A. K. (2012). *Inclusive classrooms in Ontario schools.* Toronto: Pearson.

Itard, J. M. G. (1806). *The wild boy of Aveyron* (G. Humphrey & M. Humphrey, Trans.). (1962). Englewood Cliffs, NJ: Prentice-Hall.

Jahnukainen, M. (2011). Different strategies, different outcomes? The history and trends of the inclusive and special education in Alberta (Canada) and in Finland. *Scandinavian Journal of Educational Research, 55*(5), 489–502. doi:10.1080/00313831.2010.537689

Lupart, J. L., McKeough, A., & Yewchuck, C. (Eds.). (1996). *Schools in transition: Rethinking regular and special education.* Toronto: Nelson Canada.

Ontario Ministry of Education (2002). Special education companion. Retrieved at: http://www.ocup.org/resources/documents/companions/speced2002.pdf

Ontario Ministry of Education (2005). *Education for all: The report of the expert panel on literacy and numeracy instruction for students with special needs, kindergarten to grade 6.* Toronto: Queen's Printer for Ontario.

Ontario Ministry of Education (2009). *Draft document Learning for All, k–12.* Retrieved at: http://www.edu.gov.ca/eng/elemsec/speced/LearningforAll2011.pdf

Smith, D., Luckasson, R., & Crealock, C. (1995). *Introduction to special education in Canada.* Scarborough, ON: Allyn & Bacon.

Smith, W. J., & Lusthaus, C. (1994). Equal educational opportunities for students with disabilities in Canada: The right to free and appropriate education. *Exceptionality Education Canada, 4*, 37–73.

Winzer, M. (2008). *Children with exceptionalities in Canadian classrooms* (8th ed.). Toronto: Pearson Prentice Hall.

Wolfensberger, W. (1975). *The origin and nature of our institutional models.* Syracuse, NY: Human Policy Press.

Zigmond, N., Kloo, A., & Volonino, V. (2009). What, where, and how? Special education in the climate of full inclusion. *Exceptionality, 17*(4), 189–204. doi:10.1080/09362830903231986

2

Continuing Issues in Special Education

*"My kid's handicapped. He needs somebody to fight for him, and that's me.
I'm a taxpayer, too, and if your kid can get an education so can mine.
I'm going to do what I have to do. Get used to it."*

– Laney G., parent of a child with multiple disabilities

The Paper Chase

Bill 82 stated that a special education program is a program based on, and modified by, the results of continuous assessment and evaluation and includes a plan containing specific objectives and an outline of educational services that meet the needs of the pupil with exceptionalities. The plan referred to in Bill 82 has led the Ontario Ministry of Education to establish the Individual Education Plan (IEP) and a procedure for how this plan should be created. This process, outlined in a Resource Guide published in 2004, describes the steps for board personnel to follow so the plan is co-operatively developed by education personnel, parents, and the student (if the student is sixteen years of age or older).

The IEP may be one step among many that may be generated by the assessment and programming demands of a student with special needs. Students with special needs may at times require a wide range of personnel who not only make individual reports but also must exchange them with the reports of others. Funding mechanisms tend to stir up a paper flurry, especially if unusual equipment or specialized instruction is necessary.

Fundamental to teaching students with exceptionalities is the need for adaptations in curriculum and teaching methods, adaptations that need to be recorded for pre- and post-evaluation and for dissemination to interested parties. And looming over the whole planning process is the need to collate a plan or file that makes the various parts work together toward the same purpose. The result is a great deal of paper and, for all parties, a

serious task. Just how much is necessary and who is responsible?

There is no question that written education plans have beneficial effects, especially if the plans detailing students' needs include descriptions of how, where, and when the needs will be addressed, and accounts of when and how the success (or failure) of these efforts will be evaluated. On the surface, the logic behind the practice is unassailable. A specific plan brings focus and coordination to meeting a student's needs. It helps satisfy the need for accountability: everyone involved can at least follow the tracks if funds are being spent, personnel assigned, and effort expended. A plan also offers a common basis for discussion should the need for accommodation and/or modification develop. And, far from least in importance, unfortunately, a plan provides a documented paper trail should legal issues arise.

There are potential drawbacks, however. A plan can easily become more important than the subject for whom it is designed. Once a plan becomes dominant, then flexibility diminishes and creativity disappears, and without these components, the very essence of "special" education is lost. Granted, the evaluation phase should preclude such an outcome, yet once plan supremacy is established, changes to that plan become very difficult to bring about, especially if the student with exceptionalities has complex needs. In addition, if the IEP process suggested by the Ministry of Education is followed, the time it takes to make the changes can delay the implementation of appropriate instruction for several weeks. The more complicated a case may be, the greater the number of personnel to consult and the greater the number of resources that must be shifted to effect a change – all with paper attached. Then there is the professional time taken up by record keeping. Ontario boards use online IEP forms with pull-down menus to assist in indicating accommodations. These menus may be helpful in many cases, but they may also inhibit the initiation of an appropriate approach not listed on the pull-down list.

As valuable as the detailing of information may be, it is rarely more important than the time spent interacting with the student. Nevertheless, experience has shown that, to make a significant impact, coordinated and recorded planning is essential. Finding the elusive balance between the logical boundaries of a specific plan and the art of creatively and intuitively responding to a student's needs will always be a challenge in special education. The fact that teachers and administrators continue to search for it is to their credit.

Inclusion: No Longer an Issue but Certainly a Concern

For the most part, whether students with special needs should be educated in regular classrooms is a non-issue. The vast majority of students with exceptionalities (over 80 percent in Ontario) are in regular classes. Despite these encouraging numbers, a different story unfolds when the data on specific disabilities are unpacked. In the category of developmental disabilities, 46 percent of students are still in fully self-contained classes (MOE 2009–2010). As school systems continue to adopt a more inclusive philosophy, the issue of who gets access to the mainstream and who is still excluded cannot be ignored. Advocacy groups and individuals with disabilities continue to demand equal treatment and access to educational opportunities and experiences.

That said, teachers, educational assistants, and principals – the people who deal with inclusion on a daily basis – have discarded the notion that inclusion is still a controversial issue. In academic journals, in administration offices, at professional conferences, and among advocacy groups, where the topic of inclusion was once guaranteed to brew up a storm, the winds are now relatively calm. There are a number of reasons for this, the most obvious being that inclusion today is a dominant reality, and in cases where alternatives are chosen, it is usually with the agreement of all parties involved. What most educators are concerned with now is making inclusion work.

> "I think the inclusion of students with exceptionalities continues to evolve. When I was a student in both elementary and secondary school, I did not see any students with exceptionalities. Today I rejoice when visiting classrooms where diversity is represented and students are seen learning together."
>
> – P. Blair, Superintendent, Special Education

Among those for whom the issue of inclusion still resonates, the arguments have pretty much reached a default stage in parallax positions. One side argues that all students with special needs, no matter how unique or demanding these needs are, should be placed in regular classrooms of neighbourhood schools. Supporters of no-exception inclusion contend that the mere availability of alternative settings can make integration fail for the very simple reason that it does not have to work. To a significant extent, this position is argued as much from a stance of moral superiority as from one of superior educational outcomes.

Then there are those who do not see the matter quite so unconditionally. This group contends that, whereas inclusion should indeed be sought as a first solution, some students might be better served if at least a portion of their program were delivered in a more specialized environment. They argue that to be so rigid is unrealistic, and that, out of sheer practical necessity, certain cases demand at least some form of special placement from time to time.

Much has happened over the past decades to wind this debate down. The provincial government has long declared the inclusion of students with special needs to be the norm in the province's schools, a principle that continues to be affirmed by the Ministry of Education. As mentioned in chapter 1, the *Special Education Transformation* report reaffirmed this view and recommended that when a special class placement is made, it should be duration-specific and intervention-focused. Though not in regulation, these recommendations provide guidance to IPRC and IEP developers. Educators and parents of students with special needs in regular classes now know that placing a student in a regular class is not as difficult as once thought and usually produces significant benefits for all.

The Power of Profile

The rapid expansion of special education in the final quarter of the twentieth century and in the early years of the twenty-first was marked by dramatic surges in awareness of certain special needs. One example is that of learning disabilities. In the 1970s, only a small number of teachers and parents, along with a sprinkling of academics, were deeply interested in the type of student who seems to experience serious problems in school despite apparently normal intelligence. Although the number of concerned people was growing, and the problem had acquired a name ("learning disabilities" was first proposed by Samuel Kirk in 1963), this special need still had a low profile in education and in the media. Initially, only a handful of students in publicly supported schools were actually called, or even believed to be, "learning disabled." Now, fifty years after the term was first suggested, just over 40 percent of all students officially identified for special education in the province are identified "learning disabled." More recently, autism spectrum disorder (ASD) has received a similar surge of interest and attention. In the past considered a rare disorder, it has exploded onto the educational landscape through the advocacy of interest groups and the growing concern of educators.

Raising a profile for a special need seems to follow a pattern. Initially, an advocacy group, consisting mostly of parents with first-hand experience in dealing with the need, succeeds in getting the attention of the media and – not always simultaneously – teachers and the school system. Usually, such parental advocacy is followed by a sharp rise in interest from academics. (Bureaucrats in education, interestingly, are often quite ahead of the game. For example, the learning disabilities issue had wide support among Ontario's Ministry of Education officials well before the school system at large came onside.) A final stage in profile development is getting the special need to be officially recognized administratively, thereby assuring it a permanent place on the horizon of every school and school board.

The pattern does not end here, for once a significant profile is achieved, the advocacy group instrumental in getting things started usually commits to a program of reinforcement through lobbying, information workshops, production of information literature, and, at times, litigation. An essential difference at this stage, however, is that the group now becomes more a partner in meeting the special need than an agent for awareness. Two good examples of the effect of this advocacy are the attention paid to students with learning disabilities in the 1980s through the 1990s and the positive result of advocacy efforts by parents to obtain treatment for their children with autism in the early 2000s.

Many educators acknowledge the necessity of intense lobbying to raise awareness of special needs. Yet an elevated profile is not without potential risks, especially for administrators and, by extension, for the classroom. Cynics point to the possibility that intensive media fascination may actually create a "disability du jour," a charge that, in the early years of this century, rightly or wrongly, is directed at the number of students identified with forms of ASD. Further, there is always risk that a single issue may capture disproportionate space on the administrative agenda. On balance, the benefits brought to the field by increased awareness outweigh the possible drawbacks, provided that teachers, assistants, administrators, and advocates behind the thrust keep in mind the need for a rational perspective. Education in general is extremely susceptible to cycles – fads, the cynics would say. Everyone involved with students who have special needs has a responsibility to ensure a balanced and equity-based approach to meeting students' needs and not necessarily the needs of any one agenda, no matter how passionate the discourse.

The Case of Parnell

On the surface, this case seems simple enough. Parnell lags behind his peers in achievement by at least three grades. Most serious is his apparent inability to read. The problem may be accounted for by Parnell's own explanation that he "didn't go to school much" before coming to Canada three months ago, although the teacher of the grade 5–6 split class where he is placed reports that the boy frequently manifests "learning disability–like characteristics" – adding, by way of illustration, that he frequently goes off-task, rarely follows instructions in proper sequence, seems to be easily confused, and regularly loses his personal property (and the school's). A preliminary assessment has only reinforced what everybody already knows: Parnell can't read.

On the other hand, the (half-time) assistant in the class points out that, when she is able to instruct Parnell one-on-one in skills such as phonics and letter/word recognition, he grasps the material quickly and retains it. A special reading program is not a viable option. The school's junior reading program was deleted two years ago because of budget issues and staffing reallocation. The primary program is entirely overextended and depends to a large extent on volunteers.

The classroom teacher is meeting with the school's learning resource teacher to discuss Parnell; while they agree that an IEP needs to be developed, they are still talking about whether he should be referred to an IPRC. There is an issue of some delicacy related to this situation. Only a month ago, the senior public school that shares a campus with Parnell's school was the focus of obsessive media attention after an advocacy group accused it of the over-identification of children of colour like Parnell. A subsequent investigation agreed that the number of such students identified as having special needs is indeed significantly disproportionate to the number in the general school population.

The Problem of the Purse

Concerns about funding for special education coalesce around several recurring issues, but the most basic one is, simply, adequacy: How much is enough? Unfortunately, no matter what level of funding is offered by the public purse, it will never be seen as enough. The need (demand?) always seems to outpace the number of dollars allotted. Governments have never managed to resolve this issue, which may be one reason they pursue accountability with such rigor. While accountability is a laudable goal, not to mention one that attracts positive attention from taxpayers, it is rarely achieved without significant impact on the system receiving the money. For example, a common method of funding special education, one that Ontario adopted in the late 1990s, is a system of incremental grants based on documented needs of individual students.

This system has now been abandoned in favour of an overall amount provided to school boards beyond their basic per-pupil grant (used for regular education). These funds must be used for educating students with special needs. Additional funds are also available to assist boards in providing education to low-incidence, high-need students. These funds, commonly known as Special Incident Portion (SIP), must be applied for by each school board, with documented evidence of student need. SIP dollars are made available to fund staff support to ensure the health and safety of both the student with high needs as well as others in the school. While these funds are generally used for additional staff, they can also be allocated for construction in cases where a specialized space such as a "quiet room" is needed to assist students with aggression. An additional source of funding for students with special needs is the Special Equipment Amount (SEA). These funds can be used to cover the cost of equipment (assistive technology) essential to the students' learning.

It is very encouraging that the Ontario Ministry of Education has continued to emphasize that the education of students with special education needs is deserving of a category of funding separate from the per-pupil funding provided to boards of education. This protected "envelope" must be spent on providing service to students with special needs. Ontario has tried to ensure that this funding category remains a priority. Projections for special education funding for 2010/2011 reported an increase of $65.5 million to a provincial total of $2.31 billion. One issue currently under discussion is the disparity of need among different boards throughout the province. It could be argued that boards that are geographically remote and/or have a large French-speaking population may have more need for a different level of funding to service their students with special needs than a board with a large urban and culturally and economically diverse population.

A one-size-fits-all model may not be appropriate for Ontario, but the search for the development of an equitable system is ongoing.

Against Labels

A single label, for example, "gifted," cannot sum up the complexity of a human.

Labels often stigmatize by emphasizing weakness and dysfunction.

Labels often mislead: Someone labelled "deaf" may just be hard of hearing.

Labels propagate confusion and varied interpretation (as in developmental disabilities).

A labelled person is seen in the label's terms, rather than as a human being with a special need, thereby provoking lowered expectations.

Labels tend to be lifelong.

For Labels

To be effective, academic discussion, professional development, teacher training, and research all need a common frame of reference.

Specific vocabulary permits more precise communication in hands-on situations. Caregivers, especially, must work from the same text.

Identification of a group's unique needs raises its profile.

Differentiated categories facilitate differentiated responses.

Experience shows that abolishing one set of labels simply produces another.

Labels, Categories, and Definitions

One of the most divisive issues in special education has long been the question "to label or not to label?" In 1972, Reginald Jones, in an article "The Labels and Stigma in Special Education," described the difficulties encountered by students who have a special education label. This oft-cited article brought this issue to the attention of parents and educators, and the move toward de-emphasizing labels has continued ever since. In Ontario, however, we have maintained, since the introduction of the *Education Amendment Act*, a categorical approach with labels such as Behaviour exceptionality, Intellectual exceptionality, and Physical exceptionality. (See appendix I.)

Over the intervening years, many advocacy groups within Ontario have argued vehemently for either broadening or eliminating these categories, which are seen as too limited. A case in point is students with acquired brain injury, a category that does not exist in the current definitions.

A first indication that the voices of such advocacy groups are finally penetrating the long-existing categorical model can be seen in a memo sent from the Special Education Policy Branch to Directors of Education in Ontario in December 2011. The memo clearly indicates that while the categories have not been changed, they are not meant to be exclusive. Indeed, the memo is very clear that all children who have learning difficulties are to have access to required special education assistance regardless of whether their diagnosis is contained within the categories provided by the Ministry. This memo, receiving much attention for its inclusion of AD/HD, whose advocates have lobbied tirelessly for recognition, is a clear indication that the winds of change, fanned by research and experience, are blowing in the direction of a broader and more inclusive system of providing services for all students who may be in need of them.

Some school districts in North America have already abandoned contemporary descriptors like "developmentally delayed" because of their gradual acquisition of negative connotations. It seems the need to search for ever-more-euphemistic vocabulary will never end. As new and more sensitive identifiers age, they take on negative overtones, thereby provoking the need for newer ones.

There are indications that, in this new century, the matter of labels, categories, and definitions has declined significantly as an issue for debate. As we have moved toward accepting diverse learners in our classrooms, the definition of "diverse" now expands to include students not only with racial, language, and cultural differences, but also with differing learning needs as a result of cognitive,

behavioural, physical, and communicative differences. More and more generations are growing up with people with exceptionalities in their midst as a matter of course. Parents and professional educators recognize descriptors simply as a convenience for discussion and administrative procedure. Still, it is unlikely that the vocabulary of special needs will ever be entirely free of controversy for the simple reason that the meaning of words changes over time. Also, when categories of special need broaden, as they do from time to time (case in point: the field of autism now referred to as autism spectrum disorder), a whole new battery of terms is added to the lexicon, any one of which can provoke another round of debate.

Identification and Placement Concerns

A major criticism of placement in special education classrooms is the disproportionate number of students from low socio-economic backgrounds and minorities found in these classrooms. For very real reasons, it is easy to see, rightly or wrongly, why students from these backgrounds are identified as having special needs. Children of poverty and those from some cultural minorities often have a high frequency of serious health and physical problems that affect their education. Conductive hearing loss (usually otitis media), for example, and eye infections affecting sight, occur at a much higher average rate in Aboriginal children in Canada than in the general population. Children of minority groups sometimes experience linguistic difficulties that impinge on their learning in a major way, leading to academic difficulties requiring greater intervention than normally provided. In addition, assessment procedures that do not allow for cultural anomalies may lead to an inappropriate placement or label.

It is not unusual for children from lower-income families or from recently arrived immigrant families to have difficulties simply because they are confused by the demands of the school culture. Sometimes a family's lack of precedent for educational experience, as well as lack of support for it, can have a serious effect on a student's performance. Parents all too often do not manage a child's case; they neglect to deal with the school, the education system, and support agencies (confronting them if necessary), either by choice or because they lack the sophistication.

In schools, the issue is one of delicate choice. From an educational perspective, these are indeed students with very special needs. And, very frequently, the needs can be effectively met in a special education mode. However, the educational perspective must be illuminated by consideration of what is morally and socially appropriate. Identification of a student with special needs is a major step, one that can be taken with more certainty if the basis of the decision is strictly educational. Ontario has taken a definitive step with its PPM 119 (see opposite), which attempts to build successful practice that focuses on the identification and elimination of systemic

barriers. When the basis is influenced by social, cultural, and economic factors, there is inevitably a commensurate erosion of that certainty. It is a hard nut to crack, and no jurisdiction in Canada has yet done so to everyone's satisfaction.

Policy/Program Memorandum No. 119 released by Ontario Ministry of Education, June 2009

Developing and Implementing Equity and Inclusive Education Policies in Ontario Schools states clearly that schools are obligated to review, develop, implement, and monitor equity and inclusion policies to support students' achievement. While the document focuses broadly on inclusion, it specifically notes that inclusion for students with disabilities must be part of this board-wide plan. **http://www.edu.gov.on.ca/extra/eng/ppm/119.html**

The Case of Vanessa

OF the five students still placed in the "junior resource class" at the end of the school year, Vanessa and one other have been deemed ready by an IPRC to spend part of the school day in a regular grade 5 class. The other three will remain in the resource class come September, where a teacher and two educational assistants will continue to emphasize appropriate behaviour and socialization.

Vanessa's gains after two years in the class have been considerable. She no longer screams at maximum pitch when dissatisfied. She has developed appropriate toileting skills (instead of using the floor, wherever and whenever). She seems to have discarded biting, scratching, and hair pulling as communication methods. And sessions in the regular grade 4 class indicate that, with a little help from her favourite EA, Vanessa can sustain an age-appropriate relationship with a peer group. Interestingly, what pleases the adults dealing with Vanessa more than anything is that, most of the time, with supervision, she participates in regular recess without incident. Still, hers is a situation that will bear careful watching. A similar attempt at reintegration in grade 3 failed utterly, although all agree that the outcome would have been different if the necessary accommodations had been in place.

Two assessments suggest that Vanessa is of average intelligence, and there is no indication of any physical or learning disability despite the experience of her early years. From the time she was a baby until age eight – when Children's Aid took over after her mother was jailed for voluntary manslaughter – Vanessa had moved seventeen times, had known six stepfathers, and had been treated for both TB and malnutrition. Her present school (from grade 2) is the first one she attended with any regularity, although her behaviour was so extreme initially that the principal had to arrange for one-on-one supervision. (Three EAs, the school's full complement, spelled one another off over the course of the day.)

A potential complication has developed recently. Vanessa's birth father, whom she had never seen until a few months ago, has applied to the family court for custody. Both the court and the Children's Aid Society agree that he is a responsible, mature individual (he is married with two other children) and a good parent. However, he proposes to enroll Vanessa in the same school as his other two children. This school is in a different board in a different community and has a full and absolute inclusion policy with no designated resource or withdrawal classes. The family court judge has agreed that the father can obtain custody of Vanessa, and she is now enrolled in a regular grade 5 classroom. The In-school Team in Vanessa's new school is meeting next week to discuss Vanessa's program.

Universal Design for Learning and Differentiated Instruction

The Report of the Expert Panel referred to in chapter 1 provides an approach known as Universal Design for Learning (UDL). This approach is based on an architectural premise that improved access for people with handicapping conditions is improved access for all. A ramp, for example, certainly assists a person in a wheelchair, but it also helps the parent with a stroller or a person making a delivery using a handcart. Universal Design for Learning encourages teachers to take the needs of all their students, whether academic, social, intellectual, or physical, into account when planning instruction. This consideration is to occur at the outset of planning, rather than making adjustments after the planning occurs, as has traditionally been done.

Differentiated classroom instruction, according to Carol Ann Tomlinson (1999), requires teachers to "begin where students are, not the front of the curriculum guide. They accept and build upon the premise that learners differ in important ways." Teachers following this approach begin their planning with the needs of all students in mind and present lessons and activities in a manner that effectively captures the needs and abilities of all students in their classrooms.

While some would argue that UDL and DI are new ideas for teaching, another equally vocal group would state that educators have been doing versions of this type of planning and implementation in practice for many years. The difference, indeed, may not be in practice but rather in orientation. While, for many, modifications and accommodations have become commonplace, the focus on UDL and DI comes before pencil hits paper. Certainly the use of UDL and DI is reinforced in the Ministry of Education 2009 document *Learning for All, K–12* (draft), which emphasizes the necessity of both good practice and good planning. It is an issue of orientation to planning and implementation, a perspective from which to view the individual and class as a whole, and a new lens on an age-old practice of instruction.

> *"A classroom based on the concept of UDL is specifically planned and developed to meet the special needs of a variety of students, including students who are disabled and those who come from non-dominant cultures. It is flexible, supportive, and adjustable, and increases full access to the curriculum for all students."*
>
> – Ontario Ministry of Education, *Education for All*, 2005, p. 10

Assessment and Program

The main goal of an assessment is to provide information from which program planning can be developed. Unfortunately, for several reasons, the practice often stumbles clumsily after the theory. Chief among these reasons is a strange combination of expertise and naïveté that seems to prevail on both sides of the assessment/program planning issue. Psychologists, psychometrists, or other assessors, without actual experience in teaching, often have either idealistic or simplistic notions of what actually occurs minute by minute in a classroom. Many classroom teachers, on the other hand, are not confident in their assessment skills and frequently have difficulty translating results into program. In many cases, much time can elapse between when a student is referred for assessment and when the assessment is actually conducted and the results shared with those who need to know this information. During this period, the student with special needs is expected to receive a program designed to meet his or her needs, and it is up to the teacher, confident or not, to provide one.

Frequently, teachers and those non-teaching professionals responsible for assessment are obstructed by matters not of their own making, beginning with their own training. Traditionally, neither gets much opportunity to gain more than sketchy knowledge about the other. As well – and probably more important – both sides argue that the gap could easily be narrowed, even closed, by direct communication: that if the teacher(s) and educational assistant(s) of the student under assessment could communicate directly with an assessor, the questions that need answers will at least be put on the table. Yet in many jurisdictions, bureaucracy and systems management impede this very simple expedient. It is common policy for assessors to obtain and report data only to a third party (coordinator, committee, principal, etc.).

Then, for a variety of reasons, such as privacy regulations, workloads, or in some cases, inefficiency, these data come to the classroom, if at all, in a form that is altered or diluted, or summarized to the point of irrelevance. Assessment by non-teachers would also be advanced if teachers were able to express more precisely why they are referring a student for an in-depth assessment. The referral information, the more clearly the assessor will understand what he or she needs to assess and evaluate.

It is the student who falls into the gap created by this system. Assessment personnel may well be competent; the teachers and paraprofessionals may well be effective. But unless there is opportunity for some form of direct communication, the whole point of the procedure is diminished.

Fortunately, a very positive outcome of the continuing experience in special education is an increased emphasis on classroom observation and assessment. It stands to reason that competent teachers and educational assistants who are "watching it live," so to speak, are in a crucial position to make perceptive, realistic evaluations of a student's strengths and needs. The fact that their observations are being given increasing credence in many jurisdictions is a tribute to their professionalism and to common sense.

Special Education and Research

There is much demand in education today for teachers to use "evidence–based" research approaches to working with students with special needs. In 2005, the Ontario Ministry of Education awarded the Council of Directors of Education $25 million to finance school-based research studies to develop approaches to inclusion that will lead to effective academic, social, and emotional growth in students with special needs. It is important to note that drawing firm conclusions from research can be difficult at the best of times. In education, the matter can be especially challenging for the simple reason that the variables in studies involving human interaction – the type of study much pursued in special education – are extremely difficult to control. Research in education is rarely, if ever, conducted under laboratory conditions. Despite what some might call a lack of academic rigour, the misinterpretation and misuse of data can be prevalent in any research condition whether one uses a Petri dish or not! The reality is that, with any type of research, the researchers, not to mention end-users, can never be absolutely confident about the reasons for an outcome. As a result, educators are never entirely sure that they are dealing with results that apply to their own situations.

Ironically, the two most important components in all of education, students and teachers, are the two most difficult variables to control. Simple logic forces the acknowledgment that the personality, the commitment, and the training of classroom professionals have a profound impact on outcomes in the classroom. Thus, when a study compares outcomes in two classrooms where conditions are matched, with the exception of the variable being investigated, even the most practiced researchers cannot account for the ever-so-crucial spirit and atmosphere that different professionals impart to a teaching environment. Nor can two classrooms ever be found where the collective personality generated by the students is the same.

Another problem lies in the improper use of results and data. (This is rarely a researcher's error.) For example, it has not been uncommon during the history of special education for an advocate of one point of view or another to quite blithely use research results about children who have visual impairment, for example, to support a position on children with autism. A related abuse arises from the "gee whiz" stories that frequently appear in non-refereed journals and in anecdotal newspaper columns in which success with a single subject is described in glowing terms. The implication is that a similar outcome can be expected in any student with a similar special need.

Ultimately, perhaps the most unfortunate issue is the reluctance of many teachers to attribute significant value to the role played by research. Many argue, with more than ample justification, that they simply do not have the time to "keep up." A good number insist, again with more than a little justification, that many of the results are irrelevant in any case, at least to their own classrooms. As a result, the very people who might have the most to gain from research and certainly the very people who should have prime responsibility for actually testing the relevance of results have, in fact, depressingly little involvement. This paradox has been a thorn in the side of education for a long time.

Fortunately, teachers are looking for "proven" approaches that will help them teach students with special needs in both their regular and special classes. The *Learning for All, K–12* (draft) document (Ontario Ministry of Education, 2009) was a major project of the Ministry of Education, and the end result was a compilation of effective approaches recommended to teachers to improve literacy and numeracy ability for students with special needs in grades kindergarten to grade 12.*

> *"Regular classroom teachers in Ontario serve a growing number of students with diverse abilities. According to school board statistics, most students with special needs spend at least 50 percent of their instructional day in a regular classroom being taught by regular classroom teachers. It is imperative that inclusion means not only the practice of placing students with special needs in the regular classroom but ensuring that teachers assist every student to prepare for the highest degree of independence possible."*
>
> – Ontario Ministry of Education, *Education for All*, 2005, p. 2.

* In 2010–2011, the Ministry of Education provided approximately $700,000 to support the continued implementation of this document through the support of professional learning communities in schools as well as the development of shareable resources.

Readings and Resources

Ainscow, M., & Miles, S. (2008). Making Education for All inclusive: Where next? *Prospects, 38*, 15–34.

Atkinson, D. (2004). Research and empowerment: Involving people with learning difficulties in oral and life history research. *Disability & Society, 19*(7), 691–702. doi:10.1080/0968759042000028418

Barr, S., & Smith, R. (2009). Towards educational inclusion in a transforming society: Some lessons from community relations and special needs education in Northern Ireland. *International Journal of Inclusive Education, 13*(2), 211–30. doi:10.1080/13603110701403579

Bennett, S., & Gallagher, T. L. (2011). Inclusion, education and transition to employment: A work in progress. In D. Griffiths, F. Owen, & S. Watson (Eds.). *The human rights agenda for persons with intellectual disabilities.* Kingston, NY: NADD Press.

Bennett, S., & Wynne, K. (2006). *Special education transformation: The report of the co-chairs with the recommendations of the working table on special education.* Ontario Ministry of Education. Toronto: Queen's Printer for Ontario.

Bennett, S. (2009). Including students with exceptionalities. *Research Monograph #16.* In *What Works? Research into Practice.* The Literacy and Numeracy Secretariat with the Ontario Association of Deans of Education.

Csoli, K., Bennett, S., & Gallagher, T. L. (2009). Ready or not, here they come: Inclusion of invisible disabilities in post-secondary education. *Teaching and Learning, 5*(1), 53–62.

Danforth, S., & Taft, S. D. (2004). *Crucial readings in special education.* Upper Saddle River, NJ: Pearson Education.

Friend, M., Bursuck, W., & Hutchinson, N. L. (1998). *Including exceptional students: A practical guide for classroom teachers.* Scarborough, ON: Prentice Hall.

Fuchs, D., & Fuchs L. S. (1994). Inclusive schools movement and the radicalization of special education reform. *Exceptional Children, 60*(4), 294–309.

Gallagher, T. L., DiGiorgio, C., Bennett, S., & Antle, K. (2008). Understanding disability and culture while enhancing advocacy. *Teaching and Learning, 4*(3), 30–36.

Giangreco, M. F., Edelman, S., Dennis, R., & Cloninger, C. (1993). My child has a classmate with severe disabilities: What parents of nondisabled students should think about full inclusion. *Developmental Disabilities Bulletin, 21*(1), 77–91.

Gutkin, T. B. (1996). Core elements of consultation service delivery for special services personnel: Rationale, practice, and some directions for the future. *Remedial and Special Education, 17*(6), 333–40.

Harry, B. (1992). *Cultural diversity, families, and the special education system: Communication and empowerment.* New York: Teachers College Press.

Huang, H., & Diamond, K. E. (2009). Early childhood teachers' ideas about including children with disabilities in programmes designed for typically developing children. *International Journal of Disability, Development and Education, 56*(2), 169–82. doi:10.1080/10349120902868632

Jones, R. L. (1972). Labels and stigma in special education. *Exceptional Children, 38*(7), 553–64.

Kliewer, C., & Bilkin, D. (1996). Labeling: Who wants to be called retarded? In W. Stainback & S. Stainback (Eds.). *Controversial issues confronting special education: Divergent perspectives* (2nd ed.), pp. 83–95. Boston: Allyn & Bacon.

Leake, D. W., Burgstahler, S., Rickerson, N., Applequist, K., Izzo, M., Picklesimer, T., & Arai, M. (2006). Literature synthesis of key issues in supporting culturally and linguistically diverse students with disabilities to succeed in postsecondary education. *Journal of Postsecondary Education and Disability, 18*(2), 149–65.

Lupart, J. L. (1998). The delusion of inclusion: Implications for Canadian schools. *Canadian Journal of Education, 23*(3), 251–64.

Marinos, V., Owen, F., Richards, D., Tarulli, D., & Watson, S. (Eds.). *The human rights agenda for persons with intellectual disabilities.* Community University Research Alliance and Community Living Welland-Pelham. Brock University, St. Catharines, ON.

McPhail, J., & Freeman, J. (2005). Beyond prejudice: Thinking toward genuine inclusion. *Learning Disabilities Research & Practice, 20*(4), 254–67.

Miles, S., & Singal, N. (2010). The education for all and inclusive education debate: Conflict, contradiction or opportunity? *International Journal of Inclusive Education, 14*(1), 1–15.

Ontario Ministry of Education (2005). *Education for all. The report of the expert panel on literacy and numeracy instruction for students with special education needs, kindergarten to grade 6.* Toronto: Queen's Printer for Ontario.

Ontario Ministry of Education (2009). *Equity and inclusive education in Ontario schools: Guidelines for policy development and implementation.* Toronto: Queen's Printer for Ontario.

Ontario Ministry of Education (2009). *Learning for all (DRAFT).* Retrieved November 2011 at: http://www.edu.gov.ca/eng/elemsec/speced/LearningforAll2011.pdf

Peterson, J. M., & Hittie, M. M. (2003). *Inclusive teaching: Creating effective schools for all learners.* Boston: Pearson Education.

Reynolds, M. C. (1991). Classification and labeling. In J. W. Lloyd, N. N. Singh, & A. C. Repp (Eds.). *The regular education initiative: Alternative perspectives on concepts, issues, and models,* 29–42. Sycamore, IL: Sycamore Publishing.

Salisbury, C. L., Palambaro, M. M., & Hollowood, T. M. (1993). On the nature of change of an inclusive elementary school. *The Journal of the Association of Persons with Severe Handicaps, 18*(2), 75–84.

Shah S. (2010). Canada's implementation of the right to education for students with disabilities. *International Journal of Disability, Development and Education, 57*(1), 5–20.

Tomlinson, C. A. (1999). *The differentiated classroom: Responding to the needs of all learners.* Upper Saddle River, NJ: Pearson Merrill Prentice Hall.

Vergason, G. A., & Anderegg, M. L. (1997). The ins and outs of special education terminology. *Teaching Exceptional Children, 29*(5), 35–39.

Winzer, M. (2008). *Children with exceptionalities in Canadian classrooms* (8th ed.). Toronto: Pearson Education Canada.

York, G. (1990). *The dispossessed: Life and death in native Canada.* Toronto: Little Brown (Canada).

Ysseldyke, J. E., Algozzine, B., & Thurlow, M. L. (2000). *Critical issues in special education* (3rd ed.). Boston: Houghton Mifflin.

Zigmond, N., Kloo, A., & Volonino V. (2009). What, where and how? Special education in the climate of full inclusion. *Exceptionality, 17,* 189–204.

Links

Ontario Ministry of Education website **http://www.edu.gov.on.ca**

PPM 119 **http://www.edu.gov.on.ca/extra/eng/ppm/119.html**

3

The Special Needs Population: Categories and Numbers

Ontario Student Population	
Number of Students in Publicly Funded Schools Receiving Special Education Services	
Elementary 94,364 (7.02 percent) IPRC'd	81,864 (6.09 percent) not formally identified but receiving services
Secondary 98,166 (13.67 percent) IPRC'd	32,626 (4.54 percent) not formally identified but receiving services

Table 3A   Source: Ministry of Ed., Data 2009–10

The Categories

Agreement on Generalities …

Teachers, educational assistants, and administrators in a school board usually share a common vocabulary when talking about special education. Sometimes their official terms are those promulgated by the Ministry of Education. However, it is not unusual for a board to popularize terms unique to itself. Academics may use a moderately differing special education vocabulary, especially if they have different fields of interest, say, psychology or medicine. Advocates, especially if they are emphasizing softer terminologies for special needs, may have yet another set of words. Despite the potential confusion arising from these variations, the many branches of special education nevertheless seem able to communicate, because there is a general understanding and acceptance of broad categories such as these:

- *Intellectual and developmental differences*: includes students who are intellectually gifted and those who manifest intellectual delay
- *Sensory disabilities*: includes students who are blind and/or deaf
- *Communication disorders*: includes students who have learning disabilities, those who have pervasive disorders such as ASD,

and those who have speech and language difficulties
- *Physical and health difficulties*: includes students who have genetic disorders, problems that arise from birth trauma, orthopedic conditions, and disabilities caused by disease; usually, students who have neurological disorders are included here
- *Behavioural disorders*: includes students who suffer from mental illness; those who are socially maladjusted, delinquent, or emotionally disturbed; and those who exhibit conduct disorders
- *Combinations of the above*

… but Disagreement on Specifics

The terms above appear in the literature and they are used freely in discussions, but difficulty arises when it comes to defining the terms. After some four decades of in-depth experience, special education has yet to establish a set of clear, standardized categories and definitions that everyone accepts and uses. Part of the difficulty lies in the varying purposes of different stakeholders. Administrators use definitions for identifying candidates and for determining levels of support and resource allocation. Parents, advocates, and community support associations, because they have more immediate remediation objectives, tend to emphasize extensive, symptom-based characteristics.

Some support groups argue for no definitions at all because students with special needs simply do not fit into such confines.

Other stakeholders have very individualistic perspectives. Medical professionals have their own view, one that often has limited connection with education. Researchers may develop their own definitions to limit the variables in a study. Teachers and educational assistants want definitions to provide a practical guidance point for planning and practice. Then there is the very notion of special need itself. To anyone who reflects on the fact that normalcy is not defined, it is no surprise that departure from normal is hard to describe.

In the Classroom

For those who work with students with exceptionalities on an active, daily basis – teachers, educational assistants, parents – the precision (or lack thereof) in categories and definitions of exceptionality is a minor issue in the grand scheme of things, but it is one that cannot be completely ignored.

First, classroom professionals increasingly are expected to become involved with other professionals (medical, for example) within a multidisciplinary team, and it is important that each understand the other. Within a variety of fields, efforts have been made to bridge the gap between disciplines. The Neuro Trauma Foundation of Ontario, for example, has identified education as one of the main priorities for research. There is a growing recognition that, for many children, a majority of their waking hours, and thus possible rehabilitation hours, are spent in a school setting. Given this fact, the necessity of meaningful communication and collaborative planning between previously separate treatment approaches seems obvious.

Second, for better or worse, there is an unavoidable underlay of politics in special education, so, for understanding and productive dialogue, it behooves all parties to be tuned in to all positions.

Finally, and perhaps most practically, official categories and definitions issued by a jurisdiction may well be the factor that determines which students are identified exceptional and what resources can and will be made available for their benefit. For that reason alone, teachers, for example, must be sensitive to categories and definitions.

Ontario's Official Categories and Definitions

When the *Education Amendment Act*, commonly referred to as Bill 82, made special education mandatory in Ontario, the Ministry of Education issued a set of definitions of exceptionality. The idea was for boards of education to use the definitions when identifying a student as exceptional. Initially, most boards did just that. Over time, some boards began to modify the definitions for their own use, basing their changes within the parameters of the existing Ministry definitions. Others stuck to the Ministry list, but made additions and deletions using terminology that was more suitable to and well understood within their own educational context.

In recent years, the Ministry has come under increasing criticism for its perceived unwillingness to tackle the issue of revamping the now decades-old list of exceptionalities. While changes have been proposed, they have not, to date, been implemented. In December 2011, the Ministry did release a memo stating that services for students with learning difficulties should be provided regardless of whether the cause of the difficulties can be identified within one of the existing categories. While this memo, in and of itself, does not represent a significant shift in the original categorical model, it does indicate a positive sign that the Ministry is aware that categorical labels can sometimes stand in the way of necessary programming. (See the memorandum Category of Exceptionalities **http://www.edu.gov.on.ca/eng/general/elemsec/speced/2011CategoryException.pdf** for more information.)

Certainly, agreement on the wording of the changes, as well as the implications of such a move, has been a deterrent to decision-making and implementation. Organizations that represent groups of individuals with exceptionalities such as attention deficit/hyperactivity disorder and acquired brain injury continue to advocate for the recognition of these conditions within the category list. Many feel that, as special education matures and as philosophies, scientific knowledge, and practices change, the categories and definitions should evolve as well.

Despite the fact that many boards of education took on a somewhat "personalized" version of special education categories, the result was not the hodgepodge one might expect from such independent forays. Granted, in some instances, it became possible for a student to qualify for special education in one board in the province but not in another. But, most of the time, these were unique cases that, conceivably, would have been problematic anyway. In effect, the relative independence of the province's school boards was simply a reflection of how difficult it is to describe accurately students with special needs. Many fit several definitions; others fall into cracks between definitions; still others resist the confines of such qualifiers as "mild," "moderate," and "severe." Then there is the reality of change. Students with exceptionalities, like all students, grow and develop. Their special needs are not immutable.

Despite these difficulties, there are many useful reasons for maintaining a set of official categories and definitions in a publicly funded education system, not the least of which are issues in resource allocation and other administrative factors. From the time special education first became mandatory in the province, Ontario has maintained an official set of categories and definitions. These are modified from time to time following extensive consultations. The current set, extant at publication, appears in appendix I of this new edition.

The Numbers

In 1983, the Canadian Council of Ministers of Education issued data indicating that 15.5 percent of the school-age population in the country was exceptional. That figure, developed at the time by less than rigorous science, became fixed in the consciousness of the general public, not to mention educators who usually have access to more accurate information. Despite the fact that both incidence data (number of new cases over a time period) and prevalence data (total number of existing cases) are notoriously difficult to collect and collate, there is value in examining the trends as they emerge. Current data for Ontario as shown in table 3A above present a slightly higher percentage of students at the secondary level.

While these numbers wax and wane, there is sufficient reason to pause and theorize about the larger percentage. Initiatives at the secondary school level, which include student success and transition to workplace programs, may provide part of the answer. Certainly, as secondary schools continue to implement effective initiatives to enhance learning, the number of students in need of support, in its varying forms, will increase as more students choose to avail themselves of these types of programs. Students receiving effective support and assistance may indeed be choosing to stay in school longer and benefit more from what is available to them. Placement data (see table 4B in chapter 4) imply that the majority of students receiving special education services, both elementary and secondary, are receiving programming within a regular class with various forms of support including resource teacher and EA assistance, as well as, and more importantly, the regular classroom teacher.

Yet the Numbers Are Growing

In 1986, by the end of the first year of mandatory special education in the province, Ontario's boards had identified 6.5 percent of the school population as receiving special education services. In those earlier days, many boards were still feeling their way through the process. By 1997, the percentage was 9.24, the intervening years having shown a small but steady increase in the number of students identified as having special needs. By 2001 to 2002, the percentage had continued to rise, with new information indicating that 12.8 percent of the school population was considered exceptional. This rise in numbers is, at least partly, a consequence of improved procedures of identification, along with the expansion of special education in areas where it had not previously been offered, such as autism.

The rise in identification has also been linked to a funding model that was connected specifically to a special education diagnosis. Casually referred to as "diagnosing for dollars," monies for special education increased proportionately to the number of students identified. Currently, the percentage of students receiving special education programs and services across the province sits at 14.89,* of whom 9.34 percent have been formally identified through an Identification, Placement, and Review Committee (IPRC). It would seem that the number of students receiving special education services continues to increase and that the rate of increase is somewhat greater than the rise in the total school population. There are a number of explanations for this growth, one in particular of which is peculiar to Ontario: the matter of the non-identified special education student.

_____
* Ministry of Education, 2009–10 school board reports.

Non-identified Students Receiving Special Education Services

Since the inception of Bill 82, it has been common practice that the majority of students who receive special education services in Ontario do so after having first been "identified" by an Identification, Placement, and Review Committee (IPRC). Currently, approximately 80 percent of students receiving special education in the province are placed in regular classrooms for more than half of the instructional day. Partially because of this and partially because of growing trends toward inclusion within the education field, the trend toward the identification of students through IPRCs may well be on the decline. A memo from the office of the deputy minister to directors of education across the province, dated October 2006, recommended that the IPRC process not be required when both the parents and school agree that the students should be placed in the regular classroom. The *Special Education Transformation* report (Bennett & Wynne, 2006) itself recommends that the Individual Education Plan (IEP; see chapter 5) and IPRC policy be revised to promote effective parent participation, streamline processes, and reduce administrative burden while ensuring a focus on student needs and outcomes.

The move away from the formal identification of services for students with exceptionalities is not without controversy. The IPRC, in many circles, was seen as administratively burdensome, and, in some cases, as a barrier to immediate services. However, some are concerned that the focus away from the IPRC, in some ways will reduce the legislative weight of special education services in terms of parents' ability to appeal decisions. That said, the right of any parent or principal to call an IPRC, should the need arise, is not in question.

The Case of Hobie

ACCORDING to the special education teacher, Hobie is the most loved student in the entire school. No one is certain whether Hobie knows this, but that does not matter to his classmates in grade 3, who, in the words of the teacher, "have become twenty-four willing caregivers."

Hobie has severe multiple disabilities. He is blind, has no speech, and cannot move any of his limbs.

His facial muscles respond to sound stimuli, a fact that convinces his parents – and the teacher and EA – that he can hear. No one has any firm idea at all of his mental capacities.

Hobie has outlived every one of the medical profession's dire predictions, and, despite initial grave misgivings about having him in a regular class, the school staff, and especially the students, have received him enthusiastically. He spends much of his day on a modified skateboard–looking stretcher that can be raised and lowered, and a health aide takes him out every two hours to aspirate him and see to his quite extensive health and hygiene needs. No one has yet figured out how to communicate with him. The students, for their part, go out of their way for Hobie. They vie to roll him into every group situation. They take turns holding his hand during periods such as "story time" and "the news." No one ever passes without patting his chest or gently putting a finger to his cheek, and, instinctively, they speak to him in peer-level language (no baby talk). Everyone interprets Hobie's facial reactions as proof that he is thrilled by what is happening (although recently a visiting nurse wondered whether the reactions might indicate discomfort or even pain).

Despite the very positive situation, a change looms. Hobie is in this class because the board's "fragile health needs" unit is temporarily housed in the school. Next year, the unit moves to a purpose-built facility in a brand new school and all students currently in the unit will move with it, along with the paraprofessionals and aides. When the grade 3 students, on their own initiative, asked the principal to keep Hobie with them next year in grade 4, she was deeply touched, as were members of upper-level administration and the board's trustees. Whether Hobie's thought-to-be-happy situation with the class should outweigh health, safety, and possibly legal considerations, however, must first be resolved.

Numbers, Numbers, and More Numbers?

Hard data to explain the movement in the number of students receiving special education are difficult to come by. The why and how of identification within a school board context are always linked to idiosyncratic practices of that board combined with Ministry mandates. While, overall, the number of students identified in the province continues to increase, it is within and between numbers that some interesting trends emerge and provide fodder for discussion.

The increase is most dramatic within secondary school numbers. Data indicate that in 2010, 18.21 percent of secondary students received special education programming and services as compared with the 2007 number of 16.27 percent.

Overall, the percentage of students identified as receiving special education services has increased. Between 2007 and 2012, the number of students identified as receiving services for ASD has increased at the elementary level from 6,299 to 9,020 (43.2 percent) and at the secondary level

from 1,589 to 4,071 (156 percent). It is also interesting that, in both the secondary and elementary levels, the number of students receiving special education services who were in the category of non-identified also continues to increase

Provincial trends toward the recognition and provision of services for students with ASD, as well as a movement toward the provision of services before, or, in some cases, without IPRC identification, certainly seem to be reflected in the numbers provided. Ministry initiatives within secondary schools, such as student success programs, to assist educators in recognizing and programming for students with diverse learning needs perhaps also play a role. Parent advocacy, our evolving understanding of human rights, changes in teacher education programs, shifts in provincial policy, and the introduction of documents such as *Learning for All, K-12* (Draft, 2009, Ontario Ministry of Education), also have an impact on what services are provided for students in the province.

The numbers do tell a story, but it is not

a simple tale and not one that can be told by numbers alone. Special education continues to be a dynamic field. Accordingly, most explanations are based on some empirical evidence and, to a significant degree, simply on speculation. Ultimately, the simple reality is that the number of Ontario students receiving special education service has, indeed, been increasing for some time and may well continue to do so, if only because the field, relative to general education, is still very new. Despite the fact that publicly funded schools have been offering a wide spectrum of special education for several decades now, there is still much to be learned – including how to tie the numbers down and give them meaning.

Issues Affecting Special Education Data

Getting the Numbers Right

For many years, and across many jurisdictions, the quest for the correct numbers has been an arduous one. Differing definitions and reporting procedures, access to diagnostic expertise, and even factors such as rural versus urban populations all serve to complicate the goal of numerical accuracy. Certainly, across the province of Ontario, interested parties have explored a variety of approaches to getting the numbers right.

One suggestion, that the number of students with exceptionalities be directly linked to the overall population of the board, has some curb appeal. However, this approach is often countered, and rightly so, by arguments of geographic factors, the potentially devastating effects of declining enrolments on some boards, as well as the possible dramatic shifts in funding that would accompany such a move.

Another possibility is to adopt what is termed a proxy measure for identifying the number of students with exceptionalities in a given jurisdiction. A proxy measure would take into account factors such as the average level of income, ethnicity, education level of parents, and access to

health support services of such students. The question becomes, do these factors have an impact on the number of students with exceptionalities in a given jurisdiction? To date, the identification of factors for an accurate identification of the number of students with exceptionalities in a given jurisdiction remains elusive.

The Inherent Risks in Comparison

Definitions of exceptionality vary and terminologies differ. Some school systems classify a student's need in terms of the service required, while others do so in terms of a special need. As a result, designations such as "learning disabled" and "mild intellectual disability" may be used in different schools for essentially the same case. Comparisons, therefore, must be regarded with wariness, at the very least.

In a classic comparison case in 1989, the province of Québec shocked the field by reporting a prevalence of learning disabilities three times that of Ontario and eight times that of British Columbia. Only after sorting out the differences in definition was the situation understood. (Even in the category "multiple disabilities," which is theoretically subject to more rigorously controlled description, Québec numbers that year were greater than Ontario's by a factor of 4.5.)

Chronic Problems

Another concern that affects data collection and interpretation in special education is the reality of co-occurring disabilities. In some systems, these situations are identified with terms such as "multiple exceptionalities" (as in tables 3B and 3C). However, there inevitably will be cases where, although "multi" is an appropriate identification, the decision may be taken, for a variety of reasons, to classify the individual by what is determined to be a primary special need. (Note that the reported data in tables 3B and 3C do not distinguish this – and probably could not, in any case.)

Yet another concern is the potential of certain needs to skew overall data pictures. Cases of special needs such as visual impairment or severe developmental disability are usually identified and added to the database early on, whereas something like a mild intellectual disability may not become apparent until the individual is in school, and even then, not necessarily until he or she begins to encounter difficulty. This individual may not even be added to a database under a specific disability category, becoming, instead, one of the growing numbers of non-identified students receiving support.

Nevertheless … Benefits

Notwithstanding the cautions mentioned above, the data made available by the Ministry of Education's Information Management Branch, such as may be seen in tables 3B and 3C, have significant value. These are data that confirm trends, the identifications in "ASD" being a case in point. They force us to question such things as why the total number of students in the "learning disabilities" category increases from elementary to secondary school. The numbers are vital for both long- and short-range projection, and for present and future allocation of resources. They are also useful in confirming good news. The clear decline in the number of students identified with speech impairment as they progress through elementary to secondary school, for example, strongly suggests the positive effect of remedial undertakings in this category.

Data like these in the tables permit cautious comparisons and both verify and disprove polemical claims. The data become especially valuable when compared with similar tables from other years. In short, irrespective of the problems inherent in data collection, presentation, and, especially, interpretation, without these numbers, the system would be flying blind – certainly a less appealing prospect.

Number of Students Receiving Special Education Services by Area of Exceptionality (Elementary)						
Area of Exceptionality	Fully Self-contained	Partially Integrated	Withdrawal Assistance	Resource Assistance	Indirect Service	**Total**
Behaviour	888	935	628	1370	1738	**5559**
Autism	1634	1319	1161	2141	2765	**9020**
Deaf & H. of H.	145	149	306	277	472	**1349**
Learning Disability	1387	6856	8792	10,804	8242	**36,081**
Speech Impairment	6	19	50	88	83	**246**
Language Impairment	548	903	1248	2081	1 198	**5978**
Giftedness	4784	3032	2488	738	4806	**15848**
Mild Intellectual Dis.	1802	2302	1398	1444	1213	**8159**
Developmental Dis.	2243	1091	383	627	515	**4849**
Physical Disability	321	116	153	473	652	**1716**
Blind & Low Vision	29	18	74	127	160	**408**
Deaf-Blind (alt. prog.)	0	0	0	<6	0	**<6**
Multiple Exceptionalities	915	918	696	1172	1449	**5150**
Subtotal	14,702	17,648	17,377	21,343	13,294	**94,364**
Non-identified Students	781	3249	27,568	22,945	27,321	**81,864**
(Receiving Special Ed. Programs and Services)						
Grand Total Provincial	**15,483**	**20,897**	**44,945**	**44,288**	**50,615**	**176,228**

Table 3B   Source: Ministry of Ed., Data as of January 2009–10

Number of Students Receiving Special Education Services by Area of Exceptionality (Secondary)						
Area of Exceptionality	Fully Self-contained	Partially Integrated	Withdrawal Assistance	Resource Assistance	Indirect Service	**Total**
Behaviour	160	284	1118	991	2337	**4890**
Autism	874	880	764	735	818	**4071**
Deaf & H. of H.	33	114	176	156	316	**795**
Learning Disability	237	2263	14,470	12,326	18,661	**47,957**
Speech Impairment	<6	<6	12	11	37	**66**
Language Impairment	159	761	872	723	1824	**4339**
Giftedness	26	2405	1622	1620	6667	**12,340**
Mild Intellectual Dis.	1840	1460	3162	2520	3023	**12,005**
Developmental Dis.	2512	1530	351	295	315	**5003**
Physical Disability	237	124	176	211	425	**1173**
Blind & Low Vision	9	6	55	74	103	**247**
Multiple Exceptionalities	986	908	779	938	1699	**5280**
Subtotal	**7078**	**10,736**	**23,557**	**20,600**	**36,195**	**98,166**
Non-identified Students	125	450	8099	5874	18,078	**32,626**
(Receiving Special Ed. Programs and Services)						
Grand Total Provincial	**7203**	**11,186**	**31,656**	**26,474**	**54,273**	**130,792**

Table 3C   Source: Ministry of Ed., Data as of January 2009–10

A Very Special Population

The Ministry of Education has direct responsibility for a number of very special schools in the province. The examples of longest standing, and certainly the best known, are the provincial schools. Some of these are residential schools geared to specific exceptionalities. The Ministry also participates in a number of hospital schools and care and treatment facilities at various key locations in the province, as well as schools in a number of correctional facilities. Unlike the provincial schools, where education is the primary mission, in these latter locations, the "school" aspect functions in tandem with other purposes.

Taken together, the population of provincial schools and facilities fairly consistently represents about half of 1 percent of the entire population of publicly funded schools in Ontario, and in most years, just under 3 percent of the population receiving special education services. (For more on service delivery, see chapter 4.)

Readings and Resources

Bennett, S., & Wynne, K. (2006). *Special education transformation: The report of the co-chairs with the recommendations of the working table on special education.* Ontario Ministry of Education, Ontario. Toronto: Queen's Printer for Ontario. Retrieved at: http://www.edu.gov.on.ca

Fujiura, G. T., & Kiyoshi, Y. (2000). Trends in demography of childhood poverty and disability. *Exceptional Children, 66*(2), 187–99.

Hibel, J., Farkas, G., & Morgan, P. (2010). Who is placed into special education? *Sociology of Education, 83*(4), 312–32.

Hosp, J. L., & Reschly, D. J. (2004). Disproportionate representation of minority students in special education: Academic, demographic, and economic predictors. *Exceptional Children, 70,* 185–99.

Johnson, D. R., Stodden, R. A., Emanuel, E. J., Leuking, R., & Mack, M. (2002). Current challenges facing secondary education and transition services: What research tells us. *Exceptional Children, 68*(4), 519–31.

Learning for all, k–12 (Draft). Retrieved at http://www.edu.gov.ca/eng/elemsec/speced/LearningforAll2011.pdf

The report of the expert panel on literacy and numeracy instruction for students with special education needs, kindergarten to grade 6. Toronto: Queen's Printer for Ontario: 2005.

Ysseldyke, J., & Bielinski, J. (2002). Effects of different methods of reporting and reclassification on trends in test scores for students with disabilities. *Exceptional Children, 68*(2), 189–200.

4

Service Delivery: The Infrastructure of Special Education

"Across the province of Ontario, EQAO results for students with special education needs have risen because of the excellent work being done by classroom teachers as well as a greater number of students writing these tests. When a student with an exceptionality does well on these tests and other forms of assessment, people begin to see the ability, not the disability, of this young person."

– Felice K., principal

Accessing Special Education Services: Referral Process

The process by which a student becomes a beneficiary of a special education program and/or service is basically the same in most school boards, although each board has its own policies and procedures. The following reflects what is practiced in many boards throughout the province.

Step One:	Identify a student who may need a special education program and/or service.
Step Two:	Discuss the student with the special education resource teacher assigned to the school.
Step Three:	Bring the student to the attention of the In-school Team. (An Individual Education Plan may be developed at this point.)
Step Four:	When necessary, refer the student to the attention of the Identification, Placement, and Review Committee (IPRC).
Step Five:	Implement IEP (adjust placement as necessary, as per IPRC recommendation).

Table 4A

Although the sequence seems deceptively simple in a world of procedures and policies, these five steps summarize how special education comes about for a student.

Step One: Identify a student who may need a special education program and/or service

A small number of students may come to a school with their special needs already assessed and with all or part of a program in place. Those with long-established physical or medical needs are a frequent example. A few others may come tagged, so to speak, for "careful watching," to see whether suspected needs are serious enough to be addressed. Still others, especially the very young, will arrive with extensive information about their needs prepared by parents or a preschool. Inevitably, there will be students whose special needs, perhaps for the first time ever, will become apparent only during the course of a school year.

Some, or all, of these students will become candidates for special education, a decision that will be made after an assessment and identification of their needs. Assessments vary in extent and formality, depending on the policy and the resources of the school board and the student being assessed. The purpose is to gain some insight into the subject's intelligence, strengths, needs, health, and behaviour, and to provide information that will allow for effective programming to ensure school success. For a few students, an assessment may indicate that special education is not really necessary, and the service delivery process may stop at this point. For candidates who are identified as potential beneficiaries, further steps follow, as described below. (See chapter 7 for more on assessments.)

Step Two: Discuss the student with the special education resource teacher assigned to the school

In most, if not all, schools in Ontario, a teacher qualified in special education is assigned the role of "resource teacher." Depending on the size of the school, this teacher may be present in the school for all or part of the day. One of the responsibilities of these teachers is to assist regular class teachers who may have concerns about the learning needs of some of their students. The resource teacher may provide assistance in assessing student needs, may provide approaches to improving the student's learning, or may suggest that the student be brought to the attention of the In-school Team. Note that students showing abilities indicating possible giftedness are also brought to the attention of the resource teacher.

The Individual Education Plan

The Individual Education Plan, or IEP, is a written plan of action that becomes a road map for everyone involved: student, teachers, educational assistants, parents, and administrators. Ideally, the needs highlighted by the assessment are addressed in the IEP. According to the Ministry's *Individual Education Plan Resource Guide* (2004), the development of the plan should involve all concerned parties so that the final result is not a surprise to anyone.

Overview of the IEP Process
1 Gather information
2 Set the direction
3 Develop the IEP as it relates to the student's special education program and services
4 Implement the IEP
5 Review and update the IEP

The IEP not only summarizes the student's strengths, needs, and interests (and health and behaviour profile where applicable), but also sets out individualized goals and objectives. These goals and objectives may include simple modifications of the curriculum that everyone else is studying. Sometimes, they are entirely unique to the student. As well, an IEP offers ideas and strategies for instruction, elements of scheduling, alternate assessment approaches, environmental adjustments, and other details as appropriate. For students fourteen years and older, a Transition Plan is also developed for post-secondary transition to work, community living, or further education. (For more on IEPs, see chapter 5.)

According to the Ontario Ministry of Education, the term *accommodations* is used to refer to "the special teaching and assessment strategies, human supports, and/or individualized equipment required to enable a student to learn and/or to demonstrate learning. Accommodations do not alter the provincial curriculum expectations for the grade" (Ontario Ministry of Education, 2004, p. 25). Accommodations can be instructional, or environmental (e.g., study carrel, use of headphones, special lighting), or reflect a change in the manner in which the student is assessed.

Modifications, on the other hand, are "changes in the age-appropriate grade-level expectations for a subject or course in order to meet a student's learning needs. These changes may involve developing expectations that reflect knowledge and skills required in the curriculum for a different grade level and/or decreasing the number and/or complexity of the regular grade level curriculum expectations" (Ontario Ministry of Education, 2004, p. 25).

The Cases of Sheldon and Jean-Marc

Both Sheldon and Jean-Marc were accepted into a preschool regional centre day program when they were 4.4 years and 4.2 years old respectively. Although both boys presented almost exactly the same behaviours, Sheldon had been diagnosed as having autism while Jean-Marc was diagnosed as having pervasive development disorder. Both boys were highly introverted and engaged in harmful self-stimulation. Neither used intelligible speech, and both were instant runaways if left unsupervised.

Happily, the program at the centre was successful in quickly effecting some changes. After about three months, both began to use some meaningful speech and, as well, appeared to understand much of what was being said to them. By the end of one full year, their echolalic habits diminished significantly. Jean-Marc (but not Sheldon) began to refer to himself in the first person (rather than calling himself "he" or "Jean-Marc") and directly addressed his favourite educational assistant by name, rather than as "she."

In their second year at the centre, Sheldon and Jean-Marc are now enrolled in what the staff calls the "top" group. It took a psychometrist three tries, but she succeeded in completing a preschool assessment of Jean-Marc and reported him to be of average to just below average intelligence in speech (although delayed – at 6.4, he is at the norm for four-year-olds), and improving at an accelerated pace. Jean-Marc makes eye contact spontaneously about half of the time and when directed to "look at me" will respond appropriately every time. He still exhibits some unusual behaviours. For example, he will compulsively stroke any clothing that is red in colour, no matter who is wearing it, and music of any kind will take up his total attention, not only while it is being played but also after. On occasion he will hum a melody over and over for the remainder of the day.

Staff at the centre point proudly to Jean-Marc's ability to relate to others. On the thrice-weekly field trips (to shopping malls, parks, or anywhere that people gather), he follows directions, takes responsibility, and spontaneously assists with the group.

In Sheldon's case, the field trips are a weak point. Wide-open spaces threaten him, as do large numbers of strange adults. While he copes with these situations as long as there is familiar adult support, he still turns to the comfort of repetitive, stereotyped behaviour at these times. He alternately pats his cheeks and then his ears, or spins around and around with eyes closed and arms extended – staff members have noted several times that he can persist at this indefinitely without getting dizzy.

On the other hand, Sheldon's use of appropriate language has increased dramatically. Although he refused utterly to co-operate with the psychometrist who successfully assessed Jean-Marc, she reinforced – off the record – the opinion of staff that his language usage was at, or just below, age-appropriate level.

Now, notwithstanding a possible setback incident (after a fire drill, Sheldon was found inside a heating duct in a no-go area of the building; Jean-Marc imitated the alarm bell continuously for several days), both boys are going to enter grade 1 classes in their neighbourhood schools. The receiving principals and teachers have asked for advice on how best to make the transition smooth and what modifications and/or accommodations should be included in these students' IEPs.

Step Three: Bring the student to the attention of the In-school Team

Every school will have an In-school Team, usually composed of the special education teacher, the principal and/or vice principal, a regular classroom teacher (perhaps from each division), and any other personnel the principal may believe necessary. If the resource teacher believes that the student's needs or strengths are such that further assessment and/or program strategies are necessary, the teacher will bring the student to the attention of this committee and receive ideas that are designed to help the student achieve. At this point, an IEP that permits the teacher to modify and/or accommodate the student's program may be developed.

Step Four: When necessary, refer the student to the attention of the Identification, Placement, and Review Committee (IPRC)

The IPRC may be made up of superintendents (though this is rarely the case), principals, special education consultants and/or coordinators, area resource teachers, regular education teachers, and related professionals (psychologists, social workers, etc.). This committee, after reviewing all assessment data, determines whether the student should be declared exceptional and may recommend a change in program and/or classroom placement. Once placed, a student so designated must have an IEP prepared within thirty days of placement.

> *"I try not to resent the time I spend at meetings and writing reports, but every minute it takes to do that is another minute I'm not where I want to be: helping the kids."*
> – Arlene Y., special education teacher

Step Five: Adjust placement when necessary and implement IEP

An oft-debated matter in special education is just where to implement the IEP. Most students with exceptionalities (approximately 80 percent) are based in regular classrooms and receive their special education program in that setting. For those placed in a self-contained setting (almost 50 percent for students identified as Developmentally Disabled), these settings may be anything from a school where the entire environment is devoted to a particular need (e.g., schools for students who are deaf or hard of hearing), to separate, specialized classes in a neighbourhood school. A quite frequent placement choice will be a combination of resource room (where a student will spend part of his or her day) and regular class. In many cases, the appropriate setting may be a regular classroom where resources are brought to the student.

The permutations and combinations are considerable. Whatever the choice of setting for the student, the setting is always, within reason, subject to review and adjustment.

Modify and/or Accommodate as Necessary

An essential component of an Individual Education Plan is regular re-examination, for an IEP does not just delineate the student's program; it is also a guide, an evolving benchmark for monitoring the student's progress and development. It is required that, at the very least, the IEP be reviewed at each report card evaluation period. In most cases, the IEP, from each reporting period to the next, is the baseline from which necessary additions, accommodations, and modifications are highlighted. For this reason, especially, an IEP is effective in clarifying communication with parents and other significant figures in a student's life.

Range of Placement Options

In Ontario in 2009/10, over 300,000 students were receiving special education programs and services (176,228 in elementary and 130,792 in secondary). Table 4B lists the range of options and the number of students receiving each option at the elementary and secondary levels.

Regular Class with Indirect Support

It is not uncommon for a teacher to seek assistance from the special education or resource teacher to obtain instructional ideas on how effectively to teach and/or assess a student with exceptionalities in the regular classroom. In this instance, help is provided in an "indirect" manner, in that no direct assistance is provided to the student by anyone except the regular classroom teacher.

Very often, what becomes "special" about a student's education is a simple and straightforward adjustment in his or her program within the regular class. An example would be a student who has spina bifida and requires a wheelchair for mobility. If this student has learned to manage his or her own condition, as most do, the student will participate in every aspect of the regular classroom in an entirely normal way but, at times, perhaps during a physical education program, some accommodations are likely to be made. For example, the student may not participate in basketball but would have an alternate appropriate physical activity in its place. Should the student regularly need extra time for things like personal hygiene, a teacher would accommodate by trying to present new or difficult material at times when the student is normally expected to be present.

Other assistance may be in the form of specialized equipment such as an FM transmitter system for a student who is hard of hearing.

Number of Students Receiving Special Education Services by Type of Placement				
	Elementary		Secondary	
	2005/6	2009/10	2005/6	2009/10
Fully Self-contained	18,714	15,483	7186	7203
Partially Integrated	20,562	20,897	8756	11,186
Withdrawal Assistance	61,457	44,945	27,277	31,656
Resource Assistance	42,953	44,288	30,901	26,474
Indirect Support	31,901	50,615	41,018	54, 273
Total	**175,587**	**176,228**	**115,138**	**130,792**

Table 4B
Source: Ontario Ministry of Education, *School September Report, 2005–6*, and Ontario Ministry of Education, *School September Report, 2009/10*. Includes all publicly funded schools, excluding care and treatment facilities. Includes non-identified students receiving service.

Resource Assistance

"Resource assistance," sometimes called "direct support," is delivered in a variety of ways. It is quite common for the resource teacher to enter the regular classroom and assist a student with special needs while the regular classroom teacher is providing instruction to the rest of the class. This "co-teaching" situation keeps the student with special needs in the regular class, thereby assisting in the student's socialization and ensuring that the student doesn't miss curriculum topics presented to the whole class.

In the case of a regular class in which, for example, a student who has a hearing impairment is placed, there may be direct support to the student ranging from special technical equipment to the presence of a signing interpreter. At the same time, a teacher or consultant with specialized knowledge about deafness may provide support to the classroom teacher in everything from program preparation to in-service training. Another typical example is the situation in which an educational assistant will spend specific amounts of time in classrooms providing remedial support to students in, say, language development. Still another situation is that in which the assistant provides support to a student with behaviour concerns at times in the school day when those concerns tend to manifest themselves.

Resource assistance is sometimes mistakenly construed as relatively low impact, but the assistance can be significant indeed. For example, it is not unusual for a student with intense special needs to have resource assistance in the form of an educational assistant full-time or nearly full-time.

Regular Class/Withdrawal for Assistance

For part of their program, some students with exceptionalities may benefit from an individualized learning experience that is more effectively delivered in a setting less distracting or competitive or, in some cases, more specially equipped than a regular classroom. Thus, a student may be withdrawn to a resource room, for example, where a resource teacher or an educational assistant, working in close concert with the regular teacher, will deliver the modified and/or accommodated learning experience called for in the student's IEP. In this arrangement, the student remains a member of the regular class, but part of his or her program is delivered elsewhere on a formally scheduled basis.

A fairly typical example of a student who uses this type of placement is one with a learning disability for whom reading and writing pose extra difficulty. Often, the strategies that benefit a student with learning disabilities, as well as others with special needs, can be very effectively delivered in this type of resource arrangement. Taking a student out of a class for one-on-one instruction is by no means a novel idea, especially in the elementary grades. What distinguishes the practice in special education is the specificity of the arrangement and the guarantee in a student's plan of its regular delivery.

Part-time Regular Class/Self-contained Class (Partially Integrated)

"Self-contained class" refers to a classroom setting composed of students with similarly identified special needs, e.g., learning disabled, behaviourally exceptional, gifted, or developmentally handicapped. Different boards have different policies for the composition of and criteria for placement in these classes regardless of the definitions of exceptionality provided by the Ministry of Education (see appendix I). As the designation part-time regular class/self-contained class would suggest, this is an arrangement whereby a student spends time in two settings. Unlike the withdrawal-to-a-resource-room choice, this setup is somewhat more formal in that a self-contained classroom is usually more specifically dedicated and managed than a resource room. This approach is used to help students who are making a transition from a full-time self-contained class to a regular class and offers an effective combination of intensive instruction opportunity together with a normalized experience.

Full-time Self-contained Class

It may be deemed appropriate, to generate a very specific kind of learning experience, to place a student with an exceptionality in a self-contained special education class full-time. These placements are found in some, but by no means all, school boards in the province. Ideally, students with exceptionalities who take their entire program in such classes participate in general school activities in the same way as other students. The recommendations of the Ontario Ministry of Education Working Group on Special Education suggest that any student's placement in a self-contained class "be duration-specific, intervention-focused and subject to regular reviews" (Bennett & Wynne, 2006, p. 8).

When they are placed in these settings, students rarely remain in these classes 100 percent of the school day. In most cases, the teacher arranges for the students to spend part of the day in a regular classroom (often with the assistance of an educational assistant) so they can benefit from interacting and learning with regular classroom students.

Special Schools

A number of dedicated-purpose schools in the province are run under the aegis of the Ministry of Education. In Brantford, the W. Ross Macdonald School, named after a former lieutenant-governor, has programs for students who are blind and deaf/blind. In London, Belleville, and Milton, schools named after former Ontario premiers, the Robarts School, Sir James Whitney School, and Ernest C. Drury School, respectively, offer programs for students who are deaf. The Ministry also maintains "demonstration" schools at the latter three locations for students diagnosed as having AD/HD and/or severe learning disabilities. Each is a residential school with a fairly small population. The schools are known, respectively, as Amethyst, Sagonaska, and Trillium. In Ottawa, the Centre Jules-Leger offers programs in French for students who are deaf and students who are severely learning disabled.

In addition to dedicated programs for their students, these schools also offer the standard Ontario curriculum. They are resource and training centres for both teachers and the wider community and play a role in specialized teacher training. Students are enrolled in the schools through an application process that involves the Ministry and the student's school board.

The Case of Cassie

OFFICIALLY, Cassie is 15.2 years old, although Family Services acknowledges she may be up to six months younger or as much as a full year older. There are no birth records. Cassie's physical appearance can be interpreted in a variety of ways, and nothing is known of her mother, who is believed to have been a homeless person. Equally uncertain is the origin of Cassie's intellectual disabilities and behaviour problems. Fetal alcohol syndrome is one listed cause, but a large scar over her left ear with an adjacent depression in her skull has also led to a suspicion of acquired brain injury. Nevertheless, both administration and staff at Cassie's school are quick to point out that they are less concerned with the cause of her problems than with the symptoms.

Prominent among these are deep-rooted behaviour problems that follow a pattern her teachers describe as "going on benders." Between episodes of relative calm, Cassie will become aggressive, often violent, for several days. Most recently, in a single day, she scratched a teacher who (unsuccessfully) tried to stop her from beating another student; set fire to clothing in a change room; overturned her desk after failing a test; and then spent an impressive four consecutive hours crying in the arms of an educational assistant in the school's resource room. Academically, Cassie places in the very low percentiles except for mathematics, in which she is rated Low Average.

Interestingly, the prime concern about Cassie at the moment relates to service delivery. At the beginning of the current semester, special education in her secondary school switched from a Fixed Resource model to a Mobile Resource model. In the Fixed model, over a four-period (plus lunch) day, identified students attend three regular classes and spent one specifically timetabled period in a resource room with special education staff. In the Mobile model, identified students take four regular classes, often accompanied by special education staff, with the option to "drop in" to a resource room as necessary. In theory, "drop-ins" occur after consultation with the student, the regular teacher, and special education staff. In practice, students tend to drop in at will.

Since the adoption of the Mobile model, Cassie has spent almost all of her time in the resource room to be in the company of an educational assistant assigned there. The EA is new but is very popular with both students and staff and highly regarded for her skill in dealing with students who act out.

Cassie's attachment to the EA and the resource room has generated a number of concerns. One is that sticking exclusively to the EA contradicts the goals of her IEP (not to mention that the EA has become unavailable for other duties). Another arises because the school board is very strongly and publicly committed to inclusion and sees the situation as a potential black mark.

Regular teachers, understandably, are relieved that Cassie's presence in their classrooms is limited, but that position puts them in conflict with the special education teachers. At first, no one wanted to stir the pot because Cassie has been undergoing an extended period of calm. But it is expected that Cassie spend more time in regular classrooms, and teachers are determining what approaches are likely to be most effective.

Specialized, Non-school Settings ("Section 23")

In situations where students are admitted to a care or treatment facility, group home, or custodial or correctional facility, special arrangements are usually necessary to address the students' educational needs. The educational program in these cases is part of a wider program of service that may include medical treatment or service from therapists, psychiatrists, social workers, etc. For the most part, the educational portion of the program is undertaken by a local school board under written agreement with the facility. Funding is a complex matter, for several provincial ministries are usually involved, each having its own priorities, responsibilities, and funding mechanisms.

The Ministry of Education describes these settings as Educational Programs in Government-Approved Facilities for Care, Treatment and Custodial or Correctional Purposes. In everyday parlance, these settings are typically referred to as Section 23s, this being the number and section of the funding regulation that permits these arrangements to receive provincial dollars.

It is important to note that students placed in classrooms in these settings are not officially students registered with a board and therefore do not fall under much of the legislated special education provincial requirements. They are placed in these classrooms because they have been accepted or sent to the facility, not because of an IPRC placement decision.

In terms of the placement continuum, specialized, non-school settings, along with special schools, are viewed as quite restrictive settings.

Cascade or Full Inclusion: The Debate Is Over

All school boards in Ontario now accept the premise that inclusion of students with exceptionalities in regular classes should be the normal practice. At the same time, it is Ministry of Education policy that a range of settings (such as those described above) should be available for students whose needs are best addressed under alternative arrangements. For most – but not all – school boards in the province, this approach has been pretty much standard practice since special education was first established. The standard practice is based on variations of a long-established placement model known by a variety of names such as the Special Education Cascade, or Continuum, Model (see figure 4A).

The distinguishing feature of this model is that a continuum of settings for students with exceptionalities is available on a formal and more or less permanent basis. The settings, or learning environments, are progressively more specialized, and students, if it is deemed necessary and beneficial, may be placed in these alternative settings on a short- or longer-term basis. Important philosophical principles of the model are that students always be placed in the least restrictive environment and that no restricted placement ever be regarded as permanent.

As one might expect, in a province the size of Ontario, geography and budgets have an influence on available placements. Thus, in the case of a setting organized to deal with, say, extremely difficult behaviour, a board might arrange that only one school out of several in an area would offer this special environment. Still another might have a self-contained setting for students with fragile health issues. Each school in the area, however, likely would have its own resource room or similar, moderately specialized setting for part- or full-time placements. No matter how the school board arranges matters, theoretically – and, for the most part, in practice – in the range of settings model, all students in the board have access, if necessary, to the appropriate setting for their needs.

Placement arrangements built on the principle of inclusion tend to be quite flexible and, sometimes, quite ad hoc (note the looping arrows in figure 4B below). Very often, arrangements are created – and collapsed – entirely according to needs of the moment. Most school boards where inclusion is an underpinning philosophy make at least minimal use of alternative settings, if only informally. Still, the fundamental principle of inclusion is not diluted: A student with an exceptionality, no matter where the student's special education service is delivered, is considered a full-time student in his or her regular classroom. The student is never administratively placed elsewhere. In those instances when a more restrictive setting is accessed, the goal is to return the student to the regular classroom as soon as possible.

Debate over the moral and practical superiority of inclusion versus range of settings raged hotly for several years but has diminished dramatically in the light of experience. Most educators in

Ontario, even before provincial policy was clarified, were operating from the position that regular class placement should be a first choice as a matter of course. And, over time, even the most vociferous supporters of inclusion have acknowledged that a limited number of students with special needs can benefit from specialized settings that are duration-specific and intervention-focused. It is important to note that an examination of table 4B reveals an increase in those receiving service in regular classrooms either through resource assistance or indirect service. It is evident that the primary responsibility for program delivery to students with exceptionalities lies with the regular classroom teacher.

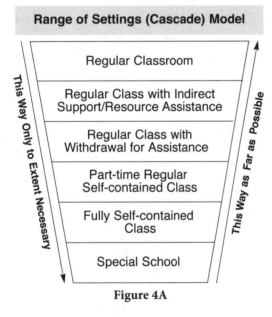

Figure 4A

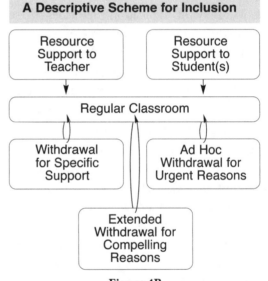

Figure 4B

Getting Special Education Underway

Under the regulations implemented after the passage of Bill 82, many boards of education tended to rely almost exclusively on formal procedures to get the process going. Hence, most decisions were made by officially constituted Identification, Placement, and Review Committees (IPRCs).

A committee would make a determination of exceptionality (if appropriate); decide on a placement; in some cases, make recommendations

regarding program; and then, if the parents agreed, begin the student's special education program. As systems and practice matured, schools began to adopt simpler procedures for some students, reserving the time-consuming and demanding formality of the IPRC for more complicated cases. The models shown in Situations I and II (tables 4C and 4D below) are reasonably typical examples of the less formal, in-school variety. The model shown in Situation III (table 4E) is considerably more formal.

Situation I (table 4C) presents a type of case

that occurs frequently. It begins when the teacher and/or educational assistant or parent becomes aware of a student's special need(s). When it is possible to bring about appropriate adjustments to meet the needs in the classroom without bringing formal processes to bear, the matter can be resolved quickly, simply, and with reasonable hope of immediate benefit. In Situation I, it is very likely that assessments would be informal and carried out by the teacher, perhaps with assistance from in-school personnel such as the learning resource teacher. In this case, the student is usually not officially identified exceptional although, for school purposes and for data reporting, he or she may be considered a student receiving a special education program and/or service.

Situation II (table 4D below) is somewhat more complex. It will likely involve more personnel. This procedure does not formally identify the student as exceptional but likely will call for somewhat more standardized actions than in Situation I. The assessment of needs usually will be more detailed and may even be supported with formal test results. As with Situation I, the student may now be considered part of the school's special education population. This latter process is becoming a more prevalent practice throughout the province.

As table 4E implies, Situation III is definitely more complex. It reflects provincially regulated practice in the province and is the approach necessary to have a student formally identified as exceptional. Naturally, this process is more time-consuming than Situations I and II and is subject to standardized procedures required by provincial regulations.

Procedures used by individual schools and boards will differ. These are examples only and have no official status. In some cases, in order to maintain flexibility and a policy of by-case response, a school will not use standard procedures at all. All schools, however, pay heed to Ministry regulations and, invariably, try to proceed with the student's best interests as the top priority. According to a Ministry of Education Memorandum signed by then Deputy Minister Ben Levin (October 12, 2006), an IPRC is not required when both the parents and school agree that the student should be placed in a regular classroom. The memo was also intended to assist principals in implementing regulation 181/91 in a way that "respects parents' rights while minimizing administrative requirements."

In those instances where school personnel and parents have difficulty agreeing on an appropriate special education program and/or service for the student, the Ministry recommends that boards put into place an alternative dispute resolution process whereby a facilitator is used to help the parties reach agreement on a program suited to the needs of the student. The document *Shared Solutions: A Guide to Preventing and Resolving Conflicts Regarding Programs and Services for Students with Special Education Needs* (Ontario Ministry of Education, 2007) offers suggestions on how this approach could be employed so that the more formal appeal and tribunal process can be avoided. (See chapter 6.)

Situation I	
Teacher and/or parent identifies special needs	
Teacher and resource teacher adjust program or instructional practice to meet specific need	*May have help of parent, school team, school resources*
Appropriate program in place	*If not, then referral to school team or to formal process – see tables 4D, 4E*

Table 4C

Situation II	
Teacher and/or parent identifies special needs	
Referral to school team	*Usually some in-class modification underway by this time*
School team helps develop a response and develops an IEP	*Input from parents and other resources is obtained; may deploy extra resources with approval of administration*
Appropriate program in place (IEP)	*If not, then referral to formal process – see table 4E*

Table 4D

Situation III	
Teacher and/or parent identifies special needs	
Student referred to In-school Team	
Principal invokes formal referral process (IPRC)	*May or may not have first gone to school team*
Committee is convened and formally identifies exceptionality and recommends placement	*Full educational assessment usually completed by this point*
Student attends at recommended placement and plan is established	*If parent agrees* *Resource support may be formally assigned – either board-managed or school-managed*
Appropriate program in place – IEP	*If not, situation reviewed for further modification and/or accommodation*

Table 4E

Service Delivery in Secondary Schools

Because of the structure of a typical high school, special education service delivery there is quite different than in elementary settings. Nevertheless, it is clear from Ontario Ministry of Education Policy documents that students with special needs in secondary schools are entitled to a program and an environment that meet their needs. Though it is recognized that the number of teachers, other students, courses, diploma requirements, and scheduling options that an individual with special needs encounters in a secondary school setting is much greater than in the elementary experience, program accommodations and modifications included on a student's IEP need to be followed by all teachers to whom the student is assigned.

Secondary schools have complex timetabling. Most are organized on a semester system, and fundamental to that structure is the completion of credits, the basis on which diplomas are awarded. Matching the typically large number of course options with the special needs of a student with an exceptionality means the role of a special education teacher in a high school frequently involves more coordination and consultation than direct intervention.

For a majority of students receiving special education services at the high school level, considerations such as course reduction, careful and strategic course selection, and scheduling of resource room time are common practices, and these must be monitored. Regular teaching staff and other school personnel need to be informed of the contents of a student's IEP and need to ensure that the IEP recommendations are implemented as indicated. Recommendations in an IEP can include:

- no accommodations and modifications, or
- accommodations only, or
- modified learning expectations, with the possibility of accommodations, or
- a non-credit (alternative) course

Student Success/Learning to Eighteen

The Ontario Ministry of Education has developed several strategies to help all students, including students with exceptionalities, succeed in high school. Key to these initiatives are six innovative programs that can be "customized" to suit the needs of the particular secondary school student.

- Student success teams: Teachers are employed specifically to assist students requiring extra attention and support.

- Expanded co-op credit: Students can now earn two compulsory high school credits through hands-on experience.

- Specialist high skills major: This program allows students to organize their courses to prepare for specific academic or skilled careers.

- Dual credit program: Students earn credits that can be put toward both their high school diploma and their post-secondary diploma or apprenticeship certification.

- Lighthouse project: Innovative local programs can be designed to help students stay in school by providing guidance, support, and alternative learning environments.

- Grade 8–9 transition: A new initiative to help students succeed in grades 8 and 9 by providing more teachers, intensive professional development, and improved tracking of students having difficulties in these grades.

Source: www.edu.gov.on.ca/eng/6ways/welcome.html

Diplomas and Credits

Currently in Ontario, successful completion of a high school program leads to an Ontario Secondary School Diploma (OSSD). This diploma requires completion of thirty high school credits, forty hours of community involvement, and successful completion of the Ontario Secondary School Literacy Test or course. For those students who fail to meet the requirements of the OSSD, an Ontario Secondary School Certificate, which requires fourteen credits, may be issued instead.

Recent changes to secondary school graduation requirements, designed to keep students in school until the age of eighteen, permit students to take more co-operative education courses and receive secondary school credits for experiential learning. These changes also provided funding to secondary schools to employ additional personnel to provide assistance to students having difficulty so that they can achieve and meet secondary school graduation requirements. The Learning to 18 and Student Success initiatives established by the Ontario Ministry of Education in 2005 encouraged all students, including those identified as having special needs, to "achieve their potential and succeed in secondary school" (Ontario Ministry of Education, 2005). These initiatives included:

- *Credit Recovery*: a program designed to help students successfully complete courses they had previously failed
- *Alternative Education*: programs designed to "re-engage" students who had difficulty succeeding in high school classrooms
- *Student Success in Grades 9 and 10*: programs designed to help students adjust to the secondary school curriculum and environment
- *Program Pathways to Apprenticeship and the Workplace*: designed to permit a combination of courses and workplace experiences to earn secondary school credits
- *College Connections*: designed to permit

secondary school students to receive credits for completing courses offered by Ontario colleges

- *Success for Targeted Groups of Students*: designed to assist targeted groups such as ESL or Aboriginal students to succeed in high school

In addition to the above initiatives, the Ministry of Education currently requires that all students fourteen years of age or older (with the exception of those identified as "gifted") have a Transition Plan in place to assist in program planning. The goal of this plan is to help these students make a successful transition from school to the workplace, to post-secondary education, or to community living. (For more on Transition Plans, see chapter 5.)

Secondary School: Modifications and Accommodations

It is certainly the goal of all high schools across the province that as many students as possible successfully complete the high school requirements for graduation. With this goal in mind, a number of programs and options are available to assist students. While specifics may vary, most high schools offer program accommodations and modifications in regular classrooms. In most cases, students are accommodated through arrangements made by the special education department. These students may spend a portion of their day receiving extra assistance in a resource room setting, either scheduled as a regular, daily item or on an as-needed basis. The same students often have modified programs in the regular classroom. Achievement based on these modified learning expectations is assessed in light of provincial requirements, and a decision is made by the principal whether to grant a high school credit in the subject area.

- *School–work transition programs*: In these programs, currently referred to as Student Success Pathways, students at risk of failure as well as those identified with learning problems have an opportunity to participate in school

work programs. These programs vary from board to board and consist of a body of course credits developed to deliver an adapted high school curriculum. Course work is delivered at a level suitable to these students, and strong connections are made between the curriculum and workplace knowledge. Students involved in these programs are not prohibited from obtaining an OSSD. However, some courses developed at the local level, referred to as Essentials courses (such as a Life Skills courses), do not provide credit toward a graduation diploma.

- *Self-contained special education settings*: Self-contained classes, for students with developmental disabilities, which focus on social and life skills, are not uncommon, though many high schools make an effort to ensure that, while a population such as this may be in a self-contained program for curriculum delivery, they are not isolated for the social aspects of the day. It is not uncommon, given the lack of post-secondary options available to students with developmental disabilities, for students with such disabilities to remain in school longer than most other pupils. Many stay until the compulsory leaving age of twenty-one.

- *Supervised alternative learning for excused pupils programs (SALEP)*: At age fourteen or fifteen, students may be considered for an alternative school environment, which may include workplace placement, life skills, or other activities that the school board deems beneficial to the students' needs. Approval for such a program must be obtained from a SALEP committee set up in accordance with Ministry requirements. Students may remain in this program between the ages of fourteen and seventeen. During that time, these students are considered registered in school and may apply any credits obtained toward an OSSD.

The Service Providers

The number and type of personnel involved in delivery of service to students with exceptionalities usually depend on the nature and extent of the needs. Naturally, service can be delivered only if personnel are available, if the system is organized to flow the service to the need, and if the ever-so-crucial element of co-operation prevails. Fortunately, the combination of professionalism among educators and members of related fields and their natural disposition to ameliorate the situation of students with special needs means that, most of the time, the right things happen.

The list of personnel – of service providers – who work with students with exceptionalities in an exceptional setting can be as varied as there are variations among students. By far the most deeply involved in every educational situation are combinations of the following:

- classroom teacher
- educational assistant
- special education teacher (there are many local terms for this role)
- special consultant

with input from:
- principals
- parents
- school teams
- advisory groups
- advocacy groups
- social agencies
- specialists

"Outside" people typically become involved when a response to special needs requires a particular expertise. They include members from fields such as psychiatry, psychology, psychometry, and social work, and those in health, speech, or physical and occupational therapy. Some boards of education, particularly larger ones, employ members of these professions directly. This is most frequently the case with professionals in the speech area and with what is often called "psycho-educational services" (or a variation thereof) – usually people who specialize in assessment and counselling. The latter are more involved at the assessment and program-planning stages, although they will also participate at times in ongoing delivery of service in situations where exceptional behaviour, for example, is a factor.

Deploying the Personnel

An abiding concern of administrators is to get the appropriate resources into the appropriate settings as efficiently and effectively as possible, all with a view to cost, co-operation, and availability. To accomplish this goal, schools and boards generally organize deployment models or service models – schemas for managing the various elements in delivering service. Once it has been decided that a student is exceptional and is to receive support, management factors must be decided, such as:

- How much support will be needed?
- Are the needed resources available?
- Who is providing support?
- How long will the support continue?
- Where does the support take place?
- Who has primary responsibility for the student?
- When and how frequently will the case be reviewed?

Who Controls the Resources?

Although resource management policies differ across the province, the most common style is a combination of board-wide control of service delivery and individual school responsibility. Schools within a board typically will have a number of resources allocated, often according to a formula based on population but that also recognizes unique school needs. Thus, within a school, one or more special education teachers will have responsibility, under the principal, for allocating available resources and personnel as needed. If there are needs that go beyond a school's allocated resources or unique situations demanding a response, the board – ideally – will enhance the allocations (an outcome, however, that is inevitably shaped by availability and funding).

School-based management, because it circumvents time-consuming bureaucracy, can bring service to bear quickly and flexibly, along with a greater likelihood of informal but immediate co-operation and approval from parents. Special needs that require very specialized expertise – blindness, for example – are often more effectively managed at the board level, even though the resources likely will be delivered in a neighbourhood school. The combination of board-wide and individual school service delivery not only seems fiscally reasonable and responsible, but it also addresses issues of immediacy, flexibility, accountability, and optimal use of resources.

The School Team

A most significant development in the late 1980s and early 1990s was the gradual realization that the mystery of educating students with special needs is not all that different from the mystery of educating any student. Experience has taught that many educational matters that at first glance imply an elaborate response can actually be addressed "in-house." No one denies that expertise continues to be important, and there is no question that dealing with certain types of exceptionality such as, say, hearing loss or visual impairment, often requires specialization of some kind. Nevertheless, the needs of most students with exceptionalities can usually be met through a healthy application of common sense, the kind of approach that effective teachers use in all of educational practice. At the same time, teachers have found that cases of special need are almost always more effectively addressed when they are the focus of broad concern and of general co-operation and support, rather than the sole responsibility of a single individual.

In many schools, this combination of insights has borne fruit in a more or less formal arrangement sometimes referred to as the In-school Team, the Teacher Support Team, the School-based Support Team, or similar title.

The School Team Concept

A support or assistance team is a committee of staff members organized to advise and consult with individual teachers who request assistance regarding students perceived as having special needs. The team neither precludes nor replaces formal special education nor diminishes it in any way. Rather, it supports special education and helps it function more effectively and more efficiently in a school. In many schools, the team is a forum of first resort to which teachers and parents may bring concerns about the special needs of particular students without formally invoking special education procedures. This practice tends to keep students in the mainstream. Also, by offering this pre-referral opportunity, a team helps to free its school's special education personnel to bring resources to bear where needs are greatest. A team can also enhance service delivery simply by offering broader involvement. Perhaps most importantly – to teachers and students equally – a team can be a vital instigator of professionalism: the kind of drive that leads a staff to seek solutions. (For more on the school team, see chapter 5.)

The Multidisciplinary Team Concept

For particularly demanding exceptional cases, service delivery is sometimes managed by a multidisciplinary team in which educators share membership with professionals who have specialized expertise. The situation, for example, of a student with multiple needs, such as severe physical disabilities along with fragile health and possibly behavioural or developmental problems, may require the services of a variety of personnel. For this student, a multidisciplinary team may come together only once or twice, on a more or less ad hoc basis, usually in an advisory capacity and most often at the initial stages when the student's placement and programming are being established. Ongoing delivery of service usually will be the responsibility of only certain members of the team.

Two areas of difficulty with the multidisciplinary

team approach in educational settings are management and organization. Since the approach is used almost exclusively in cases of extensive need, there is sometimes disagreement over prioritizing social, educational, and physical needs. Also, the mere task of bringing together a team of otherwise occupied, diverse professionals is awkward and time-consuming and usually requires the authority of someone in an upper-level administrative role responsible for such things as budgeting and allocating personnel. As well, because there is such wide involvement, ultimate responsibility for the student – even legal responsibility – may become an issue. Difficulties like these often force even a severely restricted placement, such as special day school or a residential facility, to be seriously considered simply because the situation is easier to manage in such a setting.

The Expanding Role of Educational Assistants (Paraprofessionals*)

"Something you'll notice right away is there's a lot of teachers who don't know what to do with an EA! Not their fault really, any more than it's ours, but it's an issue you have to work out."

– Kana V., graduate of an EA program speaking to undergraduates

When special education first became mandatory in Ontario, support personnel, if any such existed at all in a school, were usually found in self-contained classrooms or in a special school where students with extensive needs were placed. Rarely were they found in regular classrooms. That reality changed dramatically over time so that today educational assistants play a role in regular classrooms as a matter of course and, indeed, are much sought after as important contributors in the delivery of service. Their role expanded significantly once inclusion became established as the normative style in the province's schools. It is not unusual now for both teachers and parents to expect that if students with special needs are placed in a class, an EA will be there, too.

What Do EAs Do?

The assistants themselves and the teachers they work with, as well as principals and parents, tend to answer this question with "anything and everything!" A central role, or at least an ideal one, is active teaching of special education students under guidelines established by the teacher and the Individual Education Plan. The teaching takes many forms, from direct instruction to remediation to supervision of repeated practice. Very often an EA's instruction of a student with special needs in a regular classroom is one-on-one to expand or reinforce a concept or skill that other students have grasped more readily. This will be the case especially in larger, busy classes where there are multiple demands on the classroom teacher.

Assistants may observe and record data for a variety of purposes, particularly for assessments wherein recorded observation plays a key role. They may be involved in things as complex as helping develop an IEP, or as straightforward as responsibility for classroom supplies. Among other contributions, EAs tutor, help manage general classroom conduct, modify educational materials, become part of a school team, provide health-needs support, and – this often being a very important role – provide behaviour management support. In short, what they do is, anything and everything.

---

* As a professional designation, support personnel in classrooms are sometimes described as "paraprofessionals" just as their counterparts in medicine and law are called "paramedics" and "paralegals." In education, the term "educational assistant" (EA) continues to be popular.

Co-operative Efforts

The practice of teaming teachers and educational assistants is now fully established in most Ontario schools, and many students with exceptionalities and their teachers rely on the involvement of educational assistants to ensure that the students progress behaviourally, socially, and academically throughout the school year. Unfortunately, in many instances, the precise role of the EA is still rather undefined. It is often left to both professional and paraprofessional to establish working relationships in a classroom as best they can. The situation can be fraught with all the risks found in any human interchange. Anecdotal evidence, for example, is reported from time to time in which EAs are given (or take) ownership of a specific student, particularly one with a behaviour issue, or in which EAs are "wasting away" because a classroom teacher – who is highly unlikely to have received any pre- or post-service preparation in working with another adult in the classroom – is reluctant to share or delegate responsibility.

Fortunately, the vast majority of teacher/EA relationships work out positively. It takes time and experience to establish that the purpose of the educational assistant role is not to replace the teacher but to support what goes on in the classroom and to appreciate that, by working co-operatively, two committed adults can fulfill the ultimate goal of all educators: helping students learn and grow.

Qualifications

At time of publication, Ontario had no legislation precisely addressing the qualifications of educational assistants, although many school boards have their own prerequisites, a policy strongly supported by the Ontario Council for Exceptional Children (CEC). A number of colleges in the province offer impressive educational assistant programs.

Readings and Resources

Demchak, M., & Morgan, C. R. (1998). Effective collaboration between professionals and paraprofessionals. *Rural Special Education Quarterly, 17*(2), 10–16.

Dworet, D., & Bennett, S. (2002). A view from the north: Special education in Canada. *Teaching Exceptional Children, 34*(5), 22–27.

Fisher, D. (1999). According to their peers: Inclusion as high school students see it. *Mental Retardation, 37*(6), 65–69.

French, N. K. (1998). Working together: Resource teachers and paraeducators. *Remedial and Special Education, 19*, 357–68.

French, N. K. (1999). Para-educators: Who are they and what do they do? *Teaching Exceptional Children, 32*(1), 65–69.

Giangreco, M. F., Broer, S. M., & Edelman, S. W. (2001). Teacher engagement with students with disabilities: Differences between paraprofessional service delivery models. *Journal of the Association for Persons with Severe Handicaps, 26*, 75–86.

Giangreco, M. F., & Broer, S. M. (2005). Questionable utilization of paraprofessionals in inclusive schools: Are we addressing symptoms or causes? *Focus on Autism and Other Developmental Disabilities, 20*(1), 10–26. doi: 10.1177/10883576050200010201

Lingo, A. S., Barton-Arwood, S. M., & Jolivette, K. (2011). Teachers working together improving learning outcomes in the inclusive classroom: Practical strategies and examples. *Teaching Exceptional Children 43*(6), 6–13.

Minke, K. M., Bear, G. G., Deemer, S. A., & Griffin, S. M. (1996). Teachers' experiences with inclusive classrooms: Implications for special education reform. *Journal of Special Education, 30*, 152–86.

Ontario Ministry of Education (1999). *Ontario secondary school, grades 9 to 12.* Toronto: Queen's Printer for Ontario.

Ontario Ministry of Education (2005). *Strategies for student success.* Toronto: Queen's Printer for Ontario.

Ontario Ministry of Education (2007). *Shared solutions: A guide to preventing and resolving conflicts regarding programs and services for students with special education needs.* Toronto: Queen's Printer for Ontario.

Ontario Ministry of Education (2010). *Supervised alternative learning: Policy and implementation.* Toronto: Queen's Printer for Ontario.

Pickett, A. L., & Gerlach, K. (1997). *Supervising para-educators in school settings: A team approach.* Austin, TX: Pro-Ed.

Salend, S. J. (2010). *Creating inclusive classrooms: Effective and reflective practices* (7th ed.). Upper Saddle River, NJ: Pearson.

Scruggs, T. E., Mastropieri, M. A., & McDuffie, K. A. (2007). Co-teaching in inclusive classrooms: A metasynthesis of qualitative research. *Exceptional Children, 73*(4), 392–416.

Smith, T. E. C., Polloway, E. A., Patton, J. R., Dowdy, C. A., & Heath, N. (2001). *Teaching students with special needs in inclusive settings* (Canadian ed.). Toronto: Allyn & Bacon.

Smith, W. J., & Lusthaus, C. (1993). Students with disabilities in Canada: What rights do they have? *Education Canada, 5*(9), 45–46.

Thousand, J., Rosenberg, R. L., Bishop, K. D., & Villa, R. A. (1997). The evolution of secondary inclusion. *Remedial and Special Education, 18*(5), 270–84, 306.

Winzer, M. (2008). *Children with exceptionalities in Canadian classrooms* (8th ed.). Toronto: Pearson Prentice Hall.

Links

Authors' note: Many Ontario school boards have developed modified programs for students with exceptionalities, especially in secondary schools. The substance of these programs, along with descriptions of service delivery methods, can usually be found on board websites. School board websites can be accessed via **http://sbinfo.edu.gov.on.ca/**

Ontario Ministry of Education website **http://www.edu.gov.on.ca/eng/parents/speced.html**

5
The Individual Education Plan:
A Team Approach

"Special education cannot be defined in a single statement. It is a process, a journey that takes different shapes for different students at different times in their educational careers. An IEP provides the road map for the completion of that journey."

– Andrea J., principal

The Case of Ms. Kumar

WHEN Ms. Kumar found out she would be having a grade 2 class in September (her first job after graduating), she immediately began to develop and collect materials for the new school year. She came into the school early to decorate her class and make the room feel welcoming. Ms. Kumar learned from her principal that she would be having eighteen grade 2s, all of whom had had little difficulty in the grade 1 program.

During the first two weeks of school, despite a few minor adjustments and the establishment of classroom practices, Ms. Kumar's class seemed to settle into an active and productive routine. At the beginning of the third week of school, a new child moved into the neighbourhood. Joey was of grade 2 age, but he had not yet attended regular school. He had spent senior kindergarten and grade 1 in a day treatment program for children with social/emotional difficulties. His mother had not informed the school of Joey's history. He began school on that Monday in Ms. Kumar's room.

Within the first hour it became obvious that something was wrong. Joey had become very frustrated at journal writing time and got out of his desk frequently. At one point, Joey decided that another child was bothering him, got out of his seat, and spat on the child's desk. When Ms. Kumar reprimanded him, he responded by swearing at her and running from the room.

When Joey's mom came to get him at the end of the day, she confessed that she was extremely worried about her son. She had been afraid to tell the school too much about Joey's background in the hope that a new school might mean a fresh start. The principal explained that Joey was now a member of their school, and the staff there were committed to doing whatever was needed to plan and implement a program that would meet Joey's needs.

While Ms. Kumar agrees philosophically with the ideal espoused by the principal, she feels ill equipped to deal with a child with such complex problems. She feels some form of written guide with specific directions and ideas would be helpful.

A Road Map

Planning is an integral component of effective teaching practice. As a matter of course, teachers carefully consider how new learning is to be presented and absorbed and develop lesson and unit plans to meet those ends. For a majority of students, those who fall within what, for lack of a better term, is considered to be the normal range, lesson plans and goals are usually not differentiated to any significant degree. But in the case of students with exceptionalities, planning becomes more complex because their needs, learning characteristics, and abilities are more diverse and challenging. A different, more individualized planning approach is usually necessary. Experience in special education has taught that this differentiated approach is best achieved in what educators know as an Individual Education Plan, or an IEP. For students with exceptionalities, an IEP encompasses both the goal of the teaching enterprise and the directions needed to meet that goal. A popular metaphor for the IEP – road map – seems apt for, without such a map, the educational process can get off track and both students and educators can become lost or find themselves in a place not intended.

A properly constructed and executed IEP provides consistency, continuity, and clarity of purpose. It allows educators to act within the requirements of their job but permits them flexibility to adjust curriculum activities and assessments in a planned and systematic way to support their student. An IEP provides specific guidelines for the direction of a student's program but always allows for the day-to-day adjustments required for any teaching-learning situation. And, as a roadmap, an IEP ensures that everyone knows the destination, knows what direction to take, and agrees on how to get there.

The Road Map as Policy

Until the late 1990s in Ontario, the development of an Individual Education Plan for a student with an exceptionality was not required (albeit it was implied in a Ministry document called *Schools General*). Yet, for most Ontario teachers, as with their colleagues in other jurisdictions, using IEPs in various forms and designs had become pretty much standard practice by this time. Therefore, when the province revised and reissued its regulation governing the identification and placement of students with special needs in 1998, making IEPs a clear and official requirement, most educators in the province were already experienced with them.

The Policy Requirements*

Ontario's Regulation 181/98 requires principals to ensure that an Individual Education Plan is developed for every student identified "exceptional" by an Identification, Placement, and Review Committee (IPRC; see chapter 6). It is also the case that an IEP may be developed for students who have not been through the IPRC process but are experiencing difficulty meeting learning expectations and who are deemed by the school board to need special services or educational programs.

In each of the situations above, an IEP must include:
- a stated reason for developing the plan
- specific educational expectations
- an outline of the special education program and services to be provided to the student
- a description of the methods that will be used to review the student's progress

When an IEP is part of the IPRC process, principals must ensure that the plan is developed within thirty school days after the student is placed in a special education program and *must ensure that it is completed in consultation with the parent* (and the student, if sixteen years or older). The plan must take into account recommendations by the IPRC that identified the student. A copy of the completed plan must be forwarded to parents (and to students ages sixteen plus) within the thirty-day time frame. A copy of the plan must also be included in the student's Ontario Student Record (OSR). In those cases where an IEP is not the result of an IPRC process, the time lines are less well defined.

An IEP *is*:
✓ a written plan of action for a student whose needs require modification of a regular school program
✓ a document containing a summary of the student's strengths and needs, a statement

---

* For specifics, see Individual Education Plans, Standards for Development, Program Planning and Implementation (Ontario Ministry of Education, 2000).

of goals and expectations, and essential information regarding resources, program, teaching strategies, personnel, etc.

✓ an ongoing, flexible document, developed by school staff in collaboration with parents, and the student, where appropriate, usually under the leadership of one or two persons supported by a team

✓ a document made available to teachers, assistants, resource personnel, administrators, parents, and the student, where appropriate, so that all concerned can direct their energies to the same purposes

An IEP *is not*:

✗ a detailed account of every minute of a student's day (an overly detailed and minutely controlled plan would be impossible to implement in a classroom)

✗ an individual effort by the special education teacher to fulfill Ministry requirements (an IEP created in isolation, without the input of personnel and family directly involved with the student, risks becoming merely a superfluous bureaucratic necessity rather than an effective and meaningful document)

✗ a document that, once completed, sits in a file unexamined until the next review (for an IEP to be effective, it must be used and monitored; it is a living document that requires ongoing development and examination by everyone working with the student)

IPRC and IEP: Are Both Needed?

As noted earlier, when an IPRC is in place, an IEP must be developed within a required time frame and shared with parents. In 2007, the Ministry of Education released a recommendation that school boards consider dispensing with the IPRC process in cases where students spend a majority of their time in the regular class and where things were progressing well. In those cases, the IPRC can be seen as administratively burdensome and redundant to a process that is meeting the needs of the student. This allows schools and parents to act quickly in a collaborative manner to meet the needs of the students.

It is in those cases where the situation may be more complex or perhaps acrimonious that an IPRC is an essential. On a cautionary note, the IPRC process is currently the only legislative vehicle for ensuring the timely development of an IEP, as well as the inclusion of parents and students (sixteen and older) in the decision-making process. The IPRC process also allows for appeals by the parties involved and for decision-making that goes beyond the level of the school and school board should difficulties arise. When the IPRC process is not followed, timely IEP development, necessary collaboration, and the ability to appeal can be jeopardized. It is important to remember that parents and principals within the province of Ontario can, at any time, call for an IPRC when either party deems it necessary for the success of a student.

Preparing IEPs

All IEPs, both those that result from an IPRC process and those that are created collaboratively at the school level, follow a well-defined set of procedures for development. For all students, the implementation of an IEP is a serious undertaking and must never be confused with the types of adjustments that educators, as competent and caring professionals, do on a day-to-day basis for students within a learning environment. Moving a desk, having flexible time frames for production of work, repeating instruction, and individually instructing a student on a particular concept are all parts of what would be considered normal teaching practice. It can be difficult, at times, for educators to see a clear line between an acceptable adjustment and an adjustment that requires the development of an IEP. This determination is difficult because the line is seldom clear! As with almost every aspect of the teaching endeavour, which is by nature a dynamic process, decisions have to be made in complex and ever-changing circumstances. That is why the development of an

IEP must be a team process that takes place over a period of time, looks at existing data, collects information that is needed, communicates with stakeholders, and is monitored throughout.

In the steps that follow, there is always flexibility in who is involved, what information is collected, and when or if the process needs to be continued or stopped.

Steps in the Process

The sequence presented here represents a pattern suggested by the Ministry of Education. Although individual boards in the province frequently add their own variations, all of them generally follow these steps:

1 gathering information
2 setting the direction
3 developing the IEP
4 implementing the IEP
5 reviewing and updating the IEP

1 Gathering Information

From the OSR: For each student in the province, a continuing record called the Ontario Student Record (OSR) is maintained and continually updated. The OSR, then, is a logical place to start gathering details for preparation of an IEP. Information such as previous report cards and reports by teachers and other professional staff, medical information, and – very important – school history are customarily available in this file. Especially useful documents often found in the OSR are a student's previous IEPs.

Among other details to be gathered to develop an IEP will be the reason(s) an IEP is needed in the first place. This information may come from a recent or even a past IPRC or from a special education teacher, a parent, or school team. Additional information, e.g., whether the student requires specialized health-support services, will also be included if appropriate. Information on specialized equipment if applicable, listings of dates of consultations with parents, etc., may also be included. The information will vary case by case, and will range from specific details, such as those recorded in an OSR, to current, ongoing contributions like the following.

Insights from key persons: Information from people who have different insights and perspectives on a student is valuable in the development of the IEP. The classroom teacher and, in many cases, the educational assistant, have the most contact with a particular student, and the information they can provide is essential. Yet neither of these individuals works alone and will not have all the answers. Parents, principals, special education teachers, previous teachers, other professionals, and indeed students themselves, where appropriate, can and should contribute. Parents, most of the time, have an in-depth understanding of their child. Having seen progress (or lack of it) from year to year, they have a picture that no one else has. That picture most likely will have important features such as updated medical information, likes and dislikes, other community involvement, relevant family information, etc.

Formal tests: If the appropriate professionals are available to administer standardized assessments (e.g., an IQ test, standardized achievement tests, etc.) and if the results from such tests will help inform the process, then these are a useful resource. In most cases, test results will not be as important, at least initially, as the careful, daily, in-the-classroom observations of teachers and educational assistants. Formal tests tend to be more important in situations that are at the relatively complex or intractable end of the scale. Indeed, it is not unheard of for students to be trapped in a sort of testing limbo. The problem is complex. A recent report from the association People for Education notes that approximately 50 percent of students in the province may miss the opportunity for assessment due to caps on funding. (Go to **http://www.peopleforeducation.ca/discussion/special-education-and-parent-advocacy/** for more information.) Also, there are cases in which the school and parents see the need for differentiated programming, but waiting lists for standardized assessments are staggeringly long. Therefore, it is important that the use of formal tests be judicious and administered in a timely fashion so that development of an effective plan does not stagnate.

> "A team is everybody and that is why we have such a diversity of people: so that they will come from different backgrounds in their teaching. I know I don't know everything and I don't think there is any one person who knows everything, but if we have a group, we can pool our knowledge and come up with the best for the student."
>
> – A. Walsh, special education resource teacher

Classroom observations: For many years, special education was considered by many the realm of experts and specialists. Nowhere was this mystique more prevalent than in the area of assessment. Surprisingly, the perception persists. Special education teachers, just like teacher-librarians or computer specialists, do indeed possess some expert knowledge and training, but it does not replace the essential role that regular classroom teachers or educational assistants play in gathering crucial information. Front-line personnel can collect important information such as the students' interaction with text, how they respond to new tasks, whether they work best in groups or individually, their response to authority and routines, and their reaction to environmental conditions such as lighting and noise level. Information like this may be recorded in a variety of formats, such as anecdotal records, checklists, interviews, and even audiovisual recordings. No matter where or in what form this information is recorded, it is most valuable.

Student's work: Samples of a student's previous and current work reveal strengths, needs, and rates of progress. Portfolios of student work, test papers, journal entries, assignments, and artwork all contribute insights. Comparing samples of an individual student's work throughout the year provides not only valuable information but also much-needed validation. In teaching, because the work is in such small units, progress is hard to discern at times and the perception that "we are getting nowhere" persists. A cumulative representative sampling of a student's work over time not only can demonstrate progress but also can point out the direction to proceed.

In most cases, the types of information above will offer enough substance to develop an IEP. Naturally, there are situations in which it is necessary to return to the sources and dig deeper or wider. In some cases, additional personnel and resources may be needed to conduct other types of assessments (e.g., diagnostic tests). As well, especially in the case of students with special physical or health needs, a school may seek information from medical professionals (although this is almost always done with the help, and certainly the permission, of parents).

2 Setting the Direction

The Strength of Team

Ideally, after the basic information is gathered, a collaborative approach involving staff, parents, and the student (where appropriate) comes into play to establish the plan itself, for the simple reason that involving more than one person in the development of an IEP almost always produces a more thorough, relevant, and creative plan. Most schools in Ontario already have in place some form of active school team* that meets on a regular basis to share information about students with special needs. Accordingly, these teams, with members added on an ad hoc basis (e.g., people with a stake in the case, such as the classroom teacher, assistant, parent, etc.), are commonly used to shape and give direction to IEPs. The focus on collaboration was reinforced in 2006 in the *Special Education Transformation* report (Bennett & Wynne, 2006),

---

* Also known by other titles such as In-school Team, School Support Team, Special Support Team, or just School Team.

which recommended to the Ministry of Education that training for participation in IPRCs and the development of IEPs focus on collaborative communication, especially collaboration with parents.

A school team generally includes the principal (or designate), certain classroom teachers, educational assistants appointed by the principal, and the school's special education teacher(s), along with ad hoc members. The principal (or designate) is usually responsible for the establishment and maintenance of the team approach to IEP development, but all members of the team play an important role. Each one has a perspective in terms of the information he or she can offer and the support or services he or she may be able to provide. This is where collaboration finds its strength. Once the different perspectives are aired and consolidated with both the professional and the personal insights that everyone has to offer, the results invariably generate a more complete picture of the student's strengths and needs, along with a more informed and more creative set of strategies and actions for implementation.

The Case of Mr. Pickett

MR. Pickett has taught English to grades 9, 10, and 11 for some years now and has always felt he does a good job. His peers would agree and note that Mr. Pickett always seems well prepared for his classes, has innovative ideas, and has students who seem to enjoy being in his class.

In the past, under the direction of the previous principal, any students receiving special education support were withdrawn from Mr. Pickett's class and programmed for solely by the special education resource teacher. While Mr. Pickett has never objected to implementing some of the special education resource teacher's suggestions in his class, he has always been comfortable in the knowledge that the primary responsibility for a student's program rested elsewhere.

This year, under a new principal, the focus of special education service delivery has shifted, and the primary responsibility to oversee programming for exceptional students is now placed squarely on the shoulders of regular classroom teachers, assisted by the special education resource teacher.

This year, Mr. Pickett has two students identified as learning disabled. Both read far below grade level and require a great deal of assistance in completing any written work. He has been reluctant to take ownership for their program and is very resistant to altering his teaching practices in any significant way to accommodate their needs. Although he does not share this with the rest of the staff, Mr. Pickett has grave doubts about his ability to program for the two, fearing that he lacks the necessary expertise. He is willing to help them but does not feel he has the skills.

An In-school Team meeting has been called this week to discuss the students. Mr. Pickett, while not a regular member of this team, has been asked in advance to provide some information about these students and to attend the meeting to discuss their program and learning needs. He is unsure what kind of information he should provide and is unsure about how much he can or should tell the team about modifications and accommodations that he has already tried with the students. Mr. Pickett is feeling very hesitant and would like some guidance.

A Suggestion for Writing Goals: Smart Goals	
Popular among industry and governmental organizations, the use of the acronym SMART allows planners to organize their thinking when creating goals.	
Specific	What needs to be accomplished, who is involved, etc.?
Measurable	Are there clear targets, criteria for measurement?
Achievable	Is the goal attainable, realistic?
Relevant	Is the goal worthwhile, meaningful?
Timely	Can the goal be met within a realistic and appropriate time line?

Table 5A

3 Developing the IEP

After the information is consolidated and checked for accuracy, and after any gaps are filled and possible discrepancies resolved, the material is then summarized on the IEP form. Following a provincial collaborative review in 2006/2007, the Special Education Policy branch of the Ministry of Education released an IEP electronic template for voluntary use by school boards, made available on September 10, 2007 (Memo: Bruce Drewett, MOE for Ontario, September 7, 2007). While the use of this template, as stated, is voluntary, it was made clear that school boards must, if using their own template, meet the regulatory requirements regarding the Ministry standards for the development of Individual Educational Plans. (The authors recommend that teachers and educational assistants be familiar with both the Ministry form and, if different, the form currently used in their own school board.)

Information about the Ministry form can be found at the Ministry of Education's website **www. edu.gov.on.ca**. Whatever form a board uses, an IEP will almost always be developed with attention to the following essential components.

List strengths and needs: Much of this part will come from the observations gathered in the first phase of the process. Including the student's strengths and needs is a prelude to understanding the program modifications that need to be set up. A strength might be expressed as "… has creative ideas for stories and has good story comprehension." A need might be expressed as "… to develop an understanding and application of mathematical concepts." Strengths listed in an IEP must reflect areas in which a student has effective learning skills as well as those learning modalities or styles that contribute to the student's success in learning. Stated needs should be drawn directly from assessments and related directly to the areas for which the IEP is being developed. (In those cases where a student has been through an IPRC, strengths and needs listed in an IEP must be consistent with those listed in a student's IPRC statement.)

Establish goals and expectations: Goals state what a student would reasonably be expected to achieve by the end of a school year within a particular curriculum area or skill. The setting of IEP goals for students with exceptionalities has been shown to be related to what the teacher believes the student is capable of. High expectations related to curriculum goals can result in students spending more time in regular class settings and making better progress (Jorgensen, McSheehan, & Sonnenmeier, 2007). Goals are considered more global targets for students (e.g., "The student will develop basic computational skills in mathematics"). Expectations, on the other hand, are more specific about what the student will be doing ("The student will be able to recite subtraction facts between 1 and 18"). Expectations should reflect what a student is expected to attain within each reporting period and be written in a way that is observable and measurable. Both goals and expectations should be based directly on the Ontario curriculum when academic performance is being modified. Reporting on the progress of these expectations must be linked with the provincial report card and the progress or lack thereof will serve as a guidepost for both educators and parents as to the necessity of tweaking or continuing the goals and methods set out in the IEP. Alternative goals and expectations for such things as addressing the physical or behavioural needs of a student are also listed in IEPs and reviewed regularly.

Specify strategies and resources: Once goals and expectations are outlined, the task becomes one of choosing strategies and identifying resources, including personnel, that will be used to help the student and teachers meet them. This section of an IEP stipulates what materials will be used, what programs and teaching methods will be employed, and who will work with the student, how often, and where. The report of the Working Table on Special Education recommends that classroom teachers should be provided with ongoing training in successful practices including universal design and differentiated instruction (Bennett & Wynne, 2006). It goes on to recommend that teachers need to be supported by informed school leaders through the provision of appropriate materials and personnel.

Monitor the results: A crucial step in the development of an IEP is establishing the features of a monitoring cycle: Student progress must be reviewed at least once every reporting period and the results of that progress indicated on the provincial report card. The success of interventions needs to be considered not just in the context of whether the student made progress but also, and perhaps more importantly, in a broader context that asks whether the correct strategies and resources were used in the effort to create an environment in which the student could be successful. Decisions such as who will track the student's progress, how the record keeping will be handled, who will be responsible for communicating to whom, and what is the time frame for accomplishing the goals, need to be addressed.

What Is on an IEP Form?

Official forms vary, sometimes quite widely, from board to board and even from school to school. Fortunately, the majority of school boards now follow the template provided by the Ministry of Education. Though the headings may differ, it requires the following information.

✓ Reason for development of IEP
✓ Student profile
✓ Relevant assessment data
✓ Student's areas of strength and need
✓ Subjects, courses/codes, or alternative skill areas to which the IEP applies
✓ Reporting format
✓ Accommodations for learning, including required equipment
✓ Provincial assessments
✓ Special education program (subject, or course/code, or alternative skill area)
✓ Human resources (teaching/non-teaching)
✓ IEP development team
✓ Transition plan (if required)
✓ Log of parent/student consultation

Except for demographics, not every section of a form will be filled in every time. The ever-present problem of time constraints confronting all teachers means that, in practice, emphasis likely will be given to the issues that are most relevant in a particular case.

"An IEP is not a pristine piece of paper filed in the OSR and referred to only on occasion. Rather, it is a working document to be filled with crossed-out expectations and remedial attempts, scribbled revisions, and Post-it reminders. It resides on the teacher's desk providing easy access to all concerned during the instructional day."

R. Daigle, superintendent

Special Case: The Transition Plan

For students fourteen and older, except for students identified as gifted, regulations require schools to include a Transition Plan in his or her IEP. The plan is designed to allow for a smooth transition from school to school, workplace, or training centre. It must include specific transition goals and the actions required to achieve those goals. It must also include the person or agency responsible for providing assistance in the completion of the goal, as well as time lines for the implementation of actions. Under the regulation, the principal is responsible for consulting with appropriate community agencies and/or post-secondary institutions for the purposes of completing a meaningful Transition Plan. For more information and samples of Transition Plans, access the Ministry of Education website **www.edu. gov.on.ca** for the document *Transition Planning: A Resource Guide 2002*.

4 Implementing the IEP

Implementation of an IEP centres on communication and practical application. Teachers and/or educational assistants who will be delivering services to the student need to be informed and prepared for upcoming changes (although, if a collaborative process has been used, it is very likely that key personnel will have been involved in the plan from the beginning). Parents need to be informed of changes and adjustments. The plan itself is translated into the day-to-day operation of the classroom with all practical considerations being taken into account. At the same time, a monitoring system is established, because even though an IEP will be updated at least once every reporting period, it must always be viewed as a working document, one that evolves and develops as new information arises. There are very few IEPs that do not require some modifications early on.

Once again, it is important to point out that the IEP does not cover every minute of every day in the student's school life. It is a document that records generally how a modified-from-regular program will be conducted and monitored.

5 Reviewing and Updating the IEP

A student's IEP needs to be reviewed each reporting period. Considerations in such a review include:

- Does the plan still reflect the student's needs?
- Are the strategies and resources still effective?
- Is the student progressing at the rate expected?
- Should changes be made to the assignment of responsibility?
- Has any new information emerged that means the plan should change?
- Is the student displaying responsibility and commitment to the learning process?
- Are family/student commitments in the plan being carried out?

The IEP and Report Cards

At the elementary level, when completing report cards for students who are on an Individual Education Plan, which results in the completion of curriculum expectations varying from the regular program, the teacher *must* check the "IEP" box for the subject or strand on the Elementary Progress Report and the Elementary Provincial Report Card. On the provincial Report Card the teacher must also include the following statement:

This (letter grade/percentage mark) is based on expectations in the IEP that vary from Grade X expectations (and/or) are an (increase/decrease) in the (number and/or complexity) of the curriculum expectations.

At the secondary level, for students with modified curriculum expectations, teachers *must* check the "IEP" box for every course to which the plan applies. If the student's learning expectations for the course are modified from the curriculum expectations, but the student is working toward a credit for the course, it is sufficient simply to check the "IEP" box. If, however, the student's learning expectations are modified to such an extent that the principal deems that a credit will not be granted for the course, teachers must include the following statement in the Comments section:

This percentage mark is based on the learning expectations specified in the IEP, which differ significantly from the curriculum expectations for the course.

At both the elementary and secondary level, if the IEP requires accommodations to support only the learning in a subject or strand, teachers will *not* check the IEP box. The letter grade or percentage mark is based on regular grade expectations.

Source: **http://www.edu.gov.on.ca/eng/document/forms/report/card/BusinessRequirements.pdf**

Assigning Primary Responsibility

In most schools, IEPs are developed collaboratively, ideally by an "In-school Team" or "School Team" under the direction of the principal. However, because of the inevitable time constraints in a typical school, and for reasons of efficiency, the primary responsibility for preparation of an IEP is often undertaken by one person, or sometimes two. Very often, that primary person is the classroom teacher of the student under consideration, or is one of the school's special education teachers (often called resource teachers), or the two of them in concert, along with the educational assistant. The teacher(s) having primary responsibility almost certainly will have been central in gathering the basic information and, after consultation with the In-school Team, likely will take responsibility for writing the plan and for seeing to its implementation. They may also oversee or perhaps actually perform the monitoring of progress. In a well-run system, however, the primary persons do not work unsupported, for the school team is always there for consultation, assistance, and an insertion of fresh ideas.

The IEP: How Parents Can Help

✓ Communicate regularly with the student's teacher and attend meetings.

✓ Keep records of information that may be helpful, especially meetings or discussions that may have taken place outside the school.

✓ Share insights about the student's likes, dislikes, relevant medical information, and assessments the school may not have.

✓ Ask questions. Clarify definitions, jargon, and the roles of those participating; ask for an explanation of procedural issues that are unclear.

✓ Assume the best; professionals share your goal to develop your child's full potential.

The IEP: A Journey in and of Itself

Despite the appeal of IEPs, and even though experience has proven their value, there are some potential difficulties to be aware of, both in preparation and implementation. Some teachers feel they are ill equipped to develop what they consider a radical departure from their normal planning. Even teachers with training in special education may have little experience in coordinating a team and developing plans. There can often be confusion, if not tension, over who has responsibility for the various components of the process. And, even though a multidisciplinary approach is useful, a lack of systematic training for school personnel and sporadic attendance at meetings can make the approach difficult to maintain.

Some educators are concerned that the relatively formal nature of the IEP creates yet another level of bureaucracy and, thereby, moves education even farther away from its intended recipient, the student. The use of computer programs to spin out computer-generated strategies to complete or develop IEPs has raised legitimate concerns over weak paper compliance to the very important IEP process. Yet paper compliance is a natural response for teachers faced with increased workload, heavy demands from administration and parents, excessive paperwork, insufficient support, and lack of training.

Ultimately, an IEP is only a tool. A proven one, but a tool nevertheless. To put it to effective use requires the same skills, resources, and, above all, willingness that any other educational tool requires. One way to circumvent possible problems with an IEP and to ensure a more beneficial outcome is to manage its preparation and implementation through the power of a school team. Experience proves that a team approach to the IEP not only enhances the quality of an IEP, but also offers a greater likelihood that its contents and its ideals will take effect.

While teachers have written and implemented IEPs for many years, the calibre and effectiveness of these documents have often been of concern. The IEP Collaborative Review 2006–2007 provided much-needed insight into provincial practices. As a result of initiatives such as this, the Ministry has provided not only a provincial template, but also IEP exemplars available at the Ontario Directors of Education website (**http://www. ontariodirectors.ca/IEP-PEI/index.html**). With the inclusion of more students with exceptionalities in regular classes and a more collaborative approach to teaching, regular classroom teachers are becoming well versed in the creation and implementation of effective and meaningful IEPs.

That said, with a shift toward differentiated instruction and universal design, a vision of when an IEP is necessary can become blurred. For example, when educators use effective practices and accommodations, there may be a question whether an IEP is still useful for a student who previously may have seemed in need of one. It is through effective assessment, teamwork, and sound judgment that this question is answered.

> *"When students with special education needs interact and learn with students in regular classroom settings, they have a better likelihood of becoming part of the larger group. This type of heterogeneous configuration parallels our broader society in which everyone is included and works and lives beside each other."*
>
> – Peggy B., Superintendent, Special Education

The In-school Team

The Role a Team Plays

The role and the style of an In-school Team vary from school to school and board to board. Some schools have teams that meet on a regular, scheduled basis; others meet only when a certain number of students have been referred for discussion. Some teams meet to help a teacher with ideas for students who are having only mild difficulty, while other teams meet only if a child is already identified as exceptional or at risk of being so.

Team style and function depend on a variety of other factors, too, such as the expertise, experience, and beliefs of the staff, the nature of the student population, and the needs of the school. There are some schools, for example, that organize the team role quite bureaucratically, making it official policy that any student being considered for presentation to an Identification, Placement, and Review Committee or for the development of an IEP must first be presented to the team. Other schools involve the team only after an IPRC has identified a student as exceptional and therefore in need of an IEP. Still others use a combination of these two approaches.

Although there is wide variation in the types of In-school Teams at work in Ontario and an equally wide variation in the way their strengths are put to use, one very important, widespread, and effective role for this group is the collaborative development of IEPs.

Who Is on the Team?

Usually, a team has a relatively permanent core of people, e.g., the principal (or designate), classroom teachers, and special education teacher. Other teachers, professionals, parents, and advocates may be added to suit the needs of an individual case. The group works as a team, but each member usually has a particular role in the team process, a role defined by a variety of factors: their knowledge base, their experience with the student under consideration, or their general capacity to provide information or support at a particular level.

❋ *The principal* (or designate) is nominally the head of the team. From a purely practical perspective, administrative power is needed for scheduling and for making personnel and resources available. Usually, it is the principal who assigns one team member to carry primary responsibility for a particular IEP. The principal is also officially responsible for meeting provincial requirements (time lines for developing a plan, notifying participants, storing information, etc.). Research on effective In-school Teams suggests that strong administrative support is a key factor in their success.

❋ *A special education teacher* in a school is often the person assigned the responsibility for scheduling, chairing, and maintaining the records for team meetings. Usually, he or she is the teacher on the team with skills and training in assessment, as well as the person with the readiest access to a multitude of program modification ideas and additional resources. In most cases, the special education teacher plays a direct role in the implementation of strategies or else arranges for implementation. It may be this teacher who describes and models a new technique for a classroom teacher, arranges for support personnel, works with the student directly, etc. The special education teacher is also a gatekeeper of sorts. He or she communicates regularly with other professionals (e.g., speech and language pathologists, counsellors, assessment services) and is usually the one who can access these resources, depending on the decisions of the team.

The role of the special education teachers in an elementary setting is somewhat different from the role of special education teachers at the high school level, where students attend multiple classes and can face complex schedules and demands. In many high schools, the special education teacher, sometimes called the SERT, or special education resource teacher, has additional responsibilities of coordination in ensuring that all teachers are kept up to date with the important information they need to work with students who have difficulties. Also, at the high school level, interventions, such as student success classrooms that are set up slightly differently from board to board but whose fundamental task is working with students who are at risk, have become part of the landscape.

Initially, the relationship between these types of classrooms and practices and special education was relatively unclear, but over time and with Ministry direction, there is now an understanding that school success classes and high school special education services are fundamentally linked. After all, in any logical world, it would seem clear that in many cases the same population of students (with the exception of those with more serious cognitive and physical difficulties) is being served. Perhaps there are some lingering confusions over who is in charge, so to speak, but given that the student is at the centre of what we do as educators, including anyone who can contribute to the overall success of the student is essential to the discussion.

> *"It's not so much that I shell out advice, because if that were the case we would not hear the expertise of others. I more or less stimulate the discussion, try to encourage suggestions from other members of the team, bounce ideas off them. They bounce ideas off each other, so, in a way, I am a facilitator."*
>
> – Joan C., special education resource teacher

Many teams have **classroom teachers** as regular members who attend every meeting whether or not the student being discussed is in their class. Their role is to help generate solutions for students in difficulty and to provide support for implementing these solutions. Regular classroom teachers provide information about curriculum expectations in particular grades; they are aware of combinations of students who may be appropriate for social interventions with students having difficulty. Classroom teachers have the best line into school sports and clubs and other activities. They are also a creative source of ideas. Representation from each school division on an elementary team, or from subject areas in the case of secondary schools, provides a better-rounded pool from which to draw information and solutions.

The Case of Ms. Wall

THE grade 4/5 split that Ms. Wall was assigned this year presented quite a few challenges in classroom management. Like many experienced teachers, she has a repertoire of strategies to maintain class attention. While they have been effective for many of the students, the behaviour of one student, Audrey, has led her to seek extra support and ideas from the In-school Team.

Audrey first came to the school at the beginning of grade 3. She had been identified as developmentally delayed but had always been in a regular class. During the grade 3 year, many discussions were held with concerned individuals, including the parents, regarding how best to meet Audrey's academic needs. A suggestion that she move to a segregated class was considered but rejected. Now, with the increasing academic demands in the grade 4 setting, Ms. Wall is seeing what she considers a dramatic change in Audrey's behaviour. Audrey has become extraordinarily quiet and withdrawn. She does not participate in class discussions and spends much of her time staring out the window. In music class, which used to be her favourite subject, Audrey keeps her head down and does not seem to have learned any of the songs.

At the first team meeting, attended by the principal, special education teacher, two regular classroom teachers, and Ms. Wall, it was decided that Audrey's curriculum expectations be adjusted to focus on basic instruction. This instruction would be delivered in part by the special education teacher in a resource room, but, for a majority of the program, Audrey would stay in the regular class with Ms. Wall getting planning help from the special education teacher. It was also decided that Audrey would join the grade 1 class for music as an assistant to the teacher and to help the students learn and sing the songs. The immediate result was that Audrey seemed to regain her interest in music. She relishes being "assistant teacher" and, in her grade 4 class, has begun to participate, not just in music class, but in her other subjects as well.

As the team meets to review her case, there are several concerns. Ms. Wall is making every effort to incorporate the curriculum changes but sees a broadening gap between Audrey's achievements and what is expected of the rest of the class. Audrey's parents are encouraged by the progress but are also concerned about Audrey's ability to fit in academically and socially. Both the parents and the school are committed to inclusive practice and are seeking ways to engage Audrey more successfully as part of the class community. They are meeting to discuss plans that would create an environment to address Audrey's academic and emotional needs.

✷ *A classroom teacher*, who is an ad hoc team member because the student under consideration is in his or her class, will have similar, but slightly more onerous responsibilities. Usually, this teacher will collect much of the assessment data, often in collaboration with the special education teacher. He or she will bring in observations of the student's behaviour and work habits across a variety of settings and subject areas, samples of work, results of teacher-made tests, and information gathered through discussions with family members or other involved persons. Perhaps most importantly, the regular classroom teacher likely will be the person to carry out instructional plans generated by the team, and he or she must, therefore, make sure the rest of the team understands clearly what can be accommodated reasonably in the real world of the teacher's classroom. One real-world factor is that the teacher will probably do most of the communicating with the parents.

✴ **An educational assistant** is often an ad hoc member in the case of a student whom he or she may know better than most and can play a crucial part in the formation of an IEP. In the implementation of the developed plan, the educational assistant, under the direction of the teacher, may be responsible for particular types of instruction or assistance within the classroom setting. Along with the classroom teacher, the EA often takes on responsibility for monitoring.

✴ Other important team members are the **parents** of the student being discussed, for they have a wealth of information to be considered. The reasonableness and practicality of interventions such as a behaviour plan that would require home support is far easier to discuss productively if a parent is present. Perhaps most importantly, parent participation helps foster bonds of trust and communication. Naturally, parents are almost always ad hoc members. Experience has shown that parents often find it difficult to get to meetings, but the provincial regulations, not to mention effective teaching practice, mean they are to be kept informed and consulted.

✴ By regulation, **students who are sixteen years and older** may participate in a team meeting in which an IEP is being developed. If the student is a participant in the actual meeting, he or she may play a very special role in describing needs and perspectives and, at the very least, offering some insights into what is possible and realistic.

✴ **Support personnel** may be involved in a team meeting, but usually are not permanent members. These individuals – physiotherapists, or attendance counsellors, for example – attend meetings where their information, expertise, and intervention may be needed. Their role, as with all members of an In-school Team, is to act as an information resource. Especially with secondary school students, who have considerably more independence and a wider circle of activity, not necessarily known to their parents or classroom teachers, support personnel may be vital to the implementation and monitoring of a plan.

Initiatives in support services for students in education settings are beginning to permeate the standard drop-in type of practice that has been the norm for many boards. These practices, characterized by poor communication, lack of follow-up, and dissatisfaction on the part of service providers and educators, have led to developing and piloting an innovative service delivery model called *Partnering for Change*, which has reconceptualized the delivery of occupational delivery services for students in schools. See: **http://www.canchild.ca/ en/ourresearch/ partneringforchange.asp**

Focusing on building community and developing rapport and genuine collaboration, this model, which places OTs in school settings for regularly scheduled days, has shown positive results. Educators report that seeing the OT as part of the school community has allowed them to build trust and relationships that lead to more successful collaboration. Brown bag lunches, casual conversations, and shared problem solving over situations that emerge have been blended with the OT's historically therapeutic role in the schools.

> *"Having an OT in the school on a regular basis throughout the year led to a stronger team approach to intervention. The partnership that developed between teachers and OTs and parents enabled a wider range of students to be supported."*
> – Teacher participant in pilot study

When Educators Collaborate

Educators collaborate naturally. Before, and after, and in-between classes, in the hall, and over lunch, they share strategies they have found useful, seek opinions about their concerns for a student at risk, borrow materials, and plan mutual projects for their classes. These exchanges are part of their day (and beyond). But a team situation is more formalized, and the process, as a consequence, requires a somewhat more formal structure. To put together an IEP, most teams follow a variation of this problem-solving technique:

1 identify/clarify the problem
2 formulate a plan
3 initiate the plan
4 assess the success of the plan
5 revise as necessary

Yet even these steps can be more effectively and efficiently realized if members of a team consult and collaborate with some appreciation of team dynamics.

What Makes a Team Succeed?

For collaboration to be successful, all members of the team must, at the very least, share a common focus: a sense that they are each trying to achieve the same goal. But by itself, a mutually understood purpose is not enough. Realistically, members of a team must be voluntary participants with a sense of voluntarily shared responsibility and accountability. Above all, to truly function without impediment, team members should have parity. The latter issue can be awkward, particularly given the fact that educators exist in a hierarchical structure in which parity, even on a philosophical level, can be difficult to establish. On the plus side, however, educators are members of a profession, and, as a team, they are professionals united to achieve a goal for which they are better equipped than any others.

There is a practical side, too. No matter how professionally a team may approach its tasks, there are some simple but fundamental requirements to apply its collective strength effectively. Schools that have been benefitting from the team concept in special education for some time now unanimously attest that, to succeed, a team must:

✓ have administrative support
✓ meet at regularly scheduled intervals
✓ keep group size manageable
✓ receive pertinent information before meetings
✓ set time limits
✓ follow an agenda
✓ set review dates
✓ keep records
✓ share accountability and responsibility

Some Issues in Team Practice

Collaboration with colleagues in a school setting is sometimes a complex dance, and ensuring that everyone is in step can prove difficult. Here are a few of the issues that must be kept in mind.

Personal beliefs: In any group of individuals, there is bound to be a variety of perspectives and beliefs. This, indeed, is one of the strengths of a team: the multiplicity of perspectives. But perspectives and absolute commitment to an idea or ideal, if held to the exclusion of all else, can interfere with the problem-solving goal of an IEP. It is important to be aware and respectful of the beliefs of team members and to remember that it is the needs of a student, not the power of a principle, which ultimately must rule.

Dealing with conflict: Ideally, when discussing the important issue of how best to assist students within an educational setting, one would hope that conflicts are rare. While this may be the case in many interactions, elements such as passion, anxiety, hope and optimism, which can be part of any educational discourse, can become more pronounced when issues surrounding students with exceptionalities are at the centre of the discussion. There is a growing recognition within the province of Ontario that educators and families alike need assistance regarding how best to communicate with each other and thus avoid what may be more difficult and acrimonious discussions later. In the fall of 2007, the Ministry of Education published a document entitled *Shared Solutions: A Guide to Preventing and Resolving Conflicts Regarding Programs and Services for Students with Special Education Needs*. This document provides information and strategies to allow parents, educators, and students with special education needs to resolve conflicts and work together in a more productive and meaningful way.

Administrative support: Whether at the school level or at the school board level, administrators hold the keys to a variety of resources and decision-making powers that are not generally available to other members of the team. Within a school, the principal sets the tone for discipline and the delivery of curriculum. In team meetings, a principal's active participation as a member of the team lends a status and aura of responsibility to that team that it otherwise would not attain. Without administrative support from within the school and at the board level, In-school Teams may continue to function, but do so with their hands tied.

Time: As any teacher will attest, there is never enough time – for anything! Thus team meetings can often be viewed as an unwelcome extra in a teacher's schedule. This is even more strongly the case when a team is run inefficiently, decisions are not made or followed up, communication is poor, procedures are not well established, and there is no support. Given that time is a precious commodity, it is essential that team time be seen as worthwhile and, in the end, a time-saving activity. When teams are run well and teachers are given the opportunity to work with their colleagues in an effective way, the benefits to the school far outweigh the time spent at the meeting.

Readings and Resources

Brownell, M. T., Adams. A., Sindelar, P., Waldron, N., & van Hover, S. (2006). Learning from collaboration: The role of teacher qualities. *Exceptional Children, 72*, 169–86.

Cook, L., & Friend, M. (1993). Educational leadership for teacher collaboration. In B. Billingsley (Ed.). *Program leadership for serving students with disabilities* (pp. 421–44). Richmond: Virginia Department of Education.

Dettmer, P. A., Dyck, N. T., & Thurston, L. P. (1996). *Consultation, collaboration and teamwork for students with special needs*. Toronto: Allyn & Bacon.

Friend, M., & Cook, L. (1992). *Interactions: Collaboration skills for school professionals*. White Plains, NY: Longman.

Fuchs, D., & Fuchs, L. S. (1996). Consultation as a technology and the politics of school reform. *Remedial and Special Education, 17*(6), 386–92.

Hedda, M., Shelden, D. L., Apple, K., & DeGrazia, R. (2010). Developing a long-term vision: A road map for students' futures. *Teaching Exceptional Children, 43*(2), 8–14.

Hunt, P., Soto, G., Maier, J., & Doering, K. (2003). Collaborative teaming to support students at risk and students with severe disabilities in general education classrooms. *Exceptional Children, 69*, 315–33.

Idol, L., Nevin, A., & Paolucci-Whitcomb, P. (1994). *Collaborative consultation* (2nd ed.). Austin, TX: Pro-Ed.

Kosko, K. W., & Wilkins, J. L. M. (2009). General educators' in-service training and their self-perceived ability to adapt instruction for students with IEPs. *The Professional Educator, 33*(2), 14–23.

Lingo, A. S., Barton-Arwood, S. M., & Jolivette, K. (2011). Teachers working together improving learning outcomes in the inclusive classroom: Practical strategies and examples. *Teaching Exceptional Children 43*(6), 6–13.

Mills, M. (1994). The consultative role of school based resource teachers. *B.C. Journal of Special Education, 18*(2), 181–89.

Ontario Ministry of Education and Training (1998). *Individual education plan (IEP) resource guide.* Toronto: Queen's Printer for Ontario.

Ontario Ministry of Education (2000). *Individual education plans: Standards for development, program planning and implementation.* Toronto: Queen's Printer for Ontario.

Ontario Ministry of Education (2001). *Special education: A guide for educators.* Toronto: Queen's Printer for Ontario.

Ontario Ministry of Education (2002). *Transition planning: A resource guide.* Toronto: Queen's Printer for Ontario.

Ontario Ministry of Education (2004). *The individual education plan (IEP): A resource guide.* Toronto: Queen's Printer for Ontario.

Ontario Ministry of Education (2007). *Shared solutions: A guide to preventing and resolving conflicts regarding programs and services for students with special education needs.* Toronto: Queen's Printer for Ontario.

O'Shea, D., & O'Shea, L. (1997). Collaboration and school reform: A twenty-first-century perspective. *Journal of Learning Disabilities, 30*(4), 449–62.

Rehfeldt, J., Clark, G., & Lee, S. (2012). The effects of using the transition planning inventory and a structured IEP process as a transition planning intervention on IEP meeting outcomes. *Remedial and Special Education, 33*(1), 48–58.

Scruggs, T. E., Mastropieri. M. A., & McDuffie, K. A. (2007). Co-teaching in inclusive classrooms: A metasynthesis of qualitative research. *Exceptional Children, 73*(4), 392–416.

Stanovich, P. (1996). Collaboration: The key to successful inclusion in today's schools. *Intervention in School and Clinic, 32*(1), 39–42.

Sugai, G., & Horner, R. (2009). Responsiveness-to-intervention and school-wide positive behavior supports: Integration of multi-tiered system approaches. *Exceptionality, 17*, 223–37.

Underwood, K. (2010). Involving and engaging parents of children with IEPs. *Exceptionality Education International, 20*, 18–36.

Yell, M., & Drasgow, E. (2010). The continuing influence of the law in special education: Introduction to the Special Issue. *Exceptionality: A Special Education Journal, 18*(3), 107–8.

Zigmond, N., Kloo, A., & Volonino, V. (2009). What, where and how? Special education in the climate of full inclusion. *Exceptionality 17*(4), 189–204.

Link

Ontario Directors of Education **http://www.ontariodirectors.ca**

6

Identification Placement Review Committee: How the IPRC Works

THIS schema outlines the main features of Ontario Regulation 181/98, Identification and Placement of Exceptional Pupils, which came into force on September 1, 1998 (amended by Ontario Regulation 137, in 2001).

Step One		
Every school board is required to appoint one or more IPRCs.	**Student is formally referred to an IPRC by the school's principal.**	Principal may initiate referral (notifies parent*). Must initiate referral if asked by parent in writing.
IPRC has minimum of three members. *One must be a principal or supervisory officer of the board (or designate).*		
Step Two		
School board must publish a detailed Parents' Guide. *(See Note 1.)*	**IPRC obtains and considers educational assessment. May interview student with permission of parent.* Receives information put forward by school and parent. Shares all written information with parent.**	Medical and/or psychological data may be requested, subject to *Health Care Consent Act* (1996). Teacher interview and/or input not required by regulation, but most school boards will include these.
Step Three		
	IPRC must consider all information and proposals for special education programs and services.	Parent may present proposals in addition to those from school board.
Parent entitled to have a representative of choice present. *Parent and representative may participate in all discussions except decision-making.*		
Step Four		
Written decision of IPRC goes to parent, referring principal, school board. Parent may request that IPRC meet again to reconsider.	**IPRC decides student is not exceptional.** **OR** **IPRC identifies student as exceptional and decides on a placement. May make recommendations (but not decisions) regarding programs and services.**	Process ends, unless parent appeals or requests follow-up meeting. Decision statement must list placement, category (categories) and definition(s) of exceptionality, and student's strengths/needs. Placement to be regular class if it meets needs and if parent wishes. IPRC must give reasons if special class is chosen.
* Parent here includes parent(s) and guardian(s). Wherever parent appears, note that students sixteen years and older may be part of the process, along with parent.		

Step Five		
Within thirty school days principal of school where student is placed must see to development of IEP and, for fourteen-year-olds and older, a Transition Plan. (See Note 2.) Rights and requirements as in Steps One to Five.	**Student is placed according to IPRC decision. IEP is developed and implementation begun.**	If parent signs consent, or if consent is not signed but parent does not appeal. Step Five stayed if parent appeals.
Review		
Identification and Placement *How the IPRC works:* *A memorandum in the fall of 2006 from the then Deputy Minister outlined what for some school boards across the province would be a shift in practice with regard to IPRC. The memorandum suggested that school boards re-examine their procedures around IPRC and consider dispensing with a formal IPRC process in those cases where the board and parent were in agreement that the student's placement be in the regular classroom.*	**Student's situation to be reviewed at least once every school year by an IPRC. Parent may request review after three months.**	Reviews confirm existing situation or changes may be made. Principal to review and update IEP.
IN CASES OF APPEAL		
Step One (A)		
Parent may appeal identification as exceptional, or placement, or both. Parent and/or representative entitled to participate in all discussions except decision-making.	**School board convenes a three-member Appeal Board to review the IPRC material and decisions.**	One member chosen by board, one by parent. The two select a third as chair (in case of disagreement, chair is chosen by MOE).
Step Two (A)		
Written recommendation to parent, principal, school board, and chair of IPRC.	**Appeal Board agrees with IPRC and recommends its decisions be implemented.** **OR** **It disagrees with IPRC and makes recommendation to school board about identification, or placement, or both.**	May interview anyone Appeal Board chair feels has information to contribute. Written reasons must accompany written statement of recommendation.

Step Three (A)		
	School board considers recommendation and decides what action to take.	School board is not limited to recommendation of Appeal Board.
Written decision of school board goes to all parties.		If parent signs consent, or if consent not signed but parent does not appeal.
Step Four (A)		
	School board decision is implemented.	Step Four (A) stayed if parent appeals.
Final appeal stage is to Special Education Tribunal. (See Note 3.)		

Table 6A

On December 19, 2011, a memo from the Special Education Policy Branch of the Ontario Ministry of Education made it clear that, while the categories of exceptionalities as they exist within the current legislation are applicable, they are not to be interpreted too narrowly. The memo notes that conditions not specifically mentioned within the existing categories, such as AD/HD and fetal alcohol syndrome, are not to be excluded from special education assistance. Indeed, the memo is clear that special education resources and support should and will be provided to any student who exhibits learning difficulties regardless of diagnosis.

In October 2006, the MOE sent a memo to Directors of Education across the province stating that "an IPRC is not required when both the school and the parents agree that the student should be placed in a regular classroom." The memo was clear that this directive was in no way "intended to override the IPRC process set out in Regulation 181/98. It is intended to assist principals and other board staff to implement the regulation in a way that respects parents' rights while minimizing the administrative requirements." (Go to **www.edu.gov.on.ca/eng/policyfunding/memos/SpEdMemoOct12. pdf** for more infomration.)

Note 1: Each school board must prepare a parents' guide explaining all elements of the IPRC process, including rights of appeal and the steps involved. The guide must be available at every school in the board and, if requested by a parent, must be made available in Braille, large print, or audio form. The guide will also identify organizations and associations from which parents may seek advice and help.

Note 2: The Transition Plan requirement does not apply to students who are identified "gifted." See chapter 5 for a full explanation of IEPs and Transition Plans.

Note 3: The Special Education Tribunal (Section 57 of the *Education Act*) is a provincially appointed body that hears appeals from decisions of IPRCs upheld first by an Appeal Board and then by the school board. Tribunal hearings are complex and adversarial in structure, and are conducted under the *Statutory Powers Procedure Act of Ontario*. A Tribunal decision is final and binding. *The vast majority of IPRCs end at Step Five. Appeals are infrequent and Tribunals are rare. Where either is imminent in a student's case, the Ministry of Education encourages parents and school boards to attempt mediation before going forward.*

Also of Note …
- The regulations set specific time limits on steps in the IPRC procedure; e.g., appeals, response periods, etc.
- With a parent's agreement, adjustments are sometimes made to an identified student's situation without a formal IPRC meeting. Also, a formal Review is generally not convened to modify a student's IEP unless major change is requested or expected.
- IPRCs were governed originally by Regulation 554 issued in 1981. The procedure was modified by Regulation 305 in 1990. Fairly significant modifications were made in 1998 by Regulation 181, its current form. Regulation 137 in 2001 made a small change to Step Five, specifying a time frame for an IEP and Transition Plan. There have been no other changes.
- For the complete versions of the IPRC regulations and other documents, see **www.edu.gov.on.ca**, or the Ministry publication *Special Education: A Guide for Educators* (2001), available in government bookstores, public libraries, and school board offices.

7

Assessment: Identifying Strengths and Needs

"Whether assessed or not, my expectation is that every student will get the special education supports they need. Even if their assessment hasn't yet taken place and regardless of the outcome of the assessment, students are required to have supports at school to help them learn. In fact, one-third of students who receive special education programs are not formally identified."

– Laurel Broten, Minister of Education, Ontario, *Toronto Star*, May 2012

The Purpose of Assessment

When students are assessed, relevant information is gathered and interpreted from a variety of sources that may include teacher-made tests, observation, curriculum-based assessment, peer evaluation, portfolio development, and commercially available standardized test instruments. The results, at least theoretically, reveal some insights into the abilities, intelligence, strengths, needs, and behaviours of the students in question. The discoveries help in making informed evaluations about the students' present status and informed decisions about future instructional practice. Without a way to measure the progress of students, it would be impossible to program effectively within a school setting.

For students deemed exceptional in some way, the path of assessment, while similar to that taken for all students, can be more complicated and far more influential in determining program and placement. The assessment instruments used, the personnel required, indeed the depth and breadth of the assessment process itself, will vary from that used for more general evaluations. Ideally, the assessment process collects information, refines insight into exceptionality, and then sets the table for both programming and follow-up evaluations.

Once regarded as the exclusive realm of specialists, assessment has moved toward a more team-oriented approach with participation, responsibility, and accountability being shared by a number of key people, especially the classroom teacher, who is most likely to deliver the program. Others involved include the student's parents (and occasionally, in the case of some adolescents, the student himself or herself), the teaching assistant, the school's special education teacher (who may be responsible for some of the more formal investigations), and, if need demands and the personnel are available, various individuals with special expertise such as psychologists and speech and language pathologists.

Assessment: A Very Educated Guess

No matter how keenly we may seek specialized information about students and no matter how acculturated we may be to the belief that such truth can be revealed, the simple fact is that the very best an educational assessment can produce is a kind of loose probability. However loose, though, it is still an important probability. Education itself is not an exact science, and effective teaching is a combination of both art and science leading to effective instruction. An assessment provides information gathered in an organized way that, at the very least, confirms, in a presumably unbiased way, the view of the people working with the student. At the very best, it reveals factors that no one had known or possibly even expected.

Granted, there are reasons to harbour doubts about some of the procedures and components in an assessment and, quite possibly, reasons to be wary of the results if they differ significantly from the student's day-to-day performance. However, to ignore the possible contribution of an effective assessment to an exceptional student's case would be a disservice indeed. Assessment has an important role to play. What shapes the quality of that role is the quality of the assessment procedures and the way the results are interpreted and applied.

Assessment for Learning

In June 2009, the Draft of *Learning for All, K–12*, a follow-up to *Education for All: The Report of the Expert Panel of Literacy and Numeracy for Students with Special Education Needs, K–6*, was released on the website of the Council for Directors of Education. This report emphasized that, although research has described three types of assessment (assessment as learning, assessment of learning, and assessment for learning), the Ministry asks Ontario teachers to focus on assessment for learning. This draft states that "there is considerable research which confirms that assessment for learning is one of the most powerful ways of improving learning and raising standards because it is rooted in helping students learn more" (Ontario Ministry of Education, 2009, p. 26).

An effective assessment, according to this document, is one that reveals "where the learners are in their learning, where they need to go, and how best to get there" (p. 26). It requires collaboration among all involved (teachers, educational assistants, students, and parents) to ensure that a student receives a program and instructional approaches that are "suited to the ways they learn best" (MOE, 2009 p. 29).
Go to **http://www.edu.gov.on.ca/eng/general/elemsec/speced/LearningforAll2011.pdf** for more information.

When Are Assessments Completed?

Arguably, assessment happens at every moment of a school day. Whether they are monitoring a student's behaviour in the halls or observing while a student shoots baskets in the gym or writes a spelling test, teachers are always presented with opportunities to collect data that will identify needs and strengths. Assessment, quite simply, is an integral part of teaching. Choosing when to assess, what to observe, which piece of work to add to a portfolio, or which person to listen to in reading – these are all part of the daily challenges of classroom teachers.

Almost without exception, every student in every school setting will be subject to a screening at some time or another. A common practice, screening is a relatively formal but broad procedure that determines whether more intrusive testing is needed. Usually, groups of students are screened through an achievement test, or test of cognitive abilities, or other instrument. (Some boards have their own systems of screening to be used along with, or in place of, commercially published tests.) The purpose is to discover, in a general way, whether there are any students at risk – or potentially gifted. Then these students are usually assessed in a more formal and extensive way to confirm (or dismiss) their suspected risk or giftedness.

Screenings often take place at the preschool level where children entering school are assessed for vision, hearing, and general readiness. Farther along in the school grades, screening helps identify students who fall outside what is judged to be normal performance criteria. These students are tested further, to assess the nature and possibly the basis of the discrepancy.

Assessing Students with Special Needs

In the case of students who may be exceptional, the assessment process is more extensive.

Initially, a teacher who has concerns about a student may choose to seek assistance through the forum of the In-school Team. At this level, often referred to as the "pre-referral intervention level" because the student has not yet been referred for more formalized assessment and identification, the teacher is seeking assistance and direction from colleagues.

Generally, the teacher will prepare for a pre-referral by conducting an initial assessment based on observation, classroom performance, samples of the student's work and, possibly, a rating scale/checklist (especially in potential behaviour cases). It is not unusual for the teacher to perform a curriculum-based assessment, gathering information on the student's performance over a period of time in a particular curriculum area (such as reading or mathematics).

In many boards, a "pre-referral form" completed by the teacher requests specific information about the student's achievement and/or behaviour that the In-school Team can consider when a particular student's situation is under discussion.

With the assistance of the team, a number of suggestions may be attempted within the classroom setting. This type of intervention (e.g., moving the student to a different reading group, chunking work, or allowing for differing modes of information presentation) is often described as "intervention-focused assessment." This assessment examines the effectiveness of an intervention: Did the move to the front of the room work? Can the student complete a task better orally? Does the introduction of frequent breaks reduce the incidence of misbehaviour?

When a student's situation is more complicated or demanding, more intensive, formal, and specialized procedures (perhaps an IQ test, standardized achievement test, or even, in some cases, a diagnostic test) will be carried out. In cases where a student is formally identified as exceptional, assessment tends to be very thorough and includes assessment data obtained not only by the teacher but also by assessment personnel (e.g., psychologist, assessment counsellor, social worker, physiotherapist, speech therapist).

Usually, information is collected through a number of sources, and a variety of assessment strategies are used. The data in the identification of the student as exceptional help decide on program and placement and will be used in the development of the IEP. At the follow-up or review stage, the data will be used again with more current and perhaps further information being added.

The Case of Kyeesha

KYEESHA'S parents call her their "divine gift." She was born to them when they were in their mid-forties after they had experienced several unsuccessful pregnancies over a period of years. Both have successful academic careers (in art history and microbiology), and their home is intellectually and culturally stimulating.

When Kyeesha was four years old, the parents had her assessed for intelligence and general ability in a private clinic. The clinic's test results placed Kyeesha in the Very Superior range intellectually and, for the next two years, her parents enrolled her in a private preschool. Before enrolling her in grade 1 of their neighbourhood elementary school, the parents requested an IPRC. The committee, having little information available to it except the clinic's test results as provided by the parents, along with anecdotal accounts from them, quite readily accepted their opinion that Kyeesha should be identified as gifted and placed in a primary gifted program.

After considerable success initially, Kyeesha began to lag behind her colleagues in achievement, seriously enough that, by the end of grade 2, the school requested, and was granted by the parents, permission to conduct an assessment. The school board's chief psychologist somewhat reluctantly reported his conclusion that, intellectually, Kyeesha is in the Average to High Average range. Not unexpectedly, her parents find this difficult to believe. Because they are naturally disposed to co-operate and, no matter what, wish to make decisions that are in their little girl's best interests, they have asked for a meeting with the school.

What they want to have explained to them is how results of two assessments of the same child differ so greatly, and whether the school can provide other information that would help clarify for them what Kyeesha's real status might be and what academic program will be provided.

Who Does Assessments?

The process, quite naturally, begins in the classroom. It is the teacher who can best observe a student's response to text, reaction to physical environment, and relationship to peers and adults. Teachers collect samples of a student's work: journal entries, recordings, tests, and portfolios, to name a few. These are the materials that, along with the teacher's own professional opinions and views, establish the initial, basic, and often most important information. Further testing (and observation) may then be done by a special education resource teacher. This combination has distinct advantages in that the two (or more) teachers can then co-operate in the next step: designing the program implied by the assessment.

At the school board level, there is often a separate unit responsible for assessment known by descriptors such as "psychological services" or "support services." This unit does almost all the assessing for special education outside the classroom setting. Psychologists, or personnel working under their guidance and direct supervision (often referred to as psychometrists, assessment counsellors, or psychoeducational consultants), conduct standardized assessments measuring cognitive strengths, for example, or analysing behaviour patterns. In jurisdictions in which psychological services are not directly available, outside expertise may be hired and, where possible, classroom and special education resource teachers may be given more responsibility in conducting formal types of assessment. Most boards though, even the smaller ones, have formal assessments conducted by a person for whom this is a primary role.

Some larger school boards may employ speech and language pathologists to assess children with language difficulties. Assessments done by physiotherapists and occupational therapists are also outside the jurisdiction of the school boards, though schools may, with the co-operation of the parents, request such assessments. Parents sometimes obtain an assessment privately, even though, by law, they have access to any data the school has. If they choose, they may offer these data to the school.

Privacy Laws

Privacy regulations covering assessment information are constantly under review. Generally, whether an assessment may be performed is a matter of parental permission, board policy, and provincial and Canadian law. Similar factors govern the assessment results. Teachers and assistants must have careful regard for privacy regulations when either seeking or disseminating information about a student.

Components of an Assessment

Most, if not all, of the assessment information collected about a student revolves on:

- what the student is seen to be doing (observation)
- a systematic collection of student work products
- discussions and information sharing by key persons (including parents)
- and finally, testing

Historically, in special education, emphasis has been placed on testing. Indeed, the mystique of testing has often overshadowed and even delayed action on behalf of a student with an exceptionality. The phrase "We are getting him tested" was – and still is – an oft-heard one, and it is not unusual for a teacher to be caught in the frustrating position of waiting on results before being able to modify or make accommodations in a program. The benefits of more formalized types of testing can, indeed, inform the process of program planning. But for some time now, the experience of special education has made clear that formal tests are but one component in a much more complex process – one that starts with teachers in the classroom suspecting something, acting on that suspicion, and trying out various strategies to ameliorate the difficulty before more formal steps are taken.

The "Battery"

Curiously, the pieces that make up a formal assessment are often described collectively with the artillery term "assessment battery." What follows here is a description of the components that may be used in a battery, although certain of them will almost always be included. (It is difficult, for example, to conceive of an assessment being useful and valid without the observations of the teacher and educational assistant.)

The decision regarding what components to use is typically governed, in part, by school and board policy. For example, many boards have complex and stringent requirements for identifying students as gifted and specify that certain test instruments be used as part of the identification procedures. Some boards discourage, or even forbid, the use of certain components. However, once the school and board policies are met – and on the matter of components these matters are flexible for the most part – how an assessment is actually conducted, and what is used, typically is the choice of the professional personnel involved. That choice will vary according to their knowledge, competence, and personal preference.

Informal (Teacher-made) Tests

A growing awareness of the benefits of assessments conducted by someone working directly with the student on an ongoing basis has led to an increasing acceptance of informal measures designed by classroom teachers to meet their own immediate purposes. A disadvantage of these measures is that there are no norms for them, so they usually do not have acceptance beyond the immediate situation. But then that is not their purpose. Their advantage is that they can be truly tailored to meet specific needs. For example, an informal test can be designed to reveal the presence or absence of a very specific skill and may well provide a picture of why and when a student fails to grasp a skill (such as subtraction) instead of simply confirming that the student has not grasped it (which the teacher already knows in any case).

Informal measures may include a teacher using parts of rating scales and checklists so that he or she can be more certain to have covered all the points. Informal inventories are used here as well. Still another practice (albeit of questionable legality and efficacy) is to use parts of different formal tests to put together the desired information about a student.

> "It seems that our students living in families with complex needs get missed as they move through the education system. Students who have been enrolled in ten or more schools by the time they enrol in high school have often been missed for assessment of their special education needs. That missed diagnosis, because they were not in a school long enough to wait for their educational assessment, is a tragedy. Over and over again in my twenty-two-year career, I have had to sit at meetings and tell a parent of a fourteen-, fifteen-, and even eighteen-year-old that they were now diagnosed as developmentally delayed. This information is devastating for everyone involved and is very harmful to the esteem and well-being of the teenager. We have to find a better system to help diagnose children at a younger age and reduce the waiting lists for assessment to prevent a late diagnosis of a child. We owe it to them!"
>
> – Tracy S., principal

Formal Tests*

Intelligence Tests

Generally, tests measuring intelligence (IQ tests) give a relatively accurate assessment of what an individual has been taught (and what he remembers) and of what the student has been exposed to thus far in his or her life. In this sense, an IQ test is a measure of current performance. What continues to be hotly debated is whether the test measures intellectual potential and can thereby be legitimately regarded as a predictor of future school performance. Despite this concern, these instruments continue to be used for that purpose. Among the several commercially available IQ tests, the one most widely used in Ontario by far has been the Wechsler Intelligence Scale for Children IV (2003) known colloquially as the WISC IV.

Tests of Academic Achievement

These are the most widely used formal test instruments of all. There are achievement tests for large groups, e.g., the Canadian Achievement Tests, and there are individual tests as well, e.g., the Peabody Individual Achievement Test – Revised and the Wechsler Individual Achievement Test II. Administrators of achievement tests can be anyone from a classroom teacher to a professional psychometrist. Publishers provide detailed administration manuals and recommend that examiners attend training seminars. Very often in special education, achievement tests are used as screening tests. Other uses include general comparison, since individual test results are calculated in terms of the results – called norms – developed across a wide, randomly selected population. In other words, the test takers discover where they stand, in terms of the test, compared with a general population.

Diagnostic Tests

The term is misleading. These tests do not diagnose in any absolute sense but rather present specific information about a student's performance in a specific area. Their true purpose is to suggest areas for remediation. The Woodcock Diagnostic Reading Battery, for example, deals with specific areas such as "phonological awareness" and "oral comprehension," presumably giving indications about the extent to which a student is competent in these areas. Critics of this and similar tests question the value and even the validity of this kind of sub-skill breakdown in an area such as reading. However, they acknowledge it may have value in areas such as mathematics, where steps in the process of subtraction, for example, can be broken down and illuminated more clearly.

Tests of Cognitive Ability

Judgments about cognitive strengths and needs are inferred from a student's response to items on these tests. Memory, problem solving, and reasoning are examples of the types of skills these tests attempt to measure; the inference being that the better developed these cognitive skills are, the more successfully a student will perform in school-related tasks. The jury is still very much out on the issue of whether testing for cognitive abilities is any different from testing for intelligence with the IQ instruments already in use. Cognition is about thinking. Whether testing for thinking is any different from testing for IQ is moot. In Canada, supporters of the distinction generally opt for the Canadian Cognitive Abilities Test.

Developmental and Readiness Tests

These are primarily administered by classroom teachers, especially teachers of primary grades, to determine the level of ability of students. For exceptional students, their purpose is generally for screening. Very often these instruments are used along with checklists and skill inventories. Two popular examples in Canada are the Boehm Test of Basic Concepts – Revised and the Brigance Inventories.

---

* See appendix II for a more comprehensive overview, including publisher information, of tests currently in use in Ontario schools.

Rating Scales, Inventories, and Checklists

These instruments offer descriptive statements about areas such as attitude, self-esteem, behaviour, self-care, etc., in lists. Each item in a list is followed by a frequency ranking such as "almost all the time, frequently, sometimes, occasionally, rarely," or sometimes just by "yes" or "no." Responses are entered by the student's teacher, educational assistant, parent, social worker, or child-care worker (sometimes all of these for comparison and time/place/situation diagnosis). A reasonably popular example of this type is the Achenbach Child Behavior Checklist.

Some rating scales are designed to be completed by the student. The Coopersmith Self-esteem Inventory, for example, presents statements to the student such as, "I often wish I were someone else" followed by "like me ____" and "unlike me ____."

Most often, the results of these scales are used to determine a developmental profile from which educational or social or self-care objectives are developed. Occasionally, the information may be used to indicate a developmental level, and sometimes decisions about placement will be influenced by the level indicated. The AAMD Adaptive Behavior Scale, School Edition, often called an adaptive behaviour "test," is frequently used this way. Rating scale instruments invite considerable subjectivity and are both praised and criticized for this factor.

Keys to an Effective Assessment

For reasons of economy and the availability of personnel and appropriate instruments, as well as because of politics and the chronic problem of special education – lack of time – not all educational assessments will meet every one of the following criteria every time. But when these criteria are not met as a basic standard, the results of any assessment should be weighed accordingly.

1 Has the assessment used a broad spectrum of sources (e.g., teacher; parents; other professionals, if appropriate; test instruments, if appropriate)?
2 If test instruments have been used, are they known to be valid and reliable? Is the examiner adequately trained in the administration of the tests and the interpretation of the results?
3 Was the assessment individually tailored? Did it take into account matters such as the subject's culture, his or her language, age, school experience, and physical abilities?
4 Was the assessment ecological? Did it examine the whole student in relation to his or her whole environment and his or her program, classroom situation, and home situation?
5 Does the assessment imply or recommend avenues of remediation or enrichment (as opposed to presenting only an enumeration of deficiencies)?
6 Do key persons in the life of the subject – teacher, educational assistant, parent – acknowledge that the assessment has sampled genuinely representative factors?

Interviews and Informal Commentary: Teachers and Parents

Any effective assessment procedure will seek opinions from the adults who most directly associate with, and have responsibility for, the student. Most school boards invite the classroom teacher and, ideally, the educational assistant, to present information. Very often this face-to-face discussion is preceded by written information that may vary from a simple referral form to anecdotal information or a fully developed case study. Parents have vital information for an assessment or evaluation team. Their information is invariably current and intimate (if sometimes biased); they also have the advantage of knowing the student's full history. Both Regulation 181 and the IEP Resource Guide produced by the Ontario Ministry of Education require that parents be an integral part of the process in which a child is being considered for special education programming and/or placement.

Medical Information

This becomes part of an assessment only when it is germane, which it often is in the case of a student with special needs. Information may range from data about hearing, sight, and physical ability, to the general health and neurological conditions relevant to a student's situation. These data, if available, will come from the appropriate health professionals; they are almost never prepared by school board personnel. Experience has demonstrated that, without co-operation and impetus from parents, medical information, along with useful advice, is often hard to come by. Health professionals not only are understandably wary of privacy regulations; they also often show a curious reluctance to share more than sketchy information with schools.

Involve the Parents

What parents have to offer in assessment about a student's abilities is essential for obvious reasons. Answers to the following questions are always useful.

- What are your concerns regarding your child's learning/behaviour at school?
- How does what we do at school affect your child at home (reaction to homework, frustration level, general attitude toward coming to school)?
- Has your child had success, in the past, with a particular strategy or program?
- What other reports do you have that we may need to be aware of?
- What goals do you have for your child?
- Do you have a preference in method of communication from home to school?
- What questions do you have for us?
- When should we talk again to inform you of your child's progress?

Additional Types of Assessment Procedures

Curriculum-based Assessment (CBA)

Curriculum-based Assessment involves measuring a student's performance according to curricular expectations the school has established. Academic abilities and achievement can be systematically examined using this type of assessment. While many different variations exist, two basic components of CBA are probes of basic academic skills and content-area strategy assessment. *Probing*, which may be done across subject areas, involves ascertaining the skill and accuracy level of a student's knowledge of curriculum, e.g., letter recognition and arithmetic skills. *Content-area assessment* uses probes to establish knowledge level and examines learning skills such as note taking.

Many observers suggest that curriculum-based assessment, despite the extensive explication and argument surrounding it, does not differ very much from the way evaluation in schools was conducted well before special education became commonplace. In the case of a student with an exceptionality, they go on to say, curriculum-based measurement is not really a true alternative since all it really does is confirm that the student is not responding appropriately to the curriculum, a fact already evident. Supporters argue that curriculum-based assessment peers into a student's personal, unique, and complex characteristics as they relate directly to the curriculum and that this insight is superior to the type of assessment that merely establishes the presence of some disability.

To be effective, curriculum-based assessment must be carried out frequently and should be specific (i.e., directed exactly at what has been taught). The results should be evaluated for possible ways to adjust the instruction besides just determining how the student is doing. Assessment should also consider small, sub-skill gains in addition to the acquisition of more global matters.

Some Important Terms in Assessment

Bands of Confidence: Because of the Standard Error of Measurement factor, a test score can never be considered as absolutely correct. Thus, some test manuals note the range in connection with a given score about which there can be some confidence.

Criterion Referenced Test: A number of specific behaviours or performances are stated (e.g., Subject knows the alphabet. Can count from 1 to 20). These are the criteria. The subject's ability in the particular area is then assessed.

Grade Equivalent: A subject's raw score on a test is applied statistically to produce the school grade he or she would be in if the student were in the sample groups of students used to determine the norms for the test. (A subject's grade equivalent of 6.2 means that, if he were in the group sampled to produce the norms, he would stand at the second month of the sixth grade.)

Norms: These are the results obtained by representative populations at the time a particular test was developed. Students writing the same test have their results compared with these norms to produce scores such as Percentile, Stanine, Grade Equivalent, etc.

Norm Referenced Test: Rates a subject's performance relative to the results obtained in a known comparison group (or norm group).

Percentile Rank: A subject's percentile rank of 82 means that the student scored higher than about 82 percent of the norm group.

Reliability: The level of consistency and dependability of a test is its reliability (i.e., that it will produce similar results over variable conditions).

Split Half Procedure: This involves administering half of a test instrument (e.g., the odd-numbered questions) at a different time than the other half (the even-numbered questions).

Standard Error of Measurement: The extent to which a subject's score may be "out." These data are reported (or should be) in the technical manual accompanying a test. (See more in this chapter.)

Stanine: This is a reporting scheme for test results based on an equal interval scale of 1 to 9 (in which 5 is average, 6 is slightly above, etc.).

Validity: The degree to which a test measures what it purports to measure is termed its validity. See appendix II for more terms.

Authentic Assessment

Based on the premise that traditional types of assessment instruments fail to measure a student's performance in an authentic way, *authentic assessment* focuses on forming a "complete and realistic" picture of what a child can or cannot do. Authentic assessment allows for a collection of data based on real situations in which the students can be engaged in an interactive way and during which they can access help from teachers and peers as they most likely would in normal situations. This type of assessment is very unlike a formal test situation. The focus is on allowing students to integrate information taught in a classroom situation and to apply it in a problem-solving way. At its best, authentic assessment calls on a learner's best performance based on interaction and practice.

Portfolio Assessment

Portfolios are a collection of students' work representing growth and development over a specified time. Rather than a haphazard collection of work samples periodically collected, a portfolio is a specifically representative sampling. The goal of portfolio development is twofold: first, to provide a vehicle for the teacher to measure progress, and second (and perhaps more importantly), to allow the student himself or herself to monitor and evaluate his or her academic growth and thereby make informed decisions on how to proceed. Salend (1998) suggests the following guidelines for effective use of portfolio assessment in the classroom:

- determine the portfolio to be used (showcase, reflective, cumulative, goal based)
- establish procedures for organizing the portfolio
- choose a range of authentic classroom products that reflect the objectives of the portfolio
- record the significance of items included in student's portfolios
- review and evaluate portfolios periodically

Ecological Assessment

This concept includes an amalgam of formal and informal methods along with careful evaluation of the teaching–learning variables in the student's case. The idea is to examine the context in which the student learns, as well as the student himself or herself. Thus, matters such as the teacher's management style, the curriculum, teaching strategies, and instructional materials are examined, and work samples produced by the student are evaluated, as are the student's success and error patterns inside and outside school. Ecological assessment is attractive in principle, but management factors make it difficult to do.

Learning Style Assessment

In the 1980s, a proposal, initially well received, offered the idea that, by examining how a student learns and discovering under what conditions or through what style of presentation the student's learning is most natural and effective, remediation can become a relatively straightforward case of making appropriate adjustments when the student does not learn. While the idea was successful in promoting attention to individualized programming, as an assessment method it has proven unduly complex for the rewards it generates. Another problem is that, in the development stages of their growth, students' styles are not necessarily stable and therefore cannot be reliably measured.

Outcome-based Assessment

Outcome-based assessment requires professionals working with the student to teach and evaluate those skills important in real-life situations. Once these skills, appropriate for the individual, are determined, an assessment is conducted to determine to what degree the student has achieved those skills. After this is established, a determination is made about what needs to be learned next (similar to Task Analysis; see chapter 11). An instructional approach is then developed to help the student achieve the outcome determined at the beginning of the process.

📚 Some Issues in the Use of Formal Tests

✳ The power of test mystique. Educators, including those who should know better, seem strangely willing to ascribe to tests a kind of mystical capacity to open a window into a student's inner being and the workings of his or her mind. As a result, educators will often defer to test results even if those results contradict their own observations and conclusions arrived at over months of on-site observations and analyses. Ironically, the professionals who administer and interpret the tests are usually the ones to point out that a formal test instrument is just one of several looks at the subject. Yet so strong is the effect of a test result that almost everyone involved in a student's case will, however tacitly, acknowledges its superiority. As a consequence, the relative importance of a test in the general assessment of a student can be strongly, even shockingly, disproportionate.

✻ The aging of published tests is a serious problem. A quick review of the publication dates of any number of tests still in common use reveals disturbing results. Some standardized tests in use today were developed as early as the 1940s and 1950s – before television! Many were produced in the 1970s and 1980s – before the Internet. Thus, even though some tests are regularly updated,* it is very important for teachers and administrators to be aware of which version is being used. Given that, most of the time, the norms of a test are generated at the time of a test's original development, the results achieved by students today are sometimes compared with norms established with children who went to school decades ago. It is ironic in the extreme that educators are invariably the first to declare that our culture and our children are changing constantly and rapidly, yet seem to accept test results based, at least in part, on the performance of people from their parents' or even their grandparents' era!

✻ Bias and tacit discrimination against lower socio-economic groups and those of diverse cultures persists in testing. In older tests, normed groups may not be representative of current populations, so current scores can be misleading. As well, many test items suggest that the questions, pictures, expected knowledge base, and required skills do not take into account the diverse nature of many of today's classrooms. Producers of commercial tests claim to have addressed this matter in their revisions, but estimates of their success, as published in academic reviews, are conservative at best.

Testing Innovation

Within the field of assessment, there exists a legitimate and pervasive concern over the aging of both standardized assessments and their contents. While many of the "old reliable" tests are updated regularly, there is still the question of how much adjusting can be done before the actual premise and goal of the test need to be reexamined. Fortunately, new testing innovations are being worked on. One exciting project is the development of a test that has the potential to provide important insights into the extent that various injuries have affected the speed information is processed in certain individuals – the Computerized Test of Information Processing (CTIP). The CTIP is appropriate for individuals from fifteen to seventy-four years of age and can be used as an aid in the detection of malingering of cognitive deficits frequently associated with Traumatic Brain Injury. For more information on this test, readers are referred to MHS, Multihealth Systems Publishing Company (**www.mhs.com**).

✻ In tests administered to groups, questions are typically phrased so that answers can be machine-scored, with multiple-choice format being the most popular. Almost every question, therefore, must be responded to with a single, confined answer – a structure that invites a great many *dull and simplistic questions* and devotes an excessive amount of space, time, and effort to minutiae. Needless to say, it also leaves little, if any, room, for the reflective or creative student.

---

* Publication dates for test instruments typically show the last date an addition or revision was made. However, the change (and therefore the date) may indicate only a tiny adjustment to the content or even the layout. A publication date, therefore, does not necessarily mean the year when the instrument was last normed, updated, or otherwise scientifically improved.

The Case of Larry

EACH of Larry's eight years in the same elementary school has contributed to his reputation as a complete enigma. In fact, he is secretly (and kindly) known by the staff as "What Next Larry" because tales about him invariably attract that phrase.

In kindergarten and grade 1, Larry did not seem to learn to read, write, or even print his name. When he returned for grade 2 the next September, he immediately showed language skills well above grade level and, by Christmas, was leading the class. By the end of the year, he had begun to manifest odd behaviours, the most serious of which was eating chalk. That, too, disappeared over the next summer, but when Larry returned in the fall, it appeared he had become an elective mute. Neither his teacher nor an educational assistant, of whom he was very fond, could penetrate the mutism. His parents, who were, then as now, as baffled as his teachers, reported that not only did he exhibit the same behaviour at home, but he was being emulated in this by his next younger brother! Like the previous mysteries, this, too, passed, and in grade 4, Larry took up music. The school has a grade 7/8 band, and Larry showed he could play the clarinet well enough to join this older group and even become a soloist. Again, his parents had no explanation. Larry never had lessons, they reported, and, although they kept a clarinet in the attic, no one (except Larry, now) could play it.

Grade 5 saw sports, or rather sportscasting, enter the picture. Larry's teacher scheduled a part of each morning for current events and media study and, two or three times a week, Larry would report – pleasantly, but obsessively, and in total detail – all the scoring from the previous night's NHL games. In grade 6, Larry began his novel. He abandoned that venture before completion, but the writing took up almost all his time until winter break.

A standardized achievement test that year showed Larry at grade in language but well behind in math. However, he had been completely absorbed in his novel, especially when math was being taught. In grade 7, Larry became officially eligible for the school band but then dropped out. Instead, he got permission to form a chess club. By the end of the year, it had a higher membership than the band.

It is now the first month of Larry's grade 8 year. The principal (who is both fond of and protective of Larry – who fully returns the affection) has held a meeting of all staff who have taught or otherwise dealt with Larry. What he has proposed, with the strong support of the boy's parents, is that, since Larry will go to a secondary school next year, it would be to his benefit if his arrival there were preceded by a confidential assessment. The principal wants the teachers to suggest to him just what kind of information such an assessment should seek and how it should be obtained.

✳ ***Potential for misinterpretation***. It is not uncommon in tests of language and reading to find lists of single words, out of context, to be read aloud (e.g., see the Wide Range Achievement Test-3). These lists are often separated in sub-tests under titles such as Word Recognition, with the results interpreted, not just as a measure of word recognition, but as a measure of general reading ability. The practice also assumes that formally testing an unnatural idea such as word recognition is possible and worth doing in the first place.

✳ In tests of achievement, especially, ***each item tends to be scored with the same value*** (usually 1 or 0). School tasks typically increase in difficulty; thus, also typically, students merit proportionately enhanced recognition for dealing with these tasks successfully. In most formal, published tests, Student A, who correctly answers only questions sixteen to twenty, earns the same score as Student B, who correctly answers questions one to five. Granted, a careful item by item analysis would reveal that Students A and B attained a raw score of five by different routes, but in practice, consumers of test information rarely see, or have time to see, an item analysis.

✳ Tests are usually **rigorously timed**, with all the difficulties that causes for slow, not to mention deep, thinkers.

✳ **Misunderstanding "standardized."** Over time, commercially produced formal tests have come to be called "standardized" (distinguishing them from teacher tests, which by implication, therefore, are non-standardized). Many test consumers have come to accept "standardized" to mean these tests are based on a standard against which students are judged. This is not at all the case. Test results are, indeed, compared to a scale of values or "norms," but these norms are not an absolute standard; they are the scores obtained from the population samples used by the test publishers to establish the basis for comparison. Publishers usually contend that the norms they have established represent the range of results (in a perfect bell curve) that could be expected in a normal or typical population. That claim notwithstanding, the comparison is still relative; it is not standard. What is standard in formal tests are consistent procedures of administration and consistent scoring procedures to reduce examiner interference. It is not a standard of evaluation.

✳ Another well-established practice is to **generalize test results**. If a student takes test X in reading comprehension and scores a grade equivalent of, say, 4.2, the result is for that particular test. Yet it is regular practice by educators to assume that the student's absolute reading level is 4.2.

✳ **Ignoring the standard error of measurement.** One of the most misunderstood and overlooked features of a formal test is the standard error of measurement (SEM). Because no test is absolutely accurate, a subject's true score is never known. The score that a subject gets – the "obtained" score – is actually only an estimate of a "true" score. What the SEM does is give a statistical reflection of how close to a true score the subject's obtained score actually is. If, for example, the subject scores 110 on a test with an SEM of 3.8, then approximately two-thirds of the time, statistically, the actual score would fall between 106.2 and 113.8 (the score of 110 plus or minus 3.8). The impact of the SEM can be very powerful (not least because it is so often ignored). If students are identified for a program based on a cutoff in test scores, it is easy to see how the looseness implied by the SEM can be significant.

✳ Taken together, the problems with formal tests (not all of which, by any means, are the fault of the tests or the examiners) have led to a decrease in their use in assessing exceptional students. Although the testing tradition is still quite solidly established, alternative sources are more frequently being used and tend to have increasing credibility. What still remains for special education is to narrow the gulf between conducting the assessment of an exceptional student and developing a program for that student.

The Formal Case Study

A case study is an efficient executive summary that collates information from a number of sources into one document. In situations in which an exceptional student's case has become complicated over time – as often happens – and a variety of personnel, some of whom may not be acquainted in any way, have been involved, a case study brings together a student's history, current status, and needs. If written with some care, it can be the most effective means, by far, of bringing a group of professionals with diverse interests up to speed on a situation in which they share responsibility.

Ideally an educational case study is prepared by the teacher nominally responsible for the student in question and is written according to two principal criteria:

✓ succinctness (effective writers usually aim at a maximum of two pages)
✓ a non-judgmental, non-evaluative statement of the facts

Most often it presents information under such headings as:

1 demographic data
2 description of the educational issue
3 family history
4 physical and health status
5 social and behavioural matters
6 supplementary reports
7 assessment data
8 current program and placement
9 recommendations (most educational case studies do not include a recommendation component until after the meeting discussions, etc., for which the case study was initially prepared)

Regrettably, case studies have pretty much fallen into disuse in education today, not because of any flaws in either the idea or the process, but largely because our contemporary system seems to deny the time needed to complete them in favour of a reliance on the Individual Education Plan.

Readings and Resources

Bagnato, S. J., Neisworth, J. T., & Munson, S. M. (1997). *Linking authentic assessment and early intervention: Advances in curriculum-based assessment* (3rd ed.). Baltimore: Paul H. Brooks.

Benner, S. M. (1992). *Assessing your children with special needs: An ecological perspective.* New York: Longman.

Bufkin, L. J., & Bryde, S. M. (1996). Young children at their best: Linking play to assessment and intervention. *Teaching Exceptional Children, 29,* 50–53.

Cole, E., & Brown, R. (1996). Multidisciplinary school teams: A five-year follow-up study. *Canadian Journal of School Psychology, 12,* 155–68.

Howell, K. W., Fox, S. L., & Morehead, M. K. (1993). *Curriculum-based evaluation: Teaching and decision making* (2nd ed.). Pacific Grove, CA: Brooks/Cole.

Kleinert, H. L., Haigh, J., Kearns, J. F., & Kennedy, S. (2000). Alternate assessments: Lessons learned and roads to be taken. *Exceptional Children, 67*(1), 51–66.

Kubiszyn, T., & Borich, G. (1996). *Educational testing and measurement: Classroom application and practice* (5th ed.). New York: HarperCollins.

Mattatall, C. (2011). Using CBM to help Canadian elementary teachers write effective IEP goals. *Exceptionality Education International, 21*(1), 61–71.

Neisworth, J. T., & Bagnato, S. J. (1996). Assessment for early intervention: Emerging themes and practices. In S. L. Odom & M. E. McLean (Eds.). *Early intervention/early childhood special education: Recommended practices.* Austin, TX: Pro-Ed.

Ontario Ministry of Education (2009). *Draft report: Learning for all, k–12.* Available at: http://www.edu.gov. ca/eng/general/elemsec/speced/LearningforAll2011.pdf

Pierangelo, R., & Giuliani, G. (2006). *The special educator's comprehensive guide to diagnostic tests.* San Francisco: Jossey-Bass.

Popham, W. J. (1999). *Classroom assessment: What teachers need to know.* Needham Heights, MA: Allyn & Bacon.

Reed, L. C. (1993). Achieving the aims and purposes of schooling through authentic assessments. *Middle School Journal, 25*(2), 11–13.

Salend, S. J. (1998). In assessment (Special Issue) (1998). *Teaching Exceptional Children, 31*(2), November/ December.

Salvia, J., & Ysseldyke, J. E. (1995). *Assessment* (6th ed.). Boston: Houghton Mifflin.

Salvia, J., & Ysseldyke, J. E., with Bolt, S. (2013). *Assessment in special and inclusive education* (12th ed.). Belmont, CA; Wadsworth, Cengage Learning.

Sarouphim, K. (1999). Discovering multiple intelligences through a performance-based assessment: Consistency with independent ratings. *Exceptional Children, 65*(2), 151–63.

Stecker, P. M., Fuchs, L. S., & Fuchs, D. (2005). Using curriculum-based measurement to improve student achievement: Review of research. *Psychology in the Schools, 42,* 795–819. doi:10.1002/pits.20113

Thurlow, M. L., Ysseldyke, J. E., & Silverstein, B. (1995). Testing accommodations for students with disabilities. *Remedial and Special Education, 16*(5), 260–70.

Tindal, G., McDonald, M., Tedesco, M., Glasow, A., Almond, P., Crawford, L., & Hollenbeck, K. (2003). Alternate assessments in reading and math: Development and validation of students with significant disabilities. *Exceptional Children, 69*(4), 481–94.

Valenca, S. (1990). A portfolio approach to classroom reading assignments: The whys, whats and hows. *The Reading Teacher, 43*(4), 38–40.

Venn, J. J. (2007). *Assessing students with special needs* (4th ed.). Upper Saddle River, NJ: Pearson/Merrill/ Prentice Hall.

Wayman, M. M., Wallace, T., Wiley, H. I., Ticha, R., & Espin, C. A. (2007). Literature synthesis on curriculum-based measurement in reading. *The Journal of Special Education, 41,* 85–151. doi:10.1177/002246 69070410020401

Weber, E. (1999). *Student assessment that works: A practical approach.* Needham Heights, MA: Allyn & Bacon.

Ysseldyke, J., & Olsen, K. (1999). Putting alternative assessments into practice: What to measure and possible sources of data. *Exceptional Children, 65*(2), 175–85.

Links

About.com Special Education **http:specialed.about.com/od/assessment/ Special_Education_Assessment. htm**

Alberta Assessment Consortium **www.aac.ab.ca**

National Center for Educational Assessment **www.ncea.ca**

8

Students with Learning Disabilities

"I always thought that there was something wrong with me. When I was in the early grades, my mom arranged for me to take a taxi into the city once a week, a day-long journey, just to get an hour in a special reading clinic at the university. For years, my aunt Kit read special lessons every day with me at lunchtime. When I went to high school, even though I tried my best, I never seemed to be able to do it right. Mr. Critch, my homeroom teacher, told my mom that, if I could only say the answers instead of writing them, I would have no trouble at all. Unfortunately, back then teachers didn't know a lot about LD and oral tests didn't count. I never graduated high school."

– John C., age forty-two

Misconceptions About Learning Disabilities

1 **"Learning disability" is a social invention that excuses failure in middle- and upper-class children.**
A large body of research and an even larger catalogue of experience make it clear that a learning disability is a genuine special need and one that knows no social class barriers.

   As with any exceptionality, however, the effects of a learning disability can be aggravated by socio-economic factors.

2 **Heredity plays no role in learning disabilities.**
Although the strength and nature of the connection are unclear, evidence points to a pattern of learning disabilities in families. While anecdotal evidence is common, researchers, while postulating that there is a genetic link, are cautious about making a definitive statement on the matter. There is consensus, though, that more research into this type of linkage is necessary.

3 **Learning disabilities only show up in schools and therefore are a "school problem."**
Certain disabilities may remain hidden until the demands of school-based learning reveal them (e.g., language skills, mathematics

skills), but other specific disabilities (e.g., those concerning memory and attention or perceptual-motor processing) will become obvious independent of schooling.

4 **The main cause of learning disabilities is bad teaching.**
Not long after the term for this exceptionality was first developed, its critics offered "dyspedagogia" (bad teaching) as the real cause of the syndrome. Although ineffective instruction does have negative consequences for all students, decades of experience, careful observation, and research have demonstrated clearly that learning disabilities are a pre-existing set of special needs, independent of the quality of instruction (although the effects of disabilities are usually made worse by poor instruction).

5 **Most children will outgrow a learning disability.**
With effective instruction, the majority of children with learning disabilities manage their needs, but disabilities usually endure into adulthood.

6 **Students who are learning disabled are highly intelligent.**
Although many students with a learning disability develop clever coping strategies

and what is sometimes called substitution or diversion behaviours, there is little evidence to substantiate the claim of above-average intelligence. In fact, the weight of evidence suggests that such students' scores on IQ tests run across the same range as the general population, with what seems to be a tendency to fall into the average to below-average categories.

7 **Learning disabilities and acquired brain injury are one and the same.**
While many of the teaching and coping techniques may be similar in these two populations, they are indeed very different. Suddenness of onset, accompanied by sensory, pain, and fatigue issues, as well as the recovery period associated with acquired brain injury, make acquired brain injury a distinct condition.

8 **Students who are AD/HD are learning disabled (and vice versa).**
Hyperactivity and learning disability have become very much interwoven over the past several decades. The connection, however, is not absolute. A person with AD/HD is not always learning disabled or vice versa.

9 **Students who are learning disabled are more likely to become delinquent or criminal.**
This claim originated in the 1960s and, if nothing else, contributed to the high profile acquired by learning disabilities after that time. Some research shows a slightly higher incidence of learning disabilities in prison populations, but those findings are weakened by differences in defining learning disability.

10 **It is possible to detect the presence of a learning disability by testing.**
No test yet available can detect a learning disability in the same way that a hearing test, for example, can specify the nature and seriousness of a hearing loss. A learning disability is identified through teamwork by educators, parents, and sometimes other professionals, using observation, curriculum-based assessment, informal tests, and, to some extent, standardized, formal tests.

What Is a Learning Disability?

The question "What is a learning disability?" may be better answered, at least initially, with another question: "What isn't a learning disability?" Learning disabilities are not primarily the result of a sensory impairment, emotional disturbance, physical disability, cultural difference, or developmental delay. While these conditions do not prohibit the existence of a learning disability, they must be eliminated as a primary cause of students' inability to learn successfully. Having eliminated these other factors as a primary cause of difficulty, it soon becomes clear that learning disabilities, as an area of disability, can be the most elusive of all areas in special education. First, it is not a global impairment in which all elements of a student's performance are affected. Second, it is not a consistent, easily measured, and clear special need.

The only criterion that all students with learning disabilities seem to share is loosely described as a difficulty in dealing with information, particularly language-based information, despite any apparent freedom from intellectual or sensory handicap or cultural difference. The difficulty may be in taking in the information, or in integrating it with what they already know and understand, or in expressing what they now know as a result of taking in and integrating the information. Or – and this is where the elusiveness begins – it may be a combination of the previous three elements (or just two of the three). Students with learning disabilities may be disorganized, unable to focus attention, forgetful, and disoriented. They may be hyperactive – or hypoactive. They may be highly resistant to changing inappropriate behaviours, or so compliant that they are easily led astray. One student may manifest all of these characteristics; another student, while functioning at the same low academic level, may manifest only one of them. And either student may demonstrate some of these characteristics on one day and none the next – or may show all of them!

In effect, the exceptionality of "learning disabilities" is a syndrome of a number of behaviours. Unlike students with intellectual disabilities, in which case the impairment seems to be global, affecting all elements of an individual's performance, students with learning disabilities usually have more specific issues to cope with.

The Case of Cory

AFTER his parents' separation, Cory lived with his mother in an inner city area. For about four years, his mother regularly obstructed the father's visiting rights, contravening a string of court orders.

On the day Cory entered grade 1, his father picked him up from school at lunch hour, and the two disappeared. Eighteen months later, his maternal grandparents appeared at Pearson Airport, with the boy in tow, claiming to have rescued him from an abusive situation abroad. The Children's Aid Society (CAS) intervened and placed him with foster parents for six months, after which his mother was again awarded custody.

One year later, Children's Aid again intervened, and Cory was returned to the foster parents who had maintained him previously. Meanwhile, Cory's father returned to Canada and applied for, and was denied, permanent custody. But contrary to the recommendations of the CAS, the court granted him weekly visitation rights.

At about this time, Cory's mother suddenly remarried, abandoned her suit for restoration of custody, and moved to South America. Her parents (the maternal grandparents above) have now applied for custody, and CAS has entered an application to make Cory a permanent ward.

Cory is now almost ten. He is in a split grade 3/4 in his eleventh school and has missed about a full year of schooling. He takes medication for TB, and he has a slight hearing loss. Cory reads very poorly. Both his printing and the language and content of his stories can be easily mistaken for that of a much younger child. His math skills are inconsistent. Although his teacher suspects he may have an articulation problem, a speech consultant feels his odd way of talking is a product of mixing English and Spanish early in life. Everyone agrees that at least part of his learning difficulty is the result of timidity. A psychologist described Cory's manner as "juvenile shell shock."

The social worker responsible for Cory (a former teacher) believes that the evidence clearly indicates a learning disability and that, if he is so identified, he will get some of the help he so obviously needs. The School Team believes Cory's status is a result of his personal history and that what he needs is love and, above all, stability. To identify him as learning disabled, they argue, will add yet one more change. The principal is strongly opposed to what she calls "using the learning disability category as a dumping ground for problems that have alternate solutions." The IPRC considering the case says it will listen to any argument that clarifies whether Cory has a learning disability and will consider any and all recommendations.

Defining the Indefinable?

When the late Dr. Samuel Kirk, former head of the National Advisory Committee of Handicapped Children, proposed the term "learning disability" to a conference of parents seeking information about their "mystery kids" in the early 1960s, the response was immediate and positive. The fact that the term became widespread very quickly indicated the extent to which large numbers of concerned parents were seeking an explanation why their children did not succeed in school, despite what they, the parents, knew was not a lack of intellect. (And it was parents, far more than academics, who were responsible for placing learning disability front and centre in education.)

The new term was non-pejorative and all

encompassing. It avoided implications of low intellect and ineptitude and successfully replaced a variety of unsatisfactory general descriptors such as dyslexia, perceptual handicap, minimally brain-injured, maturational lag, and even slow learner. The dark side, however, is that "learning disability" is loose enough to permit a variety of interpretations and, although it offered a sense of focus and direction and put a consensual face on an issue that had been running in all directions, making the next step to a clear and widely accepted definition proved then – as it continues to do today – a challenging task.

A Variety of Explanations ...

Many notions and ideas about how to view learning disabilities have enjoyed periods of popularity since the 1960s. Because they continue to crop up in the literature and because none of them have been effectively and clearly disproven, they are briefly summarized here.

- *IQ score/achievement discrepancy*: Supporters contend that a difference of two years or more between the mental age obtained on an intelligence test and the grade-age equivalent obtained on a standardized achievement test indicates a learning disability. The flaw of this approach is that it reduces the complexity of an individual to numbers. Also, a two-year discrepancy has different meanings at various ages and grade levels.

- *Presumption of central nervous system (CNS) disorder*: Much of the early work in learning disability grew out of central nervous system and brain injury research of the 1930s and 1940s. Researchers, because they noted similar behaviours between children known to have brain injury and those in the new subject pool, tended to make a leap of attribution; as a result, students with learning disabilities were seen to have CNS disorder. Although by the 1980s, special education had generally retreated from the belief in brain anomalies as a cause of learning disabilities, new technologies such

as magnetic resonance imaging (MRI) have now shown subtle differences in the brains of individuals thought to be learning disabled. Although the connection remains vague and its value to education unclear, that finding has kept the file open.

- *Impairments in psychological processing*: Psychological processing includes such cognitive functions as memory and attention, perceptual-motor processing, language processing and visual-spatial integration. A strengthening conviction that diminished capacity in one, some, or all of these processes distinguishes persons with learning disabilities led a very important support group, the Learning Disabilities Association of Ontario, to give this hypothesis prominence in its definition published in 2001.

- *Exclusion of environment, culture, mental retardation, sensory impairment, emotional health*: If a learning problem is related to one of the above, that problem is usually not considered a learning disability. Unfortunately, the connection between such factors as emotional health and low generalized academic achievement is well established, so that separating them from the fact of a learning disability is difficult.

- *Classification*: Educators have favoured classifications of degree in dealing with learning disabilities, applying descriptors such as "mild," "moderate," and "severe," as well as classifications of type, usually "specific" for those cases where a student's need tends to be singular (e.g., the student has special needs in language but does well otherwise) and "general" where a student lags behind peers in most areas. Unfortunately, the lack of an adequate, objective testing instrument for learning disabilities usually means that these classifications become pretty much subjective evaluations. As well, the terms transport poorly. What is "moderate" and/or "specific" in one school may not be in another.

Transition to Post-secondary

While it is more than reasonable to assume that students with learning disabilities can and should move into post-secondary educational settings, it is important to provide support for this transition. The following suggestions provide guidance for educators at the high school level who will be in a position to assist these students.

Steps for transitioning to post-secondary:

- Begin transition planning early (probably as soon as the end of grade 9).
- Allow for a wide variety of courses that lead to programs, but focus on areas of strength.
- Involve students in the process.
- Teach self-advocacy skills (the students should know their rights).
- Be sure that students understand what a learning disability is.
- Focus on both academic and personal independence.
- Update assessment information where needed.
- Familiarize students with the resources available at the post-secondary institution.

... and a Variety of Definitions

- *Learning Disabilities Association of Ontario, adopted 2001*

Learning disabilities refers to a variety of disorders that affect the acquisition, retention, understanding, organization, or use of verbal and/or non-verbal information. These disorders result from impairments in one or more psychological processes related to learning in combination with otherwise average abilities essential for thinking and reasoning. Learning disabilities are specific, not global, impairments and, as such, are distinct from intellectual disabilities. In addition, learning disabilities:

- Range in severity and invariably interfere with the acquisition and use of one or more of the following important skills: oral language (e.g., listening, speaking, understanding), reading (decoding, comprehension), written language

(spelling, written expression), and mathematics (computation, problem solving).

- May also cause difficulties with organizational skills, social perception, and social interaction. The impairments are generally lifelong. However, their effects may be expressed differently over time, depending on the match between the demands of the environment and the individual's characteristics. Some impairments may be noted during the preschool years, while others may not become evident until much later. During the school years, learning disabilities are suggested by unexpectedly low achievement or achievement that is sustainable only by extremely high levels of effort and support.
- Are due to genetic or other congenital and/or acquired neurobiological factors. They are not caused by factors such as cultural or language differences, inadequate or inappropriate instruction, socio-economic status, or lack of motivation, although any one of these, as well as other factors, may compound the impact of learning disabilities.
- Frequently co-exist with other conditions, including attentional, behavioural, and emotional disorders, sensory impairments, or other medical conditions.

For success, persons with learning disabilities require specialized interventions in home, school, community, and workplace settings appropriate to their individual strengths and needs; these interventions include specific skill instruction, the development of compensatory strategies, and appropriate accommodations.

- *Ontario Ministry of Education, as published in A Guide for Educators, 2001*

Learning disability is a learning disorder evident in both academic and social situations that involves one or more of the processes necessary for the proper use of spoken language or the symbols of communication, and that is characterized by a condition that:

a) is not primarily the result of impairment of vision; impairment of hearing; physical disability; developmental disability; primary emotional disturbance; or cultural difference;

b) results in a significant discrepancy between academic achievement and assessed intellectual ability, with deficits in one or more of the following: receptive language (listening, reading); language processing (thinking, conceptualizing, integrating); expressive language (talking, spelling, writing); mathematical computations; and

c) may be associated with one or more conditions diagnosed as: a perceptual handicap; a brain injury; minimal brain dysfunction; dyslexia; developmental aphasia.

- *National Joint Committee on Learning Disabilities (USA), as presented, 1988*

Learning disabilities is a general term that refers to a homogeneous group of disorders manifested by significant difficulties in the acquisition and use of listening, speaking, reading, writing, reasoning, or mathematical abilities. These disorders are intrinsic to the individual, presumed to be due to central nervous system dysfunction and may occur across the life span. Problems in self-regulatory behaviour, social perception, and social interaction may exist with learning disabilities but do not, by themselves, constitute a learning disability. Although learning disabilities may occur concomitantly with other handicapping conditions (e.g., sensory impairment, mental retardation, severe emotional disturbance) or with extrinsic influences (such as cultural differences, insufficient or inappropriate instruction), they are not the result of these conditions or influences.

Characteristics of Learning Disabilities

Processing Language

Many students with learning disabilities are challenged by the task of processing language. At the receiving stage (when the student is hearing language or attempting to read it), or at the sending

Getting Technical

The use of technology with students who are learning disabled is relatively commonplace, and many educators are beginning to use it, not just with students identified with LD, but with all students. Access to laptop computers, smartboards, tablets, and even cell phones has opened up previously unexplored avenues for the transmission and teaching of knowledge. With innovations appearing daily, many educators are caught playing catch-up in learning about what is available and what may be the most effective.

In some cases, at least, and certainly in the case of students in the later grades, the students themselves may be the most valuable resource for finding and using the appropriate technology. It is important for educators to remember that students' needs for technology, just like their learning, must be reviewed frequently. Technological tools and adaptations must be suited to the students' needs and learning abilities, both of which can fluctuate across subject settings, developmental stages, and even social settings. What might have been cool in a primary setting may seem cumbersome and embarrassing in elementary. Being an informed consumer in the fast-paced world of educational technology is a challenge, and, as more expensive is not always better, it is most important, when in doubt, to ask.

stage (speaking or writing), or at the elaboration stage (when the student attempts to integrate some language with what he or she already holds), a student with a learning disability often has real problems. For some students, these happen only at one of the stages; for others, difficulties arise at two or all three stages. For example, a younger student may not be able to process an incoming set of instructions like: "Use your red crayon to colour the robins and then your yellow one to draw a line under the 'r-r-r-r' sound." The student will hear the instruction all right, but all of that linguistic information – robins, crayons, red, yellow, r-r-r-r sound – not to mention the activity, may be too much to process. The student may miss the instruction altogether, or miss a piece of it, or confuse red and yellow, or interchange pieces of information. The result will likely be a poor performance or a non-performance.

An older student may have an equally difficult time with something like this, say, from a geography teacher: "If you refer to your maps of West Africa, you'll notice a good example of how Africa was fragmented by decolonialization. Notice how Gambia is literally inserted into Senegal and then, farther down the coast, you'll see even more examples with Guinea-Bissau, Guinea, Togo, and Benin all sitting side by side." The older student may have more sophisticated language ability than the one colouring robins, but then he or she is expected to deal with more sophisticated language and, in relative terms, is going to have just as much or even more trouble.

It is not unusual for an adult working with a student who has a learning disability to confuse the student's weakness in processing of language with weakness in visual or auditory discrimination. For example, unless the student has a vision or hearing loss, this student will have no difficulty visually discriminating the letter A from a picture of a teepee, or the sound of "book" from the sound of "hook." Where the student will manifest

difficulty, however, is in recognizing the letter A as such and giving its name (or recalling the word "teepee" and saying it).

It is not distinguishing between the sounds of "book" and "hook" that is hard; it is recognizing the words and the meanings, or giving the right answers, even if the student knows them. A student who is learning disabled may also have difficulty in producing the letter A on paper (or the words "book" or "hook"). The student may draw a teepee, but it may be disproportionate. On the other hand, the student may be able to draw a beautiful teepee but when instructed to add a campfire at the left and a horse on the right will have to guess at these juxtapositions.

Non-verbal Learning Disabilities (NVLD)

Students with NVLD are often able to work with letters and numbers successfully. They gather information orally and have an excellent vocabulary, which is somewhat different from what is typically understood of as a learning disability. Students with NVLD also experience difficulties in school. These include but are not limited to:

- coordination and movement
- orienting in space
- reading social cues
- organization and sequencing
- reading comprehension
- organizing their thoughts for writing
- making and keeping friends
- adjusting to new physical and learning situations

The Case of Genevieve

As a toddler, Genevieve presented with behaviours typical of a child with a hearing impairment. She stood close to the television to hear it, and, when others spoke to her, she appeared to be puzzled by what was being stated.

Her parents took her to an audiologist, who detected a central auditory processing disorder. This was the first exceptionality that she entered junior kindergarten with. She began working with the school's resource teacher on phonemic awareness and phonological processing skills.

Genevieve's parents suspected that there were other underlying explanations for her challenges and took her to a private psychologist for a psychoeducational assessment. Genevieve was then identified with a learning disability (communication), a memory deficit, and attention deficit/hyperactivity disorder (Inattentive subtype AD/HD) when she was eight years old and entering grade 3. An IPRC meeting was called, and an IEP was put into place.

During this last year of the primary grades, the modifications were mainly to Genevieve's reading materials, which were at a primer and early grade 1 level. The accommodations included peer support when working in groups and multiple presentations of information including oral, written, and teacher reiteration. Genevieve wrote the grade 3 EQAO test, with the support of her resource teacher as a scribe, and was permitted extra time to complete it.

As Genevieve passed through the junior grades, the school began to acquire more educational technology. It acquired a class set of laptops and equipped the resource room with assistive software to support text to audio reading. Genevieve's psychoeducational assessment data were updated as she entered grade 6, and the recommendations stated at the end of the report specifically noted the value of assistive technology for her as she becomes a more independent adolescent learner.

The school board acquired a licence for a comprehensive software package that included features for assisting both reading and writing skills: scan and read, text to audio, an electronic reader, a talking dictionary, and a talking word processor. This software package was also made available for home use to the families of identified students. An information and training session was offered by the school for parents. During grade 6, Genevieve enthusiastically used the program, and it became one of her accommodations during the grade 6 EQAO.

When she entered the intermediate division, Genevieve became increasingly cognizant of her learning differences. Like a typical adolescent, Genevieve wanted to fit in with her peers and believed that using the "special" software program on the class laptops didn't constitute fitting in. She came up with an effective solution. When she needed to write, for example, she used the comprehensive software on her home computer, imported the text into MS Word, and saved it on a jump drive to take to school. This was important to Genevieve: In her mind, working in a mainstream software program such as MS Word is what students typically do.

As she prepares to enter high school, a transition plan has been collaboratively made involving her grade 8 teacher, principal, resource teacher, and the special education department head at her new high school. Genevieve will be placed in regular classes with indirect support. Fortunately, the high school is wifi appointed and laptop friendly – it is an environment in which all students are encouraged to use technology. At a critically important juncture, when teenagers crave to be accepted by their peers, Genevieve's teachers are working hard to ensure that she receives appropriate programming and support.

Variations in Ability

What makes the language-processing deficiency above so insidious is that it is so variable. If there are three students in the geography class who have learning disabilities, one of them may be entirely confused by the concept of "decolonialization" and miss everything else as a result. A second, unless there is a map right before him or her, will be overwhelmed by all the verbal details of the countries mentioned. The third may understand the point perfectly and even be able to hypothesize on it but, three days later, on the examination, prove entirely unable to put together the language that will explain what he or she thinks.

The English Language Is a Factor

The subtleties of English may pose a barrier for students with learning disabilities. For example, a teacher who says to a student, "I don't see your answer," may mean a number of different things – for example, that the answer is simply not visibly apparent, or that the answer was not completed, or that her or she does not understand the answer, or that her or she disagrees with it. Because some students who are learning disabled have difficulty not only with language, but also in reading between the lines of communication situations and social contexts, they may respond incorrectly to "I don't see your answer," or respond undiplomatically, or just not respond at all.

Language that attempts to capture time and sequence is another of the many stumbling blocks, in part because the language itself can be very complicated, and in part because chronology and sequence are problems all on their own. For example, in the sentence, "Only after it first sprouts blossoms can the tree bear fruit," the words and the syntax used to describe the sequence set up real complications. The phrase "only after" is at the beginning of the sentence. Yet it sets up a condition and presents a time frame for the rest of the sentence, which then describes what in effect must happen before "only after"! Efficient language users can usually comprehend such a sentence. Students with learning disabilities often do not.

Still another barrier exists in the pronoun "it." The listener/reader not only must hold "it" in short-term memory until its referent ("tree") surfaces, but also must perceive that "it" refers to "tree" and not some other idea. (Research shows that the difficulty with pronouns normally experienced by young language learners, aged four and five, is experienced by students with learning disabilities well into their teenage and adult years.)

Difficulties like those above are compounded by the problems students with learning disabilities have in relating one sentence to others in a passage, or in relating passages to passages, or even stories to stories, whether written or spoken.

The Case of Raghubar

RAGHUBAR's mother is fully involved in the difficulties of learning to live in a new country and a new culture, but, even though she has no other children on whom to base a comparison, she has not been too preoccupied to notice that her little boy does things differently. While he is not hard to control and definitely is not deaf, somehow he never seems to hear her. Well, that's not quite it, either. He hears her but does perhaps half of what he's asked, or starts the task and then wanders away, or more often than not, does it backwards or leaves out a step.

Raghubar almost never gets anything exactly right. Except in soccer. He is so good in soccer that older children in the community park stop to watch him. Still, that, too, is a mixed blessing. Raghubar is a natural athlete, a gifted one, probably. But he also has no fear. He puts himself at such risk that his mother is certain he will injure himself permanently one day. And that concern ties into another one. Raghubar never seems to learn from the experience of a bad fall, or a banged shin, or painful cut. The very next day, he'll go out and do the same thing that led to an accident the first time.

Although she has a fairly limited education herself, Raghubar's mom had the good sense to visit her son's teacher-to-be well before his formal schooling began. As a result, the teacher was on the lookout for what sounded to him like a learning disability, a suspicion that was reinforced when Raghubar lagged behind the rest of the class when they began to learn letters. After being in first grade for six months, it is clear that the boy is not picking up what his classmates get. He recognizes only six letters and, in counting, gets to ten and becomes confused. Over half of his class is already reading more or less independently.

When the teacher suggested to the principal that an assessment/identification might be in order, he got the two responses he expected: one, that Raghubar is far too young and undeveloped for such a major step; and two, that at this early stage the best strategy is to revise the boy's program. The teacher has now turned to his colleagues for help. He wants to know (a) if a six-year-old is too young and undeveloped to be called "learning disabled" and (b) what program steps can he take right away for a boy who does not count past ten and recognizes only six letters.

Are We on the Same Wavelength?

One of the more unsettling aspects of the problem in processing language, for teachers, parents, and certainly for the students themselves, is the frustration of discovering that an apparently successful communication has been partly, or even completely, misunderstood or misinterpreted. (Admittedly, this is a common trait in all children, but what distinguishes students with learning disabilities is how consistently this occurs.)

Because teachers, parents, and students often engage in a communication knowing that the potential for confusion is high, all parties often take extra care to be sure that the communication has meshed in such a way that what was sent is also what has been received. It is not difficult, therefore, to imagine the stress that results when what appeared to be a successful interchange turns out to have been two separate tracks of communication that overlapped from time to time but never bonded into that stage of information interchange we like to call understanding.

The implications of this problem for life in general, and for the classroom specifically, are significant. Whether it occurs solely because of faulty language processing or because of memory problems has yet to be clearly established. All that is known for sure is that it happens. Often.

Dyslexia Versus Learning Disability

The term "dyslexia" was first used by a German ophthalmologist in 1877 to describe a phenomenon in which otherwise normal individuals seem to have great difficulty extracting meaning from print. Around the same time, a pair of British doctors noted the disability but called it "word-blindness," a term that was soon discarded. Over the decades since, a combination of genuine academic research, pop psychology, and media fascination* has done much to fix dyslexia in the public consciousness. An American organization with international affiliates, the Orton Dyslexia Society, named after neurologist Samuel Orton, whose work dates to the 1920s and 1930s, has done even more to carry the idea forward so that, today, dyslexia has become familiar throughout our culture.

For teachers and EAs, the issue is not so much whether dyslexia is real. Most professionals agree that there are individuals who, although otherwise physically and intellectually normal, are unable to extract meaning from print or to produce written text in a manner that is age appropriate. But confusion arises because dyslexia is regularly used as a synonym for general learning disabilities (as is frequently the case in England, for example). For Canadian educators, dyslexia usually means a specific difficulty – i.e., processing the printed word – but such use of the term is not universal, giving rise to confusion.

The simple reality is that dyslexia and learning disability are not really one and the same inclusive term. The former describes a specific special need associated with language development. The latter has a far broader application, incorporating both language difficulties and other, non-language-based learning problems. To use the two terms interchangeably does a disservice.

* Popular press items on dyslexia regularly trot out a list of "famous dyslexics" such as Alexander Graham Bell, Pablo Picasso, Jay Leno, Cher, and John Lennon.

Memory

An apparently poor memory for learning and for new information is another characteristic that distinguishes many students with a learning disability. They may, at the moment of instruction, learn a technique or an idea, acquire information, or memorize a sequence or a formula at the same pace and in the same depth as their colleagues without learning disabilities. But unlike the latter, they will have difficulty retrieving it the next day.

Accounting for this supposed memory problem has generated considerable speculation.

One hypothesis is that the students forget because they cannot transfer learning and information from short-term to long-term memory, or at least cannot do so easily.

Another is that it is strictly a result of poor language processing – in other words, not a case of simple forgetting but of not grasping the material correctly in the first place.

Neither of these explanations is entirely satisfactory. If the students cannot transfer from short- to long-term memory, then how come teachers and parents can cite examples of phenomenal long-term memory retention in students who are learning disabled? And if language-processing problems are the sole cause, why do students with learning disabilities so often make the same social mistakes time after time? (Students who are learning disabled frequently have difficult peer relations because of a seeming inability to gain from social experience. They continue to repeat social gaffes, seemingly not remembering what happened when a similar situation cropped up previously.)

Whatever the cause, it is essential to be aware that students with learning disabilities may not have retained what everyone else thinks they have – or should have. This reality inevitably shapes how we relate to them.

Metacognition

Loosely defined, metacognition has been called "thinking about thinking." It comes naturally to the majority of students to strategize, monitor their performance, and adjust accordingly. Not so for students with a learning disability. Understanding self, being aware of the mind's activity, being sensitive to the strategies available for learning a task, and understanding the regulatory mechanisms needed to complete the task present real and persistent challenges. Teachers and educational assistants can readily attest to the difficulty that a student with a learning disability has with such tasks as studying, remembering class requirements (such as homework), and taking on a project and organizing it through to completion. These difficulties are often misinterpreted as lack of interest, laziness, or outright defiance.

Strategies as simple as providing more time, using graphic organizers, and posting reminders have proven effective in helping students with learning disabilities to be more successful in their learning environment.

Difficulties with Sequence and Order

Students with learning disabilities miss steps in a sequence, get them out of sequence, and reverse the sequence, and, as often as not, they may simply ignore a sequence. Research has not been able to demonstrate clearly whether this is a cognitive or an affective characteristic, but the weight of empirical evidence is in favour of the former interpretation.

Satisfaction with a Peripheral Understanding

An adolescent seeking a credit in chemistry, when asked for a definition of Boyle's Law, typically might answer, "Oh it's about pressure and that." The likelihood is that the student knows more: probably a definition of Boyle's Law, perhaps even an understanding of how to apply it in a problem. If this adolescent is learning disabled, however, the vague answer about pressure may well constitute the totality of his or her knowledge of the law. Yet the student will quite likely believe he or she has a thorough grasp of it and proceed comfortably in that self-assurance until confronted by a request to apply Boyle's Law to a problem.

This is the same student who in grade 2 wrote three lines in his or her journal while the rest of the class averaged twenty. And who likely responded indignantly to a comment about such a slim output with something like, "I did my journal," or "That's all I have to say!" The key features are the student's satisfaction with a vague, incomplete, peripheral piece of work and conviction that the work is adequate. This is a crucial behaviour for educators to recognize. It is not defiance; it is not shirking; and it is not an utter lack of ability. It is a misinterpretation of what constitutes completeness.

Poor Time Management

It is not surprising that a student – who rarely plans and even more rarely accommodates his or her activity to due dates and timetables – is frequently late, or in the wrong place, or in conflict with some time-specific requirement, or is just chronically off-task. Many students with learning disabilities seem to be unaware of time, or at least of time as a concept organized into sequentially discrete units.

This page in the LD catalogue accounts for a significant portion of their trouble in school. Because schools are so time-driven, so inflexibly organized into chronological chunks – sequenced, hierarchical, chronological chunks – the student often feels entirely out of place. School bewilders the student not just because of its emphasis on language (and its commensurate de-emphasis on non-language elements such as music and art and athletics, where the student may shine) but also because of its apparent obsession with time in specified units.

Regrettably, the outside world is equally passionate about time, and learning to deal with that is a necessary prerequisite in all of education. It is not unusual for a student with learning disabilities to perform better, both generally and academically, in an environment in which he or she is liberated somewhat from the demands of time.

Inconsistent and Episodic

What is at once tantalizing and frustrating for anyone who tries to view the field of learning disabilities objectively (teachers, educational assistants, parents, academics, medical professionals) is the knowledge that the profile of a student with a learning disability is never the same from day to day and that a single characteristic of learning disability is never universal. A student with this disability may regularly write "on" for "no" and "b" for "d," yet in the same sentence use all four elements correctly. He may use "on" for "no" consistently for three weeks and then suddenly and spontaneously use them correctly while simultaneously beginning to write "was" for "saw," even though those had been correctly used hitherto.

This is the adolescent who cannot remember a single irregular verb in French, or the formula for calculating the area of a circle, or the definition of alliteration, but who, on a warm Saturday, can strip down, clean, repair, and completely reassemble a mountain bike. This is the child who bumps into everyone in the queue, whose shoes are untied and whose shirttail hangs out, but who is the first in his or her age group to earn Red Cross badges for swimming excellence. This is the one who forgets where he or she put his or her clothes, books, and lunch, or who confuses his or her telephone number and address, but can recite, without error, a TV ad or the lyrics of a song.

It is an acknowledged fact by all those associated with persons who are learning disabled that no one student will be the same as another and that no one student's own pattern will ever be consistent and regular. This phenomenon, among other things, makes children's learning disabilities almost completely resistant to positive identification by formal standardized tests. It bears equally important weight for the classroom teacher who must be ever prepared to adjust to the episodic nature of these students' performance. And, of course, this behaviour is yet one more arrow in their quiver of confusion.

Some Day-to-Day School Problems Associated with Learning Disabilities

Coordination/Co-operation
- may have difficulty lining up
- often confused or anxious over taking turns
- may bump, trip, or spill far more frequently than peers

Writing Skills
- may confuse letters in writing and recitation
- mixes upper and lower case letters
- mixes manuscript and cursive styles or will continue to use manuscript long after age and grade peers use cursive
- frequently distorts letter size and shape
- attempts at continuous text are scratchy, barely legible
- often mirrors or reverses letters
- employs awkward, even unnatural, movement of the pen or pencil

Personal Organization
- forgets, misplaces things
- needs constant reminding (and often has successfully trained others to do this)
- frequently late or in the wrong place
- poor notion of chronological order
- may confuse instructions, especially if there is more than one step

Copying/Note-making
- careless, often reproduces inaccurately
- loses place often
- far-point copying very slow and inaccurate
- overprints, telescopes, omits
- may have difficulty reproducing a shape from memory
- ignores subheadings and organization cues

Arithmetic
- reverses numbers
- careless about columnar structure
- may not remember rote matters (multiplication tables)
- carries or borrows wrong digit
- skips or omits steps in problem solving

Reading/Language
- loses place regularly
- makes many flying guesses
- does not attempt a new or strange word
- ignores punctuation and other cues
- makes up words, telescopes
- reverses and transposes
- loses meaning of a sentence from beginning to end
- gets events out of sequence
- infers content that is not there
- forgets details
- seems not to retain a basic stock of spelling words
- often uses creative, phonetic spelling

Work Speed
- very often does not finish
- works more slowly than age and grade peers
- frustrated under time pressure

Social
- may relate poorly to peers
- often repeats a social error
- may fail to "read" the wishes of others
- often has difficulty keeping friends
- frequently is on the fringe of groups

Difficulty Paying Attention

It is a given that students who are learning disabled do not attend as well in class as their more academically successful colleagues. What is less clear is the cause. Do they fail to attend because years of confusion have taught the value of avoidance? Or is the habit innate? The question is part of a continuing debate in the field. Whether the characteristic is inherent or learned, the simple fact is that most students who are learning disabled do not concentrate in school (and often at home) in sufficient depth or for sufficient time to learn or acquire new information or receive instruction effectively. This attention problem is expressed in forms that vary from simple daydreaming to pervasive, counterproductive activity.

Low Self-esteem

Of all the commonly occurring traits in persons who are learning disabled, this one is not inherent but acquired. And the cause, at least as far as school is concerned, is fairly obvious. It is easy to understand the effect of a system that not only rewards but also celebrates academic achievement on a learning-disabled student who consistently fails to achieve at anywhere near the expected standards: The student will develop serious doubts about his or her whole persona. What makes this characteristic so damaging is that it feeds a continuous loop. A student with a learning disability who has become accustomed to low achievement also becomes accustomed to putting out minimal effort on the quite understandable premise that there is no point if there is no payoff. Their achievement level decreases even farther, not only because it may have been affected in the first place by the learning disability, but also because of their lack of effort.

As a result, the teacher, the parent, and the student do not get to see how good the results really could be. Even worse, the teacher and parent become so accustomed to poor achievement that, on the rare occasions of success, they often look first for the fluke that brought it about!

The next link in this chain is invariably behavioural. Students develop personas to divert attention from their disability and their failure and to attract attention to other matters. The class clown, the victim, the super-competent, the I-don't-care, the bad guy – these masks are all popular among students with learning difficulties.

Assessment and Identification

By the Teacher, Educational Assistant, and Parental Team

Experience shows that classroom professionals, working co-operatively with parents and EAs, and often with the input of other professionals, are in the best position to establish the presence or absence of a learning disability, with considerable certainty. In fact, this kind of teamwork, shaped by a few prerequisites, may be the only way to make a diagnosis with confidence. The prerequisites are disarmingly simple.

1 *Understand the exceptionality.* To diagnose and identify a learning disability, you must be clearly aware of the characteristics that make up this special need. Because a learning disability does not yield to a definable set of criteria in the same way that a hearing loss, for example, does to an audiometric assessment, to uncover the presence of a learning disability, you must first know what to look for empirically.

2 *Observe carefully.* It follows that, armed with the knowledge of what to look for (and sufficiently informed by that knowledge to go looking), an effective way of making the identification is to watch for clear evidence of some or all of the characteristics.

3 *Take time.* Since a learning disability is episodic by nature, it is a given that observation must take place over time. Learning disabilities are not revealed in a one-shot assessment.

4 *Use informal aids.* Rating scales, questionnaires, informal reading inventories, and the like can be of assistance, especially in providing specific focus on a student's needs and in collating the efforts of different observers.

5 *Teamwork.* In the best interests of the student being assessed, everyone involved – classroom teacher, special education teacher, educational assistant, parents – must share findings and attempt to achieve a consensus. A team is more likely to impose caution concerning the identification process. Because the presence of a learning disability is difficult to pin down, and because every human being exhibits some LD characteristics, some of the time, the broader view of a team helps to keep things in perspective.

Terry, age 10.1, grade 4: *My Yard Rules*
Let somebody else go first. Watch what they do.

High Paark
1 I lict the scm grhnt
2 I lict feding the dcs
3 I lict seing the Blolrn
harin

Vana, age 8.6, grade 3,
High Park
1. *I liked the scavenger hunt*
2. *I liked feeding the ducks*
3. *I liked seeing the blue heron*
("I liked" was written on the chalkboard)

By Standardized IQ and Achievement Tests

These tests are too narrow to capture the complexity of a learning disability, at least in ways that would benefit the student or the student's teachers. Often, in a standardized assessment, the testing provides the what and not the why or the how that educators need to create programs for students with learning disabilities. While this type of testing can provide useful information, these instruments simply offer a number. The translation of that number into classroom practice is difficult at best. What the number does reveal is generally what everyone knows already; the number may prove helpful, however, in prying loose some funding or to set the table for an administrative action.

Another weakness in the use of these tests lies in the episodic nature of learning disabilities: Very often the same instrument will produce an entirely different result on consecutive days, thus diminishing its reliability.

Even more importantly, at least in the classroom, tests do not point to practical, helpful, strategies that classroom personnel can use.

Nevertheless, extensive formal testing to uncover a learning disability continues, possibly because it is a long-established practice (or because it offers a feeling that at least something is being done). Therefore, in situations where this type of instrument is used, it is important that the results be seen as only one of several clues.

Some Issues in the Field

✦ *Teacher preparation* for professionals who will be working with students with learning disabilities within the regular class is a growing area of concern. Students with learning disabilities represent by far the largest proportion (just under 50 percent) of students identified with exceptionalities in the province. One could argue that, with the increased emphasis on inclusion, a thorough knowledge of learning disabilities would be an important requirement for successful teaching. Despite this, candidates in teacher education programs express great concern over what they perceive as a lack of preparation to work with students with exceptionalities.

✦ *Universal acceptance of a definition* of learning disabilities continues to elude those who care about this special need. Nor do the many existing definitions, official and otherwise, seem to be coalescing around key points in any noticeable way.

✦ *Assessing* the presence and extent of a learning disability in a manner that produces clear, indisputable results does not seem to be possible.

✦ *Co-occurring disabilities*, most commonly AD/HD and behavioural disorders, are a constant challenge. Not only is the presence of other special needs difficult to identify and assess, but the very notion is a challenge to administrators charged with service delivery and to those who must address the situation day to day in the classroom. Interestingly, empirical evidence suggests that the issue is a far greater concern at the bureaucratic level, where formal identification, funding, and placement are matters of daily importance. In the classroom, teachers and educational assistants tend to find themselves addressing co-occurring disabilities similarly to the way they approach students with (presumably) only one special need.

a BlaK roB FaS,d the windol wn It trd arwr , say it had a BlaK hod Snqlks Kam cut cF th hod

Cameron, age 15.3, grade 9, opening of a ninety-five-word narrative …
A black robe faced the window. When it turned around I saw it had a black hood. Snakes came out of the hood.

✦ *Overidentification?* Available data show that students who are learning disabled outnumber their peers in any other category of special need. (This is not an Ontario phenomenon; these data are similar to those in other provinces and in the U.S.) Such numbers continue to provoke accusations of gross misidentification and of excessive "dumping," viz., underperforming students are simply called learning disabled because that relieves the school system, the parents, and the students themselves of any blame for doing poorly. While there are few educators who would deny that that some do take this escape route, the accusation is very much unwarranted. Evidence that current numbers of identified students with learning disabilities are probably realistic can be found by examining prevalence and incidence data over the past thirty years. The sharp rise in numbers over the late 1960s and through the 1970s began to slow in the mid-1980s, and numbers have remained quite consistent since.

✦ *Quackery or experimental science?* Even before learning disability became a popular term, many unusual therapies, techniques, and teaching methods were available to deal with students who, despite apparently normal ability, spoke incomprehensibly, wrote most unusually, or generally performed in ways that are off the mark for their age. (See the writing examples in this chapter.) It would have been fairly common practice at one time, for example, to engage students such as Vana and Terry in extensive callisthenic exercises to – theoretically – develop their "visual-motor integration skills." Very often, popular support for these unusual techniques blossomed as a result of endorsements and "gee whiz" articles in non-refereed journals. Usually, the popularity of a technique declined after it was submitted to careful scrutiny.

Still, it is unfair to dismiss unusual teaching methods; given the uncertainty over just what constitutes a learning disability, any response demands at least rational consideration.

Strategies for the Classroom

1 *Differentiated instruction*: As the movement toward meaningful inclusion of students with diverse learning needs becomes more and more of a reality for educators across Ontario, the challenge of aligning the curriculum content and assignments with the learning needs of students becomes an important focal point for instruction. Differentiated instruction, while providing an enhanced learning environment for all students, can be effective for students with learning disabilities. Traditionally, differentiated instruction has been commonplace in special education settings where Individual Education Plans are the norm. Within the regular class, curriculum planning and design have traditionally been focused on large-group instruction. A move to differentiated instruction takes the focus from modifying a program after the fact to planning a program up front to meet a variety of learning styles and differing abilities.

2 *Empathy and understanding* are prerequisite qualities in any person hoping to offer instruction to students with learning disabilities (although this point is likely redundant to an effective teacher). Once one "gets inside" the particular nature of these students, making the necessary steps of accommodation follows naturally. A teacher must set up a warm, supportive climate without pandering to, or making excuses for, or drawing unnecessary attention to students' particular needs. The older the students are, the more difficult this task tends to be, for they likely will have developed, over years of practice, well-established and annoying avoidance behaviours. Yet, unless a teacher has an appreciation of what his or her students are contending with, and unless there is some sensitivity toward that, all efforts will eventually degenerate into despair and conflict. An environment of mutual trust is crucial for teaching all students with exceptionalities, but for students with learning disabilities, there is an added, subtle layer. These students usually do not appear at first to be handicapped in any way; in fact, they often seem as though they should be especially successful. But they are not, and, most of the time, they do not understand why any more than the adults in their lives do. Such is the insidious nature of a learning disability. It is why the teacher's empathy and understanding are so important.

3 *Positive, frequent feedback* as quickly as possible, especially on academic matters, is crucial. This feedback helps, practically, by keeping the student on task, and more abstractly, by reinforcing momentum, a component so necessary in continuing academic success and achievement. A student with learning disabilities, especially if the student has had a history of failure, is not willing to defer gratification as successful students do. He or she needs reassurance and reinforcement to build self-esteem to a point where the student will put forth his or her best effort. Fortunately, this kind of feedback does not have to be dramatic (although an occasional "celebration" can work wonders). Simple attention to even modest achievement is often all that is necessary to develop self-esteem in a student.

4 *A consistent, systematic approach* will help a student with learning disabilities eventually learn to interpret and accommodate expectations. Part of this approach will be a firm insistence on on-task behaviour and thoroughness. Perhaps a more encompassing term would be structure. The very nature of the day-to-day cognitive function of a student who has a learning disability means

that not only classroom instruction but also such apparently simple things as classroom regulations and expectations must be clearly outlined with the parameters firmly established. Teachers must remember that a student with a learning disability not only does not learn or manage himself or herself as effectively as he or she might, but also usually does not know how to do so. Self-management and learning become easier for such a student if the teacher establishes the boundaries and points out the steps. (And note that it is easier, once a structure is established, for the teacher to be empathetic and supportive if an operating context has been established that both parties understand.)

5 *Graphic and visual support* significantly benefits students with learning disabilities. Use of the chalkboard, whiteboard, computer, overhead transparencies, pictures, maps, and other concrete supports helps them to comprehend what might otherwise be a mass of confusion. In fact, many successful teachers assert that it is impossible to teach these students otherwise. A positive note here is that, while graphic and visual supports are essential for students who are learning disabled, they are also helpful techniques for all students. For more information on this, see appendix IV.

6 *Help in sequencing is important.* Teachers must emphasize steps and stages in the proper order as a lesson progresses. The same applies to all assignments, projects, homework, or any other item that requires independent and individual completion. Without guidance in where to begin and what organization to follow, students with learning disabilities will become confused and, likely as not, tune out or give up.

7 *Help in dealing with print* is important for many students with learning disabilities. Reading, as well as producing legible and coherent text, can be a difficult and time-consuming procedure, so a teacher not only must recognize that challenge and make allowances in time, but

also may well have to modify the challenge by simplifying instructions or providing an alternate format.

8 *Awareness of time constraints*, one of the realities of school that regular students pick up quickly, is yet another variable that teachers must factor in for their students with learning disabilities. Many of these students do not forward plan, and it may well take their entire school career before they learn the responsibilities inherent in due dates, appointments, and scheduling. Yet they can, and do, eventually acquire these skills, however imperfectly, and for that reason it is essential that their teachers persist. (Both parents and teachers attest that this issue is one of the most frustrating skills to teach and therefore one of the most tempting to avoid teaching.)

9 *"Staying-on-top of things,"* for lack of a more professional-sounding phrase, may be an apt way to describe all those apparently superficial, but in reality fundamental, behaviours that a teacher must help his or her students who are learning disabled to exercise. Drawing the student's attention to signal words, counselling about sequence and about time, reminding the student to bring and take materials, cueing things by saying, "Watch for the change here," and "This is important" – all these seemingly small things go together to help the student cope with daily life in the classroom.

10 *Making allowances* for those skills that students with learning disabilities never ever seem to master is another part of the teacher's role. Correct spelling, for example, is an expectation that many of these students almost never meet and to pursue it relentlessly is counterproductive. It is far more effective, both in the short and long term, to teach the students how to use a dictionary effectively or to get help via technology. Similarly, since these students never seem to master the memorization of multiplication tables, it

makes sense to forgo the memorization requirement. Other matters, simple on the surface to most of us, frequently escape students with learning disabilities. For example, multiple-choice questions, so time-honoured and commonly used, often have a subtlety that totally confounds. So does convoluted syntax. An attempt to persuade, for example, by saying, "Inasmuch as the field day is on Monday and the movie on Wednesday, wouldn't you be better to get the project done this week?" will not succeed as well as: "Finish the project this week because next week we have a field day and a movie. There will be no time to do it next week."

11 *Simplifying the environment*. Within the boundaries of what is practical and sensible, a teacher can make a difference simply by removing distractions. Sometimes the seating arrangement in a room or the adjacent surroundings of a student who is learning disabled can be modified to the student's benefit.

12 *Memory assists*. Strategies such as mnemonics and rehearsal can be effective and relatively easy to implement within the workings of a classroom. Essential for some and good for all is a truism that seems to apply in the case of these tried-and-true strategies.

13 *Self-monitoring*. Both academically and behaviourally, one of the greatest gifts we can give students is the ability to be cognizant of their own strengths and areas of difficulty. Checklists, role-playing, discussion, and reflection, along with allowing an appropriate degree of autonomy, create an environment in which students are able to modify their own behaviour and learning.

14 *Finally, as evanescent as* hope and optimism *may seem, they are the glue, along with trust and encouragement*, which holds the relationship of teacher and student together. A student with a learning disability, usually far more than his or her peers without learning disabilities, will respond to a stimulus, not so much because of a vague awareness that it is part of his or her education, but rather because the teacher, the one he or she trusts and respects, has asked him or her to do so. It is a reality that imposes a heavy responsibility on the teacher, but then, without that reality, the art of teaching would not be as exciting. Or as rewarding.

It is trust, and encouragement, and hope, and optimism that lead to the extra steps, the extra efforts, the one-more-times and, ultimately, the breakthroughs. Realistically, breakthroughs are not all that frequent. What is far more common is plodding progress, but progress of any kind is worth the effort.

This sentence by Cameron is the fifth rewrite of the item that appears on page 108. A resource room EA assisted Cameron with rewrites two, three, and four. This is an independent effort.

Readings and Resources

Aylwards, E. H. (2003). Instructional treatment associated with changes in brain activities in children with dyslexia. *Neurology, 61*(2).

Büttner, G., & Hasselhorn, M. (2011). Learning disabilities: Debates on definitions, causes, subtypes, and responses. *International Journal of Disability, Development and Education, 58*(1), 75–87. doi:10.1080/1034 912X.2011.548476

Büttner, G., & Shamir, A. (2011). Learning disabilities: Causes, consequences, and responses. *International Journal of Disability, Development and Education, 58*(1), 1–4. doi:10.1080/1034912X.2011.548450

Carter, E. W., Trainor, A. A., Sun, Y., & Owens, L. (2009). Assessing the transition-related strengths and needs of adolescents with high-incidence disabilities. *Exceptional Children, 76*(1), 74–94.

Deshler, D. D., Ellis, E. S., & Lenz, B. K. (1996). *Teaching adolescents with learning disabilities: Strategies and methods.* Denver: Love Publishing.

Dyson, L. L. (2003). Children with learning disabilities within the family context: A comparison with siblings in global self-concept, academic self-concept, academic self-perception, and social competence. *Learning Disabilities Research and Practice, 18*(1), 1–9.

Elias, M. J. (2004). Connection between social emotional learning. *Learning Disabilities Quarterly, 27*, 53–63.

Garderen, D., & Whittaker, C. (2006). Planning differentiated instruction for secondary inclusive classrooms. *Teaching Exceptional Children, 38*, 12–20.

Gersten, R. (1998). Recent advances in instructional research for students with learning disabilities: An overview. *Learning Disabilities Research and Practice, 13*(3), 153–72.

Gustafson, S., Fälth, L., Svensson, I., Tjus, T., & Heimann, M. (2011). Effects of three interventions on the reading skills of children with reading disabilities in grade 2. *Journal of Learning Disabilities, 44*(2), 123–35. doi:10.1177/0022219410391187

Hinchelwood, J. (1917). *Congenital word blindness.* London: H.K. Lewis.

Horowitz-Kraus, T., & Breznitz, Z. (2011). Error detection mechanism for words and sentences: A comparison between readers with dyslexia and skilled readers. *International Journal of Disability, Development and Education, 58*(1), 33–45. doi:10.1080/1034912X.2011.548466

Huntington, D. D., & Bender, W. N. (1993). Adolescents with learning disabilities at risk? Emotional well-being, depression, suicide. *Journal of Learning Disabilities, 26*, 159–66.

Jitendra, A. K., Edwards, C. M., Choutka, C. M., & Treadway, P. S. (2002). A collaborative approach to planning in the content areas for students with learning disabilities: Assessing the general curriculum. *Learning Disabilities Research and Practice, 17*(4), 252–67.

Klingner, J. K., Urbach, J., Golos, D., & Brownell, M. T. (2010). Teaching reading in the 21st century: A glimpse at how special education teachers promote reading comprehension. *Learning Disability Quarterly, 33* (spring), 59–74.

Lewis, S., & Bates, K. (2005). How to implement differentiated instruction? *Journal of Staff Development, 26*(4), 26–31.

Madaus, J. W. (2005). Navigating the college transition maze: A guide for students with learning disabilities. *Teaching Exceptional Children, 37*(3), 32–37.

Maehler, C., & Schuchardt, K. (2011). Working memory in children with learning disabilities: Rethinking the criterion of discrepancy. *International Journal of Disability, Development and Education, 58*(1), 5–17. doi:10.1 080/1034912X.2011.547335

Mammarella, I. C., Lucangeli, D., & Cornoldi, C. (2010). Spatial working memory and arithmetic deficits in children with nonverbal learning difficulties. *Journal of Learning Disabilities, 43*(5), 455–68. doi:10.1177/0022219409355482

Mavis, L., Donahue, M. L., & Pearl, R. (2003). Studying social development and learning disabilities is not for the faint hearted: Comments on risk/resilience framework. *Learning Disabilities Research and Practice, 18*(2), 2003, 90–93.

Narkon, D. E., Wells, J. C., & Segal, L. S. (2011). E-word wall: An interactive vocabulary instruction tool for students with learning disabilities and autism spectrum disorders. *Teaching Exceptional Children, 43*(4), 38–45.

O'Connor, R. E., Bocian, K., Beebe-Frankenberger, M., & Linklater, D. L. (2008). Responsiveness of students with language difficulties to early intervention in reading. *The Journal of Special Education, 43*(4), 220–35. doi:10.1177/0022466908317789

Rea, P. J., McLaughlin, V. L., & Walther-Thomas, C. (2002). Outcomes for students with learning disabilities in inclusive pullout programs. *Exceptional Children, 68*(2), 203–22.

Richardson, S. (1992). Historical perspectives on dyslexia. *Journal of Learning Disabilities, 25*(1), 40–47.

Rose, D., Meyers, A., & Hitchcock, C. (2005). *The universally designed classroom: Accessible curriculum and digital technologies.* Cambridge, MA: Harvard Education Press.

Schmid, J. M., Labuhn, A. S., & Hasselhorn, M. (2011). Response inhibition and its relationship to phonological processing in children with and without dyslexia. *International Journal of Disability, Development and Education, 58*(1), 19–32. doi:10.1080/1034912X.2011.547343

Shaywitz, S. E., & Shaywitz, B. A. (2008). Paying attention to reading: The neurobiology of reading and dyslexia. *Development and psychopathology, 20*(4), 1329–49. doi:10.1017/S0954579408000631

Sherman, G. F. (1995). Dyslexia: Is it all in your mind? *Perspectives, 21*(4), 1.

Speece, D. L., & Shekitka, L. (2002). How should reading disabilities be operationalized? A survey of experts. *Learning Disabilities Research and Practice, 17*(2), 118–23.

Strong, Scott M., Fletcher, K. L., & Stoyko Deuel, L-L. (1998). The effects of intelligence on the identification of young children with learning disabilities. *Learning Disabilities Research and Practice, 13*(2), 81–89.

Wiener, J. (2004). Do peer relationships foster behavioral adjustment in children with learning disabilities? *Learning Disabilities Quarterly, 27*, 21–30.

Wong, B. (Ed.) (2004). *Learning about learning disabilities* (3rd ed.). San Diego: Elsevier Academic Press.

Links

Learning Disabilities Association of Canada **http://www.ldac-taac.ca/**

Learning Disabilities Association of Ontario **http://www.ldao.ca/**

LD online **http://www.ldonline.org/**

National Council for Learning Disabilities **http://www.ncld.org/**

9

Students with Behavioural Exceptionalities: Students with AD/HD

"Working with secondary school students with behavioural exceptionalities causes each day, each moment, to be a new, unplanned experience. Much of the time is spent trying to develop relationships, community, and a safe place so that the students trust me to guide them through the most scary thing of their lives: school. Some days we all feel like failures, but some days the spark is there and things get accomplished."

– Jenessa D., secondary school behaviour resource teacher

Misconceptions About Emotional/Behavioural Disorders

1 **Youth violence has increased significantly since the mid to late twentieth century.**
While, overall, the rate of violent crime in Canada has decreased, there has been conflicting information with regard to trends in youth violence. Educators, legal authorities, and community workers find it too difficult to establish whether the numbers are real, whether data collection is more rigorous, or merely whether perceptions have changed. Reports of an epidemic of youth violence are sensibly tempered by recognizing factors that affect the calculation of such statistics. Changes in reporting structures, an informed perspective in terms of growth and decline percentages per total populations, and a long-range view assist in a more reasonable and realistic representation.

2 **Once a student is identified with an emotional/behavioural disorder in the school system, it is easier to get services in any education system across the country.**
Unfortunately, services for students with emotional/behavioural disorders vary across the province, and there is no guarantee that an identification of an emotional/behavioural disorder will carry over to another board inside or outside the province.

3 **Developments in mental health science have made the identification and classification of behavioural disorders simpler for educators.**
The dominating schemata for clinical description and classification is the American Psychiatric Association's *Diagnostic and Statistical Manual of Mental Disorders IV-TR** (*DSM-IV-TR* or more commonly referred to as *DSM*). The *DSM*, however, classifies disorders as either present or absent. To most classroom teachers and assistants, emotional/behavioural problems are far more subtle.

4 **Bullying is an age-old, natural schoolyard phenomenon and students learn to deal with it as part of growing up.**
While educators have long been aware of bullying as a reality of the schoolyard, it is now known that the phenomenon can have long-term consequences for the bully, the victim, and observers of the bullying.

5 **Behavioural disorders are neither age- nor gender-related.**
Most studies show that identified cases of males outnumber females by ratios of up to 5 to 1. In the last decade of the twentieth century, however, new data began to show significant rate increases for girls identified

---

* At time of publication, this is the most recently revised edition of this manual. The American Psychiatric Association is currently working on a new revision.

as having behavioural difficulties or as involved in committing crimes.

6 Behavioural disorders are manifested in patterns of aggression and frustration.
There is no doubt that outward-directed behaviour is noticeable and may well be disordered. However, symptoms of behavioural disorder can also be expressed by reticence and withdrawal, which are not as easily noticed, particularly in large classroom groupings.

7 Very often a behavioural disorder indicates a student who is bright but frustrated.
Available data suggest a correlation between behavioural disorders and average-to-low IQ test scores, with the more severe cases even lower.

8 Difficult behaviour is an external manifestation of something deep-rooted.
There is no sound evidence that all causes of behaviour are rooted deep in a student's psyche or are even necessarily connected to emotional disturbance. Especially in school, inappropriate behaviour is often spontaneous and temporary.

9 A permissive atmosphere that allows students to develop understanding and acceptance of the self is the most effective way to change inappropriate behaviour.
Evidence suggests that a highly structured, ordered, and predictable environment brings about the greatest change in students with a behavioural disorder.

10 Only the behaviour itself should be examined and dealt with. Why the behaviour is occurring is not important.
To deal effectively with a behavioural issue, it is often important to look beyond what is occurring to why it is occurring. This way, motivation, consequences, and rewards, as well as the teaching of new behaviour, can be aligned with the needs of individual students, and positive change is more likely to occur.

 Bullies and Their Victims

Bullying behaviour varies among individuals, but three behaviours appear to be common: It is a repeated action over time; it takes place in relationships where there is an imbalance of power; and it is unprovoked.

While research – and schoolyard observation – suggests that more boys than girls engage in the behaviour, many teachers insist that more rigorous investigations will inevitably reveal that girls tend to use more subtle, less visible methods to accomplish their ends.

Very often, the act of bullying is part of a wider set of behavioural problems. Bullies are often in conflict with authorities, tend to be depressed, are prone to a lifestyle that compromises their health, and often have problems with peer relationships. Victims tend to have lower self-esteem, and some manifest rather disturbed behaviour – although it is not clear whether this behaviour is a condition that arises from the bullying or is pre-existing.

Although a prevailing perception in the early twenty-first century is that bullying has become rampant, it is extremely difficult to establish hard data to support that belief. Nevertheless, research indicates that students in self-contained classrooms are stigmatized and more frequently bullied than those in mainstreamed classrooms. Students with behavioural difficulties (especially attention deficit/hyperactivity disorder) have been found to be more involved with bullying, either as bully or bullied, than those with more age-appropriate behaviour.

Ontario legislation has tried to ensure that schools pay close attention to bullying behaviour and that steps be taken to ensure that schools are a safe place for all students.

Good, McIntosh, and Gietz (2011) provide an excellent framework for how bullying prevention can be incorporated into a school-wide positive behaviour support program. The results of their study found a significant reduction in bullying behaviour and out-of school suspensions when bullying prevention was accepted as part of a school-wide behaviour support initiative.

Behavioural Disorder, Emotionally/Behaviourally Disturbed, or Behavioural Exceptionality – What Should It Be Called?

When it comes to the topic of behavioural disorders, there is some confusion over what term should be used and which students fall under this category. When Public Law 94-142 was passed in the United States (1975), the term "seriously emotionally disturbed" was used. In 1997, the term was changed to "emotionally disturbed."

In Canada, we also have some confusion over this issue. Some provinces have no term to recognize this population. Others distinguish between "mild," "moderate," and "severe" behavioural difficulties. In Ontario, the term "behavioural exceptionality" is used to represent students with behavioural and/or emotional issues and is the term that will be used for the remainder of this chapter.

To most people, behavioural exceptionality is behaviour that varies markedly and chronically from accepted norms. In a general way, then, the notion is quite widely accepted and understood, much in the way that a general notion of normal behaviour is widely accepted and understood. It is from this point that differences develop, for there seems to be remarkably little agreement exactly where on the continuum behaviour becomes aberrant. It is not difficult to see how perceptions of behavioural exceptionality arise. The wide variance of social and cultural conditions is a major contributor. Certain cultures, for example, have very permissive ideas about child rearing; others have very structured and restrictive ideas. In the same classroom, a teacher and an EA may be from different backgrounds. Indeed, there can be wide differences within a single school. The same behaviour may be seen as disruptive by one teacher but normal by another.

Then there is the reality that all children display varying behaviours and that behaviour patterns increase and decline over time within a single individual. Special educators are especially aware that patterns of conduct are affected by disabling conditions. Students with hearing problems can become extremely frustrated by their inability to comprehend. The same is true of students with visual disabilities (especially younger ones whose condition has not yet been diagnosed) and equally true of those with developmental or learning disabilities.

To create a common ground of understanding, mental health professionals, in particular, have attempted to organize behavioural exceptionalities by classification (as in the *Diagnostic and Statistical Manual* of the American Psychiatric Association, mentioned above). Unfortunately, consensus within this group is still limited. Interestingly, educators seem to have less difficulty with the issue, possibly because they have a more unified perspective and a more clearly delineated set of common objectives. Following is a brief description of the more popular views held by mental health professionals and of the general view held by educators.

The View from Mental Health

Mental health professionals tend to view behavioural exceptionalities from a particular perspective, or theory, or enveloping concept, a tendency that affects the research they do, their treatment styles, and the way they attempt to educate others. Listed here is a very brief summary of the more widely held theories.

- *Environmental*: Factors in the environment, including diet, air pollution, and metals, lead to behavioural problems. (Note that this concept is often held in concert with one or more of the others listed below.)
- *Psychodynamic*: People with behavioural exceptionalities experience deep-rooted inner turmoil, of which their deviations are a manifestation.
- *Psychosocial*: An individual's relationship with family and peers may bring on inappropriate or unacceptable behaviour.
- *Psychoeducational*: A student's behaviour may be owing to a combination of circumstances brought about by stresses in the school, home, or community.

- *Behaviourist*: Deviation from normal is the result of having been taught the wrong things or by following inappropriate role models.
- *Biophysical*: Deficiencies in genetics, neurology, and biochemistry, along with disease and malnutrition, cause deviant behaviour.
- *Combinations*: Some or all of the above theories appear in combination.

There is little doubt that children's mental health is becoming of greater concern to the education community. Below is a list of signs that will help teachers to know when to suggest to a parent that they enlist the services of a mental health professional. The ABCs of Mental Health (available at **www.hincksdellcrest.org/ABC/Welcome** prepared by the Hincks Delcrest Children's Centre) may also be of some assistance.

Identifying the Signs

Many children and youth will exhibit some of the following characteristics and behaviours at various times during normal development:

- getting significantly lower marks in school
- avoiding friends and family
- having frequent outbursts of anger and rage
- losing his or her appetite
- having difficulty sleeping
- rebelling against authority
- drinking a lot and/or abusing drugs
- not doing the things he or she used to enjoy

- damaging other people's property
- worrying constantly
- experiencing frequent mood swings
- being unconcerned with his or her appearance
- obsessing with his or her weight
- lacking energy or motivation
- hitting or bullying other children
- attempting to injure him or herself

These characteristics and behaviours may be signs of an underlying mental health disorder if they:

- are intense
- persist over long periods of time

- are inappropriate for the child's age
- interfere with the child's life

Children's Mental Health Ontario. Used with permission.

Teachers' Perceptions of Behavioural Exceptionalities

Determining whether a student falls into the behavioural exceptionality category is subjective. Note also that, while they accept the value of classifications for mental health purposes, most teachers, educational assistants, child-care workers, and others responsible for students with behavioural exceptionalities do not find them very practical on the front lines. Thus, while the classifications used by mental health professionals may be informative, or may have some administrative value, or may be used by a multidisciplinary team, the prevailing style in education is to approach the notion of behavioural exceptionality without terminology or diagnosing. In determining whether a student may be behavioural exceptional, an assessment team will almost always consider exclusionary factors such as specific sensory, social, or health-related causes. Nevertheless, even if a student's inappropriate behaviour can be explained as a direct outcome of some specific, explainable factor, he or she might still be identified as behavioural exceptional for the simple reason that, no matter what the cause, it is still the behaviour – the effect – that the educators must deal with.

When educators identify a student as having a behavioural exceptionality, they generally do so on the basis that the student:

- deviates in a significant manner from the behaviour that is normally expected in the situation
- breaks social or cultural norms that are usually well established for the age level
- shows a tendency toward compulsive and impulsive behaviour that negatively affects learning
- has poor interpersonal relationships and low self-esteem
- has low academic achievement owing to conduct
- (perhaps most importantly) manifests any or all of the above characteristics with an intensity, frequency, and/or duration such that additional assistance and/or intervention is required to improve the student's ability to maintain appropriate behaviour

Behavioural Exceptionalities: A Decreasing Population?

Behaviour that deviates from the norm attracts a disproportionate amount of attention from the media, an interest that leads to a perception that the prevalence of behavioural exceptionalities is on the increase. The increase may indeed be real. Or it may not be. Most of the time, research data simply confirm what teachers and educational assistants already know: that boys outnumber girls, particularly in aggression and hyperactivity; that prevalence rates are highest in the upper grades of elementary school and first grades of secondary school, while lowest in the primary grades; and that there tends to be a higher rate of aggressive behaviours among children from lower socio-economic groups.

Nevertheless, the value of data collection should never be disregarded. Though there was an increase in students identified under the behavioural umbrella between 2001 and 2005 – 7,701 elementary in 2001 versus 8,164 in 2005, and 4,280 secondary versus 5,015 in 2005/6 – recent figures indicate that fewer students are now being identified in the behavioural exceptionality category. In 2009/10, 5,559 were identified as behaviourally exceptional in elementary and 4,890 in secondary. This decrease may be attributed to changes in overall student population with corresponding changes to zero tolerance policies established by the government of the day. In 2006, under a new government, the zero tolerance policy established under the *Safe Schools Act* of 2000 was changed to permit principals more flexibility in handling incidents of aggressive behaviour in their schools and, though they are not yet defined, to put into place "progressive discipline" approaches designed to help a student with aggressive behavioural difficulties to learn more appropriate responses.

Causes of Behavioural Exceptionalities

Biophysical

The majority of students who are identified as behavioural exceptional appear to be physically healthy. Nevertheless, recent theory and research suggest possible links between biological makeup and behaviour. Sometimes the connection is clearly, if also distressingly, apparent. Children born with fetal alcohol syndrome or fetal alcohol effects are a case in point. (See chapter 11 on intellectual disabilities.) The causes of pervasive development disorders (e.g., autism; see chapter 12) have become an area of extensive research – and speculation – inasmuch as biology is concerned. Research in genetics is provoking a continuing reassessment of disorders such as schizophrenia.

In 2003, an Ontario judge sentenced a fourteen-year-old girl to two years of probation after she pleaded guilty to aggravated assault on a teacher. The sentencing was very much affected by testimony that the girl's behaviour was influenced by a particularly powerful premenstrual syndrome. Biology, it seems, is now being considered in cases of behavioural exceptionality, almost as a matter of course.

It is important to note, however, the suggestion of Kauffman and Landrum (2009) that "the effects of biological factors on behavioural development are considerable but frequently neither demonstrable nor simple" (p. 160). They also believe that "educators should have basic information about biological factors but focus primarily on how the environmental conditions they may be able to control might affect students' behaviour" (p. 160).

Allergies

Allergies, too, are being re-evaluated as causes of disordered behaviour. While the physical effects of allergies on some students are readily acknowledged, a more recent conception of allergies incorporates the thesis that allergenic reactions can generate learning and behavioural problems in a far deeper and more subtle way than the very obvious physical reactions.

Though rare, it may be possible that a student has a capacity to tolerate only so much substance in the environment; a combination of stale air, chalk dust, molds, and fungi in the carpet, and perfume or shaving lotion on the teacher, may exceed some students' tolerance (total load) and cause an allergic reaction expressed both physically (e.g., a rash, or watery eyes, or sneezing) and behaviourally. These reactions are often far more subtle and yet more profound than may be immediately apparent.

Speech and Language

Researchers have consistently found a higher incidence of behavioural exceptionalities among students with speech and language impairments than is found in the general population. While there is some debate in the field over whether language impairment is a cause or an effect of behavioural disorders, it seems logical to conclude that a student who has difficulty expressing his or her needs – or frustrations – may choose to act them out. Either way, it is certainly a point that classroom personnel must heed.

Psychological

Psychological explanations for behaviour vary by perspective (e.g., a psychoanalyst sees things differently from a behaviourist) and by setting (the home, the community, the school, etc.). Two very powerful influences on a child's behaviour are the home and the school. It is difficult to find a single cause for a particular child's behavioural or emotional state. Often the cause is a combination of factors that have led to the child's particular reaction to the environment. One major factor, though certainly not in all cases, is the child's relationship with his or her parents. This relationship is crucial to development, particularly in the early years. In homes, for example, where discipline is inconsistent and sometimes harsh and in which there is little reinforcement of affection, children often learn to be aggressive. Empirical evidence, supported by research, has consistently shown that the style of child rearing used by parents will have an impact on the behaviour of their children.

Still, teachers, especially those who are parents, realize that the causes of a child's behaviour may well be a two-way street in which parents may be responding to the behaviour originated by the child, as opposed to that behaviour simply being the result of what the child is taught. Unfortunately for those who work directly with a student, the cause of behavioural exceptionalities is less of an immediate issue than the effects and is, in any case, something that they are somewhat powerless to modify: This is one reason why a multidisciplinary team, which usually has a member working with the family, can be effective.

Some mental health professionals maintain that schools are a major cause of a student's behavioural difficulties, but there is no clear evidence to support this claim. Yet since schools are where students spend a major portion of their waking day, it is logical to conclude that what goes on in the classroom, under the direction of the teacher, has a major influence on behaviour. The relationship, therefore, between students and teachers, between students and their classmates, and between students and the school at large can have a significant impact in causing and correcting disordered behaviour.

The Case of Scott

WITH the co-operation of the district school board, an arrangement worked out by a social worker, the crown attorney, and the family court will keep Scott in custody for the remainder of June and for July and August. In September, he will go to a different school from the one he attended for the past two years. The school will be in a different neighbourhood, and Scott will live in a secure group home until it is decided that he can be placed with foster parents. Scott is thirteen.

The board has two possible schools for him.

One school has a full rotary timetable and a behaviour resource class called the "drop-in room" where students may be counselled depending on need, may work on their academic program, or just relax. If Scott goes to this school, he will be enrolled in a regular grade 6 class. An IPRC has confirmed his "behavioural" identification, and he will be eligible to go to the drop-in room when he feels the need, or he can be sent there by any of the teachers. The principal and staff of this school openly espouse a nurturing and personal development philosophy.

The second school does not have a drop-in room. In fact, the school has no designated class for behaviour and has only a very limited rotary timetable. If Scott goes here, he will be enrolled in a regular grade 6 class and spend most of his time with the teacher of that class. Whereas the three educational assistants in the first school are assigned to specific classes full time, the three in this school move as needed. The principal here believes strongly in academic achievement and the development of self-reliance, and she has attracted a staff with similar beliefs.

Because of privacy laws, no one knows why Scott is presently in custody. However, it is known that he has a history of aggressive behaviour, especially toward girls, and that his current brush with the courts is the latest in a string. What is also known is that Scott's full-scale IQ score is average; there is no evidence that he has a learning disability. On a standardized achievement test, he was one grade below the age-appropriate level in math and three grades below in language skills. School teams in both schools are discussing Scott's program. What issues and solutions should they be considering?

Childhood Depression

The student who quietly sits at his or her desk, rarely interacts with others, and seems to fade into the woodwork is often overlooked. Yet, this student may be dealing with childhood depression, a disorder whose prevalence has increased dramatically. Students with childhood depression may regularly appear sad, show limited academic gain, not sleep well, and have feelings of worthlessness or hopelessness. Educators need to recognize these symptoms and refer the student for more intensive mental health evaluation. Treatment for childhood depression usually involves psychotherapy and medication, but teachers can also be very helpful by assisting the student to develop social skills and encouraging an increase in activity level.

Assessment of Behavioural Exceptionality

Unless a student comes to a school already diagnosed and identified, the first step in an assessment is usually taken by a classroom teacher who calls on nothing more technical than experience and common sense to recognize behaviour that departs from the norm seriously enough and often enough to be distinguished. In fact, informal screening by teachers and educational assistants has been established throughout education as a fairly reliable first measure.

In most jurisdictions in Canada, what follows formally after this initial phase is governed by a school board's particular plans and procedures. These would include formal assessments, which in turn may be governed by the availability and the expertise of personnel and the current conceptual model for dealing with behavioural exceptionalities. The teacher, assistant, often the parents, and possibly a social worker or other community service worker will usually be asked to complete some form of observation instrument such as a behaviour checklist or rating scale. (In Ontario, The Child Behavior Checklist, Achenbach and Edelbrock, 1991, 2001, is very popular.) Once sufficient information is gathered, the next phases of program and placement are decided, sometimes by a school team, by special education teachers, or by an IRPC.

Since there is fairly convincing evidence that students who have serious behavioural problems in later grades often had difficulties in kindergarten, there is pressure to identify behavioural exceptionalities early. Doing so is not always possible, however, since disorders often do not emerge until the later grades when personal responsibilities and social and academic demands increase in complexity. Ultimately, the identification of a student as behavioural exceptional is best accomplished by teamwork, by the collaboration of classroom personnel, parents, and, where available and helpful by mental health professionals all operating in an atmosphere of mutual respect and understanding.

Reactive Attachment Disorder (RAD)

A recent addition to the list of disorders in the *DSM-IV-TR* is a condition believed to arise from an individual's failure to bond with other humans very early in life. RAD (a.k.a. AD) may develop in the very young because of the lack of nurture and attention in places such as shelters for abandoned or orphaned children during wars or other crises, or because of deliberate abuse, or even, as some would have it, because modern parents are too involved and time-driven to provide the necessary emotional support for a newborn. According to the description, "RAD Kids" develop a protective shell against what they believe is an unsafe world in which adults cannot be trusted to care for them. Among the extensive list of symptoms that these "unbonded" children are said to present are rage and destructiveness, along with frequent lying, cheating, and stealing. They are said to be obsessive, manipulative, unaware of (or unconcerned with) consequences, and have little or no empathy.

Unfortunately, RAD is easily confused with bipolar disorder, AD/HD, Tourette syndrome, and even learning disabilities. Advocates of the syndrome insist that this confusion occurs simply because RAD is still poorly understood. Critics argue it may be because it is not really a separate disorder at all.

Longstanding Issues Still Remain

◆ *As indicated earlier, agreement on an acceptable term for this exceptionality* has long been hard to achieve. Some of the more popular identifiers, some of which are still current and overlap several fields, are: socially maladjusted, emotionally disturbed, mentally ill, predelinquent, delinquent, emotionally handicapped, and socially handicapped. In education, of course, they are most frequently called behaviour disordered or behaviour exceptional. In the past, labels were developed at what seemed to be the discretion of whoever was writing on the subject.

The term "emotionally disturbed," for example, first appeared (without precise definition) at the beginning of the twentieth century. Since then, many other terms have cropped up from time to time. In Ontario, for example, "behavioural exceptionality" is used, but this term is not used in other jurisdictions in Canada. The term "behavioural exceptionality" is used because it is conceptually inclusive of a variety of problems that warrant professional attention and is less negative and stigmatizing than many of the other terms (e.g., emotional/ behavioural disorder) in use. It also tends to circumvent the suggestion of legal identification. Above all, it is sufficiently comprehensive to have wide applicability.

◆ *Developing a useful definition* has proven just as difficult, for it follows that, if the names for an exceptionality are elastic and capricious, describing the exceptionality will be just as problematic. Definitions are vulnerable to their authors' theoretical perspective (behavioural, psychodynamic), to their discipline (teacher, psychiatrist, lawyer), and to their purpose for writing a definition (research, education). The effect of these differences is a serious block to practical communication, especially in light of the fact that a multidisciplinary approach is often necessary, particularly in more serious cases.

The Ontario definition of behavioural exceptionality (see appendix I) is based on a variation of what is contained in the United States *Individuals with Disabilities Education Act*. Several groups, such as the Council for Children with Behavioral Disorders, have tried to change this definition, both in the United States and in Ontario, to one that more accurately reflects the behavioural manifestations and needs of these students. It is believed by many in the field that a more accurate definition could assist in better identifying these students and lead to more effective intervention.

On the other hand, there may be merit in the argument that perhaps this exceptionality, more than any other, should not be defined at all and that a statement of needs should suffice. Inasmuch as there is no definition of normal behaviour – which if it existed would therefore be the referent for behaviour that is not – it is only reasonable that behavioural exceptionality cannot be defined either. Even though behavioural exceptionalities are distinguished by frequency and degree rather than by their nature, these exceptionalities cannot be measured quantitatively. There is no system analogous to the IQ test. And to add to the murkiness, people who exhibit disordered behaviour also behave normally! Above all, behavioural anomalies are exclusive to an individual; there is really no set of symptoms common enough to permit a description, much less a definition, that is applicable to all cases and to be helpful to those who work with the individuals in question. Thus, unfortunately, the lack of a useful, universally accepted definition is likely to continue.

Conduct Disorder

According to Kauffman and Landrum (2009), 6 percent to 16 percent of boys and 2 percent to 9 percent of girls under age eighteen may have a psychiatric disorder referred to as conduct disorder. This term is applied to children who may have great difficulty following rules, throw temper tantrums, destroy property, bully, or regularly act in deceitful ways.

Kazdin (1998, cited in Kauffman & Landrum, 2009) believes that "the term conduct disorder is usually reserved for a pattern of antisocial behaviour that is associated with significant impairment in everyday functioning at home or school, and concerns of significant others that the child or adolescent is unmanageable" (p. 199). According to the website of Focus Adolescent Services (**www.focusas.com**), treatment for children with conduct disorders can be "complex and challenging." Treatment often involves both behaviour therapy and psychotherapy and extends over a long period of time. It is generally acknowledged that the earlier a child with conduct disorder is identified and receives treatment, the greater the likelihood of a positive outcome and a more productive adult life.

+ *Are needs being met?* An area of concern is the discrepancy between the percentage of the school population that is behavioural exceptional and the percentage that is actually being served. A Canada-wide study by Dworet and Rathgeber (1990) found that, not only are the needs of large numbers of students with behavioural exceptionalities going unserved, but this population is getting even less attention than it did in 1981. More recently, a follow-up study with data collected in 2004–2005 shows a very uneven rate of prevalence throughout the country. In some jurisdictions, such as the Northwest Territories, no reporting of prevalence was possible since they do not identify students with behavioural exceptionalities. Across provinces, Prince Edward Island reported a rate of 6.21 percent, while Ontario reported a rate of less than 1 percent, a significant decrease since information was last collected.

+ *School standards too high?* There is some evidence that schools illuminate behaviour as unacceptable because they have unrealistic and unnatural standards. Some theorists refer to this as "iatrogenic disorder." In other words, the behaviour arises as a consequence of the way the student is treated and not out of a natural predisposition. Other theorists advance the idea of psychonoxious behaviours or attention-getting styles that, over time, accumulate into a large pool of resentment in peers and teachers so that the student in question is treated as behavioural exceptional, whether the student actually is so or not.

+ *Socio-economic and class distinctions* come into play in this exceptionality. Particularly in the case of adolescents, students from lower-income families report a greater number and variety of penalties for their behaviour. Moreover, certain behaviours by lower-income students are more likely to be regarded as behavioural exceptional, whereas similar behaviours by students from high-income families are more likely to be seen as legitimate responses to stimuli.

+ *The stigma* of being identified with a behavioural exceptionality creates a lasting impression. It affects the opinions of teachers and peers, and it can contaminate matters for the student identified. Once placed in the "behavioural" category, exceptional students often find their history hard to escape and must contend with an atmosphere in which expectations govern the way others respond. As a consequence, administrators are often reluctant to apply a behavioural identification, so that some genuine cases of behavioural exceptionality may not be getting the appropriate intervention. This may certainly affect the prevalence rates referred to earlier.

◆ *Legal requirements* regularly complicate the education of a student who has become involved in crime. One of the more significant issues is the disruption of a student's education if he or she is moved through a variety of settings while a case is being decided and a sentence is being served. It is not unusual for an adolescent, particularly, to experience a variety of custodial settings through both the court hearing procedures and subsequent serving of a sentence. These settings will invariably have different educational approaches – if any – and, usually, little effort is made to coordinate these approaches. To a student with a behavioural exceptionality, such a lack of continuity can aggravate the problem.

Another issue that arises out of the legal side is the rigorous privacy stipulations in Canadian law that in some cases preclude informing teachers of circumstances surrounding a student's involvement in crime, or even of any transgression at all. While this law may have no immediate bearing on educational planning, it may require the withholding of information that, in some cases, could be important, not just to the student's program, but also to the well-being of the teacher and other members of the class.

Oppositional Defiant Disorder

Some children have a mental health condition known as oppositional defiant disorder. Children or adolescents with this condition are similar to, but present themselves with less severity than, an individual with conduct disorder. Oppositional defiant disorder may be present in a child or adolescent who is persistently oppositional, negative, and/or hostile to authority figures. These behaviours must be present for at least six months and may be accompanied by temper tantrums, aggressiveness toward peers, and the deliberate annoyance of others.

Treatment for children and adolescents with oppositional defiant disorder focuses on management training techniques, so the parent or teacher can more effectively respond to the defiant behaviour. Responses may include providing effective time outs, avoiding power struggles, and ensuring that the caregiver remains calm when confronted with frequent oppositional behaviour.

◆ *The use of drugs* to manage behaviour has provoked debate among educators and mental health professionals from the time the very first pill was swallowed. Initially, much of the argument revolved on whether moral and ethical values may be violated by chemically altering an individual's makeup and natural function. The debate is unlikely to diminish as long as drugs are used.

Other oft-voiced sentiments prevail as well, despite the fact that empirical evidence has weakened many of them. The belief that administering drugs to a child will lead to later drug addiction has not proven demonstrably true. And the argument that drug therapy is an opportunity for parents (and even teachers) to turn their responsibilities over to chemicals, while possibly of merit in isolated, individual cases, has also not found support over time. On the other hand, the jury is still out on the issue of psychological effects – for example, the impact on a child's self-esteem of regularly taking a pill. And there is evidence to support the accusation that teenagers, especially, with quantities of mood-altering drugs available, can be tempted to take illegal advantage.

Overall, however, supporters of psycho-pharmacology as a method of behaviour management can now point to some positive outcomes. Relatively long-term experience has demonstrated that many children respond positively to medication, most particularly those who are given drugs to reduce impulsivity and improve concentration. There is also fairly clear evidence that drugs are crucial in the treatment of psychotic illnesses such as childhood schizophrenia. Yet critics respond that this alleged (and rather narrow) success is a double-edged sword because it is rapidly accelerating the rate at which drugs are prescribed at the expense of other, drugless therapies. There are also concerns about possible side effects, which, according to Health Canada 2006, include, in rare cases, agitation and hallucinations. (See also Drug Therapy Approach later in this chapter.)

Conceptual Models and Their Educational Implications

Although mental health professionals tend to subscribe to a particular, and usually narrow, school of thought when it comes to treating students with behavioural exceptionalities, emphasis on a singular view of behaviour is far less common in the classroom. However, it behooves teachers and educational assistants to be aware of some of the current approaches in the mental health field.

The Case of Suzette

ALTHOUGH the school board that expelled Suzette six weeks ago has a zero tolerance policy on violence, she was given several chances before the expulsion occurred.

On one occasion, she pushed and then slapped a teacher. Action on this incident was shelved by mutual agreement when Suzette insisted she had reacted "when he grabbed me." Three student witnesses and one teacher utterly contradict that claim, but the teacher asked the principal to drop the matter because, innocent or not, he refused to be, in his words, "dragged through media mud."

On another occasion, Suzette scratched another student seriously enough to leave a scar, but an investigation of the incident gave Suzette the benefit of the doubt on the basis of self-defence.

The precipitating event for the expulsion was another fight. This time Suzette beat up another girl very badly.

Suzette's exasperated parents have prevailed on a personal friend, the principal of a large secondary school in a neighbouring board, to accept Suzette, but now he has a dilemma: Should she be placed in the school's behavioural resource class? This is an exceptionally successful unit with a highly competent teacher who places almost all of her emphasis on academic achievement. The students work hard on a full program, go on field trips, and participate in school events, but their entire program is delivered in this class.

Suzette is sixteen and was designated "behavioural" four years ago. She had been an excellent, high-achieving student, until, as her mother said to an IPRC, "she went teenage-nuts." Suzette is articulate and has a very powerful personality. At one of her several court hearings, a judge remarked, "After five minutes with you, no one would ever say 'Suzette who?' the next day."

What the principal is worried about is a struggle for power if Suzette goes to the behavioural class. He knows her potential for success is very high there, but if a power struggle erupts, the results could be very harmful to both Suzette and the other students. The principal has referred this to the In-school Team and is awaiting their input.

Psychodynamic Approach

Although it is a declining force among educators, psychodynamics continues to attract attention in television shows and popular literature. This perspective views behavioural disorders as being within the individual. Thus when this treatment approach is used, the teacher is usually part of a mental health team that seeks to develop a warm, supportive atmosphere in which it is hoped that the student will overcome his or her inner turmoil. Emphasis is placed on acceptance and toleration, somewhat at the expense of direct instruction and acquisition of academic skills.

A variation of this style is called the *psychoeducational approach*, in which more effort is directed to practical classroom outcomes.

One of the reasons for the decline of the psychodynamic approach is an accumulation of evidence that it does not improve academic achievement and, at the same time, only limited evidence that it helps to improve behaviour.

Biophysical Approach

This style emphasizes the organic origins of behaviour and postulates a direct relationship between behaviour and such things as physical defects, illnesses, diet, and allergies. Advocates of this view have generated a multiplicity of causation theories, each with a responsive therapy. Some examples include megavitamin therapy, diet control, symptom control medication, removal of offending substances (such as carpets), etc.

In the classroom, this approach is often combined with a structured, behaviour-based style that emphasizes routine, daily scheduling, frequent repetition of tasks presented in careful sequence, and the elimination of environmental stimuli that are perceived to be extraneous. Available data on the results of this treatment have difficulty separating which aspect, the therapies or the style of instruction, has more impact.

Environmental Approach

Supporters hold that individuals are a particular collective in a particular space and time, and, as such, must be regarded as the product of an ecological unit made up of themselves, their family, school, neighbourhood, and community. Educational response to students with behavioural exceptionalities, therefore, must necessarily involve the whole of the ecological unit.

Where this theory is followed in schools, teachers are expected to instruct the student in social and interpersonal environment skills. At the same time, attempts are made to modify the school's environment to meet the needs of the individual. Family counselling, and, in some cases, counselling of the student's classmates, may be part of the program.

The key element is to create, in all parts of the unit, an awareness of its reciprocal relationships and an impetus toward monitoring these relationships to the ultimate benefit of the student identified as behavioural exceptional. Classroom teachers and educational assistants with experience in this approach, while they attest to its efficacy, at least initially, also point out that the amount of coordination necessary to make it work well is almost impossible to achieve.

Video Games and Behaviour

Teachers and parents have long suspected that the violence portrayed in some video games has a negative impact on the behaviour of children and adolescents. Although there is inherent logic in that perception, and although it appears to be supported by empirical evidence in the hallways, playgrounds, and even in the classrooms of our schools, it has taken some time to reinforce the suspicion with solid research. In part, this is because the level of extreme violence in some video games is a fairly recent phenomenon, and research that might reveal a potential impact (or not) on players' behaviour must necessarily follow some time after.

It would appear, however, that the research gap is now being filled. A recent review of the literature shows that over forty peer-reviewed studies have been published, and that each one, without exception, concludes that playing violent video games has an impact on the behaviour of children and adolescents. Several well-executed studies published in the February 2004 issue of the *Journal of Adolescence* (vol. 27, no. 1) make the case with particular clarity. One study (Gentile et al., 2004), conducted on a population of over six hundred students in grades 8 and 9, concluded that, compared with controls, children and adolescents who play violent video games:

- see the world as more hostile
- get into more arguments with teachers
- have more fights
- achieve lower grades

One of the strengths of this study is that it controlled for gender, for amount of time spent playing (average was nine hours per week), and for the possibility of pre-existing hostility in the subjects being studied, all of which adds to the credibility of the results.

Other studies consistently demonstrate effects on violent-video-game players such as lack of empathy for victims, desensitization to violence generally, and a greater tendency to condone violence as an acceptable response.

It is important to highlight here the fact that the research work, particularly the studies conducted since the beginning of the current century, has focused on violent video games that have become available only in the past few years. Teachers and parents who have not reviewed contemporary game materials should realize that the relatively innocuous Pac-Man and Pong type of games of earlier generations pale in comparison with more recently available programs that portray indiscriminate mass killings and offer intensely graphic displays of violence.

Clearly, video-game violence is a phenomenon that will raise concerns in schools and homes for some time to come. For special education, the problem will be in determining to what extent the games may be a contributing, or possibly an obfuscating, factor in situations where a student is thought to be behaviourally exceptional.

Behaviour Modification Approach

Still seen as the dominant intervention style from an educational point of view, this approach follows the assumption that all behaviour is modifiable by principles of reinforcement. (It is worth pointing out that the dominance of the behavioural approach is, at least partly, owing to the vast amount of published material it spawns, much of it from American colleges and universities where the theory does indeed dominate.) Educators who adhere to this approach believe that behaviour is controlled by impinging stimuli and that it is possible to:

- create behaviours that presently do not exist
- maintain and generalize behaviours already established
- eliminate inappropriate behaviours

What happens practically is that first, a desirable behaviour or set of behaviours is established. It is hoped that the expected behaviour is within the student's repertoire, and the occurrence of the desired behaviour is slowly increased (or decreased, as the case may be) by the use of a potent reinforcer at the appropriate time. The reinforcer can be concrete, such as food or a toy, or can be more abstract, such as checks, stars, or coupons that can be traded for something concrete (commonly known as a token economy system). In every case, the reinforcer should be paired with a social reinforcer, such as praise or a smile, so that, when the concrete or token reinforcer is phased out, the student can still receive a positively perceived acknowledgment for his or her appropriate behaviour.

Educators who use behaviour modification – and many do to a degree, even those who would deny being "behaviourist" – regard every student as a candidate for learning, irrespective of whatever psychopathology may be at the root of behaviour.

Drug Therapy Approach

This treatment essentially means that a student with a behavioural exceptionality is administered psychotropic drugs, most often in pill form, to help control his or her behaviour. Research over the past thirty years suggests, fairly emphatically, that the medication does indeed succeed in this purpose, implying, therefore, a positive or at least an improved outcome for both the student and others in his school and personal life.

Classroom professionals often become involved in this therapy, first of all to administer the medication during the school day, and secondly – particularly if a drug is being used for the first time with a student – in monitoring its positive and negative effects. In the ideal situation, no medication is ever given to a student without its effects being carefully noted and duly reported, so that modifications in the dosage can be made – an outcome that is often necessary.

Regrettably, a challenge for teachers and assistants is that necessary modifications, which are always under the control of parents and medical professionals, are not always forthcoming in a timely way. Of possible interest both to parents and educators may be the claim by practitioners of naturopathic medicine that they can treat attention deficit and hyperactivity by means that do not involve administering potentially invasive chemistry.

Whatever medication is administered to a child, it must be recognized that the medication alone is not sufficient to remediate the academic and social differences a child with a behavioural exceptionality may experience. It is usually a combination of medication and appropriate behavioural and academic interventions that helps students improve socially and academically.

A Caution …

Teachers and educational assistants are often asked to become involved in the administration and monitoring of prescribed medications. It may be to their benefit, before doing so, to have written instructions from the student's parents, duly co-signed by the school principal or other authority. Some school boards have very specific policies on this issue.

The Classroom Reality: Flexible Common Sense

Teachers and educational assistants, who work with students on a day-to-day basis, often find it difficult to be entirely faithful to only one of the approaches above when they apply it in the cold (or hot!) reality of the classroom. Most combine a variety of approaches and apply them on an individual basis. For example, all teachers of all students – not just those with behavioural exceptionalities – espouse the value of a warm, supportive atmosphere.

All teachers recognize the interplay of environmental stimuli, and all are aware of the importance of these phenomena in both learning and social development. Teachers and assistants universally modify behaviour in their students, but only some will actually call it behaviour modification. And the view of each student as a dynamic, individual entity is at the very heart of teaching as a profession. Taken together, the practices followed by most educators, most of the time, could best be collected under the expression "flexible common sense." While the term may not have definitive intellectual reverberations in the field of behaviour theory, it describes pretty much the route that is followed in the classroom: doing what is effective at the time and what makes sense at the time.

According to Solar (2011), it is important for the teacher to remember that students with behavioural exceptionalities may not have the understanding of what appropriate behaviour is in all circumstances. Solar describes a situation in which the teacher requests a secondary student to be respectful of a guest speaker and the student asks "why?" What the student may be asking is "how," and the answer may be to describe to the student what "respectful" actually looks like (listening attentively with eye contact). The teacher cannot assume that students with a behavioural exceptionality actually know how to behave in all school situations – that just telling them to "behave" or "be respectful" be enough.

Kauffman and Landrum (2009) suggest, however, that regardless of the approach used, the teacher needs to establish a baseline of what behaviours are occurring. By understanding the frequency, intensity, and duration of a particular behaviour or set of behaviours, the teacher can tell if the intervention that is applied is effective.

The Case of Logan

ON just her second day in office, the (acting) principal spotted Logan under the secretary's empty chair after morning recess. He was pale, and shaking, and appeared to have been crying. Logan is a month away from his seventh birthday and is in grade 2. The principal, suspecting a playground incident, deliberately ignored Logan for a few minutes but intervened fifteen minutes later as he had not moved and was now crying hard.

In her office, Logan said his grade 2 teacher "touched me here and here and put his hand inside my pants," adding that it had happened several times. Upon consultation with family children's services, the following information was shared. Logan's parents are divorced and have joint custody of him. Last year, he told each of them, on consecutive days, that the other was abusing him sexually. Before the accusations were exposed as completely false, Logan's mother was asked by her professional association to voluntarily suspend her practice (she practices pediatric psychiatry). His father, an attorney with a prominent firm, was asked to take a leave of absence, although the firm denied that the request was connected to an interview that Logan gave – on his own initiative – to the tabloid press.

In the course of the investigation, the principal learned that, in grade 1, Logan had convinced a girl in the class that her parents were separating. She is now in a different school but, according to her parents, still has anxiety attacks even if the two of them leave for work at different times. Also in grade 1, until the teacher discovered it, Logan was quietly talking classmates into destroying their work because it was no good. The same teacher suspects, but cannot prove, that Logan is responsible for a spate of missing materials and that it was he who ruined the controls of a powered wheelchair used by a boy in the class. At the same time, she acknowledges that Logan is academically superior and that she has never actually seen him do anything remotely improper (the second grade teacher agrees) and that in terms of completing work, obeying routines, and in helping others, Logan appears to be a model student.

The acting principal's instinct is to call for an In-school Team to discuss the situation. Still, she wonders what that would accomplish.

Steps to Multidisciplinary Co-operation: Student Support Leadership Initiative

The Ministry of Education, in partnership with several other Ontario ministries, has established the Student Support Leadership Initiative. This initiative developed twenty-nine geographic "Clusters" around the province. Each cluster developed a committee made up of agencies (e.g., Community Health Centres, addiction service providers, child and youth services, etc) whose role in the community was directed to assisting children and youth with behavioural/emotional difficulties. In 2011, clusters focused their work "on the prevention of inappropriate and unsafe behaviours that may lead to suspension or expulsion and on the promotion of well-being of students" (Ministry of

Education, Special Education Update, June 2011). It is intended that schools work closely with these clusters so that students having behavioural and/ or emotional difficulties receive appropriate, coordinated services from the various agencies with whom they may be involved.

The "Popularity" of AD/HD

Throughout the final years of the twentieth century and on into the next, a confusing and controversial condition has taken a very high-profile front seat in special education: attention deficit/ hyperactivity disorder (AD/HD). The condition is being diagnosed with ever-increasing frequency by psychiatrists, psychologists, pediatricians, and family practitioners, especially in North America. As well, AD/HD has captivated the popular press, has become a regular subject of educational research, and has been almost completely – and rather uncritically – accepted by the teaching profession. Unfortunately, it is the subject of considerable debate, not just on the nature of the special needs it represents, but also on whether it requires, or even deserves, distinctive status.

Ontario, like most educational jurisdictions, does not list AD/HD as a distinct category of exceptionality. Nor is it included in the *Individuals with Disabilities Education Act* (IDEA, 1997) in the U.S. Yet, irrespective of its (un)official status and of the controversy it continues to generate, AD/HD has become a factor in both regular and special education today. The following section attempts to present a perspective for educators and parents.

Students with AD/HD

What Are the Symptoms of AD/HD?

AD/HD, or attention deficit/hyperactivity disorder, is a diagnostic category listed in the *DSM-IV-TR* of the American Psychiatric Association. When diagnosing AD/HD, medical practitioners look at three symptoms.

The first is an inability to sustain attention at age-appropriate level. The student cannot screen out irrelevant stimuli, does not concentrate on tasks long enough to complete them, and does not sustain the thought processes necessary to do school work.

The second is impulsivity. The student does things without considering consequences and often repeats the behaviour (does not learn from experience). Work patterns are erratic and scatter-focused. The student often perseverates with counterproductive behaviour.

The third characteristic is hyperactivity. The student engages in non-purposeful movement and activity that is usually not age appropriate, often at an accelerated level. This movement and/ or activity usually continues despite intervention.

(Interestingly, teachers can often see many of their students in a description like this, or members of their family, or even themselves.)

Are AD/HD Symptoms the Result of Other Factors?

Disruptive or unresponsive behaviour may be the result of anxiety or depression. Regular lapses in attention may be evidence of absence (petit mal) seizures. Fetal alcohol syndrome sometimes produces hyperactive behaviour. An uncooperative student, especially a younger one, may have lost some hearing as a result of chronic inner ear infections or have an undetected hearing problem.

In short, many things can cause the symptoms. To further confuse the matter, AD/HD is most often a medical diagnosis arrived at, supposedly, on the evidence of these symptoms. Yet professional educators see the same symptoms every day in students who are not identified as AD/HD! Supporters of the condition as a separate entity argue – often with good evidence to support them – that the distinguishing criteria of AD/HD symptoms are high frequency and severity and that the symptoms are seen repeatedly over extended time.

What Causes AD/HD?

Advocates argue that AD/HD has been around for a long time under other terms such as "hyperkinesis," "minimal brain dysfunction," and "moral deficit." They posit further that what makes AD/HD real is that it has a biological or psychological basis – or both.

As for psychological cause, proponents argue that there are some individuals who, through no fault of their own, cannot use their human will and self-control to manage themselves from within and that the pace of modern life aggravates this lack of a central control mechanism.

The majority of advocates for AD/HD, however, see it as a neurologically-based medical condition. Among the causes identified, but not yet widely accepted by both the medical and educational communities, are faulty regulation by a neurotransmitter called norepinephrine and genetic factors owing to anomalies in certain chromosomes. Recently, specific genes (dopamine transporter gene on chromosome 5 and dopamine receptor D4 gene on chromosome 11) have been discovered that appear to be related to AD/HD. Dopamine deficiency may be a cause of AD/HD, but it is unclear whether individuals with AD/HD do not produce enough of it or are unable to properly use what they do produce.

Other chemical deficiencies that may be associated with AD/HD are noradrenaline and serotonin. Noradrenaline is a substance that may act on the brain during times of stress, and serotonin is a chemical that helps the brain's ability to detect and/or possibly regulate other chemicals (Canadian Attention Deficit Hyperactivity Disorder Resource Alliance, www. CADDRA.CA).

Just a Confusion with Other Special Needs?

AD/HD has long been associated with learning disabilities because of the inattentiveness factor. The two are not, however, the same thing. Estimates vary, but the literature generally suggests that about one-third of students with learning disabilities may have some degree of attention disorder. Alternatively, the rate of learning disabilities is high in students who are diagnosed with AD/HD, possibly because lack of attention and off-task behaviour are detrimental to mastering basic skills. One special need, however, does not absolutely and automatically imply the other. (The same caution applies to combining AD/HD with other behavioural exceptionalities and with Tourette syndrome.)

Another Modern-day Phenomenon?

AD/HD is not entirely new, although it did not capture the public eye until the late twentieth century. A German doctor, Heinrich Hoffman, first described hyperactivity in 1845. In 1902, George Still, a British physician, added a moral overlay – a notion that unproductive hyperactivity is somehow associated with evil. This notion still dogs the issue. (He described "sick" children of average or higher intelligence who had an "abnormal deficit of moral control." Hence the term "moral deficit.") AD/HD was classified clinically in 1968 and acquired its current designation in 1987 (both times at the initiative of the medical profession).

When matched against other, more recent types of special need, the time frame in which AD/HD achieved its high profile seems reasonable enough, yet there continues to be intense, sometimes vicious disagreement over whether it should be seen as a distinct clinical entity, or even whether it really exists. Critics contend that AD/HD has become the label *du jour* in North America, an invention of a culture that has cast aside its obligation to parent well and now needs an excuse for the result. While such statements are unquestionably harsh and may be offered more for polemical effect, they have a powerful impact in the light of the accelerated rate of diagnosis. In 1997, the *Globe and Mail* newspaper reported that an estimated half million Canadians, mostly students, had been diagnosed – an extraordinary number for a condition that got its name only a decade earlier! Subsequent revelations in 2003 and 2004 indicate that the accelerating rate continues.

The Case of Hannah

AFTER only a month in nursery school, Hannah was secretly called "Beagle" by the staff because of her penchant for running flat out until something or someone stopped her. It was a habit she continued over the next several years.

Kindergarten passed fairly smoothly, for Hannah's teacher was a completely unruffled person committed to letting her students express themselves as much as they wished. Grade 1, however, was a disaster. This was not entirely Hannah's fault; the grade 1 teacher was having a difficult year. She had two preschool children of her own, one of whom was chronically ill, and a husband who worked shifts. But Hannah didn't help things. By this time, running about during story time, quiet time – any time – was an established habit. She regularly blurted out whatever was on her mind during instruction and seemingly could not keep from interfering with others in the class when they teamed up for an activity. Hannah regularly "borrowed" materials without asking, never returned it unless told to, and did not seem remotely aware of how annoying she was to others.

Grade 2 was marked by a field trip crisis when, because of Hannah, the class was asked to leave a petting zoo. Following this trip, Hannah's mother agreed to accompany excursions as one of the parent volunteers supervising a group. Nevertheless, because of some more incidents and because of an extensive list of complaints from other parents, Hannah's mother eventually kept her daughter at home during all subsequent field trips.

Unfortunately, the residue of this move carried over to grade 3, when several other parents used it – though unsuccessfully – as a precedent for having Hannah removed from the class altogether.

In grade 3, a pediatrician diagnosed AD/DH and prescribed medication (Ritalin), but Hannah turned out to be one of the minority for whom the side effects, especially sleeplessness, made it impossible to continue with the prescription. Hannah's mother, a nurse, ruled out a second medication, Cylert, because she had heard it may cause liver damage. Throughout grade 3, Hannah's impulsive, annoying behaviours worsened. By then it was also evident that she was lagging behind her peers academically.

Hannah is now in grade 4. Her mother reports that she had a "good summer" at a camp for children with AD/HD. Both mother and daughter have new hope because Hannah learned some self-control skills at camp and because the grade 4 teacher has a reputation for competence in dealing with AD/HD. In spite of this, there has already been an incident. The class is forming groups to put together material for a "time capsule" to be opened in June. Because no group would accept Hannah, she had a tantrum and then, for the first time anyone can remember, she began to cry in a deeply heartfelt way. The teacher sees that as a sign the time is ripe for renewed effort to address Hannah's case. An In-school Team meeting has been called to come up with ideas.

What Does Having Students with AD/HD Mean to the Classroom?

Teachers and educational assistants have long been used to "antsy" students, particularly younger ones, who find it hard to sit still. And in most classrooms, the behaviour is managed successfully most of the time. But where a strongly suspected case of AD/HD is present, teachers can expect a high level of physical activity, inappropriate responses, low frustration tolerance – the list goes on. And each of these behaviours repeats, despite intervention. Whereas it is the student's parent who must bear the ultimate costs, emotionally and physically, teachers have a burden all their own, for a student with AD/HD has a concentric effect. The student's lack of restraint and acting out will invariably draw in the student's peers, or distract them, or cause conflict, or interrupt their work, and so on.

Regrettably, there is no sure remedy in the classroom. Certainly, there is no universally accepted way to deal with AD/HD in school. Behaviour modification is often tried, but offers no guarantees. Isolating the student with AD/HD may be beneficial for the student's peers, but is not a solution for the student himself/herself, at least not long term. Ultimately, the most effective management techniques usually turn out to be those that the teacher and educational assistant work out creatively, often with the parents' help, and these techniques, most of the time, are uniquely successful for that particular student. Chances are slim that the same methods will work with the next candidate. Nevertheless, research has found that the most effective treatment is a combination of medication, effective behaviour modification practices, and, if possible, individual and family counselling.

Most teachers do find, through experience, that there are a few common threads in successful management. One is flexibility. There is not much point in banging heads with a student who seems predisposed to repeat wrong behaviours in the first place. Another is setting modest goals – objectives the student has a realistic chance of attaining. Still another is diversion. And all of these must be supported by, for lack of a better phrase, "kind firmness."

Strategies for Students with Behavioural Exceptionalities

Manage the environment: Seat the student away from distracting stimuli such as doorways and traffic areas. Try to seat the student so that particularly stimulating students are not in his or her natural line of sight. If possible, seat the student near stable peer models. Periodically use a special stimulus-reduced study area, such as a carrel. Encourage parents to do the same. Experiment with natural light versus fluorescent. Some teachers have reported that natural light is superior.

While instructing: Be simple and concise. Offer one instruction or task at a time and only after you are confident that you have the student focused and ready. Limit the use of subordinate clauses and embedded phrases, and welcome questions for clarification. Help the student to feel secure by being nearby when he or she starts work. While instructing a large group, or the whole class, use a technique commonly known as "proximity control" whereby you frequently position yourself near the student so that your physical presence can act as catalyst toward the initiation and maintenance of attentive, appropriate behaviour.

Organization of the day or period: Prepare the student for shifts in topic, setting, schedule, etc.

(Again, a teacher's or educational assistant's proximity when these shifts are about to happen can be very important.) Meet and greet with a few positive one-on-one seconds at crucial points during the day, points when the potential for hyperactivity increases: e.g., transitions such as returning from lunch, gym, recess, etc. When in-class activity is assigned (homework, too), help the student get started and then, at first, check back as frequently as you can. Help the student organize his or her output (into notebooks, files, etc.) so that the student gradually accumulates a visible, concrete, cumulative record of his or her efforts.

Other support: Enforce classroom routines and procedures consistently. And have only a few; too many rules invites disaster! Since planning is never this student's long suit, the adults in the student's life must compensate by planning for him or her and building in extra time. When a disagreement arises, do not argue. You cannot win. Reinforce "good" chunks of time, such as on-task behaviour, with just-for-her/him positive eye contact or other supportive expressions. When your experience tells you an impossible-to-resolve situation is developing, try "antiseptic bouncing," e.g., send the student on an important errand out of the room, or provide some other task that "needs doing now."

Think momentum: Not motivation, but momentum. A teacher who only motivates is forever pushing from behind. Eventually, the teacher wears out, or runs out of patience, or ideas, or, most likely, desire. On the other hand, a teacher who tries to build momentum in students and who works at developing in them a sense of personal responsibility not only will have a greater and longer-lasting impact on the students, but also will last longer himself/herself.

Note improvement: Ensure that you have an accurate understanding of the student's behaviour and note when improvements are occurring. In almost every case, a student will revert to his or her inappropriate patterns, but if this is happening less frequently, with less intensity, or for shorter duration, this is a sign of improvement that needs to be brought to the student's attention. Students with AD/HD or behavioural exceptionalities often do not see that they are doing better. Improvement, no matter how small, needs to be brought to the student's attention and to the attention of parents and the others with whom he or she may be working.

Teachers and educational assistants who work with students with behavioural exceptionalities are the first to acknowledge that there is no pedagogical magic, no secret formula for teaching success in this area of exceptionality. And those who think there is one, and go looking for it, are bound to be disappointed. Still, there is one truth, an abiding one that all educators recognize, as do students, parents, and anyone else who bothers to take a second look at classrooms. This is the truth that a teacher who is effective with "regular" students is usually more effective with "behavioural" students. It follows, then, that to emulate what effective teachers do is, at the very least, a practical beginning point for all classroom professionals.

An Effective Teacher's Attitude

Many human strengths are needed to teach effectively. Traits such as patience, flexibility, creativity, a sense of humour, and a capacity to see all sides of an issue – these, in the heat of a teaching moment, will outweigh intelligence and scholarship. Effective teachers manifest these characteristics most of the time. However, what they manifest all of the time is not a characteristic at all but an attitude, a perspective: respect. When a teacher's or educational assistant's abiding view is built on respect for students – and on self-respect – the atmosphere in their classroom immediately reflects that attitude in a variety of ways. A place where students feel respected is a safe place to make a mistake and, therefore, an ideal place to learn and grow. Where respect prevails, students recognize that, in the eyes of the significant adults there, they have value. Once students feel respected themselves, they are far more likely to show it to others. And respect for others is fundamental if students are ever to modify their behaviour.

From the instructional end of things, respect, quite simply, infuses everything a teacher does. It smoothes rapport, supports flexibility and patience, and fuels the vitality of faith and hope. A teacher who respects students plans better, prepares better, and instructs better. A teacher who respects students instinctively avoids those spontaneous, but regrettable and damaging, management errors from which recovery is so difficult. Above all, if a teacher establishes genuine respect as the central idiom in a classroom, then everyone shares a behavioural reference point. Mutual respect offers both a stage from which to begin and an objective to keep in sight.

An Effective Teacher's Style

1 *Recognizing where students are "at."* Students with a behavioural problem are often burdened by a history that shapes the expectations others have of them. And they know it. A second burden, one that reinforces the first, is in-the-classroom helplessness. Consequently, many of them do not know how to set about academic tasks or how to conduct themselves socially. An effective teacher is very much aware of this fact and begins much of his or her work from inside the student's view. It is a delicate undertaking, for one must purposefully go where the student

The Case of Deshaun

DESHAUN began his grade 11 year in the public school board after being expelled from the Catholic board. He was seventeen years old with only ten credits toward a thirty-credit diploma. Previously, he had been shifted from several schools in an attempt to find the best environment for his success and safety. His Ontario Student Record held a long list of suspensions for various inappropriate behaviours including swearing, tardiness and school uniform violations.

His teacher for the Ontario Secondary School Literacy Course (OSSLC) quickly recognized common learning issues. Deshaun struggled with grade-appropriate vocabulary, reading comprehension, and intuitive response questions (reading between the lines). He had little patience for the literacy techniques offered. He refused to keep a learning journal and would not share anything personal. Because he wouldn't share his interests, it was difficult for the teacher to "hook" him into the curriculum or the classroom community.

Although Deshaun dressed and talked like a "tough guy," his teacher observed signs of anxiety in the classroom. He refused to sit with the other students. He never read out loud or shared an idea in the group setting. He told his teacher that he didn't like it when she stood behind him; it made him nervous. He became upset if his name was written on the board or anywhere where others could see it. He asked if he could wear his hood up because it made him feel "more comfortable." He avoided eye contact, particularly with anyone in a position of authority.

However, the behaviour that got him into the greatest number of conflicts with his teachers was his refusal to come into the classroom on time. He made it a point to be the last person in the class – wandering in the hallway or hovering outside the door until the other students were settled and the teacher had begun the lesson. Then he would quietly come in with his hood and hat on and sit as far away from the other students as possible. His other teachers took this behaviour as a sign of disrespect.

When the classroom teachers confronted him about the issue, Deshaun would swear at them and storm out of the class, not returning until the next day. Eventually, Deshaun stopped coming to class altogether; however, he was in the building every day hanging out in the cafeteria or in the hallways. Even more upsetting to other teachers, Deshaun was pulling other students out of class to hang out.

The Literacy teacher called an In-school Team meeting to come up with ideas to engage him in the classroom, ease his anxieties, and discover any interests that might help connect him with the school community.

---

is "at," while at the same time continuing to be a separate, adult mentor, with all that the role implies. For a teacher or educational assistant to become a buddy is a deadly mistake. Students don't want that. What they want is an adult who is open, who listens, and who will attempt to understand what they know and do not know and to help them in a face-saving way that produces results, however modest.

2 *Realizing the importance of personal conduct.* The manner in which teachers and assistants present their professionalism is a crucial factor in preventing inappropriate classroom behaviour. Ideally, adults who deal with

students with behavioural exceptionalities are role models who don't react defensively to challenge, who have the skills to divert a troublesome situation until stability is restored (and then deal with it), and who employ fair and realistic consequences in a consistent way. These are also the people who get to class ahead of time, who are present and visible, and responsible and proactive. They are role models of adulthood who communicate to students the possibility that the world does have some sense to it. Naturally, things do not always work out this way, but even the students (or perhaps especially the students, unfortunately) don't expect things to work right every time. Yet classroom professionals must strive to model this type of conduct if there is to be any hope of modifying their students' behaviour.

3 **Establishing a realistic, consistent, and predictable learning environment.** This is the *sine qua non* of an effective teacher's style. Students with a behavioural exceptionality already have trouble making sense of the world, not to mention school. And they are notoriously poor at reading between the lines to determine what is expected of them. These are not students who know how to, much less want to, play the game of school. Teachers and assistants can make things much easier for them – make it more possible for them to behave appropriately – if procedures and expectations are clear, uncomplicated, and predictable. Particularly in the beginning, and until the students develop some confidence in themselves and in their teachers, a predictable pattern is crucial.

This sense of stability and consistency in the classroom develops naturally out of the behaviour of the teacher but also out of day-to-day organization. Effective classrooms are not hamstrung by a long list of ironclad rules that students will invariably break and for which some disciplinary response then becomes necessary. Structure, organization, sequence – these are the important features, and a minimum number of simple, reasonable procedures and routines, not rules, for ensuring that these obtain, makes sense even to students with behavioural problems. There will be some bona fide rules, of course, but most of these are the ones established by the school or the board or other more global entity. And what distinguishes them from classroom procedures and routines is that consequences for breaking them are applied. In the classroom, however, teachers and assistants who organize from a perspective of respect and who model that attitude themselves not only have a standard to refer to, but also some room for flexibility when a student pushes against it.

4 **"Catching a kid doing something good."** It may be a very challenging task sometimes, but looking for positives and discreetly praising these students will pay dividends. "Discreet" is an operative word here. Students with behavioural exceptionalities, especially older ones, often harbour a profound cynicism that walls them in and protects them from positive reinforcement, which they believe is insincere. Many of them have had unsatisfactory experiences with so-called positive reinforcement programs and, as a result, have well-developed detectors. Praise is important, but it must be proportionate to the accomplishment, sincere, and utterly free of excess. Effusiveness will only embarrass the students and may provoke them into negative behaviour just to restore the balance.

5 **Treating democracy as a very fine line.** If given the opportunity, students quite naturally wish to contribute to a classroom's plans, procedures, and even curriculum. Understandably, this is more often the case with older students. The issue is a difficult one for teachers. Anyone who has ever experienced the exchange, "What do you want to do?" "Nuthin!" is naturally wary of a suggestion that students should be consulted. And it is a healthy wariness. Students who have been identified with behavioural exceptionalities getting involved in productive interchanges about procedures and curriculum happens more often in movie scripts than in classrooms.

Still, it is worth a try. Most effective teachers would never begin a term or a relationship this way, if only because students with a behavioural exceptionality are looking for leadership and order, whether they realize it or not. After some time has passed, however, and once an atmosphere of respect is established, eliciting and then acting on a suggestion from a student with a behavioural exceptionality can produce real benefits, if only because the student has thereby taken on some responsibility.

At the very least, teachers and educational

assistants must keep in mind that they are dealing with an exceptionality where, almost always, chaos in various forms has prevailed. That reality must infuse all democratic decisions.

6 *Establishing momentum is more important than motivating.* Any teacher who operates solely on a principle of motivation quite naturally runs out of ideas over a long school term because the responsibility is always his or hers. Not that motivating is counterproductive or a waste of time, but it is only superficial; it may pay temporary dividends but rarely has a lasting impact because it is always the teacher's responsibility (a fact that doubles the potential for an all too common teaching trap: the teacher becomes an entertainer).

More effective is to plan, organize, and teach to get students rolling on their own. Each teacher or educational assistant will accomplish this in different ways, but establishing momentum has a few absolutes. One is beginning where the student is "at" and then setting achievable goals so the student can have the delightful (and hitherto unusual) experience of success. Part and parcel of establishing momentum is making those goals short term so the success can come soon. Another is arranging, even manipulating, the goal – especially at first – to make certain the student does succeed. Then, as soon as there is a success, set up opportunity immediately for another, so that the first one can be reinforced and momentum can begin.

Still another absolute, a very simple one on the surface, is arranging one's planning and teaching so that students accumulate visible products, such as notes, every day. Most students with behavioural exceptionalities have never had the sense of accomplishment that comes from accumulating a set of notes or of accumulating anything. (Worth pointing out here is that teachers who are successful in establishing "momentum" in their students report that they are then much easier to "motivate"!)

7 *Keeping academics front and centre.* With the possible exception of cases where the mental health of a student is clearly established as a serious issue, the premier classroom focus should always be on academic learning. Even if the development of social skills is a vital feature of a student's educational plan, the student's own perception should always be that he or she is "here for education." A student with a behavioural exceptionality already feels singled out. To devote the major part of a program to the development of social skills in a transparent, obvious way only reinforces the distinction. Social skill development can continue to be a principal objective, but its realization should be achieved not just by direct social skill instruction itself but also by learning it during the process of studying what all the other kids are studying. (See Fergie's enlightening comments below.)

8 *Working hard is better than sitting around.* Fergie, a fifteen-year-old student in a regular grade 9 class with a "reputation," and in which five students were identified as behavioural (including Fergie), presents this argument much better than we can:

Some teachers, they don't get much work ready for us 'cause they think we don't care about nothin' right? And they think we don't notice. But how many crossword puzzles do they think we gotta do before we figure it out, right? Don't know why they do that. I mean, we're in school, so why not give us schoolwork? But that's not everybody, now. You take Mrs. P.... Now in her class do we ever have to put out. I mean, she's got work and everything every day! Like there's always stuff on the board for us and then we get a lesson-thing. And then more work. And we got this huge ton of notes! What's cool is nobody messes around in Mrs. P.'s class. And like, it's not just that she's mean – like – it's like you're really doin' something in that class, man. It's – it's like you're learning something!

– Fergie S., age fifteen, on audiotape
(Mrs. P. was in her first year of teaching)

Some Habits of an Effective Teacher:

- establishes and then maintains consistent routines for entering the classroom and beginning the session (the point at which much of the tone for what follows is established), e.g., an effective teacher is always at the doorway to greet, manage, and intervene if necessary
- sets up and insists on specific seating arrangements (which are then altered as deemed useful in order to reduce or increase opportunities)
- is highly visible, interacts with students outside the classroom, and tries to attend anything in the school in which a student with behavioural exceptionality is involved
- uses "antiseptic bouncing" when a student is worked up or aggressive; he or she gives the student an errand to run outside the class or some other activity that may assist in letting off steam
- allows, when demerits are used in the school or class, for merits to be earned as well.
- uses proximity control and stands nearby when it appears a situation may develop; proximity also works in signaling that they are available to help and available to interact; effective teachers never spend the whole day at the front of a classroom
- rarely, if ever, makes the dread mistake of being sarcastic and always avoids yelling (a profoundly counterproductive behaviour if it is used more than once a term) or other behaviours that shred dignity
- never uses corrosive discipline techniques, e.g., writing out lines, class detentions, or using curriculum content such as math or spelling drills as a punishment
- avoids confronting students with behavioural exceptionalities in front of peers and does not get into arguments
- uses diversions; younger students, especially, can be distracted from a counterproductive path if given alternate activities and goals
- lets students know there are high expectations; if necessary, on occasion, an effective teacher will, quite willingly, but discreetly, manipulate the components of a task to ensure a positive outcome for a student who needs a boost
- sets short-term goals for students who have not yet learned to defer gratification
- makes use of reward systems such as personal progress charts, and ensures that students accumulate notes and other physical evidence that the time spent in school is producing something of consequence

---

Finally, Be Proactive: Plan Ahead

In almost every case, a student identified with a behavioural exceptionality will have behaviours that occur frequently. The teacher can be assured that if a child is non-compliant or aggressive on Monday, these behaviours will appear again throughout the week. A well-prepared teacher plans for this eventuality. The teacher either tries to avoid the misbehaviour by setting up conditions that make it less likely to occur, or provides the student with consequences, either positive or negative, if it does or does not occur. If the behaviour does take place, the consequences are implemented and little discussion (which brings undue attention to the student) needs to occur. Hopefully, over time, the negative behaviour is decreased and there is ample opportunity for reward and/or praise to be offered to the student for his or her co-operative behaviour.

Teachers need to be aware that behavioural change takes time and there can be setbacks. Many positive steps will be taken, allowing the student to be "caught doing something good" before the student needs to be in a situation where the focus is on something negative.

Readings and Resources

Aust, P. (1994). When the problem is not the problem: Understanding attention deficit disorder with and without hyperactivity. *Child Welfare, 73*(3), 215–27.

Barabasz, M., & Barabasz, A. (1996). Attention deficit disorder: Diagnosis, etiology and treatment. *Child Study Journal, 26*, 1–38.

Bennett, K., Reichow, B., & Wolery, M. (2011). Effects of structured teaching on the behavior of young children with disabilities. *Focus on Autism and Other Developmental Disabilities, 26*(3), 143–52. doi:10.1177/1088357611405040

Carbone, E. (2001). Arranging the classroom with an eye (and ear) to students with ADHD. *Teaching Exceptional Children, 34*(2), 72–81.

Clarke, S., Dunlap, G., Foster-Johnson, L., Childs, K. E., Wilson D., White, R., & Vera, A. (1995). Improving the conduct of students with behavioral disorders by incorporating student interests into curricular areas. *Behavior Disorders, 20*(4), 221–37.

Colucci, S. (1993). Peer mediation: Creating opportunities for conflict resolution. *Communiqué*, May, 25–27.

Cummins, J. G., Peplar, D. J., Mishna, F., Craig, W. M. (2006). Bullying and victimization among students with exceptionalities. *Exceptionality Education Canada, 16*(3), 193–222.

DePaepe, P. A., Shores, R. E., Jack, S. L., & Denny, R. K. (1996). Effects of task difficulty on the disruptive and on-task behavior of students with severe behavior disorders. *Behavioral Disorders, 21*(3), 216–25.

Dworet, D. H., & Rathgeber, A. J. (1990). Provincial and territorial government responses to behaviorally disordered students in Canada. *Behavioral Disorders, 15*(4), 201–09.

Dworet, D. H., & Maich, K. (2004). Canadian school programs for students with emotional behavioural disorders: An updated look at Canadian schools, Paper presented at the International Conference of the Council for Exceptional Children, Salt Lake City.

Epstein, M. H. (1999). The development and validation of a scale to assess the emotional and behavioral strengths of children and adolescents. *Remedial and Special Education, 20*(5), 258–62.

Faber, A., & Mazlish, E. (1996). *How to talk so kids can learn*. New York: Fireside.

Frey, K. S., Hirschtein, M. K., & Guzzo, B. A. (2000). Second step: Preventing aggression by promoting social competence. *Journal of Emotional and Behavioral Disorders, 8*(2), 102–12.

Furr, D. L. (1996). Now I understand the rage. *Reaching Today's Youth, 1*(1), 9–12.

Gentile, D. A., Lynch, P. J., Linder, J. R., & Walsh, D. A. (2004). The effects of violent video game habits on adolescent hostility: Aggressive behaviour and school defiance. *Journal of Adolescence, 27*(1), 5–22.

Good, C. P., McIntosh, K., & Gietz, C. (2011). Integrating bullying prevention into schoolwide positive behavior support. *Teaching Exceptional Children, 44*(1) 48–56.

Health Canada. (2006). New information regarding uncommon psychiatric adverse events for all ADHD drugs. Retrieved at: www.hc-sc.gc.ca/ahc-asc/media/advisories-avis/_2006/2006_91-eng.php

Henley, M. (1997). *Teaching self-control: A curriculum for responsible behavior*. Bloomington, IN: National Education Service.

Hincks-Dellcrest Centre (2008). The ABCs of mental health: A teacher resource. Retrieved at: www.hincksdellcrest.org/ABC/Welcome

Jenson, W. R., Rhode, G., & Reavis, H. K. (1994). *The tough kids toolbox*. Longmont, CO: Sopris West.

Kauffman, J. M. (1999). How we prevent the prevention of emotional and behavioral disorders. *Exceptional Children, 65*, 448–68.

Kauffman, J. M., & Landrum, T. (2009). *Characteristics of emotional and behavioral disorders of children and youth* (9th. ed.). Columbus, OH: Merrill/Prentice Hall.

Lantieri, L., & Patti, J. (1996). Waging peace in our schools. *Reaching Today's Youth, 1*(1), 43–47.

Lewis, T. J., Heflin, L. J., & DiGangi, S. (1991). *Teaching students with behavior disorders: Basic questions and answers*. Reston, VA: Council for Exceptional Children.

Lewis, T. J., & Sugai, G. (1999). Effective behavior support: A systems approach to practice school-wide management. *Focus on Exceptional Children, 21*(6), 1–24.

MacDonald, I. M. (1997). Violence in schools: Multiple realities. *Alberta Journal of Educational Research, 43*, 142–56.

Maag, J. W., & Reid, R. (1994). Attention deficit hyperactivity disorder: A functional approach to assessment and treatment. *Behavioral Disorders, 20*(1), 5–23.

Marini, Z. A., Fairburn, L., & Zuber, R. (2001). Peer harassment in individuals with developmental disabilities: Towards the development of a multi-dimensional bullying identification model. *Developmental Disabilities Bulletin, 29*, 170–95.

Maté, G. (2000). *Scattered minds: A new look at the origins and healing of attention deficit disorder*. Toronto: Knopf.

Mendler, A. N. (1992). *How to achieve discipline with dignity in the schools*. Bloomington, IN: National Education Service.

Miller, D. (1994). Suicidal behavior of adolescents with behavior disorders and their peers without disabilities. *Behavioral Disorders, 20*(1), 61–68.

Moore, R., Cartledge, G., & Heckman, K. (1995). The effects of social skills instruction and self-monitoring on game-related behaviors of adolescents with EBD. *Behavioral Disorders, 20*(4), 253–66.

Newcomer, L. L., Lewis T. J., Powers, L. J. (2002). Policies and procedures to develop effective school-wide discipline practices at the elementary school level. Council for Children with Behavioral Disorders.

Ontario Ministry of Education. *Student support leadership initiative*. Retrieved at: http://www.edu.gov.on.ca/eng/policyfunding/memos/june2011/SSLI_ADMmemo.pdf

Oseroff, A., Oseroff, C. E., Westling, D., & Gesser, L. (1999). Teacher's beliefs about maltreatment of students with emotional/behavioral disorders. *Behavioral Disorders, 24*(3), 197–209.

Reid, R. (1999). Attention deficit hyperactivity disorder: Effective methods for the classroom. *Focus on Exceptional Children, 32*(4), 1–20.

Rhode, G., Jenson, W. R., & Reavis, H. K. (1992). *The tough kid book: Practical classroom management strategies*. Longmont, CO: Sopris West.

Safran, S. P., & Oswald, K. (2003). Positive behaviour supports: Can schools reshape disciplinary practices? *Exceptional Children, 69*(3), 361–72.

Shippen, M. E., Simpson, R. G., & Crites, S. S. (2003). A practical guide to functional assessment. *Teaching Exceptional Children, 35*(5), 36–44.

Sprague, J., & Walker, H. (2000). Early identification and intervention for youth with antisocial and violent behaviors. *Exceptional Children, 66*(3), 14.

Solar, E. (2011.) Prove them wrong. Be there for secondary students with an emotional or behavioral disability. *Teaching Exceptional Children, 44*(1), 40–45.

Wright-Strawderman, C., Lindsay, P., Bavarette, L, & Flippo, J. R. (1996). Depression in students with disabilities: Recognition and intervention strategies. *Intervention in School and Clinic, 31*(5), 261–75.

Links

American Academy of Child and Adolescent Psychiatry **http://www.aacap.org**

Canadian Attention Deficit Disorder Research Alliance **www.caddra.ca**

Canadian Children's Rights Council **www.canadiancrc.com/bullying.aspx**

Children and Adults with Attention Deficit Disorder **http://www.chadd.org**

Children's Mental Health Ontario **www.kidsmentalhealth.ca**

Focus Adolescent Services **http://www.focusas.com**

Mayo Clinic **www.mayoclinic.com/health/drug-information/DrugHerbindex.com**

Northern County Psychiatric associates **www.baltimorepsych.com**

Website of Dr. Thomas MacIintyre **www.behavioradvisor.com**

10
Students Who Are Gifted

"Gifted kids were dealt a bad hand by Galton* with his theory that cream will rise to the top no matter what. That was a century ago, and my guess is a century from now we'll still be selling the gifted short and for the same reason – the silly notion that because of their talents they don't need help. That is utter nonsense. The gifted need support as much as any other exceptional group."

– Paul T., teacher of students who are gifted

Misconceptions About Giftedness

1 **Students who are gifted always outpace their peers.**
The level of achievement for students who are gifted does not always reflect true ability. While some fare well at school, other students who are gifted may underachieve. Cultural differences, gender, and disabilities may affect performance. Some students express giftedness in non-academic ways or in ways not necessarily curriculum-related.

2 **They work harder than their peers.**
One of the accepted markers of giftedness is strong task commitment, but the trait is not automatic. Commitment may not become evident until it is stimulated by the appropriate conditions.

3 **Students who are gifted are bored with school, disruptive, and antagonistic.**
They react to neglect, inequity, etc., like any other students.

4 **It is common for emotional instability to accompany giftedness.**
Students who are gifted usually enjoy good mental health and tend to have fewer emotional problems than the norm. Empirical evidence suggests they may be exceptionally sensitive to matters such as injustice, world issues, etc.

5 **Students who are gifted are physically inept, self-absorbed, and narrow-minded.**
For the most part, they look and act like any other students, although teachers generally report them as above average in health, moral responsibility, and social adeptness.

6 **Giftedness is a stable, absolute characteristic.**
The evidence, particularly empirical evidence, seems to show that, while a highly developed ability in a student seems to be relatively constant, it will express itself with varying intensity over time.

7 **Students who are gifted are easy to identify.**
They do not necessarily stand out in a group of age peers. Theoretically, a student who is gifted performing at age level is underachieving. Although IQ tests are a frequent means of identifying students who are gifted (and they may often score very high), these instruments are far too narrow as a sole criterion, for they are unable to measure or even highlight characteristics such as artistic ability or creativity, for example. Reliance on IQ measures may also discriminate against culturally diverse populations or populations who are disabled.

---

* Francis Galton, a nineteenth-century English scientist and eugenics advocate, was one of the first to examine giftedness. He proposed that genius would surface no matter what the circumstances.

8 Normally a school system will find 3 percent to 5 percent of the population gifted.

The percentage identified usually depends on the jurisdiction's definition of gifted and on its conception of giftedness. In Ontario, the prevalence reported by the Ministry of Education in 2007 was less than 2 percent.

Defining Giftedness

The one consistent factor in defining giftedness is the lack of a consistent definition. For decades, researchers, educators, and parent groups have attempted to settle on one universally acceptable definition, but it remains elusive. Even the term "giftedness" is seen by many as too narrow, with a preference toward the terms "gifted," "talented," and "creative" gaining popularity. There is a tension between defining giftedness broadly because of the underrepresentation of certain groups, such as persons with disabilities and ethnic groups, and a more fine-tuned approach that allows for the identification of students who are "truly" gifted.

In 2000, Alberta Learning, a provincial resource for teachers, released the document *Teaching Students Who Are Gifted and Talented: Programming for Children with Special Needs*. This resource describes giftedness as having multiple forms and being diagnostic, developmental, and process-oriented rather than static and narrowly defined through an intelligence test. Giftedness is described as broad in terms of academic ability, talent, social and interpersonal skills, and even vocational domains. The document also makes note of the fact that giftedness is also crucially dependent on context and intimately linked to opportunity, a consideration reinforced by Sternberg (2006) in his description of practical giftedness. (See below.)

No matter the approach taken, any attempt to describe the characteristics of a student who is gifted reveals just how interwoven in the human psyche are matters such as ability and desire and how crucial the matters of opportunity, environment, and circumstance. Every classroom teacher, for example, will notice in many of his or her students, from time to time, any or all of the characteristics that appear in the following list. At the same time, the teacher will inevitably reflect on whether the characteristics are situation-related and temporary, or whether they have always been genuinely present in the student, just waiting for exposure by the circumstance.

There are other concerns, too, such as distinguishing high verbal ability (a commonly accepted identifying characteristic) from mere artfulness and facility; or, distinguishing truly inherent abilities from those that show up in school as a consequence of the student's life at home. The end result is a large body of literature and a wide range of views on just what constitutes giftedness.

The field of intelligence has at times tended to "put the cart before the horse," defining the construct conceptually on the basis of how it is operationalized rather than vice versa. This practice has resulted in tests that stress the academic aspect of intelligence, as one might expect, given the origins of modern intelligence testing in the work of Binet and Simon (1916) in designing an instrument that would distinguish children who would succeed from those who would fail in school. But the construct of intelligence needs to serve a broader purpose: accounting for the bases of success in all of one's life. See p. 90 of Sternberg, R. J. (2006).

Practical Giftedness

- Intelligence is defined in terms of the ability to achieve success in life in terms of one's personal standards and within one's socio-cultural context.
- To achieve success, one must capitalize on one's strengths and correct or compensate for one's weaknesses.
- Success is attained through a balance of analytical, creative, and practical abilities.
- A balancing of abilities is achieved in order to adapt to, shape, and select environments.

Defining by "Characteristics"

Students who display giftedness appear to have characteristics and abilities that stand out from the general run of things. What follows here are many of those most cited by both educators and parents. These are but one way of defining students who are gifted and their use may well prevail more out of tradition than scientific method. However, they are at least a beginning point. The challenge, for educators especially, is to determine not just the presence and the stability of these characteristics in a student, but to decide on their relative importance as standards qualifying a student for specialized instruction.

Characteristics of Giftedness

- wide range of abilities both academic and otherwise
- well-developed attention span and deep curiosity; ability to grasp, retain, synthesize, and act on information
- ability to work independently and to take responsibility
- capacity to adjust easily to new situations and demands
- superior vocabulary and reading ability
- considerable energy and above-average health
- well-developed capacity for abstract, complex, logical, and insightful conceptualizations
- more interested in questions than answers
- enjoys learning
- self-aware and reflective
- creative and imaginative
- ability to generalize information across settings
- highly developed sense of consequence and forward planning
- motivated and goal oriented
- able to see unusual diverse relationships
- advanced sense of moral/ethical judgment
- accelerated thought processes

Note that, along with the positive characteristics above, students who are gifted may also demonstrate attributes, in a learning environment, that can be considered negative. These include:

- boredom and inattentiveness, particularly when the subject area is not of interest to them
- high sensitivity
- extreme perfectionism
- difficulty changing tasks
- stubbornly preferring certain ways of learning
- unrealistic perfectionism and overly harsh self-criticism
- unwillingness to listen to other perspectives
- insistence on dominating discussion

Defining by "Interactions"

Most educators recognize that giftedness is a dynamic exceptionality, really too complex to be confined to a list of static, observable characteristics. Consequently, it has become regular practice now to define giftedness in terms of fluid, overlapping constellations. According to this approach, giftedness is the result of a number of characteristics interacting to achieve a purpose, rather than being present in the individual in a kind of parallel isolation. One of the first, and still very much accepted, presentations of this style of identification was offered by Renzulli (1977), which deals with what he calls the Enrichment Triad Model.

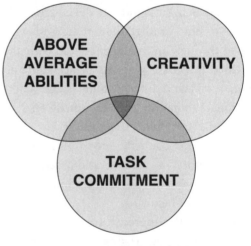

Figure 10A Triad Model

J. S. Renzulli. (1977). The model has been embellished slightly in subsequent editions.

Enrichment Triad Model

Sometimes called the "three-ring model" because it is presented as three overlapping circles, giftedness in this schema is seen as an interaction among a high level of general ability, a high level of task commitment, and a high level of creativity. Within the model, all three attributes must be present but will not necessarily be equal.

Students who are gifted, according to Renzulli, are those capable of developing this composite set of traits and applying the composite to any potentially valuable area of human performance. What is significant in this approach is it recognition of both human dynamism and the interplay of key qualities. There are times, quite naturally, when the degree of task commitment grows or fades in an individual. Everyone is more (or less) creative at some moments than at others. And to what degree abilities are utilized may well be relative to the nature of a particular task.

The Enrichment Triad Model accommodates all of this, which probably explains why it has gained very rapid acceptance among educators. Yet it has not led education for the gifted entirely out of the woods. Renzulli himself, in subsequent publications, argues that general ability is less important than specific performance in an operational definition of giftedness. (Which means, of course, that everyone can be gifted at some time: another major consideration for those responsible for definitions.)

In a later work on what he called the school-wide enrichment model (Renzulli & Weis, 1986), which has become a template for school improvement, Renzulli extends the pedagogy of instruction for the gifted to the entire school population. Educators are encouraged to create opportunities for students to develop their talents, participate in enriching activities that appeal to their interests, and allow for a wide variety of student expression. SEM has met with nearly universal appeal and is used in many countries.

Defining by "Multiples"

An increasingly popular way of looking at giftedness is to recognize that enriched abilities in a human being not only take many inherent forms, but also can be expressed in a variety of ways. Such a point of view is eminently satisfying to educators who accept that academic achievement by itself, and the traditional view of intelligence as measured by an IQ number, are entirely inadequate representations of giftedness.

The Case of Kyle

KYLE is an only child of professional parents, both very successful lawyers, and both very caring and nurturing to their son. A nanny brings Kyle to the school's day care when it opens, but one parent (sometimes both) picks him up (at varying times) from day care after school. Their home and their lifestyle are intellectually and culturally enriched. That influence was very obvious when Kyle entered grade 1 with a vocabulary and linguistic ability much beyond the norm for his age. His identification as gifted was immediately and smoothly effected. (The parents had requested an IPRC prior to his enrolment.)

Throughout grades 1 and 2, Kyle's school performance was equal to that of his also-identified-as-gifted classmates, although there was a glitch in grade 1. Kyle began the year in French immersion, but it was immediately obvious that it was a most unsuitable program for him. The parents demurred at first, but, after extensive consultation with a psychologist they retained privately, they accepted the school's recommendation, and Kyle was withdrawn.

Early in grade 3, a more serious problem developed. Kyle had increasingly demonstrated difficulty keeping up with the tasks assigned to the students identified as gifted who receive differentiated instruction to supplement their learning needs. By the end of grade 3, the gap between him and these classmates had widened.

It is now June, and the crunch has come. The regular IPRC review requested a full assessment of all students in the gifted primary group, because board policy shifts placements at grade 4 to a regular class placement with enrichment provided off-site for one day a week. Kyle and one classmate are below criterion for the weekly enrichment program on all markers but one (parent nomination). Board policy gives the IPRC latitude to withdraw Kyle's identification as gifted.

His parents are now appealing on two bases: first, that assessments of children Kyle's age (7.9) are unreliable; and second, that denying him the additional opportunity offered to the other students will damage his self-esteem and limit his opportunities to progress. The school board says that, by its widely accepted standards, Kyle's abilities do not merit the enrichment program. The Appeal Board must now make its recommendations.

Triarchic Theory of Intellectual Giftedness

Robert Sternberg has offered special education two multiple views of giftedness (Sternberg, 1997). In the first, his triarchic theory, he posits three kinds of intelligence as necessary for giftedness:

- analytic: particularly analytic reasoning and reading comprehension (the intelligence most likely to be measured by traditional IQ tests)
- synthetic: creativity, intuition; response to invention, novelty, and coincidence
- practical: ability to apply one or both of the above pragmatically

Most people have all three kinds of intelligence in their makeup, but a central part of giftedness, in this theory, is the act of coordinating the three and knowing when to use which one. A person who is gifted, then, is a competent self-manager. Such an individual not only knows what and how better than most, but also knows better where and when to use what and how. One reason for the positive reception of Sternberg's position among teachers is its appeal to the notion that creativity, adaptiveness, and old-fashioned common sense and shrewdness play a major role in gifted behaviour.

Pentagonal Implicit Theory of Giftedness

Sternberg presents another theory of giftedness that offers criteria held as implicitly valuable in a culture. The five criteria are excellence, rarity, productivity, demonstrability, and value (see table 10A). Educators who give credence to this theory are led to consider first what their culture holds dear before they propose to set out a definition of giftedness.

If nothing else, this is a theory that goes a long way toward answering a frequent criticism of education for the gifted: namely, that it ignores gifted potential in minorities because of a prejudice in favour of the dominant culture. It also adds background light to the charge that most people interested in education for the gifted, both implicitly and explicitly, limit that interest to elements that our society values most. That is to say: In our education system, to be gifted as a writer of poetry, or to be a virtuoso violinist, has more value than to be a gifted cabinetmaker because the former reflect the dominant cultural view.

A Summary Adaptation of the Pentagonal Implicit Theory		
Criterion	Explanation	Example
Excellence	Superior in some way to age peers	Writes narrative fiction much better than peers with same schooling
Rarity	Ability infrequent at age/peer level	Not just better at fiction but usually superior
Productivity	Individual produces	Other writers recognize superior skill
Demonstrability	Proven in a public way	Wins awards of consequence
Value	Ability is valued by society	Recognized by the culture in public ways

Table 10A

Multiple Intelligences (Gardner Theory)	
Type	Manifestation
1. Linguistic	Exceptional ability to use words, often prolific
2. Musical	Uncommon sensitivity to pitch, rhythm, timbre, often without training
3. Logical/Mathematical	Rapid problem solving, grasp of underlying principles of causal systems, extraordinary ability to handle long chains of data
4. Spatial	Transforms easily among elements, superb mental imagery, very highly developed perception of pattern
5. Bodily/Kinesthetic	Poise and control of body and movement evident even before training
6. Interpersonal	Capacity to "read" people even without language
7. Intrapersonal	Very mature sense of self
8. Naturalist*	Sensitivity to nature and ability to recognize and classify natural things
*A recent addition. It has not been accepted as enthusiastically as the initial seven.	

Table 10B

Multiple Intelligences: The Gardner Theory

In *Frames of Mind*, Howard Gardner (1983, 1993) proposes a theory of multiple intelligences: linguistic, musical, logical-mathematical, spatial, bodily-kinesthetic, interpersonal, intrapersonal, and naturalist (see table 10B). The theory holds that each of these intelligences is independent in function and that, if one intelligence is more powerfully developed than another, it will take over for a weaker or less developed one. (Gardner originally developed the theory while studying stroke patients.)

Gardner's very persuasive writings, supported by interesting research, emphasize the multifold aspect of human intelligence, illuminating yet again the inadequacy of IQ testing with its implied notion of intelligence as a single, internal construct.

His work has been instrumental in expanding the view that there is considerable development and plasticity in human growth. Further, even though this plasticity may be modulated by genetic constraints, humans are predisposed to certain intellectual operations and styles of operation, all of which can be addressed by education.

The Gardner theory has particular appeal to teachers, perhaps because it reflects, much more than other notions, the wide variety of abilities that they see in a classroom full of students. Not only that, but a theory of multiple intelligences reinforces the natural disposition of teachers to promote self-esteem in their students by recognizing that the world has room for many kinds of talent.

On the other hand, the theory has also been criticized as a first step in the demise of education for the gifted, for, as the definition becomes broader, it has the effect of eliminating any distinction that giftedness may have.

Emotional Intelligence

A view advanced by Daniel Goleman (1995; 1997) concludes that star performers owe their superiority to what he calls emotional intelligence. According to Goleman, this intelligence is found in people skills: social radar, political sensitivity, trustworthiness, empathy in personal relationships, and the team-building ability to create opportunity out of diversity. The theory was developed out of a survey of personnel in over five hundred organizations worldwide. Although it enjoys an exceptionally enthusiastic reception in business and industry, the theory does not have the same appeal to education. Some argue that educators are reticent because the theory appeared first in the popular press instead of acquiring official sanction through initial exposure in academic publications.

The Importance of a Balanced View

The varied explanations of giftedness (there are others beyond those summarized above) both plague and enrich the attempts of educators and parents to define giftedness and properly identify its candidates. Nevertheless, because these views tend to lead away from the notion of giftedness as a single construct (the IQ notion) toward a view of giftedness as an expression of several contributing factors, students are beginning to be more fairly identified. Above all, the idea of giftedness as a construct standing on a number of foundations gives more credence and importance to creativity, to commitment, and to the expression of ability in ways other than the narrow confines allowed by academic achievement alone.

Some Issues in the Field

✦ *Being practical in gifted identification?*
Whether one is identified as gifted may, in some cases, be more a matter of pragmatics than pedagogy. A school board with the ability to provide funding for schools for the performing arts may differ in terms of identification procedures from other boards.

Strangely, numbers of students identified as gifted in a board have also been known to vary depending on the number of seats available in a specialized setting. One year the cutoff may be 130 in terms of IQ but the next year, depending on numbers, it may have to be 135.

✦ *Discrimination and gifted identification?*
Researchers and educators alike are becoming increasingly concerned about the underrepresentation of particular groups within the category of giftedness. Persons with disabilities, students who are culturally different, and students who have low socio-economic status are often excluded from classes for the gifted due in part to the narrow identification procedures employed by some school boards. Heavy reliance on IQ measures, for example, can present difficulties for students who have learning disabilities, as well as for those with sensory impairment.

The lack of instruments normed on such groups suggests that the scores obtained by students with disabilities may not be representative of their actual ability. Certainly, continuing discussions, ongoing research, and adjustments to practice have indicated a growing awareness of the limitations of a traditionally narrow definition of giftedness. In many school systems there is still underrepresentation of minority populations as well as persistent calls for the development of a broader and more inclusive definition of what it means to be gifted.

✦ *Separate classes?* How to deal with students once they have been identified as gifted is a continuing debate. At one time, the heat arose primarily over whether the students should be placed in separate classes. Proponents of this approach argue that a totally separated (but not totally isolated) environment can offer a much more enriched experience in which the students are challenged by interchange with others like themselves, by teachers trained to work with this population, by an atmosphere of intellectual ferment, and by the momentum of exclusivity where elevated goals are obtained.

On the other hand, there are also strong arguments in favour of inclusion. A principal tenet holds that, although segregated environments may be successful, they are so specialized as to be unrealistic and are, therefore, counterproductive. By extension, experience in a rarified environment may mean that the student who is gifted will be ill prepared to perform effectively in the real world. Ultimately, like most arguments over this issue, the question of whether to congregate students who are gifted in special schools or include them in regular classes will never be fully resolved, not least because of the politics involved.

✦ *How to program?* When decisions have been taken to maintain students who are gifted in the regular class, a next stage of issues inevitably arises over how to provide the proper program.

One camp argues for enrichment: providing special activities within a regular class setting for selected students. Differentiated instruction and universal design for learning provide a vehicle for the types of specialized, yet everyday, instruction that teachers provide for all learners in their classes.

Proponents argue that this type of instruction and these flexible learning opportunities, within the regular class, provide multiple outlets for expression and learning not only for students identified as gifted but also for their classmates.

Detractors state that enrichment really does not qualify as education for the gifted, because students who are gifted in regular programs can often suffer because of the myth that they can easily teach themselves. They also point out that what passes for enrichment often just means being provided with a greater quantity of the same work, or being used as tutors, or being given busy work.

Another camp argues for a more specialized style, ability grouping, which is also offered in an inclusive environment in which the gifted are selected for instruction in more or less homogeneous groups. Supporters of this style usually advance the separate classes argument described above, while detractors say that ability grouping fosters elitism.

A third camp argues for acceleration (e.g., skipping a grade). This is one of the least-used programming methods, usually because of the fear of negative social and emotional consequences for the accelerated student.

Many school boards are moving away from any self-contained programming for students who are identified as gifted. This change in service delivery is influenced by a growing recognition within the field of education that separate does not always mean better, even for students who are gifted.

✦ *Limits to the category?* Advocates of education for the gifted wince at the fact that, despite the broadening of the concept, programming for talent (such as unusual ability in music, or athletics, or drama, or the visual arts) continues to be a poor relative in most school boards. Because these abilities are not necessarily accompanied by superior academic achievement, the issue is, first, whether to classify them as examples of giftedness; and second, and likely far more importantly, how – even whether – to offer programs aimed at developing talents.

An increasing practice in larger jurisdictions now is to develop "arts schools" for talents that come under this rubric. However, admission to these excellent academies is often tied to superior academic achievement. Also, distance means students in rural areas may have little opportunity to avail themselves of these specialized settings. (It is an interesting comment, too, on our culture, Sternberg's theory notwithstanding, that exceptional ability in areas such as carpentry, or design, or other trades receive little or no accommodation under the rubric of giftedness.)

The Case of Lydia

AT a professional development day, one of Lydia's former primary teachers (grades 1 and 2) met the girl's grade 8 teacher in her new school and was surprised to hear that Lydia, one of her brightest students ever, was "just getting by."

"Lydia can certainly handle the curriculum," the grade 8 teacher said, "and she's truly a pleasant young person – wonderful with the little children in our tutoring program, a natural who teaches as well as we do – but yes, just getting by. The work's always done, and on time. Adequate, but not much more than that.

"I've always felt she could do better," the teacher continued, "but I've got a big class. The truth is, I'm in my first year and I'm having a busy time. I just can't get around to her as I'd like to, especially with some of the demanding students I've got."

The conversation piqued the grade 8 teacher's curiosity, however, and he soon uncovered the fact that Lydia had been identified gifted in grade 4 in her former school, but neither her placement nor her program had changed at the wish of the family who had conveyed their instructions via the parish priest. Lydia's family had immigrated to urban Ontario from a mountain village in southern Europe when she was a little girl. Her parents still do not speak English and, until now, their parish priest has been their interlocutor with schools and other officials. The grade 8 teacher was also told that Lydia's grade 4 teacher, a committed feminist, had been transferred to another school after she had defiantly attempted to enrich the girl's program.

Without authorization or permission, the grade 8 teacher informally administered an achievement test to Lydia and discovered that, according to the test, she was capable of grade 11–12 work in language and even in math, although she had not yet been exposed to that subject in any significant way.

"A waste," he said to the primary grade teacher a few weeks later. "A shame and a waste. Lydia should have enrichment. Isn't there anything that can be done here?"

✦ *Gifted education for primary?* An enduring argument in the field thrives over the issue of offering programs for the very young. Many boards of education are reluctant to formally identify students in the primary grades as gifted and equally reluctant to authorize differentiated programs for them. This attitude has taken hold, first of all, because the developmental elasticity so typical from ages four to five to eight to nine can make confident identification difficult. Secondly, since primary education is usually very adaptive, flexible, and more individualized, students who are gifted can be easily accommodated in the mainstream. Further, in primary education there is an importance attached to social skills that in some schools takes precedence over even the development of academic and cognitive skills.

✦ *Building a labyrinth?* The field of education for the gifted is regularly accused of burying itself in complexity, with inordinately interwoven and complicated models for identification, equally intricate models for programming, and constant, complicated self-examination.

There is empirical evidence to support this accusation. Some boards in Ontario, for example, while recognized for their commitment to educating students who are gifted, have such amazingly intricate and time-consuming patterns of identification – and programs to match – that conceivably some students may not be receiving an appropriate program for the simple reason that they (or their parents) lack the will or the means or the stamina to crawl through the bureaucratic web.

"Termites"

Lewis Terman, sometimes referred to as the father of education for the gifted, did much to develop the founding knowledge base for this population. Between 1922 and 1928, Terman and his colleagues, using standardized intelligence testing, identified approximately 1,500 children as gifted. Researchers tracked these children (in later years known as "Termites") for three-quarters of a century. The results did much to dispel the myth of the weak, fragile, brainy child. The findings of the long-term studies indicated that, as well as being intellectually superior, the subjects were also superior socially and psychologically and were healthier physically.

How Students Are Nominated for Gifted Programs

All school boards in the province, whatever their respective policies regarding the nomination of candidates for education for the gifted, use a number of different methods for making determinations. Usually, a board relies on a combination of elements like the ones listed here.

1 Despite the acknowledged weaknesses of IQ tests, they continue to dominate as a screening device. What is administratively attractive about IQ tests is that they produce a quantified statement, a number, irrespective of whatever else they offer, and, in most jurisdictions, this number becomes a convenient entry-level border for admission to programs. The established figure varies from one school board to another. (Figures of 135 and 130 Full Scale Score on the Wechsler Intelligence Scale for Children are typical.) The work of such people as Sternberg and Gardner notwithstanding, faith in tradition has not yet been seriously shaken. Rationales for the continued reliance on a number include the presumed fairness of using an objective measure, the high correlation between IQ testing and academic strength, and good old-fashioned test mystique! Detractors argue that IQ tests discriminate against students who are culturally different and students with disabilities.

2 Tests of creativity are sometimes used to identify students who are gifted, especially in jurisdictions where creative behaviours are given credence as a major cluster. However, because the validity of these tests is so much in question, their use has less impact, generally, than IQ test scores and teacher, parent, and peer nominations.

3 Achievement tests are used as initial screening mechanisms for giftedness much in the same way as in the assessment of delayed performance. In typical practice, the student who scores significantly above his or her age level (usually two or more grades) is a potential candidate for programming for the gifted. The downside of singular reliance on these types of achievement measures is the potential elimination of students who are gifted underachievers or carry a dual diagnosis such as gifted and LD, either of which could have a serious impact on scores of academic measures.

4 The development of a portfolio has gained popularity recently with educators as a more comprehensive way to assess a student's potential giftedness. Composed of a collection of representative work, a portfolio can display talents over time and across situations. The information included is generally selected collaboratively between the student and the educator.

Gifted Underachievers?

These are students whose potential is implied by significant achievement or by high IQ test scores, but whose apparent abilities are not realized. Not that they are failures, necessarily. They may well work at grade level. However, if an individual is truly gifted, yet produces at an average level, then it may be reasonable to conclude he or she is an underachiever. On the other hand, lest students who are thought to be superior become tarred with the brush of underachievement, it is important for their parents and teachers to evaluate a number of factors before making a judgment.

Has the student learned to learn? Many very able students "coast" in the early grades because they master classroom demands effortlessly. Then, as the level of challenge increases and more is required, they may not rise to the occasion, either because their confidence is eroded, or more likely, because they have not learned consistent, effective work habits.

Do social factors permit success? Some children deliberately underplay their potential because they do not wish to be singled out. Students who are gifted underachievers also tend to have low self-esteem and peer problems that only exacerbate the underachievement.

Are expectations realistic? Learning is not automatically easy for children who are bright. Sometimes the expectations of the adults in their lives, especially parents, do not match what the children are capable of doing at particular points in their development. Flexibility, communication, addressing skills deficits, and creative programming can greatly assist students who are gifted underachievers in realizing their potential.

Is there a good "fit" between the child and the classroom? An overabundance of busywork, inflexible teaching, low expectations, and an overly competitive classroom environment are factors that contribute to poor achievement by students who are gifted. Some children who are gifted do not fare well in structured environments. Others find it difficult to conform even to the simple demands that are necessary to make a school run efficiently. Such students may well underperform as a result.

---

5 Teacher nomination is a popular method of screening. Many boards require teachers to use a clearly defined rating scale or inventory checklist to substantiate a nomination. One problem with this method is that scales usually correlate the academic behaviour of students with what is expected of them academically in the succeeding years (inevitably raising the concern that students who "play the game" are more likely to have an advantage).

6 Parent nomination is used by many school boards on the quite reasonable premise that parents have the best knowledge of their child's development. Although parent nomination is clearly a beneficial factor in the process of selection, educators must keep in mind that parents often lack opportunity for the wider view when assessing their own child's current and potential success in school.

What seems gifted ability at home may not seem so when compared with abilities across a whole class.

7 Peer nomination is yet another method for initiating referral. Although experts in the field have been favourable in their attitude to this style, there is still a serious lack of research to support it.

8 Self-nomination is most effective with older students who display specific types of talents. Very often a self-nomination accompanies a nomination by teacher or parent and, more often than not, is presented because the student has been asked to do so by one or both of the latter.

> *"The most gifted members of the human species are at their creative best when they cannot have their way."*
>
> – Eric Hoffer

B Y the end of the second grade, Colin's pranks had already made him a legend in his school. At first, most of the staff were willing to see the funny side. The upset he caused with his first major foray, for example, by putting what appeared to be soiled facial tissues (he used camembert cheese) on the tables at the school bake sale, was forgiven with chuckles. So was the time he upped the ante with seemingly used toilet tissue in his classmate's lunch boxes. However, everyone was less than amused when, during the return from a fire drill, Colin somehow convinced the entire junior kindergarten class to hide in the janitor's storeroom. Nor was the principal too pleased when Colin attached an inflated condom to the parents' notice board in the entrance hall.

Inevitably, the litany of mischief gradually became more serious. Colin discovered that he could bring police to the school by activating the overnight security system with a handheld laser pointer. On one occasion, he pulled the fire alarm at dismissal time and, in the ensuing chaos, disabled two school buses by plugging their tail pipes with Styrofoam. It was a carefully planned endeavour, for the plugs were precut to size and the chosen vehicles were at the very front and very back of the bus lineup. When a large order of pizza arrived at the school during the first week of school in grade 3, it was widely concluded that Colin was warming up for another year and that something would have to be done.

Serendipity intervened, at this point, in the combination of an educational assistant with three years' experience in a class for the gifted and a teacher with a passion for Renaissance art. In response to a group project they devised for the class, Colin produced a mural that duplicated da Vinci's *The Last Supper*, but from a ground-level perspective. Thirteen very large pairs of feet exactly paralleled the positioning of the famous work! Among the reactions to this mural was the educational assistant's strong push to have Colin assessed for giftedness. The outcome confirmed her intuition. He was found to be off the scale in creativity and very superior in IQ test results. As well, Colin became caught up in the "Renaissance passion," and the pranks stopped, or at least went on hold.

Plans are now underway to accommodate Colin's needs in the regular class with support, but programming is a challenge, and Colin's teacher feels overwhelmed. She has referred this to the In-school Team. Everyone is concerned that if Colin is unchallenged, ever-more-serious pranks will return.

Organizational Models

Organizing the Students: Programming and Placement Options

It is quite common practice for boards to organize students identified as candidates for education for the gifted into differing levels in terms of the provision of services. While terminology may vary, students are usually differentiated by ability and placed in, generally, one of three groups.

The largest group will likely spend most of its time in the regular classroom but will receive some enriched or differentiated curriculum. This may be in the form of a theme study undertaken independent of, but in addition to, the regular curriculum.

The classroom teacher may be helped by a resource teacher, or the latter may have responsibility for the venture entirely on his or her own. (Many schools encourage the teacher and resource teacher to co-operate and to involve all of the students in the class as much as possible.)

The second group may also be assigned to a regular class, but may be withdrawn more frequently for independent pursuits under the guidance of a resource teacher. These students may also be somewhat more involved in projects that involve several schools at once and that culminate in special presentations, workshops, etc.

The third group is more likely to be in separate classes in which the entire curriculum is differentiated.

Organizing the Programs

School boards invest considerable time and effort in developing organizational models to fulfill programming requirements for students who are gifted. One immediate outcome is that the programs are thus established on a broad basis so that there can be a good deal of interaction among schools with sharing of resources, expenses, etc. To a greater extent, too, than in most other areas of special education, there tend to be more board-wide excursions, co-operative projects, and involvement with what the community at large has to offer. Whether a board formally divides its students who have been designated as gifted as described above depends on the delivery of program service around a particular style or model.

Following is a discussion of some of the models that continue to be in popular use in Ontario. Almost without exception, they are implemented with local variations.

The Enrichment Triad

With modifications, the Enrichment Triad (Renzulli, 1977) continues to be very widely used in the province, indeed throughout Canada. It proposes three levels of activity.

- General exploratory activities: designed to expose students to exciting topics, ideas, and fields of knowledge not ordinarily covered by the regular curriculum. There are extras such as visiting speakers, field trips, demonstrations, and interest development centres.
- Group training activities: methods, materials, and instructional techniques designed to develop thinking processes, research and reference skills, and personal and social skills.
- Individual or small-group investigations: students investigate real problems and topics using appropriate methods of inquiry.

An important modification of the Enrichment Triad is the Revolving Door Identification Model (Renzulli & Reis, 1986). In this model, the resource room teacher is a consultant and the classroom teacher is directly involved in the students' special projects. Students are not permanently in or out of the program, but can apply for special consideration to work on projects of their own choosing. The resource teacher helps the student frame the area of interest into a researchable problem, suggests where the student can find appropriate methodologies for pursuing the problem, such as a professional inquirer, helps the student to obtain appropriate resources, provides assistance and encouragement, and helps find appropriate outlets and audiences for the creative work.

Both styles above enjoy more popular use than a third notion developed by Renzulli (1988) called the Multiple Menu Model, which focuses on ways to teach content in efficient and interesting ways.

Twice-exceptional Learners

A term coined by James Gallagher, "twice-exceptional," refers to students who are both gifted and disabled. Generally, these students show patterns of extreme strengths accompanied by significant difficulties. These students are at risk of underachievement as well as misidentification. Unfortunately, the make-up of school systems can place educators in a position to choose only one type of programming or identification, an unfortunate dilemma for students and educator alike.

Students who are twice-exceptional can be inquisitive and impulsive, have high levels of creativity but poor memory, and display a superior vocabulary but poor work production. These students need programs that focus on their areas of talent, learning opportunities that are flexible and provide compensatory and remedial assistance, as well as, and perhaps most importantly, a nurturing environment that recognizes their unique way of learning.

The Autonomous Learner Model

This is a program developed by Betts and Neihart (1986)* principally for the secondary school. It adapts to the departmentalized structure of high schools and anticipates that students will be withdrawn for single periods at specified times of the week. The student progresses through five stages:

1 orientation
2 individual development: learning the attitudes and concepts necessary for lifelong learning
3 enrichment activities: exploring outside the curriculum, becoming aware of resources
4 seminars: presenting results of personal pursuits and findings to larger groups for evaluation
5 in-depth study: opportunity to pursue an area of interest on a longer-term basis

The Purdue Three-Stage Enrichment Model

This is a half-day or full-day withdrawal program (Feldhausen & Kolloff, 1986), used mostly in elementary schools. The Purdue type of program is popular (under names such as Challenge, Upward Bound, etc.) because it offers enrichment and opportunity without taxing the already scanty resources of many elementary schools. The quality of these programs varies dramatically according to the teacher in charge. There are three basic components:

1 divergent and convergent thinking in which the program concentrates on problem solving, decision-making, forward planning, etc.

---

* Note that almost all of the models listed here continue to undergo modest revisions (with later publication dates), but, in all cases, their basic structures are the same. As it is, very few schools or school boards adopt a model without making adaptations.

2 creative problem solving, which offers strategies and techniques in dealing with real problems
3 development of independent learning, which requires the student to engage in the development of a product through learning and investigation and then to share it with an audience

Other Styles

Here are some other responses to the need for educating students who are gifted use more time-honoured approaches:

◆ *Enrichment in the classroom*: This is a differentiated program of study offering experiences beyond the regular curriculum. This model is delivered by the regular classroom teacher with or without assistance from a consultant or resource teacher.

◆ *Consultant teacher program*: Enriched instruction is provided within the regular classroom by the classroom teacher with the assistance of an educational consultant or specialist (occasionally delivered by the specialist).

◆ *Community mentor program*: Students interact on an individual basis with selected members of the community to study topics of special interest.

◆ *Independent study program*: Projects are supervised by a qualified adult.

◆ *Learning enrichment service*: Generally, this is a networking system that combines many of the above ideas in an organized way.

Stategies for the Classroom

"Achieving potential" is admittedly a buzzword in all of special education, but its use requires no apology for it identifies what special education is all about. The phrase has extraordinary personal and societal significance in the case of students who are gifted.

A program for students who are gifted must be based on the idea of achieving potential and, from that premise alone, proceed to accommodate their unique needs. Part of that program – in some cases perhaps all of it – will be met in the role played by the classroom teacher. Each individual teacher of students who are gifted brings to a program, or a class, or a student, his or her own unique nature, as well as his or her own unique talents and interests and skills and background, all of which, in the right circumstances, go a long way toward fulfilling the notion of achieving potential. In other words, as with any teaching–learning situation, the teacher is the key.

There are, however, certain absolutes to which teachers should subscribe, regardless of their own preferences, styles, and areas of interest. These are planning goals that include the following:

1 *Establish an environment that shows clearly that intelligent thought, analysis, and creativity are valued.*

2 *Encourage students to discover and develop their special abilities.* Provide the time, space, technology, materials, and opportunities for them to do this at the sacrifice, if necessary, of the laid-on curriculum. (In this sense, the teacher is much more of a facilitator than an instructor.) Arrange learning experiences that go beyond the normal acquisition-of-knowledge level. Students who are gifted need to go higher, deeper, and wider in their pursuit of a subject, pushing past the usual limits. Very often the teacher acts as a consultant, using maturity and experience to help the student find a productive critical path or a method of investigation.

3 *Provide opportunities for students to interact with adults, other students, and various experts* so they will be challenged, not just to know about things, but about people, and so they will learn to see their own place and their responsibility in the human connection.

4 *Create an atmosphere in which risk-taking, speculation, and conjecture can be undertaken safely.* The teacher recognizes that trial and error are part of learning and that the only real failures in a classroom are those that erode self-esteem. If the teacher takes risks and fails, the student invariably will learn from this, too.

Readings and Resources

Ambrose, D., Allen, J., & Huntly, S. B. (1994). Mentorship of the highly creative. *Roeper Review, 17*(2), 131–33.

Betts, G. T., & Neihart, M. (1986). Implementing self-divided learning models for the gifted and talented. *Gifted Child Quarterly*, 30 (4), 174–77.

Chamberlin, M. T., & Chamberlin, S. A. (2010). Enhancing preservice teacher development: Field experiences with gifted students. *Journal for the Education of the Gifted, 33*(3), 381–416.

Clarke, B. (2002). *Growing up gifted: Developing the potential of children at home and at school* (6th ed.). Upper Saddle River, NJ: Merrill/Prentice Hall.

Colangelo, N., & Davis, G. A. (1997). *Handbook of gifted education* (2nd ed.). Needham Heights, MA: Allyn & Bacon.

Coleman, M. R. (2005). Academic strategies that work for gifted students with learning disabilities. *Teaching Exceptional Children, 38*, 28–32.

Davis, G. A., & Rimm, S. B. (1998). *Education of the gifted and talented* (4th ed.). Needham Heights, MA: Allyn & Bacon.

Delisle, J. R., & Gailbraith, J. (2004). *When gifted kids don't have all the answers: How to meet their social and emotional needs*. Minneapolis: Free Spirit Publishing.

Del Prete, T. (1996). Asset or albatross? The education and socialization of gifted students. *Gifted Child Today, 19*(2), 24–25, 44–50.

Feldhausen, J. F., & Kolloff, P. B. (1986). The Purdue three-stage enrichment model for gifted education at the elementary level. In J. S. Renzulli (Ed.). *Systems and models for developing programs for the gifted and talented*. Mansfield Center, CT: Creative Learning Press.

Feldman, D. (1993). Child prodigies: A distinctive form of giftedness. *Gifted Child Quarterly, 37*, 188–93.

Fetzer, E. A. (2000). The gifted/learning disabled child: A guide for teachers and parents. *Gifted Child Today, 23*(4), 44–50.

Flint, L. J. (2001). Challenges of identifying and serving gifted children with ADHD. *Teaching Exceptional Children, 33*(4), 62–69.

Ford, D. Y., & Harris, J. J. (Eds.). (1999). *Multicultural gifted education*. New York: Teachers College Press.

Friesen, J. W. (1997). The concept of giftedness in First Nations context. *Multicultural Educational Journal, 15*, 26–35.

Gallagher, J., & Gallagher, S. (1994). *Teaching the gifted child* (4th ed.). Boston: Allyn & Bacon.

Gardner, H. (1983). *Frames of mind: The theory of multiple intelligences*. New York: Basic Books.

Gardner, H. (1993). *Multiple intelligences*. New York: Basic Books.

Gardner, H. (1999). *Intelligence reframed: Multiple intelligences for the 21st century*. New York: Basic Books.

Goleman, D. (1995, 1997). *Emotional Intelligence. Why it can matter more than IQ*. New York: Bantam Books.

Hong, E., Greene, M., & Hartzell, S. (2011). Cognitive and motivational characteristics of elementary teachers in general education classrooms and in gifted programs. *Gifted Child Quarterly, 55*(4), 250–64. doi:10.1177/0016986211418107

Lidz, C. S., & Elliott, J. G. (2006). Use of dynamic assessment with gifted students. *Gifted Education International, 21*(2–3), 151–61. doi:10.1177/026142940602100307

Louis, B., & Lewis, M. (1992). Parental beliefs about giftedness in young children and their relationship to actual ability level. *Gifted Child Quarterly, 36*, 27–31.

Maker, C. J., Nielson, A. B., & Rogers, J. A. (1994). Giftedness, diversity and problem solving. *Teaching Exceptional Children, 27*, 4–19.

Masse, L. (2001). Direction of gifted education in the first decade of the 21st century: A step back, continuity, and new direction. *Journal of Secondary Gifted Education, 12*, 170–73.

Matthews, D. J., & Foster, J. F. (2005). *Being smart about gifted children: A guidebook for parents and educators*. Scottsdale, AZ: Great Potential Press.

Michael-Chadwell, S. (2010). Examining the underrepresentation of underserved students in gifted programs from a transformational leadership vantage point. *Journal for the Education of the Gifted, 34*(1), 99–130.

Montgomery, W. (2001). Creating culturally responsive inclusive classrooms. *Teaching Exceptional Children, 33*(4), 4–9.

Nielsen, M. E., & Higgins, L. D. (2005). The eye of the storm: Services and programs for twice exceptional learners. *Teaching Exceptional Children, 38*(1), 8–15.

Pirto, J. (2001). *"My teeming brain": Understanding creative writers*. Cresskill, NJ: Hampton.

Reis, S. M., & Westberg, K. L. (1994). The impact of staff development on teachers' ability to modify curriculum for gifted and talented students. *Gifted Child Quarterly, 38*, 127–35.

Renzulli, J. S. (1977). The enrichment triad model: A plan for developing defensible programs for the gifted and talented. *Gifted Child Quarterly, 21*(2), 227-33.

Renzulli, J. S. (1988). The multiple menu model for developing differentiated curriculum for the gifted and talented. *Gifted Child Quarterly, 32,* 298–309.

Renzulli, J. S., & Reis, S. M. (1986). The enrichment triad/revolving door model: A school-wide plan for the development of creative productivity. In J. Renzulli (Ed.). *Systems and models for developing programs for the gifted and talented*. Mansfield Center, CT: Creative Learning Press.

Rinn, A. N., Reynolds, M. J., & Mcqueen, K. S. (2011). Perceived social support and the self-concepts of gifted adolescents. *Journal for the Education of the Gifted, 34*(3), 367–96.

Shaywitz, S. E., Holahan, J. M., Freudenheim, D. A., Fletcher, J. H. M., Makuch, R. W., & Shaywitz, B. A. (2001). Heterogeneity within the gifted: Higher IQ boys exhibit behaviors resembling boys with learning disabilities. *Gifted Child Quarterly, 45*, 16–23.

Shore, B. M., Cornell, D. G., Robinson, A., & Ward, V. S. (1991). *Recommended practices in gifted education*. New York: Teachers College Press.

Silverman, L. K. (1994/1995). To be gifted or feminine: The forced choice of adolescence. *Journal of Secondary Gifted Education, 6*(2), 141–56.

Sternberg, R. J. (1997). A triarchic view of giftedness: Theory and practice. In N. Colanelo & G. A. Davis (Eds.). *Handbook of Gifted Education* (2nd ed.). Toronto: Allyn & Bacon.

Sternberg, R. J. (2005). WICS: A model of giftedness in leadership. *Roeper Review, 28*, 37–44.

Sternberg, R. J. (2006). Practical giftedness. *Gifted Education International, 21*(2), 89–98.

Sternberg, R. J., Nokes, K., Geissler, P. W., Prince, R., Okatcha, R., Bundy, D. A., & Grigorenko, E. L. (2001). The relationship between academic and practical intelligence: A case study in Kenya. *Intelligence, 29*, 401–18.

Winner, E. (1996). *Gifted children: Myths and realities*. New York: Basic Books.

Links

Association for Bright Children **http://www.abcontario.ca/**

Government of BC resource guide **http://www.bced.gov.bc.ca/specialed/gifted/**

Kids Source **http://www.kidsource.com/ kidsource/ pages/ed.gifted.html**

Mensa **http://www.mensa.org/**

Teaching Gifted Children **http://www.canteach. ca/links/ linkgifted.html**

11

Students with Intellectual and Developmental Disabilities

"When I first started teaching I knew for certain that kids with developmental disabilities 'belonged' in special classes. Now, so many years later, I can't believe I used to think that way. As a principal in an inclusive school, I see every day that all kids belong in regular classes and that, with support, all children can succeed."

– Gary O., principal

Misconceptions About Intellectual and Developmental Disabilities

1 **Developmental disability is a condition like an illness.**
Development disability is not something one has, like a heart condition, or big feet, or schizophrenia, but rather a state of functioning characterized by limitations in both intelligence and adaptive skills.

2 **An intellectual or developmental disability puts a cap on learning.**
An individual's intellectual functioning is not a static thing. (If it were, the role of education would be much different!) Intensive and early instruction in both academic functioning and adaptive behaviour can make a major difference.

3 **The disabilities occur equally across class and gender.**
Data collected over decades by the American Association on Intellectual and Developmental Disabilities (AAIDD) and others show that, for a variety of reasons, the number of boys identified is greater than that of girls by a factor of five to ten. The disability also has a significantly higher prevalence in children from lower socio-economic classes.

4 **Developmental and intellectual disabilities are reflected in physical appearance.**
Certain groups of students, including many with Down syndrome, do appear physically different from their peers, but the vast majority of students with intellectual or developmental disabilities look just like any other student.

5 **A low intelligence quotient (IQ) test score is evidence of at least borderline disability and means the subject's adaptive skills are below normal.**
An IQ test may predict academic or school matters, but an individual's level of adaptive skills is more a factor of training, motivation, and social environment and generally is not tapped by IQ tests.

6 **Students with intellectual or developmental disabilities are always compliant/difficult.**
Like everyone else, these students experience both happiness and emotional stress and react accordingly. Regardless of a similar label, there is no "always" in the population of individuals with intellectual disabilities.

Definition and Classification

Changes Over Time

For the first half of the twentieth century, significant numbers of people with intellectual and developmental disabilities were housed in large institutions. At this time, the prevailing definition was one established in 1920 by American psychologist H. H. Goddard. Goddard divided the exceptionality into four categories of declining ability, beginning with feeble-minded, followed by moron, idiot, and ending with imbecile.

By the 1950s, Goddard's categories were overtaken by the general term "mental retardation" with adjectives of degree such as "mild," "moderate," "severe," or "profound" added to differentiate. In the minds of those who advocated for using the term "mental retardation," the change represented the best science of the time (and was less offensive than the Goddard terminology). The term, however, was nevertheless loaded with implications, for it suggested an incapacity that is both permanent and comprehensive.

By the end of the twentieth century, this term was pretty much replaced by "intellectual" and "developmental," usually in combination with a "disabilities" or "challenged." This change occurred in part out of a gradual realization that classifying people as retarded is a gross oversimplification that ignores the importance of adaptive behaviour and in part out of a passion for political correctness.

The result has been, by and large, positive. Although there is some confusion, even among professionals, whether terms such as "intellectually disabled" or "intellectually challenged" are most appropriate – or whether either term is as comprehensive as "developmental" – the language reflects a clear shift in attitude. Not just educators and medical professionals but also the public at large now generally view persons with these disabilities as equal citizens in the community, capable of learning and deserving of an education.

The State of Things Today

Regrettably, there is still no universally accepted definition of intellectual and developmental disability. However, a large body of research, along with intense advocacy by interested parties and thoughtful application of empirical evidence by educators, has led to a more or less general acknowledgment that three interrelated factors describe the exceptionality. These are:

1 sub-average intellectual functioning
2 problems in adaptive behaviour
3 both of the above occurring during the developmental period

1 Sub-average Intellectual Functioning

This aspect is usually addressed by using IQ test scores to indicate levels. Prior to 1973, school boards commonly followed the policy of the dominant professional body in the field, the American Association for the Mentally Retarded (AAMR – now called the American Association on Intellectual and Developmental Disabilities [AAIDD]), which recommended an IQ test score of 85 and below as the cutoff for identification as "mentally retarded." This is only one standard deviation below the mean, or norm, of 100. In 1973, the AAMR recommendation was changed to an IQ test score of "approximately 70 to 75," or two standard deviations below the mean, thus significantly lowering the barrier. This change recognized the importance of other factors (such as adaptive behaviour) and reinforced the notion that IQ tests are an aid, not a diagnostic magic wand.

Although there is no "official" set of scores, school boards that use test scores to classify intellectual and developmental disability generally apply the following ranges, each with its own set of general expectations or needs.*

---

* Some jurisdictions correlate IQ ranges with "classification by degree." The four most frequently used terms are "mild," "moderate," "severe," and "profound."

IQ Score	Expectations
Below 25	Student may learn basic self-care and communication skills.
	Full time ed. assistant or tech. support (or both) likely.
	High level of supervision and structure required.
25–40	Part- to full-time support providing instruction for limited independence. Self-help and social skills emphasized.
	Some lifelong assistance likely needed.
	May be able to live in a group home
40–55	With support may learn independent life skills, self-care, and basic academic skills.
	Supervised independence possible.
55–70	Academic achievement to grade 5 or more is possible with intermittent support.
	Secondary school academic-focused programs may present a challenge.
	Can become fairly self-sufficient
	And with community and in some cases, with support, can live independently.

Table 11A

2 Adaptive Behaviour

Generally, adaptive behaviour refers to how well an individual is able to meet – to adapt to – demands made by his or her environment. It is a dynamic construct, one that is influenced by factors such as cultural norms, the demands of a particular situation, and the age group to which the individual belongs. Including adaptive behaviour in the assessment of intellectual and developmental ability, a practice that began in the 1970s, has proven to be instrumental in shaping a more positive view.

Taking adaptive behaviour into account recognizes that many individuals who might score poorly on an IQ test can actually live and learn quite well in a variety of environments. As well, it encompasses recognition of an individual's strengths, not just weaknesses. An assessment of adaptive behaviour, how one fits into his or her academic, social, and family environment, is instrumental in helping to determine the extent and effect of any intellectual and developmental disability and thus the program that will be provided.

The Case of Christina

THE annual review of Christina's case took longer to complete this year because she is in grade 8 and the committee requested a full psychometric assessment. It was the first such undertaking since she was in grade 3, five years ago, and confirmed the assertions of the special education resource teacher in the school that Christina is not only an improved but also an improving student.

Her IQ test score (both verbal and performance) on the Wechsler scale is Low Average to Borderline (as it was in grade 3). But standardized achievement scores show significant gains in academic skills. Christina reads grade 4/5 material comfortably. (She has had a particularly rewarding experience this year as a "reader" in the kindergarten class.) Creative writing is still a challenge, although this may be a physically related issue; Christina has a disabled left arm and is naturally left-handed. Even with the classroom's several computer programs to help her, however, she has trouble writing even minimally coherent prose.

Math gains are significant and measurable. Five years ago, she could not do any basic arithmetic. This year she is working one-on-one with the EA out of the grade 4 textbook.

All of the adults who have immediate contact with and responsibility for Christina – her mother, the grade 8 teacher, and the educational assistant who has known her since grade 6 – confirm independently that she has had "a very happy year." Everyone agrees that this fact is very much a result of efforts to manage her occasional bursts of unusual behaviour, and of the fact that Christina's classmates now accept her completely.

In light of these advances, Christina is going to be promoted to grade 9 and go with her classmates to the neighbourhood secondary school. Christina's mother is very concerned about what the secondary school program will look like and is meeting with the secondary school resource teacher to obtain this information.

3 The Developmental Period

This is the period up to the chronological age of eighteen.

Defining by Support Needed

In 2002, the AAMR (as this association was called at the time) made yet another major revision to its definition of mental retardation, a change that still includes the intellectual functioning, adaptive behaviour, and developmental period factors but that places new emphasis on the importance of supports. A primary purpose in describing an individual's limitations, the association insists, is to develop a profile of needed supports that, over time, will improve that person's life functioning. Rather than classifying an individual according to a pre-existing diagnostic category – usually one tied to available models of service – a supports approach evaluates the person's needs and then tries to find strategies to address those needs.

Although skeptics say there is nothing new in this approach except the name and that it is exactly what effective teachers and educational assistants do when they are given the freedom to act in the name of good common sense, advocates point out that, at the very least, the approach puts the student ahead of the program and the paperwork.

Ontario's Definition

The categories and definitions of exceptionalities, as published in the Ministry of Education's *Special Education: A Guide for Educators* (2001), present two levels of disability: "mild intellectual" and "developmental," the difference in degree being implicit in the terms (see appendix I for the complete definitions). Using both the "intellectual" and "developmental" terms, rather than confusing matters, makes the issue of classification administratively simpler. At the same time, the expansion of each term is worded in a manner that anticipates practical response without adding undue complexity. Such a positive accomplishment is relatively rare in government literature. These terms, however, are open to interpretation by boards of education, and there are discrepancies across the province with regard to which students may belong in a particular category.

"My first year, and I get not one, but two developmental kids in my class! I have to be honest; at the end of September, I was going to quit. Sure glad I didn't, though. Now that I've had some time, well … it's no different from having any other kids in your class. Not really. But then, these two were pretty good kids. I sure could have used more time on special kids in my teacher training. We never talked about them enough, and well …"

– Alexandra P.

Some Issues in the Field

✦ *Terminology*: An abiding concern is what to call an intellectual disability – or whether to call it anything at all! Part of the tension arises out of the desire of administrators, researchers, clinicians, and academics to have a neutral, scientific, and widely accepted term to identify a consonant group for their various purposes. Balanced against this desire is the far less scientific but equally important desire of parents and advocates to expunge terminology from the field for the simple reason that descriptive terms for this exceptionality, no matter how carefully they are chosen, invariably seem to imply limitations and, very rapidly, are adopted for pejorative use in popular parlance. There appears to be no simple way out of this dilemma. To professionals, terminology is part and parcel of scientific, educational practice.

In 1993, the Ontario Ministry of Education changed the label for this population. For many years, students with limited intellectual and developmental abilities in Ontario schools were referred to as "trainable retarded" or "educable retarded," depending on the degree of intellectual and developmental limitation. But in the mid-1990s these terms were changed to "developmental disabilities" and "mild intellectual disabilities" (for the specific definition of these terms, see appendix I).

Recently, as mentioned above, the American Association on Mental Retardation, a highly respected organization representing professionals in this field, changed its name to the American Association on Intellectual and Developmental Disabilities. Though the term "mental retardation" is still used throughout North America, a change of terminology is slowly gaining acceptance.

The Case of Robyn

At age seven, Robyn spent several months in a day program at a development centre but then became ill (she has severe respiratory problems) and remained at home where she was visited daily by a special services at-home worker. At age eight, she attended her neighbourhood school in a regular grade 1 for three weeks but, with the agreement of her parents, was transferred to a special resource class full time. This placement continued until grade 4, when she was gradually integrated into a regular class. Robyn moved with her classmates to grade 5 and spent that year with them. She is now in grade 6.

Robyn is identified as seriously developmentally disabled. Her language abilities are below age norms. Her speech is babyish and mostly in the third person, e.g.: Teacher: "Hi, Robyn! How are you today?" Robyn: "Robyn OK." She does not seem to be able to read but greatly enjoys being read to. She does not participate in any meaningful way in the curriculum; however, she likes to be part of a group when it pursues a task and enjoys being paired with other students when seat work or other individualized tasks are assigned.

Attempts to present "parallel curriculum" have been singular failures. Since grade 4, Robyn has never once worked on her own. She seems content only when she is part of others' endeavours. An occasional exception to this behaviour is her willingness to spend time at an art table where she will colour with crayons and magic markers. But she tends to have temper tantrums when she tires of this activity if she is not immediately diverted. Robyn destroyed a keyboard when she became bored with a computer program.

Until now (February of grade 6), the fact that there is no assistant available to this class (and will not be) has been blunted by the willingness of two classmates, both girls, to befriend, guide, and patiently assist

---

Robyn. But almost simultaneously, the two – in the words of their teacher – "have just discovered boys" and now actively avoid her, not just inside the classroom, but outside, too.

Robyn's tantrums are now frequent and severe, and her skills have regressed. Motivated, at least in part, by complaints from parents of other children, the principal has called for an IPRC review. At the committee's first meeting, Robyn's mother made it clear that she will not agree to a special class placement. The committee has asked the school, as a first step, to prepare a new IEP for Robyn, working within the resources presently available.

✦ *Normalization*: The principle of normalization suggests that people with disabilities should be seen for their similarities with their non-exceptional peers rather than their differences and be interacted with in a manner consistent with these individuals' strengths, not their weaknesses or diagnostic label. They should be allowed to thrive in the larger society to the maximum possible extent consistent with their chronological age and adaptive ability.

Though this principle is widely accepted today, in the nineteenth century the gradual development of institutions to care for persons with intellectual and developmental disabilities was regarded as a major step forward. And no doubt it was, for institutions that offered care when the alternative was often abandonment reflected a degree of social and moral responsibility hitherto unknown. But institutions have a potentially insidious nature. For reasons of economy, ease of management, and sometimes ignorance, the environment in an institution is often impoverished in terms of stimulation and opportunity. Given what special educators now know about human development, it is apparent that many of the behaviours historically associated with a disability are consequences of institutional living.

With the growing trend toward deinstitutionalization, individuals with intellectual and developmental disabilities, for the most part, are living in their homes with their families and attending their neighbourhood schools where the necessary supports are provided. When they complete their education, the very large numbers of people with disabilities live in the mainstream, many of them on their own or with some supervision, many with gainful employment who acquire and enjoy the benefits of education.

✦ *Inclusion*: Ontario classrooms are quite diverse, containing students from different cultures, socio-economic backgrounds, languages, and learning abilities. The inclusion of students with limited intellectual and developmental disabilities, once thought revolutionary, has now become commonplace.

The emphasis on Universal Design for Learning contained in the *Education for All* document (Ontario Ministry of Education, 2005) and the draft of *Learning for All, K–12* (Ontario Ministry of Education, 2009) clearly supports the principle of inclusion: that is, keeping all students in the regular classroom as the preferred instructional location.

Including persons with intellectual and developmental disabilities, without reservation, in mainstream society is still an issue, in large part because of conflict that seems to arise out of the impatience of the supporters of inclusion and the guarded hesitancy of the larger society. At the most liberal end of the spectrum are those who argue that all persons should be fully included in society immediately, most especially in schools. The view is that total inclusion at once is the only possible position that a society can morally and ethically adopt. Regrettably, this position often sets up an adversarial context, particularly when educators argue that for some students a modified school environment may produce better results.

It is not that educators reject inclusion, but rather that some prefer a more cautious approach or are concerned that appropriate supports are not provided. Teachers regularly argue that students should be considered on an individual basis, for not all students are ideally suited for immediate inclusion, particularly if resources and support are not in place in the inclusive setting. Unfortunately, the different perspectives often harden because, instead of being able simply to recommend this position, educators are made to defend it and find themselves using arguments that can be interpreted as pro-segregation, whether or not this is indeed what they believe. The risk for students is that the significant developments of the past few decades are sometimes jeopardized by hasty decisions, emotion, polemics, and blanket policies.

Empirical evidence shows that, generally, children who begin their school lives in inclusive classrooms treat that environment as natural. And, most of the time, the inclusion is successful and continues to be so for all children as they grow. Where success is limited is in those situations in which the inclusion does not start until later grades, where it is arbitrary, and where supports are not provided.

◆ *Time to learn*: Early theory held that a developmental or intellectual disability implied an absolute limit to potential. This notion was handily reinforced by supposed empirical evidence (especially bizarre behaviours that often turned out to be institutional behaviours) and by notions of incurability. Especially since the success of the normalization movement, it has become

evident that, with stimulation, support, and direct instruction, there is literally no limit to students' learning capacity. However, the process for some students takes longer. They are learners, but they are slower learners. The time factor becomes an issue because many jurisdictions make school enrolment terminal (usually tied to chronological ages of students) either through funding limitations or simply by decree. While continuing education programs go a long way toward circumventing this problem, it is still an issue that has not yet been satisfactorily resolved by school boards and governments.

Prerequisites to Successful Inclusion

Almost two decades ago, Scruggs and Mastropieri (1994) offered a lucid and comprehensive summary of useful research that identified seven factors as crucial to successfully integrating students with special needs. Interestingly, these elements remain as important today as when first identified. They are:

▶ administrative support
▶ support from special education personnel
▶ accepting, positive classroom atmosphere
▶ appropriate curriculum
▶ effective general teaching skills
▶ peer assistance
▶ disability-specific teaching skills

◆ *Employment and vocational training*: In the past, and periodically now, but with much less frequency, some adults with intellectual and developmental disabilities have found employment in industries described as "sheltered workshops," where they are paid for relatively simplistic and repetitive industrial tasks. On one side of this issue is the appreciation that these adults are thus given an opportunity to contribute to their own support by a gainful activity that is within their capacity under supervision. On the other side is an opinion that such employment is exploitation and is simply an unsubtle extension of institutionalization. The issue is an awkward and difficult one to resolve in a free economy, and proponents of both sides are able to refer to many practical examples that support their respective arguments.

For educators, the disagreement is uncomfortable, since they must resolve for themselves the importance of this potential employment when determining learning objectives for their students. As acceptance of individuals with intellectual and developmental disabilities is increasing in society, opportunities in the private sector are also increasing. Through the development of co-op programs and school-to-work transition programs, individuals with intellectual and developmental disabilities are able to demonstrate what they can do in the workforce, and, as a result, in many cases they are obtaining gainful employment.

◆ *Greater challenge in the classroom*: Changes in definition, especially the lowering of the "IQ cutoff"; changes in placement, especially including students in classrooms; as well as the steadily growing awareness that people who are intellectually and developmentally disabled are learners mean that teachers and educational assistants today encounter greater numbers of students with special needs in their classrooms. Although few would disagree with the premise that these changes have been positive, at the same time the shift has not been without impact. For example, Ontario's category of disability called "educable mentally retarded," now called "mild intellectual disability" (referring to an IQ test score approximately two standard deviations below the mean), were almost always segregated in separate classrooms with separate, dedicated programs whereas currently, students identified under this category are generally found in regular classes with support.

Today, while progress has been made in terms of inclusion, students with developmental disabilities remain the most segregated of all special needs populations in the province. In school boards that practice inclusion, students with more severe intellectual and developmental disabilities are placed in regular classrooms, often with the support of an educational assistant. Whether an assistant is provided or not, the teacher is ultimately responsible for the student's program and for assessing how well that program is being achieved.

Should Cause Be a Concern for Educators?

Although insight into the reason for a particular student's disability may satisfy intellectual curiosity and the natural desire to know as much as possible about a student in order to support the student effectively, several factors diminish the value of this knowledge.

The amount of hard science in the field, not to mention theory and speculation, is extensive and bewildering, even to medical specialists. Causes range from trauma (e.g., anoxia at birth) to chromosomal abnormality (e.g., Down syndrome, tuberous sclerosis, Klinefelter syndrome) to metabolic (e.g., phenylketonuria, Prader-Willi syndrome) to infectious/toxic conditions in the pregnant mother (e.g., rubella, syphilis, alcohol, cocaine). More than one name is used for some conditions (e.g., epiloia for tuberous sclerosis), and, very often, the terms are poorly or incompletely described or are presented in language that is comprehensible only to the thoroughly initiated.

Scientific complexity regarding causes is problematic not only because of the confusion it can create but also because a practical educational response can rarely be inferred from a description of cause. Even worse, it is not unknown for a child's case to be given up as educationally hopeless on the basis of a scientific description of cause.

For these reasons, some educators argue that causes should be tendered only for very compelling reasons. (Boards of Education in Ontario, as a matter of practice, if not official policy, do not state the cause of a student's disability on the record unless it has treatment implications.)

The Special Case of Down Syndrome

One area of disability in which cause may have significance for educators is the chromosomal difference called Down syndrome, estimated to account for 5 percent to 6 percent of all cases of intellectual retardation. Students with Down syndrome are often recognizable because of certain common characteristics such as a generally smaller stature, thick epicanthal folds in the corners of the eyes, and a smaller oral cavity that results in a protruding tongue. (Less easily noticed, but typical, are speckling of the iris, a wide gap between the first and second toes, and a single palmar crease on short, broad hands.)

These physical factors provoke an issue of importance when they are juxtaposed with a typical factor that is non-physical. Most persons with Down syndrome are in the mild to moderate range of intellectual limitation and have generally been shown to have what is called "trait plasticity" (malleable intelligence). Research suggests their early development is normal, particularly in infancy, although it seems to slow as they age. Thus, because the physical aspects of Down syndrome are quite recognizable, it would be a mistake to assume automatically, as many uninformed people do, that a child with the syndrome is intellectually limited and, ipso facto, incapable.

A second issue accruing to Down syndrome comprises the physical health factors of which teachers and assistants should be aware. Persons with Down syndrome are at greater risk of congenital heart defects and upper respiratory infections. Many have hyperflexible joints with a high potential for orthopedic injury. Taken together or singly, these characteristics have implications for what goes on in a classroom or schoolyard.

Instructional Implications

As with all students, students with intellectual and developmental disabilities bring with them to class a variety of characteristics that teachers need to take into consideration when designing their students' program. Students in this category usually require new material to be taught in a variety of ways and then need much drill and repetition (conducted in a motivating manner) to help them retain new information.

In addition, teachers should be aware of the following factors.

Learning and Memory

Problems here, as with other areas, become more marked and more easily observable in tandem with levels of severity, but, in almost all students with intellectual and developmental disabilities, learning and memory problems are usually significant. Specific areas of difficulty include ability to pay attention, verbal communication, motivation, ability to generalize, and the ability to understand similarities and differences.

Quite typical is difficulty with short-term memory. The students do not tend to use memory strategies spontaneously, although they will learn to use mnemonic strategies if explicitly taught to do so. It is important to point out that, once a thing is learned and filed in long-term memory, the students will recall it as well as anyone else when conditions are appropriate.

Learned Helplessness

Poor short-term memory, combined with an apparent lack of motivation and a tendency to be off-task, often leads to a passive pattern wherein the student allows a significant adult (often the EA; sometimes a fellow student) to manage everything. Viewed from the other side, so to speak, the student with disabilities manages to train a significant adult to do everything for him or her simply by being universally passive. Educational assistants often report this behaviour as a recurring problem.

Key Facts About Fetal Alcohol Syndrome (FAS)

▶ Consumption of alcohol by an expectant mother, even in small amounts, can damage a developing fetus leading to an organic disorder generally known as fetal alcohol syndrome (FAS). The disorder very often has a major impact on the child after birth, and, by extension, on his or her parents and teachers.

▶ FAS usually manifests itself in a combination of physical, behavioural, or intellectual problems ranging from minor to very serious. The condition is lifelong.

▶ A number of other terms for the syndrome are in use, fetal alcohol spectrum disorder (FASD) and alcohol-related neurodevelopmental disorder (ARND) being more recent examples. Perhaps most germane for educators is that medical science now tends to distinguish the full-blown syndrome, FAS, from less severe cases by describing the latter as fetal alcohol effects (FAE).

▶ Characteristics associated with FAS and, to a lesser extent, with FAE, are extensive and usually have a major impact on the individual's education and general lifestyle. Physical anomalies are often skeletal, showing up in deformed limbs and growth deficiency and may appear in a range of heart and urino-genital problems. Individuals born with FAS also have a high rate of epilepsy, especially in the early years. Very often, the more severe cases will have a facial appearance not unlike that associated with Down syndrome. Severe learning difficulties and even the inability to live independently as an adult are possible outcomes of FAS. The learning problems typically found in students are similar to those usually classified as developmentally disabled (poor visual scanning, reading problems, inattentive to or unable to absorb detail, difficulty generalizing and deducing, etc.). Indeed, FAS is now considered to be the second major cause of intellectual and developmental disability in Western countries. In addition, significant behavioural problems, such as hyperactivity, indiscriminate forming and severing of bonds or attachments, difficulty expressing emotions, and low rate of task completion, are common.

▶ Medical science has been certain of the effects of alcohol on a fetus only since the 1970s. Research into FAS, therefore, and experience with the syndrome as a separate condition are still fairly slim. Nevertheless, strong evidence already suggests that for an individual with FAS, or even FAE, the manifestations of the condition intensify rather than lessen with age.

▶ Although conclusive data on the prevalence of FAS are still being developed, some estimates are as high as 2 in 1,000 births. These numbers have a sharp relevance for special educators since most of the individuals with the condition may end up in their hands. Even more frustrating to professionals, such as teachers and educational assistants, who must deal with the effects of FAS is that the syndrome is not a genetic accident but an entirely preventable condition.

For the most part, practical classroom response is similar to the methods applied in the case of other students with intellectual and developmental disabilities (see Strategies for the Classroom later in this chapter).

Academic Achievement

It requires little effort to recognize that academic achievement is an issue. Achievement deficits seem to be most pronounced in reading comprehension, arithmetic reasoning, and problem solving. Nevertheless, a steadily growing body of research evidence suggests that time is an important factor.

In many cases, students pass through the same phases of cognitive development as non-disabled students, particularly childhood phases, but do so more slowly and often attain lower levels of achievement. Accordingly, it is safe to infer that many students can and should be taught from the standard Ontario curriculum but their academic learning will be slower and likely less efficient. This fact makes time and regular practice crucial items in the educational planning process.

Speech and Language Problems

The frequency of speech defects is considerably above the norm. Mutism and primitive speech are quite common among those who are severely disabled. Typically, the language level, both oral and written, but especially the latter, is below commonly accepted age norms.

Social Adjustment

Many of the students experience difficulty in social interaction because they do not find it easy to "read" a social setting. It is not uncommon for them to participate inappropriately, perhaps by being inappropriately loud or ebullient, for example. Some students in an inclusive setting may at first function in what is called "parallel existence." That is, because they do not know how to naturally ingratiate themselves with their peers, they simply go along in their own world, without really becoming a part of the general social environment. This behaviour occurs most frequently when students with disabilities and so-called normal students interact with one another for the first time, especially if there has been no preparation. (It is very encouraging, however, to observe a class of very young children. The mutual acceptance one invariably sees forces the conclusion that interactions like this can be natural if inclusion begins early.)

Genetic Research and the Future

Persons with Williams syndrome are usually mildly to moderately intellectually limited (typical IQ test scores are about 60) and have profound difficulties with spatial relationships, abstractions, and logical sequences. They typically have an elfin-like facial structure, an above-average incidence of heart problems, and, very often, hyper-sensitive hearing. At the same time, persons with Williams syndrome have strikingly developed vocabularies, are often warm, compassionate, and outgoing, and – what intrigues researchers most – may have prodigy-level talent in music. What is believed to be the cause of the syndrome was discovered in 1993: the loss of some genetic material on Chromosome 7. Researchers believe that this site also influences concentration levels and visual and spatial skills. Discoveries in this type of research may one day revolutionize education.

Perseveration

Perseveration is the persistent repetition of a specific behaviour. Some individuals develop behaviours that the rest of the world may look on as bizarre and tend to indulge in these behaviours repetitively in times of stress or discomfort. As a consequence, a large part of educational planning is sometimes devoted to teaching self-control. Proponents of inclusion argue – with considerable empirical evidence to support them – that inappropriate behaviours are eliminated more easily and quickly in the mainstream.

Physical

Milestones such as learning to walk, using the toilet, etc., tend to be attained up to nine months or a year later than the norm. There is also a tendency to perform below age-related standards in motor areas, and features of height, weight, and skeletal development are often at the extreme ends of age norms. Persons with moderate (as opposed to mild) disabilities often show even more complex physical differences and tend to be markedly less able motorically. Very often, severe intellectual limitations are part of a multiple set of disabilities suffered simultaneously, with the consequence that simple locomotion and other basic activities become an issue.

Self-injurious Behaviour

Behaviours that lead to harm of a subject's own body is not infrequent, especially among those with severe developmental disabilities. These behaviours cover a wide range such as head-banging, scratching, pinching, hitting, and rectal digging. Unfortunately, research has yet to shed light on the causes of these behaviours or the keys to remediation. Empirical evidence suggests stress and a lack of stimulation as possible causes.

The Importance of Self-help Skills

For obvious reasons, the most immediate of which is physical health, an important part of an education program deals with items such as hygiene, eating, dressing, use of the toilet, physical appearance, etc. While these items will be part of an educational plan only to the extent necessary, and that necessity will vary according to the degree of need, learning these culturally significant skills is nevertheless crucial to a student's sense of well-being and sense of self. For students with intellectual and developmental disabilities, there is much truth in the age-old wisdom that connects feeling good to doing well.

Self-esteem

Self-esteem tends to be low. A combination of discouraging social experience and repeated failure often leads to self-expectations of poor performance. When this expectation is overlaid with learned helplessness, it is easy to understand why students with disabilities avoid or ignore challenging tasks. The "if-at-first-you-don't-succeed-quit" syndrome is tempting and comfortable. Educators must avoid the trap of becoming a controller – the easy route; instead, by judicious encouragement and behaviour modification, they can demonstrate to a student that he or she can do an assigned task and should feel proud because of it.

Transition

As part of the IEP process, all those involved with the student must consider future goals and plan accordingly. Decisions about high school programming, post-secondary education, or entering the community after high school need to be made early. Once these decisions are made, those responsible for the student's education need to implement curriculum and instructional strategies related to these transition expectations. These strategies may lead to co-op programs, adaptive programming, and/or social skill instruction.

Assessment and Classroom Placement

Individually administered tests of intelligence such as the Wechsler Intelligence Scale for Children – IV continue to play a role in the determination of a student's level of intellectual and developmental functioning. However, in practice, anecdotal reports by parents, teachers, and EAs also play an important part in completing a picture of needs. So do a range of instruments known as Rating Scales, Achievement Inventories, Personal Checklists, etc.

These instruments vary in length and nature of information sought, but are similar in principle. They are completed by the individual or by adults who have been able to observe the student in different situations and are able to judge the student's skills in a number of areas. Usually, the skills are rated on a comparative basis (fair, good, excellent, etc.). And, most often, the questions deal with areas of general performance such as family, community and peer relations, self-care skills, cognitive abilities, and so on.

Although these instruments are usually quite

informal and are often constructed locally to meet local needs, published adaptive behaviour scales are available (e.g., Vineland Adaptive Behavior Scales, 2nd Edition, Pearson Assessments). In practice, an Identification, Placement, and Review Committee (IPRC) will quite regularly accept almost any information about a student with developmental and intellectual disabilities when it is making determinations regarding identification and classroom placement.

As tables 3B and 3C, chapter 3, indicate, relatively more students in this area of special need are placed in full-time and part-time self-contained classes, despite the vigour of advocates who favour inclusion. Nevertheless, compared with the days before the passing of the *Education Amendment Act* in 1980, when it was rare for a student with disabilities to attend a regular school, there have been very great changes. Specially dedicated schools for the "mentally retarded," where these students were enrolled – if they went to school at all – for the most part have been closed. Students with intellectual and developmental disabilities, even though some may be placed in special classes, are part of neighbourhood schools now, and by far the majority of students are placed in classes on the basis of what their teachers and their parents together believe is in their best interests.

The Case of Blaine

BLAINE has just completed his first year at secondary school. He is eighteen. Although the school is committed to inclusion, three self-contained classes are available on an ad hoc basis. No one is officially placed in these classes full time, but during the past year four students have spent their entire school time there. For the final quarter of the year, Blaine became the fifth, mostly because of his overwhelming moroseness and his apparent unwillingness to do anything for himself.

In Blaine's medical report, fetal alcohol syndrome is noted as a primary cause of his disability. He also has chronic health problems and spent three years in a hospital school. Academically, Blaine works at approximately the level of a nine- or ten-year-old, but every teacher who has had responsibility for him insists that he is significantly more capable than his output indicates. They are unanimous in the belief that the academic performance gap is a product of an attitude that – also unanimously – they call "learned helplessness."

The school's physical education department has proposed to the In-school Team (IST) that, next year, the senior football team make Blaine one of the school's "inclusion pals." He would be made an honorary player, attend all practices, and be at all games dressed in equipment and uniform. Although he would not actually compete, he would be part of every other activity. Football team members would also be expected to invite Blaine to their social events and involve him after school. The coach did this once before with a special student, Mel, and the project was so successful it attracted enthusiastic reviews from the media.

Blaine's parents, however, are aware of a dark side. When the football team graduated and scattered to universities, colleges, and employment, Mel was, in effect, suddenly abandoned. So traumatic was the experience that he has still not recovered. Mel was then twenty-two, and he, too, left the school, but now his guardian (a grandmother) reports that "… for nigh on a year now he sits, and eats, and stares. Won't talk. Won't look at me. Won't do anything."

Blaine's parents are willing to do anything for their son but want some assurance from the IST that the football team's undertaking will not end up the way Mel's case did and want more information on what the secondary school program will provide.

"I do not want to overly protect him from the norms of society; rather, I want him to learn from his experiences in more challenging social situations. As an example, I mentioned to you about an experience at the drop-in centre when a teen told him 'dude you stink!' This had a bigger impact on shaping his behaviour in a positive way, toward the life skill of proper hygiene, self-care, and how to handle social situations, much more than mom telling him to have a shower and more than a social skills classroom talking about abstract concepts. He is capable of more, he expects more, and I expect more."

– Jennifer K., mom (letter to her son's school)

Strategies for the Classroom

1 The importance of a positive attitude. For teachers and educational assistants working in this area of special need there is a prerequisite understanding that must be accepted for appropriate educational planning and instruction to occur. The prerequisite, quite simply, is a positive attitude: recognition and acceptance that these are students like any others with strengths and needs, likes and dislikes, idiosyncratic behaviours, and a capacity to learn. What distinguishes them, perhaps more than any other trait, is that they tend to learn more slowly. The implications of that slower learning speed (perhaps "learning rate" is better) are significant, but the students can and do learn. Classroom professionals, by nature, accept this, but when they have such students in a class, they need just a bit more of that faith – that quality reflected in the patience, the effort, the flexibility, and the sense of humour that, together with enlightened instruction, make classrooms successful. Without these intangibles – in liberal quantities – no amount of tactic or technique can be effective. The educator, as always, is the key.

2 A collaborative approach. It is common administrative practice to assign educational assistants to classrooms where one or more students with developmental disabilities are enrolled. A principal reason for the popularity of the practice is that, time and again, assistants

have proven their immense value. However, doubling the number of adults in a room does not automatically double the achievements. Whether an assistant is assigned to a whole class or specifically to a student (this latter option has come in for serious criticism as a form of de facto segregation), it is crucial that both teacher and assistant work together in an atmosphere of mutual respect and appropriately shared responsibility.

3 Teamwork. In a similar vein, teachers and assistants recognize that, when students with special needs are in their classes, they are expected to co-operate extensively with other professionals and certainly with parents. In the case of students with developmental or intellectual disabilities, this support circle often widens considerably. Very active involvement by advocacy groups, for example, often leads to the development of a team of key players in a student's life that shares information, ideas, and concerns about that student and then takes some wider responsibility for promoting his or her inclusion in the life of the community. Since school is a major part of a student's community, it is only natural that such a team will often involve and overlap the classroom role. Thus, in addition to their responsibility for individual instruction, teachers and assistants often find themselves part of a larger circle of action that includes other students, parents, and interested members of the community.

4 *Careful attention to structure* both in direct individual instruction and in the general learning environment is another important factor. Experience in both integrated and modified environments suggests that the students are much more comfortable when classroom routines and expectations are regularized. In this case, familiarity breeds not contempt but comfort, and the security engendered by this comfort can usually assure more effective learning. Establishing a structured environment may mean that the teacher or assistant arranges for and continually repeats certain sequences until they are fully assimilated by the students. It may mean temporarily reducing the number of choices a student is expected to make. Very often, a great deal of effort is expended on what, in the grand scheme of things, may seem relatively trivial: colour-coded notebooks, for example, with red for one purpose, green for another, etc. Yet these are precisely the kind of arrangements that protect the students from confusing and overlapping demands and allow them to bring their available cognitive strength to bear on a learning task. Without a carefully established structure in which to learn, students tend to expend a prohibitive amount of energy trying to establish it on their own. In an unstructured environment it is easy to seek the comfort of learned helplessness or perseverative behaviour.

The challenge is finding the right balance of structure and flexibility so that organization does not become more important than learning. An additional challenge is finding this balance in an inclusive classroom where there are many students whose need for a structured and carefully sequenced instruction may not be the same. Professionals in this type of classroom can argue, with considerable authority, that such a placement for a student with serious developmental or intellectual disabilities, despite its benefits, may also mean having to forgo some of the vital learning support that occurs in a carefully arranged structure.

5 An effective practice for all students, and especially for those with cognitive limitations, is *drill and repetition.* However, it is essential that teachers attempt to design drill and repetition in a motivating manner such as through games, puzzles, or activities. The simple fact is that all students seem to need the opportunity to go over material a certain number of times until it is taken in – and students with this disability perhaps more so.

6 *Momentum*, or commitment within the individual, is another concern. Students with a disability regularly and successfully invite others to do their work for them and, equally regularly, back away from challenge and opportunity. Encouragement by significant adults is very important, therefore. In fact, a teacher who establishes a sense of commitment in a student has usually led him or her through one of the most important steps of development.

7 *Use of technology.* Students with intellectual and developmental disabilities can be highly stimulated and helped to maintain attention through the appropriate use of a variety of software designed to meet their instructional needs in language and numeracy. Technologies, including voice creation and voice recognition software, may be very helpful in assisting the instruction of students with limited intellectual ability. For more information, see appendix IV.

Task Analysis

Task analysis is a method of breaking down a general concept or skill into its component parts. The component parts are then presented in a logical sequence. Particularly for students whose needs are fairly extensive, the method has proven very successful because it is based on sequencing and operant conditioning and offers a sense of accumulating success.

An example follows. Teaching begins at baseline: the level where the student is functioning prior to instruction (or, possibly, one step below, so that success is assured). Each step is taught in a variety of ways until "overlearning" has taken place. Overlearning means practicing the concept beyond the point of original mastery – the instructor cannot assume a student has mastered the concept on the basis of a single correct response. Instead, the instructor should present the concept on numerous occasions over a time period, expecting the student to respond correctly most of the time before being satisfied that the concept has been mastered. (Some instructors determine in advance the criteria for mastery, e.g., four correct responses out of five consecutive trials.)

1st step:	state expectation; e.g., accessing the Internet
2nd step:	list all steps, operations, and prerequisite skills necessary to do step 1
3rd step:	order these in hierarchy or logical teaching sequence
4th step:	find out where in this sequence the student is functioning (baseline)

An Example of Task Analysis: (Steps 1–3)	
Expectation: Student can read and print in words whole numbers to twenty, using meaningful contexts.	
1	student can attend to task
2	student can follow instructions
3	student can count from 1 to 20
4	student can read the number "one"
5	student can read the number "two"
6	student can read the number "three"
7	student can read the number "four"
7–20	same as above, progressing to the number "twenty"
21	student can print the number "one"
22	student can print the number "two"
23	student can print the number "three"
24–40	same as above, to number "twenty"
41	student can demonstrate the correct use of numbers "one" through "twenty" when reading or writing these numbers in context
Note: The final task is a demonstration that the expectation has been achieved.	

Table 11B

Readings and Resources

Abbott, S., & McConkey, R. (2006). The barriers to social inclusion as perceived by people with intellectual disabilities. *Journal of Intellectual Disabilities: JOID, 10*(3, 275–87. doi:10.1177/1744629506067618

Bennett, K., Reichow, B., & Wolery, M. (2011). Effects of structured teaching on the behavior of young children with disabilities. *Focus on Autism and Other Developmental Disabilities, 26*(3), 143–52. doi:10.1177/1088357611405040

Bennett, S., & Gallagher, T. L. (2011). Inclusion, education and transition to employment: A work in progress. In D. Griffiths, F. Owen, & S. Watson (Eds.). *The human rights agenda for persons with intellectual disabilities.* Kingston, NY: NADD Press.

Bialas, J. B., & Boon, R. (2010). Effects of self-monitoring on the classroom preparedness skills of kindergarten students at-risk for developmental disabilities. *Australasian Journal of Early Childhood, 35*(4), 40–52.

Certo, N. J., Luecking, R. G., Murphy, S., Brown, L., Courey, S., & Belanger, D. (2009). Seamless transition and long-term support for individuals with severe intellectual disabilities. *Research & Practice for Persons with Severe Disabilities, 33* (3), 85–95.

Cipanni, E., & Spooner, F. (1994). *Curricular and instructional approaches for persons with severe disabilities.* Needham Heights, MA: Allyn & Bacon.

Crealock, C., & Bachor, D. (1995). *Instructional strategies for students with special needs* (2nd ed.). Scarborough, ON: Allyn & Bacon Canada.

Drew, C. J., Hardman, M. L., & Logan, D. R. (1996). *Mental retardation: A life cycle approach* (6th ed.). Upper Saddle River, NJ: Merrill/Prentice Hall.

Feldman, M. A., & Walton-Allen, N. (1997). Effects of maternal mental retardation and poverty on intellectual, academic, and behavioral status of school-age children. *American Journal on Mental Retardation, 101*, 352–64.

Freeman, S. F. N., & Alkin, M. C. (2000). Academic and social attainments of children with mental retardation in general education and special education settings. *Remedial and Special Education, 21*(1), 3–18.

Goddard, H. H. (1920). *Human efficiency and level of intelligence.* Princeton, NJ: Princeton University Press.

Graziano, A. M. (2002). *Developmental disabilities: Introduction to a diverse field.* Boston: Allyn & Bacon.

Hankin, J. R. (1994). FAS prevention strategies: Passive and active measures. *Alcohol Health and Research World, 18*(1), 62–66.

Herr, S. S., & Weber, G. (1999). *Aging, rights, and quality of life: Prospects for older people with developmental disabilities.* Baltimore: Paul H. Brookes.

Hutchinson, N. L., & Martin, A. K. (2012). *Inclusive classrooms in Ontario schools.* Toronto: Pearson.

Newman, L. Wagner, M., Cameto, R., Knokey, A. M., Shaver, D. (2010). *Comparisons across time of the outcomes of youth with disabilities up to 4 years after high school: A report of findings from the National Longitudinal Transition Study – 2 (NLTS2).* Menlo Park, CA: SRI.

Parette, H. P. (2011). Using animation in Microsoft PowerPoint to enhance engagement and learning in young learners with developmental delay. *Teaching Exceptional Children, 43*(4), 58–67.

Reiss, S. (1994). Issues in defining mental retardation. *American Journal of Mental Retardation, 99*, 1–7.

Sands, D. J., & Wehmeyer, M. L. (Eds.). (1996). *Self-determination across the life span: Theory and practice.* Baltimore: Paul H. Brookes.

Scruggs, T. E., & Mastropieri, M. A. (1994). Successful mainstreaming: A qualitative analysis of three representational cases. *American Educational Research Journal, 31*(4), 785–811.

Smith, T. E. C., Polloway, E. A., Patton, J. R., Dowdy, C. A., Heath, N., McIntyre, L. J., & Francis, G. C. (2006). *Teaching students with special needs in inclusive settings* (2nd Canadian ed.). Toronto: Pearson.

Snell, M. E. (1993. *Instruction of students with severe disabilities* (4th ed.). New York: Macmillan.

Taylor, S., Bogdan, R. (1989). On accepting relationships between people with mental retardation and non-disabled people: Towards an understanding of acceptance. *Disabiity, Handicap and Society, 4*(1), 21–31.

Weaver, H. R., Adams, S. M., Landers, M. F., & Fryberger, Y. B. (1998). Meeting the life skills of students with developmental disabilities in integrated settings. In A. Hilton & R. Ringlaben (Eds.). *Best and promising practices in developmental disabilities* (87–106). Austin, TX: Pro-Ed.

Wolfensberger, W., Nirje, B., Olshansky, S., Perske, R., & Roos, P. (1972) *Normalization in human services.* Toronto: Leonard Crainford.

Links

American Association on Intellectual and Developmental Disabilities **http://www.aamr.org**

Canadian Association for Community Living **http://www.cacl.ca/**

Canadian Centre for Substance Abuse (FAE/S) **http://www.ccsa/CCSA/EN/Topics/ Populations/FASD.htm**

Canadian Down Syndrome Society **http://www.cdss.ca**

Council for Exceptional Children **http://www.cec.sped.org**

Division on Autism and Developmental Disabilities **http://www.daddcec.org**

Ontario Association for Community Living **http://www.communitylivingontario.ca**

12

Students with Autism Spectrum Disorders

"Having a child with an ASD has fundamentally changed who I am, from where I live in the country to what kind of home I live in, how I spend money, how I parent, my career path, how I spend my spare time, how I react to stress, and how I view the world and react to it. Having a child with ASD has not-so-gently forced me to put my world into perspective, from the big picture of looking ahead to my child's adult years to everyday decisions and situations and how I choose to react to them. He has taught me what is important, what should be let go, and how to struggle and advocate not only for his needs, but also for the needs of the children and families I teach and support as a professional. So far, it has been a truly awe-inspiring journey. During the very difficult years, one of my many wishes was that I had more hope – or had someone to give me that hope for the future – that things would get better. They did."

– Kimberly M., mother of Robert

Misconceptions About Autism Spectrum Disorders (ASDs)

1 **ASDs are a kind of mental illness.**
Although ASDs appear in the list of mental disorders presented by the *Diagnostic and Statistical Manual* of the American Psychiatric Association, there are no known psychiatric causes.

2 **ASDs are untreatable.**
Intensive intervention, especially if begun early, can often make a significant impact on an individual's development. Not all treatments, however, are effective for all children with ASDs.

3 **Preoccupied, career-oriented parents are most at risk for causing ASDs.**
Although this was once a popular theory, there is no concrete evidence to substantiate it.

4 **ASDs are the result of our socially-disconnected urban culture.**
The nexus of relationships once regularly present in families and communities may indeed be disappearing, but the effects have not been connected to ASDs.

5 **ASDs can be caused by vaccinations.**
The study that led to this belief, published in *Lancet* in 1998, was retracted by most of its authors and by the journal in 2004. There is no evidence to indicate that vaccinations cause ASDs.

Autism Spectrum Disorders

Autism spectrum disorders (ASDs) is an umbrella term used to describe a range of neurodevelopmental disorders classified in the *Diagnostic and Statistical Manual-IV-TR* (*DSM-IV-TR*) of the American Psychiatric Association. It represents a range of behaviours that originally were classified as "autism," a severely incapacitating disability that can affect all aspects of an individual's development; if not treated, these behaviours can be lifelong. ASDs, however, describe individuals who have characteristics ranging from what was once called only autism, which can be very severe, to those with characteristics that have a lesser, but still serious, impact on communication and behavioural, cognitive, and/or social growth. People with ASDs are believed to have anomalies in both the structure and the chemistry of the brain. The characteristics of behaviours associated with ASDs are not due to psychiatric or emotional difficulties but rather are linked to neurological and/or genetic causes.

For several decades after autism was first described in 1911, the disorder was customarily known by that single term. By the end of the century, "autism" was seen as too narrow to encompass the many manifestations of the disorder. Both professionals and public alike began to acknowledge a range, or spectrum. Hence, the more or less accepted term today is autism spectrum disorders, although in general discussions, in symposia, and even in academic papers, "autism" is regularly used as a kind of shorthand. A further development must be noted in that the *DSM* now presents five different categories of autism under the heading Pervasive Developmental Disorders (PDDs), so this term, too, is now part of the mix, though less commonly used in everyday conversations.

A simple caveat for teachers and educational assistants is to be aware that terminology used to describe autism spectrum disorders is somewhat elastic and that explanations of cause, characteristics, and prevalence continue to evolve, as well.

The DSM *and Pervasive Development Disorders*

As noted earlier, recent editions of the *DSM* divide ASDs into five separate categories under the heading of Pervasive Developmental Disorders. For practical purposes within the education community, the first three disorders described below represent the spectrum referred to as ASDs. That said, the five contained in *DSM-IV-TR* (the most recent version of the *Diagnostic and Statistical Manual* of the American Psychiatric Association at the time of writing) are summarized in what follows.

Autistic disorder: includes impairment in social interaction, communication, and imaginative play prior to age three, with restricted interests and repeated behaviours.

Asperger's disorder, sometimes colloquially referred to as Asperger syndrome: is usually applied to individuals with apparently normal language development and average to above average intelligence but who are impaired in social interactions and have unusually restricted or specialized interests.

Pervasive developmental disorder – not otherwise specified: may also be called "atypical autism." This is a somewhat vague category that picks up individuals otherwise not classified by the other categories but who, nevertheless, have severe impairments of an autism-like nature.

Childhood disintegrative disorder: characterized by the presence of a range of autism-related behaviours that appear after typical development for at least two years.

Rett's disorder is progressive and, so far, seen only in girls. There is a period of typical development followed by the loss of acquired skills. A key symptom is replacement of purposeful hand movements with repetitive actions (e.g., hand-wringing) between ages one and four.

Looking ahead, the American Psychiatric Association's proposed revisions to these definitions, which will appear in *DSM* due out in 2013, include a single category entitled Autism Spectrum Disorder, divided only by severity level from 1 (requiring substantial support) to 3 (requiring support).

A Note on Terms and Labels

From Autism Society Canada (used with permission): "It is important to distinguish between the clinical terms and descriptions of ASDs and our understanding and knowledge of people who live with ASDs. We need to understand clinical terms used in medical settings, during diagnosis, and in certain treatment or intervention settings. However, it is wise to keep in mind that these terms may also be seen as limiting labels to some people with ASDs who feel that ASDs have been medicalized to the point where individuals who are unique in their skills, abilities, and value to their communities have been forgotten or eclipsed by the 'disorder.'"

Characteristics of Autism Spectrum Disorders

Whatever definition of ASDs eventually prevails, a reality in the classroom is that students who have one of these related disorders generally present certain characteristic manifestations or symptoms. These vary in style and intensity from individual to individual in one or several of the following clusters.

- *Communication**: Speech may be delayed, diminished, or entirely absent. May use gestures rather than words; may often use words without attaching their usual meaning. Many students with ASDs demonstrate "echolalia" – the repeating of a word or phrase spoken by another person. This may be words or phrases just heard, or may be words, phrases, or even detailed dialogue heard at an earlier time (e.g., movie scripts).

- *Social interaction*: May find relating to others difficult or even impossible, reflected in anything from lack of eye contact to total withdrawal. May show little interest in making friends or in shared play and will spend inordinate amounts of time alone. Seeming unawareness of social interplay and an absence of intuition are typical (e.g., student does not read body language of others; talks, but does not seem to listen; seems unaware of protocols).

- *Behaviours*: Behaviour is described as atypical. May become obsessed with a theme (e.g., hockey scores) or object (spinning objects, flags, fans). Will often engage in repeated ritualistic actions (e.g., rocking in place) and demand close adherence to routines and schedules.

- *Responses to sensory stimuli*: May find sights, sounds, conversational "buzz," crowds (e.g., as at recess or an assembly) overstimulating.

---

* The Ministry of Education includes autism under "Communication" in its definitions. (See appendix I of this book.)

Responses are often seen as unusual. Tolerance for some stimuli may be fine while specific noises (e.g., the sound of a ringing telephone, fire alarms) may cause great upset. Reactions may be under-sensitive or over-sensitive and may vary from sense to sense within each individual with an ASD.

- *Transitions*: Change of any type is often difficult for a child with an ASD. Even slight differences in classroom or school routine may be extremely upsetting (e.g., shifting to group work after quiet seat work). Shifts into and out of recess or lunch hour or dismissal time are often difficult. Changes in personnel (e.g., educational assistant or supply teacher) can cause an extreme response.

Current evidence suggests that ASDs typically appear in the first three years of life, especially between the ages of two to three, and are four to six times more common in males than in females.

Exploding Numbers

Obscure Beginnings ...

In 1943, American psychologist Leo Kanner (pronounced "conner") published a paper identifying what he called "autistic children." Of course, this exceptionality did not suddenly appear in the mid-twentieth century! Rather, what Kanner did was separate out a small group, who, to this point, had been classified as emotionally disturbed, or mentally retarded, or both. Kanner pointed out that the group he called autistic (borrowing the term from Eugen Bleuler, who also coined the term "schizophrenia," in 1912) was not as slow learning as the "mentally retarded," and did not fit the pattern typical of the "emotionally disturbed."

A year later, in 1944, Austrian psychologist Hans Asperger independently published what was essentially a similar hypothesis, but, unlike the group Kanner described, the people Asperger identified all had language. Hence "Asperger's disorder" came to be used to distinguish children with autism who use language.

In the 1980s, prevalence rates for autism were held to be 4 in every 10,000. And, for the most part, few people had any awareness, much less understanding, of this exceptionality, for many identified cases were institutionalized, often for life. By the end of the twentieth century, prevalence rates were being revised sharply upward to ranges of around 1 in every 1,000 births.

By 2007, Autism Canada was citing a prevalence rate of 1 in every 200 births, and the U.S. Centers for Disease Control and Prevention reported in 2012 that ASDs occurs in 1 of every 88 births. If accurate, that figure means that the rate has nearly quadrupled in only a few years. Autism Canada reports that ASDs are the most prevalent neurological disorder or severe developmental disability of childhood.

Research as recent as 2011 by Ozonoff et al. also found that siblings of those with ASD were at significantly greater risk for developing ASD, particularly if they are male and/or have more than one sibling with ASD.

The Case of Raven

RAVEN, age fifteen, has spent the past three years in a self-contained classroom with four other students with severe ASDs where she has made great strides under a dedicated teacher and very patient educational assistant. Because school board officials repeatedly point to this classroom as proof of "what is possible," it has become a popular spot for visitors. Curiously – or perhaps not – despite all of the positive features in the setting, what visitors remember most is the sight of Raven's palms. Both her left and right hands have thick scars that match the concentric rings of electric stove elements. One day when she was nine, Raven turned the elements on and put her palms down until they – quite literally – cooked!

Six years later, Raven still has an inexplicable insensitivity to physical pain. (She nearly died at age twelve from a ruptured appendix; an abscessed molar went unnoticed until huge swelling made it obvious.) Yet she is extremely sensitive to other, seemingly innocuous, stimuli, especially sounds. Only in the past year, for example, and only if warned in advance, can she tolerate the sound of paper being shuffled or folded. Although music is an important part of her program – the EA discovered some time ago that Raven's tantrums could be calmed by soft classical music – the classroom piano had to be removed because just one note would send her into a frenzy.

Raven still does not communicate verbally, but she will now mouth certain nouns softly if she wants something. She still rocks when bored or stressed or faced with change in her routine or surroundings but no longer pulls out her hair. She has stopped throwing her food and waits her turn for the classroom lavatory. Recently, she undertook responsibility for the aquarium.

Raven has also learned to acknowledge the presence of others, even strangers, although she does not make eye contact. She now sits in "circle" after lunch each day without prompting. In sum, a comparison of Raven's profile today with the base line established three years ago shows major, continuing progress.

The IPRC is placing Raven in an inclusive high school setting in which the school is able to provide an EA and, if necessary, resource room support. It is time to prepare Raven's IEP, noting changes in strengths, needs, and placement.

"Having Asperger's is like being a coyote in a city park.
You survive but it's the wrong environment. You just don't fit."
– Jon K., age nineteen, diagnosed with Asperger syndrome

Why the Rapid Acceleration?

Although such a profound increase in prevalence rate challenges credibility, an issue that will likely confront the field for some time, there are a number of explanations for it, some satisfactory, some otherwise. This increase is attributed to changes in areas such as diagnosis, awareness, and service eligibility (Johnson & Myers, 2007). More specifically, once the *DSM* included ASDs there was an increase in the number of diagnoses, if only because a wider range of medical professionals became more aware.

Educators, faced with the presence of vastly increased numbers of special education students in the 1980s and 1990s, became far more sensitive to the needs of students with ASDs. Increased publicity led to greater awareness in the public at large. With more awareness has come more research, greater attention to empirical evidence, more elaborated definitions, and more informed diagnoses.

📚 Red Flags for Parents

Children do not attain developmental goals according to a timetable. Yet, it may be important for parents to seek referrals for further medical advice and early intervention. After all, "early specialized intervention is considered best practice for ASD and may represent the best hope for reducing symptoms and overall disability" (Ozonoff et al., 2011, p. 493). One reason for such a referral may be if parents notice that their child demonstrates any of the following issues, all of which are examples of communication, social, and behavioural red flags:

- does not babble by one year of age
- hears, but does not respond to, his or her name
- avoids eye contact, may avoid cuddling
- begins developing language and/or skills, then regresses or is slower than other children in developing language skills
- does not point to things, seek attention, or look where others are looking
- may have unusual hand movements

The Cause

Scientific research has not yet established the specific cause of ASDs, but theories are plentiful. Some theories have appeal, based as they are on empirical evidence, a good example being the current dominance of the genetic cause. Indeed, much of the current research has revealed a genetic basis, with the hypothesis reinforced by apparent patterns of ASDs in twins and in families. According to the United States National Institute of Mental Health, recent neuroimaging studies have shown that abnormal brain development, beginning in the infant's first months, may relate to later anatomical abnormalities often seen in children with ASDs that may be caused by genetic defects in brain growth factors.

Diagnosis

Diagnosing a child with ASD is often very difficult because there is not yet a biological marker or medical test to definitely determine that a child has an ASD. It is through an understanding of the child's development and behaviour that a diagnosis of an ASD is made by a medical practitioner or psychologist.

A list of criteria for each type of pervasive developmental disorder is included in the *DSM-IV-TR*. Diagnosis of ASD is based on a consideration of three areas: the degree of communication impairment, the degree of social impairment, and the degree of the child's repetitive interests and/or activities. Currently, there are a variety of assessment instruments that can assist, but not definitively determine, whether a child has an ASD.

Examples of these assessment instruments include the Autism Diagnostic Observation Schedule (ADOS), which allows clinicians to observe and evaluate behaviours; the Autism Behavior Checklist (ABC), which is used by teachers and parents as a screening instrument; and the Autism Diagnostic Interview – Revised (ADI-R), which can be used to semi-structure a parent interview. This interview is conducted by a clinician and can help identify characteristics in the child that can be associated with the diagnosis of ASDs and pervasive developmental disorders.

Ideally, a child should be evaluated by a multi-disciplinary team, the members of which are familiar with ASD in its various manifestations. Again, ideally, the conclusions of the team will be reached only after extensive observation – the sole diagnostic technique with any solid history – as well as after a collation and comparison of the various results and after informed discussion. Needless to say, unless the child's case is managed thoroughly, an ideal evaluation is not often achieved.

In practice, a diagnosis that actually places a label such as PDD-NOS or Asperger's disorder on a child is ultimately in the hands of a medical professional. Once that label is attached to a student, the education system may go forward with its own approach to both a placement and a program that accommodates the student's needs.

The Case of Larry

BECAUSE his mother has been offered a major career opportunity, Larry's family is considering a move to another community. The stress of relocating is exacerbated by Larry's situation. He is eight years old and has Asperger's disorder. Although the parents insist he is not a "savant," Larry does things that other eight-year-olds do not. He can, for example, recite an entire weather forecast verbatim, having heard it only once (provided that weather is his *passion du jour*). When he became interested in the Korean War, he could cite the regimental names and personnel numbers of every country contributing to the UN forces. At the moment, Larry is obsessed with astrolabes, sextants, and compasses. He can describe their origins, history, function, and construction with a degree of accuracy known to only a few scholars.

Larry is also afraid to use any bathroom except the one in the basement of his family home. He has yet to master tying shoelaces and, to prevent anxiety attacks, must be escorted to and from the school bus by an adult he trusts. Although he has an impressive vocabulary and clear speech, Larry has difficulty carrying on conversations with others. And he does not get on well with his peer group. As the EA explained, "It's not so much that his peers can't understand him; it's more that they can't stand him!" Larry, it seems, prefers his own world and actively excludes others from it.

His current placement is in a regular grade 3 class where both the teacher and the EA not only are qualified in special education but also have taken a particular interest in ASDs.

Together, they have made extensive efforts to create an atmosphere of positive acceptance and community in the class. (Larry is not the only student with special needs included here.) They have been successful in generating a feeling among the other students that human differences are a matter of degree and that "we're all different."

They have also made strides in "softening Larry's corners," as the EA puts it, teaching him to respect the feelings of others.

It is apparent that Larry will continue to develop important social skills in this environment. The concern is over Larry's move to a new classroom. What issues and interventions should be considered in Larry's new placement?

"I still remember, in the delivery room, I had visions of flooding the backyard, skating, shinny. He'd be a right winger; that was my dream. But when Kev stopped talking to us – stopped looking at us – and started all that strange stuff, I knew hockey was going to be the last thing on the agenda."

– Alf R., parent of a child diagnosed with childhood disintegrative disorder

Treatment

Taken generally, interventions fall into five principal categories: behavioural (intensive behavioural intervention and various other forms of behaviour modification); biochemical (vitamin supplements, medications, special diets); neurosensory (patterning, sensory integration techniques and auditory training); psycho-dynamic (holding, body contact therapy, psychotherapy); and developmental. An Autism Speaks survey showed that the average child with ASD was involved in an average of five different treatments simultaneously.

For every treatment style there are vociferous supporters and equally vociferous critics, although comparatively few styles are actually backed (or claim to be) by scientific studies. One such approach, Applied Behavior Analysis (ABA), is based on the principles defined by B. F. Skinner in 1953. In an article reported by Heflin and Alaimo (2007), Baer, Wolf, and Risley (1968) suggested that ABA should contain the following five dimensions:

1 *Applied and effective*: New behaviours being taught to the child should have goals that benefit the student and are valued by the community. Procedures employed should be minimally invasive and considered acceptable in terms of the outcome; all of the outcomes and procedures should be acceptable in improving the quality of life for everyone involved.

2 *Technological*: This approach represents the strategies employed to change behaviour. Teachers must ensure that the items they use for reinforcement are in fact appropriate and attractive to the student. If the behaviour is not changing or is getting worse, then what is being employed is not a reinforcement. In addition to reinforcement, strategies include "prompting," i.e., providing assistance so that the appropriate response can be obtained. Once the reinforcement and prompting is determined, discrete trial training occurs. This step defines a basic unit of instruction that presents an opportunity for the student to respond correctly.

3 *Behavioural*: This step takes a functional view of the behaviour and requires the teacher or parent to try to determine the function of a particular behaviour. Once it is understood why the child is behaving a certain way, interventions and/or changes in the environment can be made to make it easier for the child to behave in an appropriate manner.

4 *Analytic and conceptual*: It is important that, when ABA is being applied, there is an element of accountability – in other words, measurements of changes in behaviour are occurring and the interventions being applied are working. Baselines need to be established before ABA is applied, and data need to be regularly collected to determine the program's effectiveness.

5 *Generalization*: Once the behaviour is learned, it can be repeated in a variety of settings. Using the newly learned behaviour often does not happen automatically and needs to be encouraged as part of the intervention procedure.

Treatment Standards

According to Autism Society Canada (used with permission), an effective treatment program should be one that is supported by scientific research and includes:

- early and intensive treatment and education techniques to help people with ASDs develop and learn new skills
- clear guidelines and expectations for behaviour
- a highly structured, specialized, and consistent education plan tailored to the individual
- parental and family participation in assessment and curriculum planning
- instruction, monitoring, and evaluation by those people who know the person best and will have the clearest understanding of the individual's history and learning style

> *"It's difficult. People treat you differently when they know. If they first saw you and they didn't know, they treat you like a normal person, but if they do know, they treat you weird and different. Either they act like jerks, or they are overly polite. People seem to pester you with things you don't want to do, and it's annoying."*
> – Robert, a young adult diagnosed with an ASD at age nine

Intensive Behavioural Intervention*

Intensive Behavioural Intervention (IBI) is a highly structured program based on Applied Behavior Analysis principles. It is designed to develop age-appropriate skills and independence in a child with ASDs (or other disabilities). Originally, IBI was conceived for and applied to children from the ages of approximately two to approximately five or six, but there is pressure from advocates to expand that target group. The program follows behaviour modification principles and is very intensive and hands-on, typically involving twenty to forty hours per week of direct service from professionals. Parents and/or caregivers are crucial to its implementation and are expected to follow the regimen faithfully and precisely.

An IBI program is individualized and built around needs in communication, daily living and safety skills, social skills, motor skills, pre-academics, self-management, and attending skills. It is formally administered, supervised, and evaluated by qualified service providers, typically a clinical psychologist in tandem with other qualified personnel. IBI is very effective with some children and, when the intervention is early, is said to produce dramatic, positive results.

Currently, though there is a waiting list, the province of Ontario provides IBI for children with ASDs. For the past several years, there was cutoff once the child reached the age of six, but this cutoff has been the subject of much legal action brought on by parents against the government of Ontario. In March 2005, the trial judge ruled the age criterion discriminatory against the children on the basis of age and that the refusal to provide or fund IBI and appropriate educational services discriminates against them on the basis of disability.

This decision, however, was overturned by the Ontario Court of Appeal, in July 2006. This court ruled that the Ontario government's refusal to provide IBI beyond age six was not discriminatory and did not contravene the *Canadian Charter of Rights and Freedoms*. The parents then applied to the Supreme Court of Canada. On April 12, 2007, the Supreme Court indicated that it would not grant the parents "leave to appeal," essentially upholding the decision of the Ontario Court of Appeals.

Despite this decision, the Ontario government is continuing to fund IBI beyond age six and has also increased funding to school boards so that students with ASDs can be provided appropriate educational interventions with collaborative support between the Ontario Ministry of Education and the Ontario Ministry of Children and Youth Services.

Current Ontario Policy

In May 2007, the Ontario Ministry of Education issued a Policy/Program Memorandum providing direction to school boards regarding how to support their use of Applied Behavior Analysis in the school setting for students with ASDs. This memorandum requires school boards to:
- offer students with ASDs special education programs and services, including, where appropriate, special education programs using ABA methods
- plan for the transition between various activities and settings involving students with ASDs

---

* Though not the same, IBI, which is a therapeutic, clinical intervention, and ABA, which is used in the educational environment, often are inaccurately used interchangeably in the media. IBI is one form of ABA and represents a very structured and intensive approach to teaching behaviour and skills to individuals with ASDs.

In addition, the Ministry published the document *Effective Educational Practices for Students with Autism Spectrum Disorders* as an additional resource to help teachers understand and teach students with ASDs.

Examples of Other Treatment Programs

In 2009, the National Autism Center published its National Standards Report, an evaluation of various interventions as having either an established, emerging, or non-established evidence base.

Some of the following examples are classified as non-established and are described as ineffective or harmful.

Facilitated communication is an example of this latter category. Facilitated communication (FC) is a program in the neurosensory category that attracted a rash of front-page media attention during the 1990s. This idea operates on the premise that a child with an ASD (or other person) who does not use speech can peck out words or symbols on a keyboard if a "facilitator" gently props that person's arm above the keyboard. FC continues to be used, although it is heavily criticized for lack of validation. The Autism Society of Canada reports it as "potentially harmful."

Another treatment example is the *Tomatis method*, an auditory integration training concept in which an individual spends hours a day listening to specially created sounds and classical music, particularly that of Mozart, with the low frequencies filtered out. Over time, the frequencies are added back, along with voices and other everyday sounds. The assumption is that children with ASDs may overcome extreme oversensitivity to certain sounds and may be sufficiently soothed to decrease hyperactivity. Like FC, the Tomatis program is criticized for lack of validation.

The TEACCH program (Treatment and Education of Autistic and related Communication Handicapped Children), established in 1972 by Dr. Eric Schopler, has a positive profile in the field; its continued use after more than thirty years is a tribute to its efficacy. This program begins with an exceptionally detailed assessment to uncover the individual's potential for acquiring communication skills and competencies for independent living. TEACCH is not behaviour modification in that it does not work on behaviours directly (except in the case of endangering behaviours). Rather, it tries to give the student a better understanding of his or her environment to reduce anxiety (and the reactions that develop from that) and emphasizes communication skills so that the student can deal better with the world around him or her.

Picture Exchange Communication System: For many students with ASDs, verbal communication is limited. In place of fluent speech, alternative and augmentative communication systems may be used. One of the most popular is the Picture Exchange Communication System whereby pictures are used to represent what a student may need. By selecting appropriate pictures, the parent or teacher can indicate what they expect of the student; the student, meanwhile, can indicate his or her particular needs and wants. In tandem with a speech-language pathologist, PECS, sign language, and technology can be used to assist students with ASDs to communicate without using speech.

Social Stories: This approach, developed by Carol Gray in 1991, is designed to help students with ASDs better understand the world around them. Social Stories, according to the Gray Centre for Social Learning and Understanding, are stories that describe a situation, skill, or concept in terms of relevant social cues and common responses. Social stories can be used to help the student understand social cues, react better to social situations, and feel more comfortable in both familiar and unfamiliar social situations. (See the Reading and Resources section at the end of this chapter for further information.)

Self-monitoring: Recent research by Holifield et al. (2010) indicated that teaching students with ASDs to self-monitor increases their ability to attend to tasks and improves their academic accuracy. Self-monitoring was described as teaching students to record whether they were paying attention and assessing their own academic accuracy.

Do the Treatments Work?

An enduring problem for both professionals and parents is true validation of the many methods proposed to treat ASDs. For parents, who, understandably, are interested in almost any proposal that may offer help to their child, whether to adopt a particular treatment program can be a real dilemma. Very often they learn of a program through enthusiastic anecdotal tributes, and the impetus to try it becomes almost irresistible. But once launched into a program, they typically face significant costs in time, effort, and money, and, since very few programs produce immediate or even early results, the ever-present worry that they may not have chosen wisely.

Implications of Specific Treatments for the Classroom

Very often, a student identified with an ASD comes to the classroom with a treatment program already in place. The teacher – and the EA if the classroom is fortunate enough to have one – is then expected to adhere to the tenets of that program and sometimes even be in charge of implementing it whether or not the teacher or EA agree with its principles or have received training in it.

This can be a particular problem because of the amount of time and resources the program may require, not to mention its potential for disruption. Even more troubling to many teachers is that a predetermined treatment program may well deny them opportunities for creative response.

As well, especially in inclusive classrooms, a method with laid-on requirements has the potential of denying the purpose of inclusion by isolating the student, however unintentionally.

On the other hand, teachers can be just as confused and challenged by a student with an ASD as anyone else, and the clear plan of response typically outlined in a treatment program may well be a relief.

Some Issues in the Field

✦ While rational doubt should be enough to make most people view these accounts with caution, a strong wish to believe, on the part of some parents, together with a lack of information, can easily subvert natural wariness. *A bandwagon effect* even accrues to programs in which positive results are supported more scientifically.

For example, both empirical evidence and investigation now leave little doubt that, for the most part, IBI can improve matters for a child with ASD, particularly if that child is very young and the treatment begins early. By the beginning of the millennium, the program was being pursued by parents regardless of the type of ASD with which their child was diagnosed. And by the middle of the decade, there was an added twist. The apparent success of IBI with very young children had led parents to advocate for its extension beyond the time (age five to six) at which the program has typically ended so this intervention could take place in schools.

The position of the Supreme Court of Canada (as indicated above) is that schools do not have to provide this treatment; cases challenging this issue are still before the courts.

✦ The *cost of implementing a program* continues to beleaguer parents and governments. ASDs are not unique in this, but the intensity of need that distinguishes ASDs usually requires a response of equal intensity – with heavy expenses attached. The delicacy of the issue lies not in whether the program is worth the price but in who will pay for it. A program such as IBI, which requires twenty to forty hours of service a week from qualified personnel, along with training, travel, and other supplementary expenses, is way beyond the income of most Canadian families.

Although government funding is available in most provinces, Ontario included, those monies are not unlimited. The demand by parents for greater funding and expanded programs has thus led to an increase in litigation and human rights appeals.

✦ The media have had a powerful impact on *the public impression of ASDs* over the past decade or so, and, as usual, the impact comes as a mixed blessing. The performance of actor Dustin Hoffman in the popular 1988 Hollywood movie *Rain Man* did much to create awareness of an exceptionality hitherto known only vaguely. Yet the same movie did much to create a false impression. The person with an ASD played by Hoffman was obsessive, quite charming, and a savant (he could recall information from the telephone book). As any special educator can quickly attest, neither language nor savant abilities are present in all people with ASDs. Those with savant characteristics or "splinter skills" represent only about 10 percent of

the population with ASDs. Since this seminal movie, more television shows (such as ABC's *Grey's Anatomy* and NBC's *Parenthood*), movies (such as *Adam* in 2009 and *Temple Grandin* in 2010), and books (such as Jodi Picoult's *House Rules*) are representing ASD more accurately.

✦ Students with ASD are now *more frequently placed in regular classrooms* with the classroom teacher responsible for programming in co-operation with the Learning Resource Teacher and, if assigned, an educational assistant. In the case of students with ASD who exhibit behaviour problems, the debate over appropriate classroom placement continues. The behaviours can be a major challenge when supporting the child in a regular classroom.

> *"If you let your students pick their own groups, we'll always be picked last. Defeats the purpose of having groups, doesn't it?"*
> – Jon K., age nineteen, diagnosed with Asperger syndrome

Strategies for the Classroom

• *Intuition.* With ASDs, perhaps more than any other exceptionality, there is less commonality from case to case, and what "works" in one situation often will not translate to another. Thus, in the regular classroom, especially, intuition, along with trial and error (and, therefore, good record keeping!), are two essential arrows in the quiver shared by teacher and assistant.

• *Teaching essential skills.* Teachers and educational assistants must be prepared to offer instruction in skills that most students acquire as a routine part of the process of growing up. For example, it follows that a student who needs to be taught to pay attention to his or her name (not unusual in ASDs) will likely find it difficult to follow simple instructions. This is not necessarily

owing to diminished intelligence but more to a style of processing information. Usually, a student with an ASD needs more time to switch focus in order to attach meaning to the words being tossed at him or her and to follow through on requests.

• *Understanding the ordinary.* A major challenge is getting a student with an ASD to understand and accept the very ordinary, frequently occurring phenomena that characterize the behaviour of students in a classroom. Getting the student to understand, for example, that a classmate's movement from point A to point B is not necessarily an "invasion of his or her space" or that physical contact among peers is normal is not something most classroom professionals have to encounter on an ordinary day. At the same time, a teacher or assistant who tries to educate a student with an ASD in these matters must realize that the aversive behaviours are real – that they are not something to be punished, but part of a condition to be acknowledged so that alternatives can be taught. The suggestions below offer a few simple procedures that generally are helpful.

- *Provide a "safe person" and a "safe place."* The noise and disorder of recess, a pep rally, an assembly, sometimes even normal classroom noise (such as on the day before a holiday break) may overwhelm the student. It may be advisable to have a quiet place for the student to go, or to develop a routine response in these situations (e.g., by having him or her pair with a calm classmate). Perhaps more important is to anticipate and watch for signs that the student is approaching meltdown. It may also be useful for these times if the student can be taught to recognize the signs himself or herself and be taught how to act accordingly. There may be a trusted adult (nurse, another teacher, EA, or person in the office) for the student to go to. Some students find it helpful to overcome stress by listening to music for a brief period.

- *Prepare for changes in routine*. Until the student develops the appropriate skills, it may be necessary for the teacher and/or EA to be at the student's side when change is imminent, quietly coaching and helping the student through such changes with the use of visuals.

- *Structure group work very deliberately*. Ensure that the task, roles, and time lines are clearly understood by all group members.

- *Seating plans are useful*. Because of the potential for intense reactions to stimuli and for unusual behaviours, attention to where the student sits, relative to the entrance, work areas, etc., and relative to who sits near him or her, may pre-empt "situations."

- *Technology may help.* Many students find the use of technology an ideal medium of communication because it offers the opportunity for interaction, cognition, and language use without the impact of nearby human presence and is often motivating for students with ASDs. The key for the teacher or EA, of course, is to use the tool judiciously lest it become an escape. For more information, see appendix IV.

- *Be a positive interlocutor*. The teacher or educational assistant, especially at first, may be the only one in a classroom who understands that the student with ASD lacks the intuition necessary for successful social and intellectual exchange. It will probably be necessary to coach both the student with ASD and the student's classmates in this reality – the special student in the impact he or she is having, and the classmates in not taking abruptness personally.

- *Educate peers of children with ASD.* Teach other students about sameness, differences, and/or directly about ASD. Although it is difficult to fully experience an ASD, peers can be taught information and/or take part in activities to develop empathy and an awareness of diversity. For example, students can take part in experiential activities (e.g., demonstrating and experiencing gross motor issues by walking on a line of tape with backward binoculars), watching videos focused on other students sharing what ASD is like (e.g., Autism Ontario's "A Chance to be Me"), or reading about ASD through fictional or non-fictional accounts that centre on characters or students who have ASD themselves (e.g., "Looking After Louis").

- *Capitalize on special interests*. Having a student with ASD in a class, especially one with Asperger's, may mean that you have an "expert" on a specific topic in your class. There may be reward for everyone and personal satisfaction for the student if he or she is allowed to educate others on this personal intense interest.

- *A caring community.* As much as it sounds like an overbeaten cliché, there's no substitute for a classroom where understanding, accommodation, and forgiveness prevail. It takes the professionals in the room to make it happen.

- *Environmental arrangement.* Try to determine what precipitates a specific inappropriate behaviour, then design the environment to decrease the likelihood that these precipitating events will occur. For example, if you notice that a student with ASD acts inappropriately when another student sharpens his or her pencil, perhaps sharpened pencils can be provided throughout the day so that the inappropriate response can be avoided.

The following is from an adult who was diagnosed with an autism spectrum disorder at age three:

- My head is like a video. The only way I learn is to see things. That's why nouns and verbs are easier to learn than other words. When you teach an autistic kid things, show him.

- You need blocks and sticks and things like that for math.

- Use art a lot.

- Phonics is best for reading. So are poems. And music and songs.

- Autistic kids stick with special things they like. I loved trains. Still do. My best teacher used math trains. We had train records and we read train stories. Ms. King was so cool.

- When you talk, don't say so much at once. Don't talk slow. We're not idiots! Just don't say so much at once! I wish we had computers when I was in school. With computers you control the information coming in.

Readings and Resources

Akshoomoff, N. (2000). *Neurological underpinnings of autism* (vol. 9). Baltimore: Paul H. Brookes.

American Psychiatric Academy (2010). *DSM-5* development: Autism spectrum disorder. Retrieved from http://www.dsm5.org/ProposedRevisions/Pages/proposedrevision.aspx?rid=94

Attwood, T. (1998). *Asperger's syndrome: A guide for parents and professionals.* London: Jessica Kingsley.

Bauer, S. (1995). Autism and the pervasive developmental disorders. *Pediatrics in Review, 16,* 130–36.

Boutot, E. A., & Smith Myles, B. (2011). *Autism spectrum disorders: Foundations, characteristics, and effective strategies.* Upper Saddle River, NJ: Pearson.

Brownell, M. T., & Walther-Thomas, C. (2001). An interview with Stephen Shore: Understanding the autism spectrum – what teachers need to know. *Intervention in School and Clinic, 36,* 293–305.

Cattell-Gordon, D., & Volkmar, F. R. (1998). The development of an effective applied behavior analysis program for young children with autism: A parent's perspective. *Infants and Young Children, 10*(3), 79–85.

Cohen, D. J., & Volkmar, F. R. (1997). *Handbook of autism and pervasive developmental disorders.* New York: John Wiley.

Donnellan, A. M. (1999). Invented knowledge and autism: Highlighting our strengths and expanding the conversation. *The Journal of the Association for Persons with Severe Handicaps, 24*(3), 203–36.

Dunlap, G., & Fox, L. (1999). Supporting families of young children with autism. *Infants and Young Children, 12*(2), 48–54.

Gresham, F. L., & MacMillan, D. L. (1997). Autistic recovery? An analysis and critique of the empirical evidence on the early intervention project. *Behavioral Disorders, 22,* 185–201.

Gresham, F. L., & MacMillan, D. L. (1998). Early intervention project: Can its claims be substantiated and its effects replicated? *Journal of Autism and Developmental Disorders, 28*(1), 5–13.

Hall, L. (2009). *Autism spectrum disorders: From theory to practice.* Upper Saddle River, NJ: Pearson Education.

Heflin, J., & Alaimo, D. F. (2007). *Students with autism spectrum disorders: Effective instructional practices.* Upper Saddle River, NJ: Pearson/Merrill/Prentice Hall.

Holifield, C., Goodman, J., Hazelkorn, M., & Heflin, L. J. (2010). Using self-monitoring to increase attending to task and academic accuracy in children with autism. *Focus on Autism and Other Developmental Disabilities, 25*(4), 230–38.

Johnson, C., & Myers, S. (2007). Identification and evaluation of children with autism spectrum disorders. *Pediatrics, 120*(5), 1183–1215.

Klin, A., Volkmar, F. R., & Sparrow, S.S. (2000). *Asperger syndrome.* New Haven, CT: Child Study Center, Yale University.

Lovaas, I. O. (1981). *Teaching developmentally disabled children: The me book,* Baltimore: University Park Press.

Lovaas, I. O. (1987). Behavioral treatment of normal educational and intellectual functioning in young autistic children. *Journal of Consulting and Clinical Psychology, 55,* 3–9.

Maich, K., & Belcher, E. C. (In Press). Using picture books to create peer awareness about autism spectrum disorders in the inclusive classroom. *Intervention in School and Clinic, 47*(4).

Maurice, C. (1996). *Behavioural intervention for young children with autism: A manual for parents and professionals.* Austin, TX: Pro-Ed.

McGee, G. G., Morrier, M. J., & Daly, T. (1999). An incidental teaching approach to early intervention for toddlers with autism. *The Journal of the Association for Persons with Severe Handicaps, 24*(3), 133–46.

McLaughlin-Cheng, E. (1998). *Asperger syndrome and autism: A literature and meta-analysis. Focus on Autism and Other Developmental Disorders, 13* (4), 234–45.

Mostert, M. P. (2001). Facilitated communication since 1995: A review of published studies. *Journal of Autism and Developmental Disorders, 31,* 287–313.

Myles, B. S., & Simpson, R. L. (Eds.). (1998). *Educating children and youth with autism: Strategies for effective practice.* Austin, TX: Pro-Ed.

Myles, B. S. et al. (2001). *Asperger syndrome diagnostic scale.* Austin, TX: Pro-Ed.

Myles, B. S., & Simpson, R. L. (2001). Understanding the hidden curriculum: An essential social skill for children and youth with Asperger syndrome. *Intervention in School and Clinic, 36,* 279–386.

National Autism Center. (2009). *National standards report.* Randolph, MA: Author.

National Research Council. (2001). *Educating children with autism.* Washington, DC: National Academy Press.

Ontario Ministry of Education (2007). *Effective educational practices for students with autism spectrum disorders: A resource guide.* Toronto: Queen's Printer for Ontario.

Ontario Ministry of Education. Policy/Program Memorandum No.140 (2007). Incorporating methods of applied behaviour analysis (ABA) into programs for students with autism spectrum disorders (ASD). Retrieved at: www.edu.gov.on.ca/extra/eng/ppm/140.html

Ozonoff, S., Young, G., Carter, A., Messinger, D., Yirmiya, N., Zwaigenbaum, L., Bryson, S., Carver, L., Constantino, J., Dobkins, K., Hutman, T., Iverson, J., Landa, R., Rogers, S. J., Sigman, M., & Stone, W. (2011). Recurrence rate for autism spectrum disorders: A baby siblings research consortium study. *Pediatrics, 128,* e488-e495. doi:10.1542/peds.2010-282

Picoult, Jodi. (2010). *House rules*. New York: Washington Square Press.

Prizant, B. M., & Rubin, E. (1999). Contemporary issues in interventions for autism spectrum disorders: A commentary. *The Journal of the Association for Persons with Severe Handicaps, 24*(3), 199–208.

Quill, K. A. (1995). *Teaching children with autism: Strategies to enhance communication and socialization.* Baltimore: Paul H. Brookes.

Rapin, I. (1997). Current concepts in autism. *New England Journal of Medicine, 337*(2), 97–104.

Rogers, S. J. (1998). Empirically supported comprehensive treatments for young children with autism. *Journal of Clinical Child Psychology, 27*(2), 168–79.

Ruble, L. A., & Dalrymple, M. J. (1996). An alternative view of outcome in autism. *Focus on Autism and Other Developmental Disabilities, 11*(1), 3–14.

Ryan, J. B., Hughes, E. M., Katsiyannis, A., McDaniel, M., & Sprinkle, C. (2011). Research-based education practices for students with autism spectrum disorders. *Teaching Exceptional Children, 43*(3), 56–64.

Safran, J. A. (2002). Supporting students with Asperger's syndrome in general education. *Teaching Exceptional Children, 34*(5), 67–70.

Schopler, E. et al. (1998). *Asperger syndrome or high-functioning autism?* New York: Plenum Press.

Siegel, B. (2003). *Helping children with autism learn.* New York: Oxford University Press.

Wilkinson, K. M. (1998). Profiles of language and communication skills in autism. *Mental Retardation and Developmental Disabilities Research Reviews, 4*(2), 73–79.

Williams, K. (2001). Understanding the student with Asperger syndrome: Guidelines for teachers. *Intervention in School and Clinic, 36*, 287–92.

Wing, L. (1988). The continuum of autistic characteristics. In E. Schopler & G. B. Mesibov (Eds.). *Diagnosis and assessment in autism.* New York: Plenum Press.

Links

Autism Internet Modules **autisminternetmodules.org/**

Autism Society of Canada **autismsocietycanada.ca**

Autism Ontario **autismontario.com**

Autism Resources **autism-resources.com**

Autism Speaks **autismspeaks.ca**

Canadian Autism Intervention Research Network **cairn-site.com/en/index.html**

Geneva Centre for Autism **autism.net**

The Gray Centre for Social Understanding and Learning **thegraycenter.org**

Global Autism Collaboration **autism.org**

Ontario Ministry of Education: Effective Educational Practices for Students with ASD **edu.gov.on.ca/eng/general/elemsec/speced/autismSpecDis.html**

Special Education Technology British Columbia **setbc.org/pictureset/**

Treatment and Education of Autistic and Communication related handicapped Children **teacch.com**

13

Students with Neurological Disabilities:

Chronic Health Needs • Musculoskeletal Impairments • Acquired Brain Injury

"What I don't get is: What's with everybody! The way they treat us!
I mean – so I've got tics. And sometimes I hum. What's so bad about that?
So I've got Tourette's. Big deal! And Eddy … he's got CP. So he jerks. So what?
I mean, what's the big deal? Why do people treat us like we're some kind of
freaks or something? It's not like they're perfect either, you know."

– Paulo, age sixteen

Misconceptions About Neurological Disabilities and Chronic Health Needs

1 **Students with special health conditions are automatically candidates for special education.**
Usually the distribution of intellectual abilities, hearing, and vision among students with chronic health conditions is similar to that of the rest of the population. While learning may be affected in some cases, making small accommodations around the way students learn is often sufficient. Some students with chronic health needs may miss a great deal of school, however, and may benefit from a remedial program that includes special education programming.

2 **Students with Tourette syndrome swear and "talk dirty."**
This characteristic is known as coprolalia. Only about a third of individuals with the syndrome manifest this trait, which waxes, wanes, and often disappears altogether.

3 **The physical condition of students with cerebral palsy cannot be remediated or improved.**
Cerebral palsy involves damage to the brain and is considered irreversible, but occupational and physiotherapy, orthotic devices, mobility aids, and sometimes surgical procedures can make a positive change to students' physical function and ability to

participate, especially if intervention is begun early.

4 **When chronic health conditions are neurologically based, students have diminished intellectual capacity.**
There is a slightly higher incidence of intellectual problems among students with conditions such as cerebral palsy, but the severity of the physical condition does not tell you whether a student has intellectual disabilities. Other neurological conditions, such as spina bifida, muscular dystrophy, or convulsive disorders, generally have no direct connection with intellectual abilities.

5 **Students with epilepsy and Tourette's have mental illnesses.**
Students who have conditions such as epilepsy and Tourette's may have secondary mental health issues such as anxiety, but they do not necessarily experience a serious mental illness.

6 **Students with spina bifida will be incontinent.**
Lack of bowel and bladder control is a genuine problem that accompanies more severe cases of spina bifida, but students are taught at an early age how to manage these issues. Students with milder cases of spina bifida generally do not have this problem.

192

7 **Arthritis is found only in elderly adults.**
Arthritis can be found in all ages. Juvenile rheumatoid arthritis is one example of a health condition that starts in childhood.

8 **Medical science is reducing the incidence of physical disabilities and chronic conditions.**
Some conditions, such as spina bifida, are actually decreasing due to medical advances. The number of children with health conditions such as cerebral palsy, however, is staying stable because medical advances have improved conditions at birth. More children are surviving who are very premature or who have low birth weights that could result in medical and learning problems.

Describing the Needs

The primary characteristics of students with a physical disability or other neurological or health needs are usually the concern of the health professions. Because a majority of students with these types of conditions attend neighbourhood schools, it follows that teachers and educational assistants need to be familiar with the characteristics and implications of these types of conditions. From an educational perspective, some medical knowledge can be useful for educators who are developing an appropriate program. The knowledge can be very helpful in understanding a student's emotional needs and learning patterns. In most cases (with the occasional exception of some neurologically based conditions such as Tourette syndrome), students with a significant physical or health need will have been identified before they arrive in school. These cases are usually already classified by health personnel and will have been presented to an IPRC. Thus, classroom personnel should receive a fair amount of information in advance.

It is important to recognize that a physical, health, or neurological condition will manifest itself in a variety of ways. It is even more important to remember that the student with the condition is, first and foremost, a student. Teachers should approach medical information, therefore, from an educational and co-operative perspective, not from the perspective of diagnosis or treatment. In addition to learning about a particular condition, it is also wise to seek out the specifics of the individual student's case, since conditions can present very differently with a wide variety of symptoms.

The descriptions that follow offer only a brief overview. The authors have avoided presenting a catalogue of the very long list of chronic health conditions encountered in the schools of the province, for despite the drama implied by the conditions, most are of very low prevalence, and each student inevitably will be significantly different from others.

Cerebral Palsy

Cerebral palsy (CP) is an umbrella term for a type of brain damage that occurs in children before, during, or shortly after birth. It usually presents as a motor disorder that may vary in type, severity, and also in the number of limbs that are affected. It is not progressive, nor is it contagious. It does not go away, however. Whatever type of cerebral palsy a child has does not change for that child over the course of his or her life. About 2 or 3 of every 1,000 children have cerebral palsy. Cerebral palsy cannot be "fixed" but occupational, physiotherapy, and speech and language therapy can often be helpful in improving function, communication, and mobility.

The most common type of CP is *spastic* cerebral palsy. This type describes cases in which children have increased muscle tone (stiff, tense muscles) and arms and legs that are often in tight reflex positions with arms curled up and legs extended. Movements are often slow, poorly coordinated, and uncontrolled.

Another type is *dyskinetic* CP, which includes *athetosis* (continuous slow, writhing movements, usually of the hands and feet), *chorea* (irregular, involuntary movements of the limbs or face), and *dystonia* (abnormal muscle tone). Students with dyskinetic CP usually seem more floppy and have difficulty maintaining posture, even in a wheelchair.

Students with *ataxic* cerebral palsy also have low muscle tone and their movements are uncoordinated and jerky.

Some students with cerebral palsy have a combination of types and the presentation in all of these cases can vary from mild, to moderate, to severe.

Other conditions associated with cerebral palsy are intellectual and developmental delays (not an absolute connection, but the incidence is higher than in the general population), speech and language problems, visual and auditory difficulties, and seizures. An ongoing debate over cerebral palsy arises from the fact that intelligence test scores for children with this condition tend to be lower than the general average. However, one wonders about the appropriateness of IQ tests and the way they are administered and interpreted.

Motor disorders such as cerebral palsy and also some types of paralysis (for example, after a spinal cord injury) may be classified according to which limbs are most involved. Although the extent of a student's limb involvement is not a fundamental issue for teachers and educational assistants, it may have an impact on classroom planning. The terms that are generally used are: *paraplegia* (both legs are involved); *diplegia* (legs are more involved than the arms but all four limbs might be affected); *hemiplegia* (one side of the body is involved); *quadriplegia* (all four limbs are affected).

Spina Bifida

Spina bifida results from a neural tube defect that occurs before the child is born. The tube around the spinal cord does not close completely, and this defect can occur anywhere along the spinal cord from the brain right down to the bottom of the spine. Like cerebral palsy, spina bifida is not a progressive condition and can vary from quite minor impact to very severe. Wherever it occurs, the area below the lesion is usually paralyzed. Spina bifida occurs in about 1 in 2,000 births.

Spina bifida *occulta* is the mildest form of spina bifida and occurs when there is a gap in one of the vertebrae but the spinal cord stays within the vertebral canal. There may be no symptoms, or there may be some bladder and motor problems, depending on how many vertebrae are involved.

Spina bifida *cystica* occurs when the spinal cord actually sticks out through the defect in the vertebrae. It is called *meningocele* when the covering of the spinal column (the meninges) protrudes from the defect in the spine, creating a sac of cerebrospinal fluid. This condition is usually corrected surgically shortly after birth, but students may still need to have multiple surgeries as they grow.

Always Innovation …
A new prototype developed by Jan Andeysek, a professor at the Institute of Biomaterials and Biomedical Engineering, University of Toronto, provides a low-cost prosthesis that will allow individuals who may, in the past, have been unable to afford a prosthetic leg to have access to the most modern technology for only a fraction of the cost. The leg, estimated to cost less than $100, mimics the functionality of the more expensive technologies. The prototype is being tested across the world and has great potential to provide mobility for individuals who would have been unable to access such a device.

The most severe type of spina bifida cystica is called *mylemeningocele*, which describes a situation in which the spinal cord itself, as well as the meninges and cerebrospinal fluid, protrude outward into the sac. This type of spina bifida usually results in quite significant disability including lower body paralysis as well as loss of bladder and bowel control. This form is often accompanied by hydrocephalus, an enlargement of the head caused by an accumulation of fluid in the brain that causes increased pressure inside the head. Students with hydrocephalus will usually have a shunt (a short tube) installed in the spinal column to help this fluid drain from the brain into the abdomen.

Children with spina bifida sometimes have language abilities that seem to be very advanced, with speech that has been called "cocktail speech" because they speak well but have difficulty giving meaningful explanations.

Muscular Dystrophy (MD)

Muscular dystrophy is an umbrella term for a number of genetically inherited disorders that can affect people at various stages of life. In MD, there is *myopathy* (disease of the muscle) that results in the destruction of muscle fibres and the gradual wasting away of skeletal muscles. The most common form of childhood muscular dystrophy is Duchenne muscular dystrophy. Affecting more boys than girls, Duchenne MD is generally evidenced in the early school years by frequent falling, a "waddling" gait, and difficulty climbing stairs or getting up from the floor. This disorder, which progresses steadily, is characterized initially by weakening of the pelvic girdle and progresses to a stage where the child is in a wheelchair. Lifespan estimates for children with Duchenne MD have been increasing with medical treatment, but the degenerative process eventually leads to a premature death.

Children in a school setting may be assisted by access to technology and mobility aids, as well as physical adaptation of their learning environment. Muscular dystrophy does not affect the student's ability to learn, but programming for these students must take into account the progressive nature of the disease and the need to plan for accommodations over time. Consideration should be given to the social aspects of the student's educational environment: Opportunities need to be provided for peers to adjust to changes in health and functioning.

Developmental Coordination Disorder (DCD)

Developmental coordination disorder (DCD) is a less well recognized but much more prevalent chronic health condition that affects about 5 percent of children, or one child in every classroom. DCD is a motor learning problem that interferes with children's ability to perform many common, everyday tasks. It is often noticed first when a child's motor coordination difficulties begin to affect his or her academic achievement (e.g., handwriting, copying from the blackboard, and playground and physical education activities) or their independence in the activities of daily living (e.g., dressing, managing juice boxes, opening lockers). Students may appear to be clumsy or just to be less physically fit. Teachers may notice these behaviours in addition to noticing difficulty in completing their desk work.

Children with DCD have difficulty learning new motor skills and may have trouble performing the fine motor and gross motor skills that they have learned. While they may appear awkward, they sometimes just look lazy and unmotivated when they avoid tasks that require motor skills such as writing a story or colouring a map. DCD often co-occurs with attention deficit/hyperactivity disorder (AD/HD) and language disorders. If unrecognized, many children with DCD experience secondary emotional and behavioural problems. By adolescence, many children with DCD have poor self-esteem and mental health issues, including depression and anxiety. Teachers have a large role to play with these children as they will often progress through school without much difficulty if accommodations are made. Information about how teachers can support children with DCD can be found on the CanChild website. (**www.canchild.ca**).

Seizure Disorders (Epilepsy)

Epilepsy is not a disease but a symptom of a brain disorder that leads to seizures. There are several types of seizure, the two most common being tonic-clonic and absence seizure (formerly called "grand-mal" and "petit-mal").

In a tonic-clonic seizure, an individual loses consciousness, often convulses, and may fall. Breathing may stop temporarily. The individual may lose bowel and bladder control or bite the tongue. After one to five minutes, the person regains consciousness but may experience confusion and headache and often goes into deep sleep.

Absence seizures, on the other hand, are very brief and often go unnoticed. They may occur several times a day and are characterized by what is often called a "clouding of the consciousness," during which the individual's eyes may stare blankly, or the hands move aimlessly. Return to a normal state is usually abrupt. It is not unusual for teachers and educational assistants to be the first to suspect absence seizures since one-on-one learning situations are good opportunities for observation, especially if there is an effort to find out why a student's style is marked by significant ups and downs in understanding.

Students with idiopathic epilepsy (epilepsy of unknown origin) seem to function entirely normally between seizures. Those with symptomatic epilepsy (for example, following a brain injury) often have to cope with the consequences of a different primary condition, of which epilepsy is one factor. Epilepsy itself usually is not the reason a student is referred to an IPRC. More often, it is the primary condition (brain trauma), or the side effects of seizure-control medication, that lead to consideration for special education.

Many students who have tonic-clonic seizures are extremely sensitive about the episodes, and teachers may find themselves more challenged by the emotional than the physical consequences of a seizure. How a teacher deals with a post-seizure classroom atmosphere can have a major impact. Reassurance and emotional support for the student who had the seizure is crucial. Equally vital is how the teacher educates the other students about epilepsy. (The Epilepsy Association has excellent materials to assist with this issue and has up-to-date information on new medications for seizure control.)

How to Deal with a Tonic-clonic (Grand-Mal) Seizure in the Classroom

- Do not try to restrain the student; you cannot stop the seizure.
- Remove, or try to protect the student from, furniture and sharp objects.
- Do not force anything between the teeth.
- After the seizure, turn the student to one side to allow saliva to drain.
- Loosen the collar and other tight clothing.
- Put something soft under the student's head.
- Do not offer a drink until the student is fully awake.
- Let him or her rest afterward. (Often the student will sleep.)

If it is known that a student has epilepsy, it is useful to be prepared. Simple aids kept in the classroom – a blanket, for example – will be helpful.

N.B. Treat the situation as a medical emergency if the seizure lasts beyond five minutes or seems to pass from one seizure to another without the return of consciousness.

The Case of Xianan Yu

AT the age of ten, Xianan had many friends and, except for mathematics, did well in school (even in math he was keeping up with his grade level). He was a talkative boy who enjoyed video games, social networking, and, of course, hockey (which he played or practiced almost every day in winter).

A week before his eleventh birthday, Xianan was a passenger in a friend's car when a drunk driver went through a red light and hit the car almost head on. Xianan sustained serious head injuries.

Xianan's level of functioning has changed dramatically. He uses a motorized wheelchair, which he operates by blowing into a tube. He has speech, but frequently has trouble finding the right word, which causes him to become very frustrated. His comprehension is good if what he is reading or having read to him is not too lengthy.

Special education personnel of the board are in a dilemma. While the medical community and the insurance providers define him as having an Acquired Brain Injury (ABI), there is no category of this type under current Ontario Ministry of Education definitions. As a result, he has been classified in the Multiple Exceptionality category, which represents a very diverse population of students. The parents are quite upset about this because they believe that this category does not accurately capture the extent of their son's situation.

Nevertheless, Xianan is attending school (grade 6) with the assistance of a full-time educational assistant provided by the insurance company. He has a voice-activated computer attached to his wheelchair so that he can dictate notes, read, respond to assignments, and get onto the 'net. Due to Xianan's ABI, he is currently not up to grade level in any of his subjects and knows that he is behind where he once was. He gets angry when he is given academic tasks below where he thinks he should be. His teacher, the school resource teacher, and his educational assistant work together very effectively, but progress is slow. His parents want more individual assistance than is currently being provided and have also requested a new computer since the one Xianan is currently using is too slow.

The In-school Team is meeting to discuss how more assistance can be provided.

Tourette Syndrome (a.k.a. Tourette's or TS)

Tourette's is a neurological disorder that usually manifests itself in childhood and is frequently characterized by motor and/or vocal tics. In a small percentage of cases, the sounds are obscenities or curses (coprolalia). Although the condition was once thought to be limited to these manifestations, recent and more careful study of Tourette's suggests that other behavioural features may also be involved, such as hyperactivity, obsessive behaviour, and uncontrolled rages. Teachers and parents have noticed the frequent co-occurrence of these behaviours, but health professionals are not certain whether these constitute part of the syndrome.

Although Tourette's is usually a lifelong disorder, symptoms have been known to disappear for long periods or even altogether, with and without medication. There is no medical test for Tourette's, so a diagnosis must be determined clinically, i.e., by observation. Most health professionals appreciate the input of teachers in considering the criteria for a diagnosis.

Students with Tourette's can have difficulty in getting tasks started (or finished), problems with comprehending verbal instructions, and confusion over space–time directionality. Given those difficulties, it is not hard to understand why Tourette's is confused with other conditions such as a learning disability, intellectual handicap, or mental illness. Medications are frequently used, and their side effects may have an impact on classroom function.

The role of the teacher and educational assistant, as usual, is vital in the case of a student with Tourette's. Understanding, empathy, common sense support, and remediation strategies are obvious needs. Perhaps the most crucial matter in assuring the student's security and sense of well-being is the way in which classroom professionals respond to the symptoms and manage their effect on peers.

The chronic health conditions described above are the most common and are presumed to be present either at birth or to become evident as the child grows and develops. Following is a discussion of some health conditions that will also be encountered by most teachers at some point, but are conditions that are acquired more suddenly.

Acquired Brain Injury

Acquired brain injury (ABI) or traumatic brain injury (TBI) are terms used to describe any type of sudden injury that causes temporary or permanent damage to the brain after infancy. Motor vehicle accidents, near drowning, and sports-related injuries are among the leading causes.

ABI can seriously affect a student's cognitive,

behavioural/emotional, and physical well-being. The list of potential problems can be intimidating but, like the other health conditions, will vary considerably across students. Cognitively, students may experience difficulties with attention, processing, judgment, anticipation, perception, problem solving, transfer of learning, memory initiation, and fatigue.

As for behaviour, students may experience agitation, disinhibition, sudden outbursts of anger, impulsivity, and have general difficulty controlling their emotions. Students with ABI may become isolated and withdrawn or overly aggressive, difficulties that are often exacerbated by a lack of social awareness and an inability to self-monitor.

Physical difficulties after an acute injury may include central and peripheral nervous system problems, as well as orthopedic complications. Students may experience difficulty in other areas, including fine and gross motor skills, speech, hearing, vision, taste, olfaction, muscle spasticity, contracture, paresis or paralysis, and physical fatigue.

Students who experience an ABI usually need specialized help when returning to school. Often the period following the injury can be difficult, not only because of the sudden change in a student's functioning but also because of the variability of performance during the recovery period, which can last for up to two years. A team approach, involving parents, school, and medical personnel, is the most effective way to meet these challenges.

The Case of Matt

THE car crash that disabled Matt also caused serious injury to three of his friends and killed two others, but Matt was the only crash victim with permanent spinal cord injury. Although his condition was at first diagnosed as diplegic (legs more involved than arms), after about six months of therapy, he had a stroke and went into a coma. Doctors were sure he had another stroke, for, when he awakened, he had developed extreme choreoathetosis (abrupt, involuntary writhing movements) in all four limbs. This condition was so intense and painful that, after three months, it was decided to relieve the condition with a non-reversible surgical procedure that has made Matt a quadriplegic.

The accident happened after a weekend field party when Matt was fifteen years old and in grade 10. At the time, he was an identified gifted student and had been placed part-time in a self-contained class with gifted peers, and part-time in advanced grade 12 language and math classes.

Matt is now nineteen. He returned to school about a year ago and, to everyone's delight, demonstrated immediately that, although his body was immobilized, his intellectual abilities were not impaired.

An admirable piece of creative thinking by a special education teacher solved a potentially serious obstruction to Matt's rehabilitation. Rehabilitation engineers at the hospital had fashioned a "headstick" so Matt can tap a computer keyboard. Matt speaks normally; he uses a computer for writing, problem solving, and a range of activities. Leaning over the keyboard with a headstick quickly exhausted him, so the teacher mounted the keyboard above the computer monitor so that Matt's neck brace could support most of his movements. (Today, a voice-to-text program would likely have been introduced.)

Matt did exceptionally well after his return and graduated with honours. He asked for career counselling and is considering a liberal arts degree or a career in accounting. Matt's teachers recognized that they needed to support him to prepare for whatever choice he makes.

Spinal Cord Injury

Catastrophic accidents (e.g., car accidents, skiing, diving) may lead to an ABI by damaging the spinal cord. A spinal cord injury results from a fracture of the vertebrae or severe compression of the spinal cord leading the spinal cord to be cut or compromised. Usually paralysis occurs below the site of the damage. As outlined earlier, quadriplegia is the term used to describe weakness or paralysis of arms and legs while paraplegia means that only the legs are involved.

In severe cases where the spinal cord has been damaged at a very high level, the student may even require a ventilator for breathing. Nearly all students who have experienced a spinal cord injury will require a wheelchair for mobility.

If there has been no accompanying brain damage, there is no reason for the student to have difficulty with learning. The sudden onset of this type of serious injury, however, means that many students who have recently been injured may experience accompanying depression.

Information About Low-incidence Chronic Health Conditions

Finding information on rare conditions and disorders has become easier in recent years with the use of the Internet (though Internet information must be evaluated with caution).

Tuberous sclerosis and Mobius syndrome are two examples of rare disorders that may impact a student's performance in the classroom.

Tuberous sclerosis is marked by lesions in the brain and other organs, often the skin, and is frequently accompanied by serious developmental delay. Students may have seizures or manifest obsessive-compulsive and rage behaviours, not unlike those seen in students with autism or Tourette's.

In Mobius syndrome, first described as congenital facial diplegia, the muscles of the face gradually weaken so much so that the student cannot make facial expressions, even when crying or laughing. Atrophy of the tongue is common, and, in some cases, the forehead and eyebrows may even droop over the eyes, making vision difficult. Although there usually is no intellectual delay, Mobius is a condition that generates special needs both at home and in the classroom.

Health conditions such as these do not automatically indicate a need for special education, but the circumstances accompanying them may mean that special education intervention is preferred. Teachers and educational assistants will often find it useful to ask families for resources, get information from reliable Internet sites, or contact consumer groups.

Multiple Disabilities

Students identified as multiple-disabled or multi-handicapped typically have more than one special need. There is limited evidence that certain disorders will always be accompanied by others. In fact, a prevailing myth is that all students with multiple-disabilities are severely intellectually delayed. Another myth is that all students with multiple disabilities will have no oral language. There may, however, be a higher prevalence of disability associated with certain exceptionalities. Children with cerebral palsy, for example, may have a disproportionately high prevalence of visual impairment and epilepsy.

A student with multiple disabilities often requires considerable administrative attention. Establishing an appropriate placement, for example, may be difficult. A jurisdiction may have only one student who is diagnosed deaf/blind, physically disabled, or medically fragile. And it may have three students diagnosed as severely autistic, one of whom also has a visual impairment. In the past, the tendency was to identify these students as multiple exceptionality and place them together in a self-contained class. The rationale for such a placement was, generally, that doing so allowed individualized programming and easy access to support services and was economically feasible. This option has become less frequently used as the impact of segregation has become better known and parents have become stronger advocates for keeping their children with their siblings and peers. School boards throughout the province have worked hard to distribute services and allow students to remain in their home schools, though in some areas, partially due to practical realities such as finances and infrastructure, this has proven, as of yet, an ideal rather than a reality.

Whatever the identification and placement of a student with several special needs, his or her program usually:

- will be highly individualized
- will have a significant amount of specialized support
- will be marked by extensive communication and co-operation with the student's home so that education and habilitation can be coordinated beyond the school day

Other Chronic Health-care Needs

Modern medical science continues to improve the survival, growth, and development rate of children born with profound needs. Children go on to attend school, and their special health-care needs must be met, sometimes before their learning.

Teachers and assistants will encounter students with cystic fibrosis, scoliosis, congenital malformations, diabetes, cancer, severe allergies, asthma, and other chronic health conditions that preceding generations may never have even imagined. As a consequence, among items that distinguish modern classrooms, in addition to learning tools, are oxygen tanks and Epi-pens. With that reality comes the necessity for some knowledge of health conditions. Classroom professionals should not be medical managers, but for obvious reasons it is important for them to have an understanding of both daily and emergency procedures.

What makes this an even trickier challenge is

that their primary responsibility is still to educate, not to treat, with all the latter implies. Attending school, simply being in school, is a crucial element in the growth and development of all students: teachers and assistants have powerful roles to play in that process.

As outlined previously, a chronic health-care need does not automatically predestine a student to special education, especially in terms of placement. If a student's health requirements can be met in a regular school, there is no reason why they cannot be met in a regular classroom. A chronic health condition also does not, in itself, automatically generate the need for an Individualized Educational Program. However, management of the health condition (missed time, frequent medical and/or therapeutic interventions) may mean that special programming is required. Either way, students with chronic health conditions are in neighbourhood schools today.

Some Issues in the Field

◆ While it has been well established *that the role of the educational assistant* has proven to be extremely valuable in the successful delivery of services for students with exceptionalities, the role is most visible and essential within the area of health needs Many children with complex health needs require a specialized type of knowledge and treatment that, in general, is not within the standard teaching repertoire. A successful partnership between teachers and educational assistants (or health aides, or support workers) is characterized by mutual respect for the knowledge base of each, as well as rapport and trust. With these professionals working together, many children with complex needs can participate with their peer group and enjoy a successful experience within a school setting.

A particular concern to teachers is how to react in an emergency. This concern sometimes leads them to resist the placement of high-risk students in their class. Usually, this resistance can be overcome with information and education about the particular exceptionality. However, a constant – and justified – complaint of frontline classroom personnel is that they are not kept adequately informed about students with health needs. Changes in medication, environmental triggers (e.g., of a seizure incident or allergy), and crucial times of day are factors that can be very important to the accommodation of a student with special health needs.

✦ Teachers, quite rightly, argue that *poor communication* from health personnel, inefficient bureaucracy in a school or larger system, and stringent privacy regulations make their jobs more difficult and may even put the student at risk. Regular, direct communication with parents will likely be both helpful and informative.

✦ Families often experience *practical and emotional havoc* when they have a child with physical disabilities, neurological conditions, or chronic health needs. Such a child may demand a disproportionate amount of the family's resources in energy, money, and time. Needless to say, families react in different ways, and their feelings usually have a profound effect on the way the child reacts, in turn, to the world at large. In whatever way the family – and the child – react, the teacher, educational assistant, and a wide number of personnel in a school may be drawn into this reaction. Relative to their other students, they may also find themselves expending disproportionate amounts of energy, money, and time. How these demands are dealt with in a school, morally and practically, can become a matter of serious debate.

✦ *Responsibility by default* is not unusual in the case of students with severe disabilities. Most of the time, it occurs when an educational assistant becomes the sole teacher, classroom caregiver, or even, unfortunately, the sole companion of a student with profound needs. The issue is a particularly difficult one to solve, for the student's needs are usually very demanding, and it is both realistic and sensible for the needs to be dealt with by the person who is most familiar and competent. Often this is the educational assistant.

This type of management runs counter to the purpose of an inclusive classroom placement and is also antithetical to the objective behind placing a student in a self-contained class in a neighbourhood school. Even in a specialized setting, it is expected that the student will interact with as wide a variety of people as possible. The issue is a challenge for educational assistants, for their inclination and professional training orients them toward a wider use of their talents.

The Case of Tamhana

THE grade 4 teacher had met Tamhana two years ago while substituting in a grade 2 class for several months. At the time, the teacher had taken note of the young girl's persistent and unusual behaviour, but followed the advice of a colleague and did not pursue the matter.

Now, as the grade 4 teacher, he regrets that decision, for Tamhana's apparent oddities are much more pronounced and obsessive. She has continued a grade 2 habit: returning from the schoolyard according to a very specific walking pattern. But whereas she would permit intervention two years ago, Tamhana now blows into a frightening rage, if interrupted. She enters the classroom by a patterned path as well (and her peers have learned not to get in her way). Her lunch is eaten in a specific sequence, and she has taken to counting aloud while chewing to ensure an identical number of "chews" each time.

Tamhana's facial tics, very evident in grade 2, have ceased, but she now makes strange sounds when sitting alone (which, regrettably, is most of the time), ranging from growls to oohs and eehs, and on one occasion, the teacher is certain, barking. Lately, Tamhana has taken to impulsively running from the room. She allows herself to be brought back and is very remorseful for causing a disturbance. However, she cannot explain why she runs out and often, if questioned the following day, denies any knowledge of the event.

The teacher, like many of the staff, believes Tamhana has Tourette syndrome and wants the principal to refer her to an IPRC. Unfortunately, this was attempted in grade 3 and then abandoned after a friend of Tamhana's family told her parents that girls don't get Tourette's. As a result, the parents refused all requests from the IPRC for co-operation.

The staff has now learned of an additional complication: Tamhana's father does not want attention focused on a female child in any way that might bring disgrace on the family. What the teacher knows he must do is somehow convince the girl's parents that some kind of intervention is necessary, for Tamhana's behaviour is intensifying daily.

Implications for Social Aspects of the Classroom

North Americans live in a culture obsessed with beautiful bodies. Health and strength are not enough for us; we feel we must also be well formed and attractive. It is not surprising, therefore, that students with physical exceptionalities may face a battle to overcome the limitations imposed by their own bodies as well as to be accepted by others without stigma.

The same phenomenon applies to behaviour. To students with Tourette syndrome, for example, the band of acceptable or typical behaviour in our culture may appear very narrow; when their condition expresses itself, they feel very much singled out. A teacher with one or more of these students in class may deal as much with behaviours – that of the students with the disabilities, his or her own, of other students, or of the community at large – as with curriculum and instruction.

Students with exceptionalities may have negative feelings about themselves, especially if it is obvious that others around them do. Conversely, they may become independent and self-sufficient in response to the expectations of others. Self-acceptance and self-awareness will develop with the open and honest appraisal of significant people in their lives. It is essential that teachers and educational assistants alike become aware of the profound influence that their actions and attitudes can have on a class when it comes to interacting with students who are disabled. A look, a turn of phrase, and subtle body language can send clear messages of inclusion or exclusion, a message that will be heard and acted on by those who look to the teacher and educational assistant for instruction. Working in inclusive settings with students with exceptionalities goes far beyond reading, writing, and math to include acceptance by attitude and example.

Treatment of conditions such as epilepsy or Tourette syndrome often involves the use of medication that has sedating side effects. Teachers sometimes find themselves adjusting not to an exceptionality but to its treatment. It is not uncommon for a student to be in need of special accommodation because of the effects of the medication used to control a primary condition.

The normal adjustments that every teacher makes to accommodate his or her students' individual needs are often intensified in cases of chronic health need. Students often miss a great deal of instructional time through illness and absences for therapy. Teachers also have to make allowances in scheduling and in monitoring so students' personal hygiene can be addressed. As well, students with particularly serious disabilities may have attendant behavioural, even psychiatric problems, which can call on the full extent of a teacher's patience and stamina.

A chronic health condition may affect progress through the natural stages of development; teachers can anticipate that some students may not be able to work at the same academic level as their peers, and must therefore make adjustments in program and evaluation.

Strategies for the Classroom

1 Students in both regular and self-contained classes – especially younger children – will invariably take their cue from adults when seeking out how to react to and behave toward people with disabilities. Teachers and EAs have a positive leadership and modelling role, tactfully showing other students how to be helpful without taking over, how to ask for direction from the individual with the disability, how to react with empathy not pity, and how to manage their peer's exceptionalities with common sense.

2 If there are no secondary exceptionalities to deal with, such as developmental delay, teachers of a student with non-sensory physical limitations, neurological impairments, or chronic conditions will likely interact with a student in the same way as everyone else, making allowance only for special needs in day-to-day functioning. These special needs might include help in ensuring that medication is administered and help in the effective use of a prosthesis (artificial replacement for a body part), or some other adaptive device necessary for daily living.

3 Developments in computer technology accelerate far ahead of the capacity of texts like this to describe them, and classroom professionals need to stay abreast as best as they can to use this progress on behalf of their students. For more information, see appendix IV.

4 Because children with health conditions may be absent from school, co-operation in out-of-school assistance can be important to academic success. Some jurisdictions appoint "itinerant" teachers, who provide on-site instruction at home, in hospital, or in other settings.

5 It is rare, but possible, for the classroom teacher or EA to be a catalyst in the discovery of a condition (absence seizures, for example) that may go unnoticed in a family setting but become evident at school given its more structured demands. Less-known conditions such as Tourette syndrome sometimes go undiagnosed even through adolescence.

6 Effective communication among teachers, parents, and health-care professionals is absolutely essential, but such communication is ignored with discouraging frequency. It is often incumbent on the teacher or EA to initiate the communication, usually by direct and regular contact with the parents.

Help from Support and Advocacy Groups

Support and advocacy groups can be helpful in a variety of ways. Members of condition-specific organizations such as the Epilepsy Association, the Tourette Syndrome Foundation, the Canadian Hearing Society, the Canadian National Institute for the Blind, and many more are usually well informed and current in seeking out evidence-based information, supporting innovative practice, attempting to advocate for students and families who are dealing with slow-moving bureaucrats, or facilitating access to services and timely management by health professionals. All of these issues may be faced by classroom professionals, and, most of the time, the appropriate advocacy group can be quite helpful in addressing them. Associations, for example, generally have education programs in kit or video form that are useful for enlightening both students and adults. Advocacy groups are also often an effective first line of emotional support and information to a family who has just learned their child has been diagnosed.

Readings and Resources

Bennett, S., Good, D., & Kumpf, J. (2003). *Educating educators about acquired brain injury: Resource manual.* St. Catharines, ON: Brock University and the Ontario Brain Injury Association. www.brocku.ca/abieducation

Bennett, S., Good, D., Zinga, D., & Kumpf, J. (2004). Children with acquired brain injury: A silent voice in the Ontario educational system. *Exceptionality Education Canada, 14* (1), 115–30.

Buyer, D. M. (1999). Neuropsychological assessment and schools. *The Brain Injury Source, 3*(3), 18–20.

Dormans, J. P., & Pellegrino, L. (Eds.). (1998). *Caring for children with cerebral palsy: A team approach.* Baltimore: Paul H. Brookes.

Egilson, S. T., & Traustadottir, R. (2009). Assistance to pupils with physical disabilities in regular schools: Promoting inclusion or creating dependency? *European Journal of Special Needs Education, 24*(1), 21–36. doi:10.1080/08856250802596766

Emms, L., & Gardner, H. (2010). Study of two graphic symbol-teaching methods for individuals with physical disabilities and additional learning difficulties. *Child Language Teaching and Therapy, 26*(1), 5–22. doi:10.1177/0265659009339820

Giangreco, M. F. (1997). Persistent questions about curriculum for students with severe disabilities. *Physical Disabilities: Education and Related Services, 15*(2), 53–56.

Kurlan, R., et al. (2001). Prevalence of tics in schoolchildren. *American Academy of Neurology, 57,* 1383–88.

Lash, M. H. (2000). *Resource Guide: Children, adolescents, and young adults with brain injuries.* Wake Forest, LA: Publishing/Training.

Missiuna, C., Pollock, N., Campbell, W., Bennett, S., Hecimovich, C., Gaines, R., De Cola, C., Cairney, J., Russell, D., Molinaio, E. (2012). Use of medical research council framework to develop a complex intervention in pediatric occupational therapy: Assessing feasibility. *Research in Development Disabilities, 33*(5) 1443–52. doi: 10.1016/j.ridd2012.03.018

Missiuna, C., Pollock, N., Levac, D., Campbell, W., Sahagian Whalen, S., Bennett, S., Hecimovich, C., Gaines, B. R., Cairney, J., Russell, D. (2012). Partnering for change: An innovative school-based occupational therapy service delivery model for children with developmental coordination disorder. *Canadian Journal of Occupational Therapy, 79*(1), 41–50.

Richardson, P. K. (2002). The school as social context: Social interaction patterns of children with physical disabilities. *American Journal of Occupational Therapy, 56,* 296–304.

Schenker, R., Coster, W., & Parush, S. (2006). Personal assistance, adaptations and participation in students with cerebral palsy mainstreamed in elementary schools. *Disability and Rehabilitation, 28*(17), 1061–69.

Shu-Li, L. (2000). Coping and adaptation in families of children with cerebral palsy. *Exceptional Children, 66*(2), 187–99.

Tyler, J. S., & Wilkerson, L. R. (1999). Planning school transition for students with TBI. *Brain Injury Source, 3*(3), 14–16, 54.

Zinga, D., Bennett, S., Good, D., & Kumpf, J. (2005). Policy and practice: Acquired brain injury in Canadian educational systems. *Journal of Educational Administration, 43* (June), 1–23.

Zinga, D., Bennett, S., Good, D., & Kumpf, J. (2003). Brief report: Educating educators about acquired brain injury – a program description. *Journal of Developmental Disabilities, 10*(1), 159–63.

Links

CanChild Centre for Childhood Disability **www.canchild.ca/en**

Cerebral Palsy Canada **http://www.cerebralpalsycanada.com/**

Educating Educators About Acquired Brain Injury **http://www.abieducation.com**

Muscular Dystrophy Canada **www.muscle.ca**

Ontario Brain Injury Association **http://obia.on.ca/**

Spina Bifida and Hydrocephalus Association of Canada **http://www.sbhac.ca/**

Spina Bifida and Hydrocephalus Association of Ontario **http://www.sbhao.on.ca/**

Tourette Syndrome Foundation of Canada **http://www.tourette.ca/**

14
Students Who Are Deaf or Hard of Hearing

"Being hearing impaired, it was almost impossible to participate in class the same way as other students. Teachers thought that, because I wore a hearing aid, the problem was 'fixed,' I could hear 'normally' and therefore should be able to participate in classroom or group activities like the others were expected to. Nothing could have been further from the truth. I never knew what I missed hearing or heard incorrectly, therefore my responses were more often than not off topic. Even if I could hear what the teacher was saying, I could rarely hear others in class. To avoid feeling ridiculed and stupid because of inappropriate contributions, I withdrew as much as possible."

– Lynda P., forty-five, hearing impaired since birth

Misconceptions About Deafness

1   **Deafness diminishes intellectual ability.**
    The range of intellectual ability among individuals who are deaf is the same as among those who hear normally. Nevertheless, students who are deaf may lag academically because of difficulties communicating with people who can hear and use spoken language easily.

2   **Deafness leads automatically to muteness or to an inability to speak.**
    People who are born deaf or become deaf before acquiring speech (usually called prelingual deafness) sometimes have difficulty learning to speak clearly, but the connection between deafness and the inability to speak is not absolute.

3   **People who are profoundly deaf live in a world of total silence.**
    People with profound deafness can respond to some sounds or to the vibrations of sound.

4   **Hearing aids restore normal hearing.**
    Hearing aids do not restore normal hearing, but the technology has become very sophisticated now and allows for extensive customizing to individual needs.

5   **It is counterproductive and potentially harmful for people who are deaf or hard of hearing to socialize almost exclusively with others who are also deaf or hard of hearing.**
    Some members of the deaf community argue that an exclusive "deaf culture" is entirely natural and should be encouraged. Others argue the opposite with equal vigour. There is no conclusive evidence yet that the desire of some people who are deaf or hard of hearing to associate primarily with one another is anything but normal.

6   **Teaching signing to people who are deaf or hard of hearing will retard their development of spoken language.**
    There continues to be much controversy about the relationship between the development of spoken language and the age at which sign language is introduced. Teaching of sign language does not, of itself, retard the development of spoken language. However, if a person who is deaf or hard of hearing chooses to learn or to use sign exclusively, the development of facility in spoken language may be affected.

7 Individuals who are deaf compensate by reading lips.

When reading lips, the reader notes facial expression, hand gestures, and other body language in addition to simple lip movement. This skill does not come more easily to individuals with hearing loss than to anyone else. Reading lips alone is often not helpful because of similarities between words and inconsistencies in the lip movements of speakers. Some experts estimate that perhaps 30 percent of spoken language can be understood using this technique.

8 American Sign Language (ASL) is a universal sign language characterized by a loose style of gesturing primarily used to convey concrete ideas.

ASL is one (sign) language among many. Just as there is no universal spoken language, there is also no universal sign language. ASL is a sophisticated language with its own set of grammatical rules and can be used to convey levels of abstraction just as oral language does. See more about signing later in this chapter.

9 With the increasing movement toward the inclusion in regular classrooms of students with special needs, teachers have become better prepared to deal with students who have hearing impairments.

While many schools boards provide professional development as well as support services and personnel, on balance, within the field of special education, the proportion of students with deafness is small and the time for professional development short. Preparation at the preservice level is, at best, site-specific. In many cases it is non-existent.

Types of Hearing Loss

The Canadian Association of the Deaf defines hearing loss as having little or no functional hearing which results in an individual being dependent on visual rather than auditory communication (e.g., sign language, lip reading, reading, and writing). Most hearing losses are conductive or sensorineural (and sometimes, but not frequently, both).

In the case of *conductive hearing loss*, sound is reduced or blocked before it reaches the inner ear. This may occur as the result of trauma, wax buildup, or (most commonly) middle ear infection (otitis media). Sometimes the blockage can be cleared or the sound amplified to reduce the effects of conductive hearing loss. Conductive hearing loss can often be treated successfully and does not generally result in the need to access special education services.

In *sensorineural hearing loss*, the problem is in the reception of sound in the inner ear or in the transmission of electrical impulses along the auditory nerve. Sound may reach the inner ear, but because of problems in the inner ear structures, it may not be transmitted meaningfully, even with amplification. There are many possible causes for sensorineural hearing loss, which include a family history of permanent hearing loss, such apparently simple diseases as mumps and measles, more complex viral infections such as meningitis, as well as a range of congenital disorders and types of trauma.

Attempts to correct sensorineural loss tend to be more radical and the results less predictable than corrections of conductive hearing. As a result of more advanced screening methods, early intervention for hearing loss has been shown to be related to positive school achievement.

Hearing Loss and Other Disabilities

Data reported from the U.S. suggest that approximately 40 percent of students with hearing loss who receive special education services are also identified as having another type of impairment (Galladet Research Institute, 2008). These impairments, which include learning disabilities and intellectual disabilities, must be considered within the context of both physiological (whether part of a syndrome or genetic) and environmental factors (poor intervention, late school entry).

Possible Indications of Mild to Moderate Hearing Loss in Children

In primary classrooms, especially, children who experience more than the usual frequency of colds, earaches, sore throats, etc., need to be watched carefully for signs of the hearing problems that may follow. The following signs merit attention if a teacher or educational assistant notices them consistently:

- poor articulation, especially of consonants, not attributable to factors such as age or a different first language
- loud or soft speech that is at an inappropriate level for the environment
- physical signs (such as constantly cocking the head)
- trouble following directions or answering simple questions
- unusually frequent requests for repetition
- unusual inattentiveness
- requests that the volume be turned up
- failing to respond when being called on
- complaints of pain or earache

The possibility of a hearing loss should always be considered when assessing a student's behaviour problems and/or failure to meet academic potential.

Classifications of Hearing Loss

Specialists in the field of hearing generally include four markers to classify an individual's hearing loss.

These are:

- *site of loss*: whether the loss is conductive, or sensorineural, or both
- *age of onset*: whether the loss is pre- or post-lingual
- *etiology*: whether the individual's loss was present at birth (congenital loss) or has arisen since birth (acquired loss)
- *severity*: acuity of hearing, measured by an individual's response to intensity or loudness, as measured in decibels (dB), across a range of frequencies measured in hertz (Hz). A simple metaphor for the severity measure can be found in the controls on a radio. The volume control of a radio increases or decreases the decibel rating of sound issuing from the speaker, while frequency or pitch is modified by how carefully the tuner is set to the signal and by the degree of clarity achieved by adjusting the tenor/bass setting

A Caution About Severity

It is important to note that the characteristics used to describe the implications of hearing loss are by no means all there is to know about persons who are deaf or hard of hearing. Just like those who hear normally, people who are deaf and hard of hearing are as completely individual as anyone else – and therefore attend or tune out just like anyone else.

Another difficulty with classification is that, despite a certain presumed level of function in a person who is deaf or hard of hearing, that function invariably will be affected by the style and expressive quality of the person sending the communication.

Degrees of Hearing Loss*

Sound intensity is measured in decibels (dB). The faintest sound that a person can hear is measured at 0 dB.

Mild: Loss range is 25 dB-40 dB. Subject may have difficulty with faint or distant sounds and with conversations; may have loss when in groups, or in settings with ambient noise.

Moderate: Loss range is 41 dB-55 dB. Subject frequently has difficulty hearing normal speech, especially in groups, class discussions, etc.

* A hearing loss is also described as bilateral (both ears) or unilateral (one ear), with the severity of loss of each ear indicated individually.

Moderate/severe: Loss range is 56 dB-70 dB. Subject frequently has difficulty comprehending speech. Voices must be loud or amplified.

Severe: Loss range is 71 dB-90 dB. Subject has great difficulty understanding even loud or amplified speech. The latter may seem faint and distorted. Subject usually requires amplification and intensive speech and language training.

Profound (deaf): Loss range is 91 dB+. Subject may be aware of loud sounds and vibrations, but may not comprehend even amplified speech without training.

Common Sounds	dB Rating	Usual Effect
rustling leaves	20	pleasant
whisper	30	barely audible
2 or 3 people conversing	0–65	varies
hair dryer on high	70	interferes, disrupts
occupied cafeteria, food blender, motorcycle 5 m. away	80–95	annoying (85dB for 8 hrs begins hearing damage)
chainsaw, snowmobile, jet flyby 5 m. away	105–110	regular exposure without protection can damage
sound system at 100+ watts	120	pain threshold is 125 dB
concert, or jet takeoff	110–140	

Table 14A

Oralism Versus Manualism

Although several matters have a high profile, the single most overwhelming and consuming issue is that of communication method or style. On the surface, the issue appears to be a simple one of oralism versus manualism (signing): that is, should a person who is deaf or hard of hearing learn to develop and fully use whatever residual hearing he or she has available in order to communicate with people who hear, or should the emphasis and energy be devoted to learning how to sign in order to communicate with other signers (who, by and large, will be other people who are deaf or hard of hearing, family members, and teachers).

The Deaf Culture

Supporters of manualism argue that being deaf means being part of a culture that is distinguished by, among other things, its own language. They argue that, because experience shows that most people who are deaf or hard of hearing do not become comfortable participants in the hearing culture, to deny them their own language denies them their own culture and force them into one in which they are not full participants and may even be at risk. The phrase "deaf community" is frequently used (especially by those who are deaf or hard of hearing) to describe people who are deaf or hard of hearing as a cohesive group who share their own entertainment, activities – and language. This tendency toward self-exclusion does not prevail to the same degree among other groups with an equally apparent special need.

Supporters of oralism counter that the world is dominated by, and made up mostly of, people who hear. Persons who are deaf or hard of hearing who do not avail themselves of the opportunity to be part of the dominant culture are denying reality and relegating themselves to what is, in effect, not a culture but a subculture, with all that this implies. Some advocates on this side of the issue suggest that it may be advantageous for persons who are deaf or hard of hearing to develop skill in both styles of communication, either simultaneously or separately, so they can make a choice.

The issue of oralism versus manualism can present parents of a young child with an agonizing decision, for it is advantageous to begin either method as early as possible.

Educators, too, are inevitably involved in this issue, both practically and ethically. Learning to read, for example, can be significantly affected if a student is using ASL as the predominant means of communication. For example, a phrase that in print is written, "Yesterday I went to the store" is typically signed in ASL as, "Yesterday me store go."

Because sensitivity to syntax is such a powerful component in learning to read, it follows that some children who are deaf or hard of hearing and who are using ASL may have an extra challenge to face when learning to read English text.

Still another matter for educators is sensitivity to the intensity of this debate. While their primary role is to teach, that role can be more complex if the student (or his or her parents) is intensely committed to one side or the other of this communication and culture issue.

Further complicating the matter of educating students who are deaf or hard of hearing is the intensity of debate inside the respective oralism and manualism philosophies themselves. Even after a decision has been taken to emphasize one approach or the other, there is the potential for further disagreement over technique. For example, among supporters of manualism, American Sign Language has become an overwhelming, but not unanimous, choice.

In recent years, sophisticated surgical implantation technology has generated more possibilities – and difficult decisions – for dealing with significant hearing loss. One of the more vigorously debated technologies is the cochlear implant. In this procedure, a receiver is implanted either within or outside the cochlea (part of the inner ear) and an external component transmits signals to this receiver.

The present state of cochlear implant technology does not restore normal hearing, but there is evidence to suggest that it can dramatically improve a subject's ability to interpret speech and to make sense of environmental sounds, both natural and artificial. Controversy about the procedure and the technology arises over the suitability of candidates, the type of implant to use, and the impact on the subject.

Also of concern is what some consider the primitive state of the technology and the risk of damage to the cochlear nerve, which might prohibit future use of newer and more advanced devices that may be developed with further research.

Despite these types of controversies, the use of cochlear implants continues to grow.

A personal stereo system at maximum volume has been estimated to have a decibel level of between 100 dB to 110 dB. At a level of 105 dB, exposure over one minute can risk permanent hearing loss.

The Prevalence of Hearing Loss

An issue that plagues researchers, and one that has more than a peripheral impact on educators, is determining the true prevalence of hearing loss in Canadian populations. In 2007, the Canadian Association of the Deaf, using the traditional "one in ten" formula, estimated (with strong disclaimers) that there were approximately 310,000 culturally deaf Canadians and 2.8 million hard-of-hearing Canadians. The association states clearly that, in their opinion, no credible census has ever been conducted in Canada (Canadian Association of the Deaf **http://www.cad.ca/**).

In the United States, numbers are similarly difficult to ascertain. The National Association for the Deaf reports that approximately two to three in every thousand children in the United States are born deaf or hard of hearing (**http://www.nad.org/**).

Inconsistent definitions across jurisdictions, differences in the style of collecting and reporting data, and difficulties in assessing hearing loss among individuals with other disabilities (especially if these disabilities are multiple) lead to some confusing numbers in the field. Difficulties in reporting hearing problems are also compounded by an aging population. Depending on the parameters for reporting, the percentage of individuals with hearing loss can grow rapidly as older populations are included in the results.

Typical School Placements

- *Special residential schools*
  There are five special residential schools in Ontario, each of which also offers day programs. These are the Sir James Whitney school in Belleville, the Robarts school in London, the Ernest C. Drury school in Milton, the W. Ross MacDonald school in Brantford for students who are blind and deaf/blind, and the Centre Jules-Leger in Ottawa, which focuses on students with learning disabilities, visual impairments, and deafness.

Interestingly, over the past decade and more, the population of students who are deaf or hard of hearing at these schools has declined somewhat. This has led to the inference that there is an increase in students with hearing loss being educated in their neighbourhood schools.

In 2012 the Drummond Report (**www.fin.gov.on.ca/en/reformcommission**) recommended the closing of demonstration schools and the amalgamation of existing schools for the deaf into one site to achieve a greater critical mass. It also recommended that dollars saved from these closings/amalgamations be reinvested into enhanced opportunities for learners who are deaf or hard of hearing in school boards, colleges, and universities.

- *Special classes within regular elementary or secondary schools*
  Self-contained classes of students who are deaf and hard of hearing, though once common, are now decreasing as a placement option. Numbers reported by the Ministry of Education for 2009–10 indicate that, of students defined by the province as deaf or hard of hearing, 145 of 1,349 at the elementary level and 33 of 795 at the secondary level are in self-contained classes.

- *Part-time inclusion programs*
  Students may attend some regular classes in a regular school. A signing interpreter or an FM communication system or other support might be used. This type of program may have a resource room component, especially if a trained teacher of students who are deaf or hard of hearing is available to work directly with the students and to consult with the regular class teachers.

- *Itinerant teacher programs*
  Specialist teachers of students who are deaf or hard of hearing offer assistance in classrooms. In this program, students are usually in a regular class full time.

Communication Approaches and Supports

Oral Approaches

A child who is deaf or hard of hearing, and who learns via an oral approach, typically is taught to take advantage of auditory, visual, and tactile input. Much attention is given to auditory training, talking, speechreading, and amplification. Usually, oral programs emphasize the development of intelligible speech. Research suggests that significant successes in this type of program tend to occur in fully integrated school programs and in students with above-average IQ test scores whose parents are fully involved and supportive and who have above-average socio-economic status. Some of the methods used under the rubric of oralism are described below. Educators and parents who wish to investigate further usually begin with information from the Canadian Hearing Society.

Speechreading

This is a process in which a person receives a message principally by observing a speaker's face, paying special attention to the lips, facial expressions, and to the speaker's hand gestures and body language. Speechreading is enhanced if the receiver is aware of, and familiar with, the context of the speech. Complications, such as poor lighting, or any instance where the educator's face may not be in clear view, make this method only one of several avenues for people who are deaf to receive information. Very few people who are deaf or hard of hearing rely exclusively on speechreading.

Auditory Training

This process teaches a child to use what residual hearing he or she has. Also called the auditory method and auditory learning, the process operates on the principle of teaching a child to learn how to listen rather than just learning how to hear. Advocates argue that only a very few children are unable to benefit from this training, especially if it is begun as early as possible. Essentially, the method involves first the development of awareness of sound, then the ability to make gross discriminations between sounds in the environment, and finally the ability to discriminate between speech sounds. Supporters argue for the earliest possible use of amplifications, as well as simultaneous training in speech production.

A Signing Interpreter in the Classroom

Frequently, in this situation, the interpreter, teacher, and student will discuss the most appropriate location, one that will work best for the student's learning while providing minimal distraction for others in the class. Ideally, the student should be able to see the interpreter and any visual aids provided in the learning environment. Some pointers and recommendations:

- Be prepared for significant distraction at first.

- Provide, when appropriate, a notetaker.

- Get lesson summaries to both interpreter and student in advance.

- Allow time for the student to both read material provided visually and watch the lesson as the interpreter presents it. The student will need time to see and understand both.

- Be conscious of the lag between oral speech and its translation into sign.

- A visual aid means the student who is deaf has two stimuli to process with one sensory organ. (This is not dissimilar, in the case of a person who hears, to being addressed by two people at once.)

Specialized Approaches

A number of individual and unique ideas continue to appear in the field from time to time, some of which attract attention because of active support – and active criticism. Two that have attained a high profile, even though they are not widely used, are the cued speech method and the acoupedic method.

The cued speech method uses a combination of oral and manual styles. Attempts to develop the individual's residual hearing capacity and the capacity for speech are supported by eight manual configurations and four hand positions to supplement the visual manifestations of speech. The originator of cued speech, Orin Cornett, claims it can be learned in twelve to fifteen hours by anyone of average intelligence.

The acoupedic method, on the other hand, excludes all visual clues in order to encourage the individual to use residual hearing to the maximum extent possible.

Manual Approaches

American Sign Language (ASL)

In May 1993, Ontario became the first Canadian province to authorize the use of ASL (and LSQ, Langue de Signes Québécoise) as a language of instruction for students who are deaf or hard of hearing. Ontario schools for students who are deaf now use ASL and written English and allow students opportunities to use and develop their auditory and speech potential.

ASL is a true language in itself, quite different from spoken language, and most emphatically not a translation of English into manually communicated words. ASL has its own vocabulary, its own grammar, its own word order, and its own history. American Sign Language is founded on combinations of symbolic gestures produced by the shape, the location, and the movement of the hands. Whereas methods such as Total Communication (see below) very often employ iconic signs in which the shape of the sign encodes English as much as possible, the signs of ASL are unique. Many of these signs symbolize concepts rather than individual words. ASL has no signs for grammatical markers such as "ed" and "ing" that express verb tense and condition. Rather, users depend on facial expression and body language to replace voice intonation and enhance meaning.

ASL tends to be learned by children who are deaf or hard of hearing in special settings like schools, rather than being passed on by parents in the way language is learned by most hearing people. (The predecessor of ASL is FSL, French Sign Language, developed as a one-hand signing system by Abbé Charles Michel de l'Épée, 1712–1784, who founded an institution in Paris in 1770 for people who were deaf.)

Fingerspelling

This method spells out the letters of the English alphabet by using various finger positions on one hand. As a technique, it is often used as one part of the Total Communication method. Members of the Canadian Hearing Society have varied in their endorsement of fingerspelling. Critics generally hold that it is exceptionally inefficient and time consuming and requires an inordinate amount of attention for a style that has large potential for error. Supporters, especially those who are competent in the use of the method, say it is ideal for filling in those times when a communication doesn't get through and when it is useful for the communicator to spell out a word or words just as hearing people sometime feel the need to do.

Combination Approaches

Although the communication approach of a person who is deaf or hard of hearing is likely to emphasize one, rather than several, methods, he or she will invariably avail himself or herself of other sources for information such as facial expressions, body language, etc., in the same way as a person who hears. Within the taxonomy of communication styles advocated for people who are deaf, there are approaches that operate from this multi-source position both practically and philosophically. Two of these approaches are the Rochester Method and Total Communication.

The Rochester Method uses fingerspelling in conjunction with speech, speechreading, and amplification.

Total Communication may be defined as the use of speech, speechreading, fingerspelling, and amplification, along with the simultaneous use of a school-based manual system. In a school-based Total Communication system, signs are usually taught in the same order as language. This teaches the child to communicate manually using English syntax. Also, unlike ASL, the signs tend to attempt to reflect English syntax.

Worth noting is that some classrooms use ASL as part of a Total Communication approach. As well, even advocates who strongly support ASL to the exclusion of all else acknowledge the potential usefulness of other supports such as speechreading and hearing aid technology.

Hearing Aid Technology

There was a time, not long ago, when fitting someone with a hearing aid meant installing a device that simply amplified incoming sound. While the basic advantage of such a system is obvious, the accompanying drawbacks were often significant. Although straight amplification is still available today, and in some cases is entirely adequate for a user, the technology has become far more sophisticated and versatile.

Today's hearing aids are much smaller and more efficient, often fitting behind or in the child's ear. As technology progresses, so, too, does the ability to adjust the sensitivity of the device to the needs of the child. Using digitally programmable hearing aids, factors such as background noise and the teacher's voice can be accounted for in the device's functions.

In most cases, professionals who assess hearing (audiologists and audiometrists) not only can point to where on the decibel and hertz range an individual has hearing problems, but also can identify assistive devices that can be customized to address those problems. This technological step represents somewhat of a revolution for people with a hearing loss for it means that, in many cases, they are able to acquire hearing aids, although often at significant expense, that compensate for loss without adding new problems by amplifying other sounds unnecessarily.

In the classroom, technology can be generalized across a very wide spectrum. One example, and there are many, is a system that uses FM radio band technology. In this system, the teacher (and/or other students) wears a transmitter and those students with hearing loss wear receivers. For the student who is deaf or hard of hearing, the amount of classroom ambient noise is usually less obtrusive as they principally hear sounds coming from those wearing transmitters.

This is only one of many systems recently developed primarily for classroom use. Educators involved in choosing technological support for students who are deaf or who have a hearing loss need to investigate the options thoroughly, particularly in seeking out recent developments and in seeking out possibilities for customization of the support. Ironically, in an age that turns readily to technology in almost every facet of life, fewer than one-third of people who could be helped by hearing aids own and use one.

Educational Implications of Hearing Loss

✦ Students who are deaf or hard of hearing often do not have an easy time in school, mostly because of what is, in effect, a language barrier. Some researchers suggest that up to 50 percent of the learning difficulties experienced by students who are deaf or hard of hearing in school are the result of instructional factors. Studies over several decades suggest the academic achievement of such students is affected by five specific factors more than any other. These are the severity of the hearing loss, the chronological age at onset, intelligence, socio-economic status of the family, and hearing status of the parents (a student who is deaf or hard of hearing with parents who are also deaf or hard of hearing is considered to have a better chance of academic success than one with hearing parents).

◆ Achievement test scores for students who are deaf or hard of hearing, even on adapted test instruments, are often significantly lower than the scores of students who hear. However, it behooves educators to consider whether this lower performance is simply the result of a bad fit between the real abilities of students who are deaf or hard of hearing and the way achievement is measured. Even though students who are deaf may lag in reading and other language skills, teachers must be on guard against interpreting a difficulty with language as an inherent lack of ability. Yet the issue of language development and its effective use is inevitably a principal consideration in any evaluation of ability.

◆ The difficulties students who are deaf or hard of hearing have in communicating often lead to exaggerated compensatory behaviours or to frustration expressed in ways that cause the students to be unfairly labelled as disturbed, or odd, or even developmentally disabled. In the past, it was not unusual to find deaf students of normal intellectual and emotional development placed in segregated classes because of this mistaken label. There has even developed, over time, a so-called psychology of the deaf in which the characteristics of people who are deaf or hard of hearing are sometimes described in very unflattering language. One result of this perception of people who are deaf, no matter what its accuracy or its origins, is reinforcement of the isolation that students who are deaf or hard of hearing frequently describe as the worst part of living in a hearing world. Being aware of and responding to this factor is very important for teachers and educational assistants.

> *"It happened in grade 4. I was nine. I was concentrating on math – I love math; the numbers follow a pattern, not like words where the rules always change. I was aware other kids were moving. Nothing unusual about that. Class of thirty. But then the lights went out! I looked up. Everyone, including the teacher, had disappeared! I was so scared! I ran to the door and there was a class monitor waving at me. Probably yelling, too. Looked like it, anyway. It was a fire drill. Mustn't run, mustn't talk. But when I caught up with the class, I was shaking and sobbing. Once again, I felt ignored."*
> – Vivienne T., profoundly deaf from birth

◆ Classroom environment plays a major role in accommodating the needs of a student who has a hearing loss. Although matters such as locating the student's desk are always taken into immediate account by most teachers and educational assistants, there are other issues that recent findings have shown to be important. One of these is the amount of echo in the classroom, technically referred to as reverberation (the amount of time it takes for a sound to decrease to 60 dB after it ceases). Naturally, the more reverberation can be reduced, the less likely a student with hearing loss will experience interference. Interestingly, the impact of reverberation on students with normal hearing can be very significant, too, a fact that makes reverberation reduction through carpeting, acoustical ceiling tiles, and drapes (which may introduce allergy considerations – nothing is simple!) a matter of serious consideration.

◆ Yet another issue is signal-to-noise ratio. This ratio is the decibel level of the speaker divided by the decibel level of the ambient sounds in the room. The higher the latter, the lower the ratio and, naturally, the lower the ratio, the more difficulty a student who is deaf or hard of hearing will experience.

◆ Whether a student with hearing loss has an interpreter, or has amplification devices, or uses Total Communication, communicating is very hard work, both as a consequence of the concentration needed to receive information and of the effort needed to send it. Students who are deaf or hard of hearing get very tired, usually more so than their peers who hear, and teachers must recognize this. (It is important for people who hear to realize, too, that signing is very tiring work; an interpreter has an intensely energy-consuming job.)

◆ Social relationships for students with hearing loss in inclusive settings have been shown to be enhanced by participation in extracurricular activities. Having the opportunity to build friendships around common interests is essential for students to develop meaningful relationships. It is important for educators, who are modifying programs for students who have hearing loss, to look outside the curriculum and take into account the whole school environment by ensuring that opportunities for interaction are provided for students with hearing concerns.

◆ Meaningful co-operation with the hearing world can be difficult to achieve. People who are deaf or hard of hearing often describe their experiences with others in societal control (e.g., police and other officialdom) as unsatisfactory. An important responsibility of educators, because of their potential for extensive contact with students who are deaf or hard of hearing, is to sensitize the hearing public to this matter.

The Case of Nils

NILS' thirteenth birthday was more dramatic, if not traumatic, than most such days for a young adolescent. To begin with, on that day, he boarded a plane in Stockholm with his mother to come to Canada. She had accepted a three-year diplomatic posting, with an option of a three-year extension.

On the day of their arrival, Nils and his mother learned their first lesson in Canadian geography. The school for students who are deaf which had agreed to accept Nils was too far away from his new home for him to be a day student. They learned the even more distressing reality that the school used a communication style quite different from what Nils used. From age six, Nils had attended a private residential school for the deaf that uses sign exclusively. Moreover, the style of signing is one the school itself has developed and it is quite significantly different from any form of sign used in any general way in North America. This difference might not have been an issue for Nils in his home country, for the school provides personal interpreters for students who leave to enrol in neighbourhood schools. However, with Nils' move to Canada, the matter has become far more complicated.

Over a series of meetings during the first month of his life in Canada (during the summer vacation), Nils and his mother decided, and the local (Ontario) board has agreed, that he will enrol in the neighbourhood school. At this point, however, the boy and his mother have a further decision to make: choosing one, or a combination, of the following options.

1 The Swedish diplomatic service will provide, and pay for, a personal, in-class, signing interpreter trained in the signing style used by Nils' former school.

2 Given that Nils has some residual hearing (his loss is severe to profound, but he wears two powerful aids), a type of Total Communication can be used.

3 Nils is already familiar with sign. He could continue sign but use ASL.

One piece of good news for Nils is that the teacher of the class where he will attend is both qualified and interested in special education. She acknowledges that she has preferences in the matter of communication but has pointed out in meetings with Nils and his mother that she will happily accommodate whatever decision is made. Nils' school career has demonstrated that he is very bright and very resourceful and, although his language skills are typically lagging behind those of his peers who hear, his superiority in subject areas such as mathematics suggest that he would likely respond to any or all of the above. The question to be solved: What is best for him?

Strategies for the Classroom

The following suggestions have been collected from students who are deaf or hard of hearing. They were asked to offer advice to teachers and educational assistants involved in regular classes.

1 *Seat the student toward the front of the room and to one side, with the better ear toward the teacher and class.* Otherwise, seat them in the second seat from the front, second row from the window, or similar setting, but always in such a way that the teacher's face will be illuminated.

2 *Permit the student to move his or her seat if the teaching centre moves to another part of the room.*

3 *A student who is deaf or hard of hearing needs to see the speaker's face.* Seat the student two to three metres away from the place where you do most of your talking. Keep your hands away from your face.

4 *From time to time, attempt to keep your mouth near the level* of the student's eyes. For example, instead of always standing, sit at your desk at certain times.

5 *Be sure to have the student's visual and aural attention before giving assignments or announcements.*

6 *Where appropriate, make a practice of asking both students who are hearing and hard of hearing to repeat directions for the benefit of the whole class.* Ask the student to repeat instructions to ensure that he or she understands.

7 *Do not turn your back while talking.* Do not talk while writing on the chalkboard/whiteboard. A moving speaker is impossible to speechread. Do not walk around the room while talking about important things.

8 *Don't use loud tones or exaggerated mouth movements.* Use the tone of voice and inflection you use for everyone else. Avoid gestures, which draw attention away from the face and lips. They're embarrassing, too.

9 *Many words sound the same,* such as blue/blew or tax/tacks. This is confusing enough. But many words that do not sound the same look the same on the lips, e.g., bat, pat, and mat, and bad, pad, and mad.

10 *It may be helpful to explain to other students that many words look alike.* Let the class try to speechread a few sentences. This procedure will help others in the class to understand. Understanding helps to eliminate teasing and unfair judgments.

11 *During a discussion, ask questions to ensure that the person with hearing loss understands.* If the student does not understand, restate the material in a different way. Perhaps the student was not familiar with the key words that you used, or some of them may have looked like other words.

12 *Names of people and places, especially new ones, are very difficult to understand.* It is helpful to place new words or terms on the chalkboard/whiteboard and discuss new material from this vocabulary.

13 *A buddy can explain things.* A buddy can be a great fallback, but there may be potential for too much dependence.

14 *Try rephrasing rather than repeating,* but be sure a rephrase does not add confusion.

15 *If the person with a hearing loss is completely lost, say quietly, "I'm talking about …"* This often gives the student a fresh start. But be discreet!

16 *If the student seems to have trouble with certain words repeatedly, use these words often in as many ways as possible.*

17 *If your class has group discussions or co-operative learning activities, a round table is better for a student who is deaf or hard of hearing than a rectangular one.*

18 *Quietly and discreetly tell the student when his or her voice is too loud.*

19 *Encourage participation in extracurricular activities.* Students who are deaf or hard of hearing are like any others. They take their lead from their teachers.

20 *If a visit is being planned or a visitor is coming, prepare for it.* Write new and unusual words on the chalkboard; help the student with hearing loss become familiar with the names of persons or objects the student will be seeing. Explain any special rules ahead of time, when you can be sure that the student understands them. The brief discussion will help the student associate lip movements with new words and promote understanding of their meaning. By telling the student in advance what unit of activity will be studied, the student has an opportunity to find material on the subject and will be able to follow along much better because he or she will be more familiar with the vocabulary. Always, in history, science, and geography lessons where there will be new vocabulary or new concepts, try to give the student a brief written statement, e.g., "Today's topic is the Introduction of The War of 1812. Key words are Niagara Frontier, Sir Isaac Brock, York, James Madison."

21 *Students who are deaf tire more easily than others do.* You can help by planning the day's work so the periods when they must pay careful attention are interspersed with other activities.

22 *Encourage the student to keep trying.* Please be patient. Repeat instructions as often as necessary.

23 *If possible, try to help the student learn to use a dictionary pronunciation key.*

24 *Be aware that many students hear better on some days than others.*

25 *Talk with the students who are deaf or hard of hearing every day.* Talk often, rather than for a long time. Ask questions about movies, TV programs, hobbies, travel, work, etc.

26 *A regular hearing aid makes speech louder, but not always clearer.* It often amplifies all other noise, too. See if some of the other noise can be reduced.

27 *If it has not already been investigated, look into the possibility of using an FM system.* This system can be more effective in a classroom than a hearing aid.

28 *There is a lot of helpful technology (e.g., voice to text), and computers don't get tired of repeating something.* If the student controls the keyboard, then the number of repeats will be just what is needed. Not too many. Not too few. Earphones are always better for people with a hearing loss. They concentrate the sound and block out all the background. Half the time it is the background that's the problem. For more information, see appendix IV.

Authors' note: The following is verbatim (orally) from a very bright twelve-year-old student with a severe hearing loss.

> "Our teaching assistant this year was the best help I ever had. And she wasn't a hearing specialist. Couldn't sign or nothing. But she was helpful. You don't always need a specialist. Just a good T.A."

Readings and Resources

Akamatsu, C. T., Stewart, D. A., & Mayer, C. (2006). Is it time to look beyond teachers' signing behavior? *Sign Language Studies, 2*(3), 230–36.

Antia, S. D., Jones, P., Luckner, J., Kreimeyer, K. H., & Reed, S. (2011). Social outcomes of students who are deaf and hard of hearing in general education classrooms. *Exceptional Children, 77*(4), 489–504.

Calderon, R., & Naidu, S. (2000). Further support for the benefits of early identification and intervention for children with hearing loss. *The Volta Review, 100*(5), 53–84.

Furlonger, B. E., Sharma, U., Moore, D. W., & Smyth King, B. (2010). A new approach to training teachers to meet the diverse learning needs of deaf and hard-of-hearing children within inclusive Australian schools. *International Journal of Inclusive Education, 14*(3), 289–308. doi:10.1080/13603110802504549

Gallaudet Research Institute (November 2008). *Regional and National Summary Report of Data from the 2007–2008 Annual Survey f Deaf and Hard of Hearing Children and Youth.* Washington, DC: GRI, Gaullaudet University.

Hardonk, S., Desnerck, G., Loots, G., Hove, G. V., & Van, E. (2011). Congenitally deaf children's care trajectories in the context of universal neonatal hearing screening: A qualitative study of the parental experiences. *Journal of Deaf Studies and Deaf Education.* doi:10.1093/deafed/enq055

Hintermair, M. (2011). Health-related quality of life and classroom participation of deaf and hard-of-hearing students in general schools. *Journal of Deaf Studies and Deaf Education, 16*(2), 254–71. doi:10.1093/deafed/enq045

Kushalnagar, P., Topolski, T. D., Schick, B., Edwards, T. C., Skalicky, A. M., & Patrick, D. L. (2011). Mode of communication, perceived level of understanding, and perceived quality of life in youth who are deaf or hard of hearing. *Journal of Deaf Studies and Deaf Education, 16*(4), 512–23. doi:10.1093/deafed/enr015

Lartz, M. N., & Litchfield, S. K. (2006). Administrators' ratings of competencies needed to prepare preservice teachers for oral deaf education programs. *American Annals of the Deaf, 150*(5), 433–42.

MacDougall, J. C. (2004). Irreconcilable differences: The education of deaf children in Canada. *Education Canada, 44*(1).

Marschark, M., Spencer, P. E., Adams, J., & Sapere, P. (2011). Evidence-based practice in educating deaf and hard-of-hearing children: Teaching to their cognitive strengths and needs. *European Journal of Special Needs Education, 26*(1), 3–16. doi:10.1080/08856257.2011.543540

Meadow, K. P. (2005). Early manual communication in relation to the deaf child's intellectual, social, and communicative functioning. *Journal of Deaf Studies and Deaf Education, 10*(4), 321–29. doi:10.1093/deafed/eni035

Mitchell, R. E., & Karchmer, M. A. (2006). Demographics of deaf education: More students in more places. *American Annals of the Deaf, 151*(2), 95–113.

Moores, D. F. (2001). *Educating the deaf: Psychology, principles, and practices* (5th ed.). Boston: Houghton Mifflin.

Ontario Ministry of Finance: *The Drummond Report.* www.fin.gov.on.ca/en/reformcommission.

Patel, H., & Feldman, M. A. (2011). Canadian Paediatric Society Position statement. Retrieved at: http://www.cps.ca/english/statements/CP/cp11-02.htm

Punch, R., & Hyde, M. (2011). Social participation of children and adolescents with cochlear implants: A qualitative analysis of parent, teacher, and child interviews. *Journal of Deaf Studies and Deaf Education, 16*(4), 474–93. doi:10.1093/deafed/enr001

Schirmer, B. R. (2000). *Language and literacy development in children who are deaf.* Boston: Allyn & Bacon.

Schirmer, B. R., & Woolsey, M. L. (1997). Effect of teacher questions on the reading comprehension of deaf children. *Journal of Deaf Studies and Deaf Education, 2*, 47–56.

Seewald, R., & Tharpe, A. M. (Eds.) (2011). *Comprehensive handbook of pediatric audiology.* San Diego: Plural Publishing.

Shirin, A., Luckner, J., Kreimeyer, K. H., & Reed, S. (2011). Social outcomes of students who are deaf and hard of hearing in general education classrooms. *Exceptional Children, 77*(4), 489–504.

Links

Canadian Association of the Deaf **http://www.cad.ca/definition_of_deaf.php**

Canadian Hearing Society **www.chs.ca**

Government of British Columbia **http://www.bced.gov.bc.ca/specialed**

Hearing Foundation of Canada **http://www.thfc.ca**

Ontario Association of the Deaf **http://www.deafontario.ca**

15

Students Who Are Blind or Partially Sighted

*"If there was only one thing about sighted people that I could change,
it would be to make them think of me as just a normal person who can't see.
So that when I do something normal, like find a CD and slip it into the player
and turn it on – stuff like that – nobody will say 'Isn't he something?'
When we blind people do ordinary things, it's because we're ordinary people.
It's not like we should be in a circus."*

– Corey P-N, age twenty-nine, blind from birth

Misconceptions About Blindness and Partial Sight

1 **People who are blind have no sight at all.**
Only a small percentage of people who
are legally blind have absolutely no vision.
The majority have a useful amount of
functional vision.

2 **People who are blind use Braille as their
primary method of reading.**
The majority use print – often large type – as
a primary source of reading. An increasing
trend among people who cannot see print is
to use audio technology rather than Braille.

3 **Individuals who are blind automatically
develop better acuity in their other senses.**
Through concentration and attention, persons
who are blind often learn to make very fine
discriminations in the sensations they obtain.
This is not automatic; rather, it represents a
better use of received sensations.

4 **Almost any person who is blind would
benefit from the use of a guide dog.**
While guide dogs can, indeed, provide much-
needed assistance, in actuality only a small
percentage of persons who are blind use one.
Individuals who use guide dogs must be over
sixteen and demonstrate that they are able to

care for the animal. Given the age restrictions,
the use of such an animal would be rare in a
school setting.

5 **If students who are partially sighted use their
eyes too much, their sight will deteriorate.**
Only in rare conditions is this true; visual
discrimination ability can actually improve
through training and use. Strong lenses,
holding books close to the eyes, and using
the eyes usually does not harm vision.

6 **Students who are blind automatically
become good listeners.**
Good listening is primarily a learned skill.
Although many individuals who are blind
develop good listening skills, it is the result
of effort because they depend on these skills
for so much of their information.

7 **Instructing children in mobility techniques
should wait until elementary or even
secondary school age.**
The adage of "the earlier the better" applies to
children who are blind as well as to their peers
who are sighted. Even the use of a cane at an
early age has been shown to have advantages.

Definitions and Prevalence of Blindness

Legal blindness in Canada is defined as distance acuity of 6/60 m, or 20/200 ft, or less in the better eye after the best available correction. That means the person must stand at six metres or closer to see an object that normally would be seen at sixty metres.

Persons whose visual field is reduced to an angle of twenty degrees or less at its widest diameter are also legally blind. (People with normal sight have a visual field of 180 degrees.)

A person who is partially sighted is one whose distance acuity is 6/13 or less in the better eye.

It is important to recognize that someone with visual acuity of 6/60 can probably read, or at least see, print. Total blindness, i.e., the inability to see anything at all, is actually uncommon.

In the Participation and Activity Limitation Survey (PALS) conducted by Statistics Canada in 2006, 836,000 Canadians reported themselves as having a "seeing disability." Of that 836,000, only 19,700 were children under the age of fourteen (National Coalition for Vision Health). For educators, three important facts underline the matter of prevalence.

The first of these is that blindness and visual impairments are both low-incidence conditions.

Second, they are conditions that affect adults at significantly greater rates than children and teenagers.

A third is that, while the conditions do not appear with high frequency in North America, their prevalence in many Asian, African, and South American countries is much greater. Lack of sanitation, vitamin deficiency (particularly Vitamin A), poor sanitation, and the high potential for water-borne illness raise the numbers in these countries.

> *"Sighted people have all these ways of saying shut up without actually saying it – you know? Like – they turn away, or they stand up suddenly. Stuff like that. I never interpreted that as shut up, even when I knew it was happening, until someone told me about it. I'm glad I was told though. Helps to know. That's one of the things about being blind. Everybody treats you with kid gloves. We don't need that. We've got to be told to shut up, too, just like everybody else."*
>
> – Ginny de V., age seventeen

Classifications of Blindness

Near normal vision: able to function without special training, but will use corrective lenses.

Moderate functional impairment: requires specialized aids and lighting.

Reduction in central vision: moderate field loss; may qualify for special services as legally blind.

Low vision: even after correction, vision is lower than normal, although correction is usually helpful.

Poor functional vision (and possible poor central vision with marked field loss); standard correction is of little or no benefit; usually strong reading aids and other technologies are needed.

Blind: total field loss as well as total detail loss; may be able to perceive light.

Vision can be further classified as congenital (from birth) or adventitious (acquired later in life, most likely through illness or injury).

Some Typical Causes of Blindness

Retinal detachment: retina can become separated through injury or disease, making the eye incapable of receiving images.

Retinoblastoma: a genetic disease that presents with malignant tumors; treatment usually involves chemotherapy and localized eye-saving measures.

According to the Ontario Cancer Institute, the majority of eyes are saved. The Institute advises genetic counselling for the families involved.

Retinopathy of Prematurity (formerly known as Retrolental Fibroplasia): a condition occurring in babies who are exposed postnatally to a greater than normal concentration of oxygen.

Rubella: a syndrome occurring as a result of maternal rubella infection during the first months of pregnancy; fortunately, immunization against Rubella has significantly reduced the risk.

Sympathetic Ophthalmia: when there is a penetrating wound to one eye, the other eye may reflect the same characteristics as the injured eye.

Classroom Checklist of Possible Vision Problems

Although the ultimate diagnosis of a student's visual problem – or even its existence – would naturally be determined by an optometrist or ophthalmologist, teachers and educational assistants can play an important role in early detection. While these problems are more common in the very early grades, teachers of older students should not exclude themselves, since eye disease and poor vision can begin at any stage in life and grow serious rapidly. Any of the characteristics in the Classroom Checklist, especially if observed over time, might indicate real or potential visual impairment.

1 Appearance of eyes
- One eye turns in or out at any time?
- Reddened eyes or lids?
- Encrusted eyelids?
- Frequent sties on lids?
- Eyes tear excessively?

2 Complaints by student
- Headaches in forehead or temples?
- Burning or itching of eyes after reading or desk work?
- Nausea or dizziness?
- Print blurs or moves after reading a short time?

3 Behavioural signs of visual problems
- Head turns while reading across the page?
- Loses place often during reading?
- Needs finger or marker to keep place?

- Tilts head abnormally while working at desk?
- Rereads or skips line unknowingly?
- Too frequently omits or substitutes words?
- Complains of seeing double (diplopia)?
- Misaligns number columns regularly?
- Squints, closes, or covers one eye?
- Orients a worksheet unusually?
- Must feel things to understand?
- Disorderly placement of words or drawings on page?
- Blinks to clear view of chalkboard after near task?
- Squints to see chalkboard?
- Holds book too closely?
- Avoids all possible near-centred tasks?
- Closes or covers one eye when reading?
- Rubs eyes a great deal?

Some Typical Causes of Partial Sight

Albinism: genetically transmitted disease in which the eyes are light sensitive; minimum illumination is needed and tinted glasses are usually prescribed.

Astigmatism: defect causes an error in refraction; images are blurred and there is generally poor visual discrimination; glasses are prescribed, usually with positive results; good illumination usually helps, too.

Cataracts: lens opacity is a cataract; such opacity causes blank areas in what is seen; depending on the nature of the opacity, adjustments in lighting are usually necessary.

Colour deficiency (a.k.a., colour blindness): inability to distinguish colours; more boys than girls are affected.

Glaucoma: a problem caused by increased intra-ocular pressure; glaucoma patients require regular medical attention and sometimes suffer headaches;

if untreated, peripheral vision may become limited; good illumination is recommended.

Hyperopia: hyperopic eye is far-sighted; student with this condition usually functions well in gross motor activity but finds reading and other near work difficult and tiring until correction is provided.

Macular degeneration: centre of the field of vision blurs causing most detail to be lost; some limited peripheral vision usually remains; there are two common forms: "wet," which usually progresses rapidly, and "dry," which develops more slowly.

Monocular vision: disease, accident, or defect leaves a person with only one functioning eye.

Myopia: distance vision is blurred so that gross activities can be difficult; student with this condition is more comfortable with reading and other close work.

Nystagmus: involuntary movement of the eyeball caused by this problem makes focusing and fixation difficult.

Optic atrophy: optic nerve sustains permanent loss of its ability to carry clear images to the brain; may result in restricted fields of vision.

Peripheral vision: ability to see only those activities and objects outside the direct line of vision; because of defective central vision, the student may have to tilt head or raise or lower eyes to read.

Retinitis pigmentosa: pigment deposits in the retina cause loss of peripheral fields resulting in tunnel vision; major difficulties occur in dim light; good illumination is needed.

Strabismus: imbalance of the eye muscles causes failure of the two eyes to focus on the same object; eyes can cross or deviate upward or downward; early treatment is vital or a "lazy eye" condition (amblyopia) can result.

Tunnel vision: field of vision is so reduced that a child sees only what is directly in front; it creates the same visual image that others see when looking through a tube, severely affecting mobility and the collection of information from the environment.

Working with the Resource Teacher for the Visually Impaired

Many students who are blind or visually impaired spend a majority of their day, if not all of it, in a regular class with peers. While many of their learning opportunities need not take a great deal of adjustment, specialized interventions and techniques may definitely be necessary. Because the percentage of students with blindness and visual impairments within a given population can be very low, it is not always a reasonable expectation that all classroom teachers will have the specialized knowledge needed to be as effective as possible. Because of this, it is not uncommon for boards of education to have what would be referred to as itinerant teachers or resource persons for the following types of things.

- explanation of the student's impairment to educators at the school level
- assessment of the student's residual vision
- provision, training (teacher and student), and integration of specialized equipment
- strategies for instruction
- provision of Braille
- provision of and training in appropriate technology
- socialization and adaptation strategies (student, teacher, and sometimes classmates)
- orientation and mobility information
- available resource support materials and organizations

Some Issues in the Field

✦ A most significant issue for individuals who are blind or partially sighted is ***successful adjustment to the world at large***. This adjustment calls for mobility and a sensitivity to the environment that is natural in persons with sight but not so in those whose vision is limited. A great deal of the energy, life force, education, and time of persons who are blind or only partially sighted is devoted to this matter, especially when they are young. At the same time, because they are normal human beings in every other respect, persons who are blind naturally wish to live the life that the rest of the world does. Much of the initial social exchange between people who are visually disabled and the people in their lives who are not is devoted to finding a mutually comfortable, appropriate, and effective means of associating.

✦ The failure of individuals and families to have ***regular eyesight examinations*** continues to be a nagging concern for health-care professionals and educators. Infants as young as three months can now be tested with considerable accuracy. Optometrists urge that all children be examined by three years of age and again at school entrance. This is because many vision problems are more correctable if a response is made early. It is also important to begin teaching visual efficiency early, if visual acuity is poor or weakening. Testing is especially important if there is a familial pattern of such problems as strabismus, cataracts, etc. Despite the logical and impassioned arguments of both educators and health professionals, the response of families and even educational jurisdictions is, surprisingly, less intense than one might expect given the ease and limited expense with which these examinations can be conducted.

✦ In an increasingly technological world, it is not unexpected that ***technological innovations*** would find a place in the area of disabilities. Computerized programs that automatically scan and enlarge print for students with limited vision, voice-activated cell phones, personal data assistants, and even GPS tracking devices to assist in mobility are only some of the options available for persons with vision difficulties. While technology holds out great promise, it is not without its limitations. Braille users point out that scanning for information, reading a speech, and taking notes are far more easily done using Braille than other types of recorded information. Mobility devices that use a method similar to echolocation are only in their preliminary stages and should not be used in place of the long cane. There are also concerns about access and affordability of this technology for all persons who are blind. Certainly, technology should not be seen as a panacea. It provides another set of options for persons who are blind to use judiciously where maximum gain can be achieved.

The Case of Lori

At age three, Lori seemed to bump into things and fall over her playmates far more frequently than seemed normal for her age. Both parents suspected a vision problem. That suspicion was reinforced two years later by a very observant kindergarten teacher and an equally perceptive educational assistant. After the first week of school, both instructors began to keep an "Events Journal" on Lori, noting specifically those behaviours suggesting Lori had impaired vision. Within ten days they were both convinced their young student was using peripheral vision to accomplish what other students did by focusing face on.

A conference with Lori's parents led to a visit with an ophthalmologist and confirmation of what the two suspected: Lori had macular degeneration.

The quick and careful thinking by Lori's kindergarten teacher and educational assistant made a huge difference in her life. Macular degeneration usually means that the individual has blurred or completely obscured centre-of-field vision while retaining some vision at the edges of the field. Very often it is progressive and intensifies over time. The early intervention in Lori's case meant that she was able to receive special training at a crucial time in her development. Lori's average to above-average ability and what every adult in her life calls "high-profile spunk," along with this training, meant that she was able to progress quite smoothly through the next years of her school career. She was in a regular class in her neighbourhood school during this time.

Now, in the seventh grade, a problem has arisen. Lori's condition has worsened over time so that, essentially, she has lost all of her vision. For several years now, for funding purposes, she has been identified as legally blind. In spite of this, she participates fully in all class activities, something she and her parents insist on even though her mishaps have increased in number and seriousness – most recently, a broken arm in gym. Other difficulties have arisen as well. Lori is in the school band, but she does not have a natural ear, cannot see the notes, and plays her trombone badly – and loudly. Because of an incident during a natural science field trip last year (Lori fell over an embankment and pulled two other students down with her; no one was hurt), this year's class trip is being reconsidered.

A meeting of Lori's teachers, assistants, and parents has been called for next week by school officials. They are committed to keeping Lori involved in all activities. The administration wishes to discuss what is best for Lori and her schoolmates in terms of their education and social development. What should her program be?

Some Educational Implications of Teaching Students with Special Visual Needs

✦ Empirical evidence suggests that, in the classroom, especially among younger students, cognitive abilities in those who are blind and partially sighted tend to develop more slowly than the norm. There is a good deal of support for the view, however, that this apparent lag is owing more to differentiated early learning experiences than to any inherent intellectual difference. Children who are blind simply have not had the opportunity to experience some of the things that children with sight have.

✦ Children who are blind or partially sighted need explicit information to accompany their vocabulary. It is important for teachers to realize that, despite the fact a child can verbalize that a cow gives milk, he or she may have no context for that statement. The student may know the information but not have any idea of what an udder is or the mechanics of how milk is collected. Ensuring that information is contextualized is essential for the development of understanding and learning.

✦ It is difficult for students with serious vision problems to develop a spatial map of their environment. However, it is possible to develop the concept of space with other senses, such as noting the time it takes to walk various distances, or feeling the dimensions between objects. Because the amount of information that can be taken in at one time is limited, the process is understandably slower. This fact makes the time to acquire learning an important factor – as it is with almost all students with exceptionalities.

- For students who cannot see, or who see poorly, it is often difficult to understand abstract concepts without the aid of concrete materials. Such students will benefit from three-dimensional models, and games and materials that focus on manipulation.
- Students who are blind or partially sighted are often overprotected by the adults in their lives and treated over-delicately by fellow students. Although this is not an unnatural response, it is important that independence be a prominent and continuing objective in the education of students with vision problems. Fostering this independence calls for frequent and delicate judgments by the teacher and educational assistant.
- Students who are blind often require additional mobility and orientation training. Children learn, not only from moving but also from watching others move. The lack of these opportunities for observation, combined with the overprotection mentioned above, can result in the necessity of additional support to develop fluid mobility skills.
- Students who are blind must be taught social and communicative skills that many persons with sight acquire naturally. Most cultures, for example, attach great importance to whether or not a speaker looks at his or her listener, and many advocates for the blind urge that this habit be taught. However, some so-called natural skills are much more difficult to teach. For example, people with sight make constant use, subconsciously, of body language, using it to convey responses such as reinforcement, enthusiasm, reluctance, disagreement, uneasiness, etc. Body language can alert a speaker to modify a particular communication and sometimes even indicates whether a communication is finished – or should be! For obvious reasons, the very notion of body language and the means of dealing with it is something that students who are blind and partially sighted cannot be expected to acquire naturally.

- The less a person is able to know the world through sight, the more important it becomes that he or she be a good listener. Although it was once assumed that good listening skills automatically develop as a consequence of sight deprivation, it is now known that such skills must be taught. It is also important to keep in mind that classroom environments need to be adjusted to allow for that listening to take place.
- Professionals dealing with the very young must be particularly conscious of the fact that many children are not aware of a visual problem if they have one. Or, if they are aware, they often do not understand its extent or its implications. This is important for classroom professionals, not just in discovering the presence of the problem, but in helping the child to deal with it.
- Academic success is more closely related to social, cultural, and familial factors than to degree of visual impairment.
- Opportunities to build social relationships, as well as skills, can be enhanced by ensuring that extracurricular opportunities are not developed or orchestrated in a way that excludes students with visual impairment.
- As with any type of impairment, early intervention seems to be best. Evidence is clear that an early focus on mobility and communication reaps significant benefits.

Visual Stimulation

As recently as the 1960s, students with low vision were encouraged to "save" their visual capacity to keep it from "wearing out." Today, the belief is that the more one's residual vision is used, the stronger and fitter it may become. Thus, educators now encourage students with low vision to attend to light and objects, to use tracing and scanning techniques, and to exercise their residual vision in a variety of ways (e.g., a popular technique with children, especially younger ones, is to have them sort, classify, sequence, and creatively rearrange pictures). With students who have low vision, many of the technical devices mentioned in this chapter can be very useful, but the students must be trained to use them.

Assistive Technology

Braille

This well-known writing system is named after Louis Braille, but its origins go back to Charles Barbier, an officer in the army of Napoleon Bonaparte. Barbier devised a system of raised dot writing that could be read by touch in the dark. Braille published his modified system in 1834. Within twenty years, this system was adopted by the Paris School for the Blind, but it took another half century for Braille to penetrate North America. By the mid-1950s, more than half of all persons who were blind or seriously visually impaired were Braille users. By the end of the century, however, the number had dropped to below 10 percent. More recently, there has been resurgence in the use of Braille, partly in recognition of its usefulness as a means of communication.

Braille is a tactile communication method. Cells of from one to six raised dots on paper represent the letters of the alphabet (and numbers). Although it is a direct transliteration of English (or other language), Braille regularly resorts to contractions to save time and space. For example, in English Braille, the letter "r" by itself means "rather." Although it has been established that Braille is easier to read than raised letters of the alphabet, it is still a much slower process than reading print is for the average reader with sight.

Students can begin learning Braille in the first grade or earlier and have a number of technologies available to them, beginning with Braille books. A brailler is a six key device not unlike a typewriter.

Computer-assisted Technology

Computer technology continues to develop at a rate that almost outpaces the capacity of special education to use it effectively. The BrailleNote allows junior-to-intermediate Braille users to take notes efficiently and has other functions such as a day planner. This device allows for translation from print to Braille and Braille to print. Brailling options that require a lighter touch, such as the Mountbatten Brailler, are also available for young Braille users. The Mountbatten Brailler has speech/read options that allow students to hear what they are brailling with the use of headphones. It also has other functions, such as translating text into French! Commercially available products, such as the Apple iPad, allow textbooks to be downloaded and print enlarged. Many of today's laptops are also able to enlarge print easily, with available software even providing options for surfing the web in this format. Portable CCTVs and smartboards allow for adjustable viewing and methods of interaction with images and text that seemed impossible only a few years ago. Other computer innovations allow for the subtle, seamless and unobtrusive recording of class sessions for later playback. For more information, see appendix IV.

Mobility Assists

The long cane is one of the simplest and most effective devices yet devised for safe, efficient mobility for persons who are blind or sight impaired. It is important to note that, although the use of one seems simple to people who can see, learning to use a cane effectively requires some training and practice.

Users of guide dogs report that they are extremely helpful in alerting them to potential dangers and changes in the immediate environment and in guiding them through complex situations.

Electronic devices, such as GPS devices for the blind, laser canes, and sonic guides (worn on the head), are becoming more readily available, though they are not without glitches.

Educational Placement

Increasingly, and with marked success, students who are blind or partially sighted are being educated in the regular classroom. Special assistance may be delivered by an itinerant specialist teacher who provides advice on strategy, materials, and, possibly, on curricular modifications and/or accommodations. Such modifications and/or accommodations may include intense instruction on how to listen, how to make "mental mobility maps," etc. The assistance may also take the form of one of the educational aids listed above, or it may be a combination of aids from several sources. As in all other areas of special education, educational assistants in the classroom have proven to be invaluable for students who are blind or partially sighted.

For some students, a resource room may play a central role in their educational setting. Using this type of setting may offer a more certain guarantee of the specialized instruction the students may need.

A more specialized placement, used particularly for students whose vision problems are quite seriously disabling, is an entirely self-contained classroom, or even a residential school devoted to students who are blind (some of whom may have other special needs as well). In these environments, where there are usually very low student–teacher ratios, students receive a regular school curriculum adapted to their needs, along with very specialized instruction related to their blindness. While these types of placements can provide certain types of specialized instruction, considerations such as the lack of a diverse social environment and, in the case of residential placements, separation from family, are very real concerns. In recent years, these types of settings have been decreasing in number.

Strategies for the Classroom

1 It is usually very beneficial for a teacher of a regular class that includes a student who is blind or partially sighted to establish the practice of holding regular, informal, and private discussions with that student to work out special means of communication.

2 It may be necessary for a teacher *to set up the classroom with the expectation that physical arrangements will not be altered,* at least for a significant period of time. While this may contradict the style a teacher likes to follow, it may be a necessity for simple reasons of safety.

3 At the same time, *there is the student's normal need to be physically mobile, to explore, and to expand his or her capacity,* as well as the need to perceive themselves as both part of and separate from the environment. A great deal of professional skill is demanded of teachers and educational assistants in marrying this need with the obvious requirements of safety and efficient function described above. The key phrase is "responsible independence."

4 Common sense. A student with partial sight, for example, should always be permitted to sit near the chalkboard/white board/smartboard and to borrow notes or access their material by computer. (Yet the exceptionality need not be emphasized. If other students are blindfolded in an activity, the student who is blind should be, too.) Print can be enlarged, or an alternate version using large print can be provided for a student's laptop. Students who are partially sighted almost always respond to better lighting. They may require additional time for tests or a variety of other activities. Doors should always be fully open or fully closed. Name students being addressed; if an instruction is given to another child without such specification, a child who is blind may automatically follow it, with perhaps disastrous results. By the same token, be explicit in giving instructions, particularly those involving movement from one place to another.

A student who is blind cannot be expected to compensate for obstacles. If told to "come here," he or she may well come in a straight line, regardless of hazards, because of his or her trust in the teacher.

5 **Teachers, assistants,** *and fellow students with sight often have to make allowances for communication style.* Students who are blind or partially blind usually do not reinforce others' understanding with eye contact or facial expression – a phenomenon that takes some getting used to. In the same vein, these students often place great interpretive value on the expression and tone of their teacher's voice. This can be very important in some situations. Also, if an individual who is blind responds to a communication with total silence, it may be because he or she is taking in and interpreting available cues. This, too, requires adjustment from the teacher.

6 **"Blindisms"** *are characteristic mannerisms such as rocking, head shaking, hand shaking, and eye poking.* Most advocates suggest that teacher and educational assistants adroitly discourage these behaviours, for they may isolate the student as irremediably different in a way that goes beyond merely being blind.

7 **Many people who are blind** *have grown to associate physical contact with being guided.* Gestures such as patting and hugging may have negative connotations for some students or may be misinterpreted. When an individual who is blind is being guided, let him or her be the one who maintains and controls the physical contact. Don't grab the person's arm and steer; let the person hold your arm.

8 **When individuals who are blind** *are lost or disoriented, they may need to be repositioned in order to work out their position.* If a person with sight has occasion to help in this situation, it is important to make the person who is blind understand where he or she is first. Once the student is oriented as best as possible, an explanation about direction can follow. A subset of this issue is the matter of snow-covered surfaces. People who are blind often describe snow as their fog because the snow covers surface references they use to orient their position. It follows, then, that they will often need more assistance in winter.

9 **A tactful classroom buddy** *or advocate is always helpful,* but this arrangement should never be an unnaturally long-term arrangement.

10 **Perhaps the single most** *important role a teacher plays is being the classroom leader in developing a positive attitude.* Students with sight will take their cue from their teacher in determining how to react to and interrelate with a student in their midst who is blind. An accepting atmosphere for this student, with realistic expectations, will build the student's self-esteem, sense of success, and willingness to deal with the world. It will also contribute in a major way to the maturing of all students in the class.

Readings and Resources

Andreou, Y., & McCall, S. (2010). Using the voice of the child who is blind as a tool for exploring spatial perception. *British Journal of Visual Impairment, 28*(2), 113–29. doi:10.1177/0264619609360285

Bishop, V. E. (1996). *Teaching visually impaired children* (2nd ed.). Springfield, IL: Charles C. Thomas.

Bowen, J. (2010). Visual impairment and its impact on self-esteem. *British Journal of Visual Impairment, 28*(1), 47–56. doi:10.1177/0264619609349429

Canadian National Institute for the Blind (CNIB). (1993). *History of the CNIB.*

Chein-Huey Chang, S., & Shaler J. (2002). The views of students with visual impairments on the support they received from teachers. *Journal of Visual Impairment and Blindness,* August.

Davis, P., & Hopwood, V. (2002). Including children with visual impairment in the mainstream primary school classroom. *Journal of Research in Special Education Needs, 2*(3).

Donley, P. R. (2002). A touch of class: Teaching languages of the blind and visually impaired – some suggestions. *The Canadian Modern Language Review, 59*(2).

Douglas, G., McLinden, M., McCall, S., Pavey, S., Ware, J., & Farrell, A. M. (2011). Access to print literacy for children and young people with visual impairment: Findings from a review of literature. *European Journal of Special Needs Education, 26*(1), 25–38. doi:10.1080/08856257.2011.543543

Erin, J. (1996). Children with multiple and visual disabilities. In M. C. Holbrook (Ed.). *Children with visual impairments: A parents' guide* (287–316). Bethesda, MD: Woodbine House.

George, A. L., & Duquette, C. (2006). The psychosocial experiences of a student with low vision. *Journal of Visual Impairment and Blindness*, March.

Hallahan, D. P., & Kauffman, J. M. (2006). *Exceptional learners: An introduction to special education*. Boston: Pearson Education.

Herold, F., & Dandolo, J. (2009). Including visually impaired students in physical education lessons: A case study of teacher and pupil experiences. *British Journal of Visual Impairment, 27*(1), 75–84. doi:10.1177/0264619608097744

Hill, E. W., & Snook-Hill, M. (1996). Orientation and mobility. In M. C. Holbrook (Ed.). *Children with visual impairments: A parents' guide* (259–86). Bethesda, MD: Woodbine House.

Kirchner, C., & Diament, S. (1999). Estimates of the number of visually impaired students, their teachers, and orientation and mobility specialists. *Journal of Visual Impairment and Blindness, 93*(9), 600–06.

Minor, R. J. (2001). The experience of living with and using a guide dog. *RE:view, 32*, 183–90.

Rooks, D. L., & Maker, C. J. (2009). Inquiry: A teaching approach for gifted visually impaired learners. *Gifted Education International, 25*(2), 172–87. doi:10.1177/026142940902500207

Sacks, S. Z., & Wolffe, K. E. (1998). Lifestyles of adolescents with visual impairments: An ethnographic analysis. *Journal of Visual Impairment and Blindness, 92*(1), 7–17.

Sharma, U., Moore, D. W., Furlonger, B. E., Smyth King, B., Kaye, L., & Constantinou, O. (2010). Forming effective partnerships to facilitate inclusion of students with vision impairments: Perceptions of a regular classroom teacher and an itinerant teacher. *British Journal of Visual Impairment, 28*(1), 57–67. doi:10.1177/0264619609347409

Taylor, K., & Preece, D. (2010). Using aspects of the TEACCH structured teaching approach with students with multiple disabilities and visual impairment: Reflections on practice. *British Journal of Visual Impairment, 28*(3), 244–59. doi:10.1177/0264619610374682

Links

American Foundation for the Blind **http://www.afb.org/**

Canadian National Institute for the Blind **http://www.cnib.ca/**

National Coalition for Vision Health **http://www.visionhealth.ca/**

World Health Organization **http://www.who.int/health_topics/ blindness/en/**

16
Students with Speech and Language Disorders

"Try this. Just for a day, or even an hour. Stop in the middle of each sentence. But leave your mouth open and make it clear you're trying to talk but can't. Then watch how people look at you. Like you've got two heads. Now think of living your life like that."

– Ronnie K., diagnosed with aphasia at age eleven

Misconceptions About Speech and Language Disorders

1 **Speech and language disorders are synonymous.**
While they can often be found together, it is indeed possible for a person to have no difficulty with speech production or articulation but have difficulty communicating thoughts, ideas, wants, and needs. Language is the system for understanding and putting words and sentences together.

2 **Stuttering affects all ages and both genders equally.**
Stuttering affects more boys than girls and more children than adults. The child over adult ratio is usually ascribed to the fact that, by adulthood, many people with a stutter have been helped by speech and language specialists.

3 **Speech and language disorders are not related to intelligence.**
Prevalence data show that, although the disorders may occur among very intelligent individuals, they are found more frequently among persons with lower intellectual ability.

4 **Articulation disorders in very young children, especially, are not serious, and correction is rarely worth the effort or the risk of trauma.**
Many small children have unique speech patterns, but articulation disorders should never be dismissed as insignificant, especially if the child is very difficult to understand or his speech patterns make him stand out or seem unusual. "He'll grow out of it" is often an inappropriate substitute for remedial action.

5 **If an individual has a speech or language disorder, that individual also has a learning disability.**
The connection is not an absolute one, although difficulties with language affect both areas. Speech and language disorders also overlap other areas of special need, such as hearing impairment and deafness. Some estimates say up to 50 percent of students in special education receive speech and language intervention.

Defining Speech and Language Disorders

For most children, the process of acquiring language, though seemingly complex, follows a relatively straightforward path. From birth, children are exposed to a language-rich environment. Parents and caregivers are responsive, motivating teachers who provide ongoing opportunities for infants and toddlers to develop the necessary language skills to build a solid foundation for future language use. As a result of this early and continuous interaction, a majority of children develop language naturally. The successful acquisition of language can have a dramatic effect on a child's ability to understand and function in both the social and academic worlds. Communication, the exchange of ideas, can take many forms: a word, an expression, a movement of the body.

When a child lacks the ability to engage effectively in this interactive exchange of information, the child's learning capacity is compromised and socialization is potentially limited. Without such learning and socializing opportunities, the acquisition of language becomes more difficult and the opportunities to improve more limited. Because of this, it is essential that students with speech and/or language difficulties receive some type of structured intervention to assist them in developing effective communication skills.

An Important Distinction

The distinction between a speech disorder, a language disorder, and a communication disorder is an important one.

Speech disorders are characterized by impairments of voice or difficulties in the fluency or articulation of sounds. In essence, a student who has difficulty with the oral production of language is considered to have a speech disorder.

Language disorders, on the other hand, encompass both understanding (receptive) and using (expressive) language and, therefore, may result in a problem receiving information and/or formulating an acceptable and adequate response.

A communication disorder is one in which the child has difficulty using his or her speech and language skills effectively to communicate thoughts, ideas, wants, and needs. A child can have clear speech production and can understand and produce words and sentences but not necessarily communicate effectively with others.

Types of Speech Disorders

Speech disorders, while more common in particular types of populations such as individuals with lower intellectual ability and those with neuromotor difficulties such as cerebral palsy, are not exclusive to those populations and can be found across a wide range of students. Diagnosis and treatment are generally the province of professionals in the field, in particular speech and language pathologists, although often it is a teacher or educational assistant who first notices that something may be amiss.

Students with speech disorders have difficulty with the production of voice and/or speech sounds. This can be a result of a number of factors such as inability to manipulate the tongue, lips, and jaw, breath irregularities, and damage to the vocal cords. The cause of many speech disorders remains unknown, however. Speech disorders are generally divided into three distinct yet related categories: articulation, voice, and fluency.

Clues to Identifying a Speech or Language Disorder

- Does the student follow simple directions?

- Does the student understand the meanings of words that others understand?

- Does the student have a limited vocabulary compared with age peers?

- Does the student understand longer, more complex sentences?

- Does the student follow the general rules of grammar?

- Does the student have more than normal difficulty finding the correct word?

Articulation Expectations

By age eight, most children have a repertoire of the sounds that they will use for adult speech, and most acquire these sounds in a similar sequence. In a normal population distribution, for example, nine out of ten will master these sounds:

By the end of age 3	/m/, /n/, /ng/, /p/, /f/, /h/, /w/
By the end of age 3.5	/y/
By the end of age 4	/b/, /d/, /gl, /k/, /r/
By the end of age 4.5	/s/, /sh/, /ch/
By the end of age 6	/t/, /l/, /v/, /th/ (as in then)
By the end of age 7	/z/, /zh/ (treasure)
	/j/, /th/ (three)

An average three-year-old child will say 50 percent of the sounds in English correctly and will be 90 percent intelligible.

Articulation Disorders

By far the most common type of speech disorder, articulation disorders are characterized by atypical production of speech sounds in a language. These vary from omissions (e.g., "nana" for banana) to substitutions ("wam" for swam), additions ("sawl" for saw), and distortions ("streep" for sleep). For obvious reasons, an articulation anomaly must be a regular and typical element in the student's speech and cause communicative breakdown before it is regarded as a disorder.

Voice Disorders

Everyone's voice is unique. Individuals may have a quiet or loud voice, one with a nasal quality, or one with variations in pitch. All of these variations of speech can be considered normal. When the variations become so pronounced that they cause the speaker difficulty in communicating successfully, or they draw undue negative attention, they are considered voice disorders. Voice disorders are characterized by atypical production of vocal quality (e.g., hoarseness), pitch (high/low, squeaky), loudness, and resonance (e.g., nasal).

Fluency Disorder

When a person's flow of speech is unusually irregular, or marked by stoppages, repetitions, unusual pauses, and atypical rhythms, a fluency disorder may be present. Stuttering is the most common fluency disorder and is characterized by the repetition of a particular syllable or sound of a word, prolonging some sounds (e.g., sssssstay here), or blocks (e.g., inability to express a word or sound for a noticeably long time). It can be a normal part of language development. A child with a family history of stuttering and whose stuttering persists for more than six months is at greater risk of chronic stuttering.

Types of Language Disorders

Language disorders are characterized by difficulty in the use and understanding of language and are found across a wide spectrum of the population. Students with language disorders can be at risk in the development of literacy. Children begin to acquire language skills in infancy, responding to vocal sounds by turning their heads and smiling. At two to three months, they start to coo and, by the age of four, have approximately 1,000 to 1,500 words though they understand many more. By the time a child starts grade 1, more complex parts of language, such as the use of irregular verbs, are being mastered. Not all children reach these milestones at these times for a variety of reasons. Some may have difficulty hearing; some lack intellectual ability; others may not be sufficiently exposed to language.

Some children may experience difficulty with expressive language (the formulation of phrases and sentences), as in the use of incorrect words (e.g., "puppy" for all four-legged animals) or sentence structure ("me go my house," or "I goed to the store yesterday"). Others may have difficulty with receptive language (the ability to comprehend spoken, written, or other symbol systems). A set of directions, for example, "Get your red jacket from the closet and make sure to put on your scarf and mittens," may overwhelm. In the latter situation, it is not hard to understand why the complication intensifies in a school setting where a student may be told to: "Discuss the impact of urban society as a root cause for the Civil War." Most often individuals with language disorders have some combination of both expressive and receptive difficulties.

Some Common Language Problems

Language is composed of a variety of components including morphology (word endings), phonology (speech sounds in words), syntax (word order in sentences), semantics (word meanings), and pragmatics (communication function of sounds, words, and sentences). These components, when impaired or not developed in any way, result in language disorders.

Someone having a problem with the morphology of language, for example, may have difficulty understanding and using sections of words that have meaning (e.g., "the dog bark when the car went by" for "the dog barked when the car went by").

With problems in phonology (combining sounds to form words and manipulating sound sequences to form coherent speech), the person may say "nana" for "banana," "pasketti" for "spaghetti," or "bwush" instead of brush.

Syntax, the rules that govern the combining of words to form coherent sentences, can be a challenge (e.g., What he is doing?), while problems with the semantics of a language (combining words and sentences to convey meaning) often indicate the individual just doesn't "get it," particularly if an expression is idiomatic or metaphorical. For example, the baseball metaphor "I'll go to bat for him," in reference to defending a person, may well be interpreted literally as referring to an actual baseball game.

Problems with pragmatics, using language socially to greet others, to request needs or information, to protest, pretend, and respond, mean that an individual may be unresponsive to normal social interchange.

Selective Mutism

Selective mutism is not generally considered a communication disorder. Rather, it is categorized under psychiatric disorders. Formerly known as elective mutism, it is characterized by a child's inability to speak in certain social settings. The student may speak with family and/or select individuals at school, but, due most likely to intense anxiety, is unable to speak in a variety of social settings. Students with selective mutism may communicate through facial expression, gestures, and other types of body language and despite their inability to speak in certain settings be otherwise developmentally normal.

Central Auditory Processing Disorders

Some students seem not to be listening even though their hearing may be perfectly intact. More and more professionals in the speech and language field believe this apparent lack of listening is owing to a "central auditory processing disorder" (CAPD). It is characterized by a difficulty recognizing meaningful acoustic signals sent to auditory areas of the brain. Normally, people use both ears to fuse information and to "tune out" auditory distractions (selective attention). People who demonstrate CAPD may lose messages, mix them up, or fail to integrate the information coming in via both ears.

Students with CAPD generally exhibit the types of behaviours listed to the right, even though their hearing is normal. (However, it should be noted that these behaviours might also be associated in many students with other types of difficulties; this is likely why the notion of central auditory processing disorder has not yet been fully accepted across the broad area of special education.)

Indications of Possible CAPD

- inconsistent response to oral speech and other sounds
- better response to oral speech in quiet environments than in noisy environments
- poor response to speech in environments that are noisy or where speech is distorted, such as a gym or cafeteria
- difficulty telling the difference between two similar-sounding words or speech sounds (e.g., pat versus bat, oh versus ah)
- frequent requests for information to be repeated or clarified

The Case of Brent

BRENT, in senior kindergarten, is the eldest of five children. For the first two months of school, his only form of communication was a slight nodding of the head. Brent seemed unwilling to follow class routines, did not socialize with other children, and refused to comply with direct requests by the teacher. While Brent eventually did begin to speak, his utterances were mumbled and scant. At times, it seemed as though his answers were designed to cause difficulty or mock the teacher.

Following kindergarten, Brent was placed in a self-contained class that emphasized behaviour modification. In the new setting, his disruptive and non-compliant behaviour persisted. Brent's special class teacher suggested to the In-school Team that he be assessed by the board's speech and language pathologist, a request supported by the principal and Brent's parents. Test results showed that, in both expressive and receptive language, Brent was functioning at the age level of two and a half years: results with profound implications.

The IPRC review is to be held next week to discuss Brent's situation. Neither the teacher nor the educational assistant in the behaviour class has any special training in areas of speech and language, but both are willing to undertake any program to help Brent, as long as they are given professional advice and supervision. The school board has one full-time speech and language specialist with a very busy schedule. She visits the school twice weekly where she works with two children in a regular grade 1 class. If Brent were placed here, she would include him in her twice-weekly sessions.

The grade 1 class, though, is a very busy and somewhat noisy setting in a pod-style room with three other primary classes. The specialist feels that, given the intensity of Brent's language needs, this may not be as helpful a setting as the behaviour class where things are much quieter and more controlled. The principal is now seeking opinions from the In-school Team.

Getting Help

Most students with speech and language difficulties are in regular classroom settings. To assist them and their teachers, many school boards either employ or retain the services of speech and language specialists. The availability of these professionals to provide direct intervention on an ongoing basis varies from board to board. Often, there are just too many students requiring support for the therapist to work directly with all students needing help. Thus, a special education teacher, or classroom teacher, or educational assistant, under specific direction from a speech and language specialist, may be enlisted to work directly with students. Intervention may involve working on a particular sound, or playing a word game to develop expressive language skills, or other relatively straightforward activities.

Where more extensive assistance is required but is unavailable at the school board level, a speech and language specialist may refer children to support services outside the jurisdiction of the board. Some parents may also choose to get services and support privately.

Students Who Rely on Augmentative and Alternative Communication

We communicate for many reasons each day, such as greeting people, commenting, sharing information, telling stories, making requests, directing others, asking and answering questions, agreeing or protesting, expressing emotions, sharing humour, and for other reasons. Communication enables teachers and students to engage effectively in their roles as facilitators and learners of the curriculum.

Everyone communicates using a combination of many methods. These may include body language, facial expressions, gestures, sounds, spoken words, pointing to objects and people, and writing. Other ways to communicate include sign language, pointing to pictures/photographs/words, typing words, and operating speech-generating devices. For some students with impairment in the production of oral language, speech alone is insufficient to convey what they would like to communicate. These students often rely on Augmentative and Alternative Communication (AAC). AAC refers to using one or more communication methods to supplement speech (Augmentative Communication) or replace speech (Alternative Communication). Students who rely on AAC use various combinations of communication reasons and methods depending on their unique profile of speech, receptive and expressive language, cognition, and physical capabilities and challenges. The goal of AAC is to close the gap between receptive and expressive language and between students' thoughts and ideas and their ability to communicate them.

In Ontario, individuals who need an AAC assessment can be referred to a multidisciplinary team at a designated Augmentative Communication Services Clinic, under the Ministry of Health and Long Term Care. An AAC team may include speech-language pathologists, occupational therapists, communication disorder assistants, technologists, and educators. AAC teams work with individuals, their families, educators, and other professionals to develop AAC skills. If equipment is required, funding is available through the Ministry of Health and Long Term Care. AAC teams provide ongoing consultation and/or training to further develop AAC skills, provide training and support for communication partners, and provide consultation regarding curriculum adaptations and inclusion.

Inclusion and programming for a student who relies on AAC will require an exploration of resources including past IEPs, school board therapy reports, and reports from external services such as Augmentative Communication Services. Discussions with the student, his or her family, past educators, therapists, and other involved professionals provide invaluable information for the classroom teacher. Observation of the student communicating using methods identified within these reports and discussions is also important. By understanding a student's communication reasons and methods, the teacher can incorporate purposeful communication throughout the school day. Strategies to support AAC in the classroom vary according to the needs of each student but typically include modelling, encouraging, and providing opportunities for a variety of communication reasons and methods, giving students enough time to communicate, and responding naturally.

The development of an AAC system is a long-term process as individuals are constantly learning to communicate more effectively and communicative demands vary in different settings and life situations. Teachers have an important role in facilitating this development. Collaboration will help to ensure the student's communication continues to develop as an essential part of his or her life.

This submission was created by: Mary Harrison, OT, Debbie Hayne, AAC Resource Teacher, and Rebecca Shultis, SLP, of the Communication Assessment and Support Team (CAST), Niagara Peninsula Children's Centre.

Note: For more information on the integration of technology, see appendix IV.

Vital Roles for the Teacher and Educational Assistant

Very often, in fact in most cases, a specialist in speech and language will evaluate and recommend ways to help support the needs of the student. The more severe the case, the more likely the teacher and educational assistant will be part of a team collaborating to develop programming ideas. However, since nothing in practice is as straightforward as it appears in theory, it will still be incumbent on regular classroom personnel to provide leadership in several ways. These would include providing extended opportunities for the student to communicate, making the classroom a comfortable and safe place for the student to work on his or her speech and language, and modelling an appropriate response to the child's communicative attempts for peers to follow. In short, the teacher's role with speech and language disorders is similar to his or her role with all students: to be a compassionate professional who takes responsibility for developing the whole individual.

Strategies for the Classroom

For Listening

• Allow students to ask for clarification and be willing to repeat instructions. You may wish to set up a system with the child so that he or she can signal a need for clarification (e.g., a green card that he or she places on his desk). Many children do not like to ask for clarification because other children might think they are not very smart. Also, the signalling system helps to ensure that the child is not just impulsively asking questions – he or she has to signal and then wait for the teacher to provide assistance.

• Avoid long periods of instruction in which only listening is required. Use pictures, videos, written notes, and other visual support for spoken material and break up listening with activities.

• Gain attention before speaking (indicating that the information you are about to present is important, asking students to look in your direction before speaking, tapping a student who appears to be drifting on the shoulder).

• Be aware of your delivery style. Decrease

your rate of speech; use repetition, simple explanations, and short sentences.

- Use many types of expression besides oral (gestures, miming).

- Use figurative language carefully (providing an explanation, watching to make sure all students understand, and asking students to discuss the phrase).

- Check for comprehension by asking the student to repeat what has been said. Make sure this is done in ways that permit the child privacy and dignity.

- Paraphrase your own ideas after speaking, to ensure comprehension.

- Be conscious of noise levels and, where possible, improve classroom acoustics. Encourage all students to indicate when they are finding the classroom too noisy.

- Offer preferential seating, away from pencil sharpeners, open windows, doorways, or ventilation systems, for students who have difficulty with listening and/or processing information.

- Use visual support to supplement information (e.g., written material, pictures, photos, videos).

For Speech and Language

- Restate a student's phrases in a more accurate and/or grammatically correct way when

appropriate, making sure that undue attention is not drawn to the student's error or inaccuracy.

- Structure the physical environment to increase opportunities for interaction.

- Be sensitive to the student's current speech and/or language development so that he or she is asked to use expression in possible and positive ways.

- Provide opportunities for interactive games and activities.

- Create situations that promote the use of oral language (e.g., "forget" to provide enough supplies for an activity, such as paint or brushes, to prompt the student to ask for them).

- Avoid placing undue pressure on a student to express himself or herself verbally.

- Reinforce the correct use of language by commenting in a way that does not draw undue attention to the student.

- Introduce new words in a variety of contexts that are meaningful to the child and use repetition to reinforce them.

- Avoid overcorrecting the student's language; doing so may discourage the student from speaking.

- Encourage the student to express thoughts and ideas when discussing topics that interest him or her.

Readings and Resources

Ajodhia-Andrews, A., & Berman, R. (2009). Exploring school life from the lens of a child who does not use speech to communicate. *Qualitative Inquiry, 15*(5), 931-51. doi:10.1177/1077800408322789

Anthony, J. L., Aghara, G., Dunkelberger, M. J., Anthony, T. I., Williams, J. M., & Zhang, Z. (2011). What factors place children with speech sound disorders at risk for reading problems? *American Journal of Speech-Language Pathology, 20* (May), 146–61. doi:10.1044/1058-0360(2011/10-0053)b

Asher, S., & Gazelle, H. (1999). Loneliness, peer relations, and language disorders in childhood. *Topics in Language Disorders, 19*(2), 16–33.

Bauman-Waengler, J. (2000). *Articulation and phonological impairments: A clinical focus.* Boston: Allyn & Bacon.

Butler, K. G. (Ed.). (1999). Children's language, behaviour, and emotional problems. (Special Issue). *Topics in Language Disorders, 19*(2).

Calandrella, A. M., & Wilcox, M. J. (2000). Predicting language outcomes for young prelinguistic children with developmental delay. *Journal of Speech, Language and Hearing Research, 43*, 1061–71.

Clegg, J., Hollis, C., Mawhood, L., & Rutter, M. (2005) Developmental language disorders: A follow-up in later adult life – cognitive, language and psychosocial outcomes. *Journal of Child Psychology and Psychiatry, 46*, 128–49.

Conti-Ramsden, G. M., Durkin, K., Simkin, Z., and Knox, E. (2009). Specific language impairment and school outcomes I: Identifying and explaining variability at the ends of compulsory education. *International Journal of Language and Communication Disorders, 44*, 15–35.

Filla, A., Wolery, W., & Anthony, L. (1999). Promoting children's conversations during play with adult prompts. *Journal of Early Intervention, 22*(3), 93–108.

Hart, S. L., & Banda, D. R. (2009). Picture exchange communication system with individuals with developmental disabilities: A meta-analysis of single subject studies. *Remedial and Special Education, 31*(6), 476–88. doi:10.1177/0741932509338354

Letts, C., & Hall, E. (2003). Exploring early years professionals' knowledge about speech and language and development and impairment. *Child Language Teaching and Therapy, 19*, 211–29.

Loeb, D. F., Gillam, R. B., & Brandel, J. (2009). The effects of Fast ForWord language on the phonemic awareness and reading skills of school-age children with language impairments and poor reading skills. *American Journal of Speech-Language Pathology, 18* (November), 376–87.

Ownes, R. (1996). *Language development: An introduction* (4th ed.). Boston: Allyn & Bacon.

Schraeder, T., Quinn, M., Stockman, I., & Miller, J. (1999). Authentic assessment as an approach to preschool speech-language screening. *American Journal of Speech-Language Pathology, 8*(3), 195–200.

Wang, P. P., & Baron, M. A. (1997). Language and communication: Development and disorders. In M. L. Batshaw (Ed.). *Children with disabilities* (4th ed.), 275–92. Baltimore: Paul H. Brookes.

Wellington, W., & Stackhouse, J. (2011). Using visual support for language and learning in children with SLCN: A training programme for teachers and teaching assistants. *Child Language Teaching and Therapy, 27*(2), 183–201. doi:10.1177/0265659011398282

Links

AAC Intervention **www.aacintervention.com**

American Speech, Language, Hearing Association **www.asha.org**

Canadian Association of SLP and Audiologists **http://www.caslpa.ca/**

Closing the Gap **http://www.closingthegap.com/**

Kids Health for Parents **http://kidshealth.org/parent/medical/ ears/ central_auditory.html**

OACRS links to the children's treatment centres in Ontario **www.oacrs.com**

Ontario Association of SLP and Audiologists **http://www.osla.on.ca**

Definitions and Categories of Exceptionalities in Ontario

Exceptional Pupil

A pupil whose behavioural, communicational, intellectual, physical, or multiple exceptionalities are such that a committee considers the pupil to need placement in a special education program.

Special Education Program

With respect to a pupil with an exceptionality, an educational program that is based on and modified by the results of continuous assessment and evaluation and that includes a plan containing specific objectives and an outline of educational services that meet the needs of the pupil.

Special Education Services

Facilities and resources, including support personnel and equipment, necessary for developing and implementing a special education program.

The following five categories included in the definition of an exceptional pupil – behaviour, communication, intellectual, physical, and multiple – were clarified in, and are quoted from, a memo to school boards on January 15, 1999.

Behaviour

A learning disorder characterized by specific behaviour problems over such a period of time, and to such a marked degree, and of such a nature, as to adversely affect educational performance, and that may be accompanied by one or more of the following:

a) an inability to build or to maintain interpersonal relationships
b) excessive fears or anxieties
c) a tendency to compulsive reaction
d) an inability to learn that cannot be traced to intellectual, sensory, or other health factors, or any combination thereof

Communication

Autism

A severe learning disorder that is characterized by
a) disturbances in: rate of educational development; ability to relate to the environment; mobility; perception, speech, and language
b) lack of the representational symbolic behaviour that precedes language

Deaf and Hard of Hearing

An impairment characterized by deficits in language and speech development because of a diminished or non-existent auditory response to sound

Language Impairment

A learning disorder characterized by an impairment in comprehension and/or the use of verbal communication or the written or other symbol system of communication that may be associated with neurological, psychological, physical, or sensory factors, and that may

a) involve one or more of the form, content, and function of language in communication, and
b) include one or more of: language delay; dysfluency; voice and articulation development, which may or may not be organically or functionally based

Speech Impairment

A disorder in language formulation that may be associated with neurological, psychological, physical, or sensory factors; that involves perceptual motor aspects of transmitting oral messages; and that may be characterized by impairment in articulation, rhythm, and stress

Learning Disability

A learning disorder evident in both academic and social situations that involves one or more of the processes necessary for the proper use of spoken language or the symbols of communication, and that is characterized by a condition that

a) is not primarily the result of impairment of vision; impairment of hearing; physical disability; developmental disability; primary emotional disturbance; cultural difference

b) results in a significant discrepancy between academic achievement and assessed intellectual ability, with deficits in one or more of the following: receptive language (listening, reading); language processing (thinking, conceptualizing, integrating); expressive language (talking, spelling, writing); mathematical computations; and

c) may be associated with one or more conditions diagnosed as a perceptual handicap; a brain injury; minimal brain dysfunction; dyslexia; developmental aphasia

Intellectual

Giftedness

An unusually advanced degree of general intellectual ability that requires differentiated learning experiences of a depth and breadth beyond those normally provided in the regular school program to satisfy the level of educational potential indicated

Mild Intellectual Disability

A learning disorder characterized by

a) an ability to profit educationally within a regular class with the aid of considerable curriculum modification and supportive service

b) an inability to profit educationally within a regular class because of slow intellectual development

c) a potential for academic learning, independent social adjustment, and economic self-support

Developmental Disability

A severe learning disorder characterized by

a) an inability to profit from a special education program for students with mild intellectual disabilities because of slow intellectual development

b) an ability to profit from a special education program that is designed to accommodate slow intellectual development

c) a limited potential for academic learning, independent social adjustment, and economic self-support

Physical

Physical Disability

A condition of such severe physical limitation or deficiency as to require special assistance in learning situations to provide the opportunity for educational achievement equivalent to that of pupils without exceptionalities who are of the same age or development level

Blind and Low Vision

A condition of partial or total impairment of sight or vision that even with correction affects educational performance adversely

Multiple

Multiple Exceptionalities

A combination of learning or other disorders, impairments, or physical disabilities that is of such a nature as to require, for educational achievement, the services of one or more teachers holding qualifications in special education and the provision of support services appropriate for such disorders, impairments, or disabilities

In December 2011 the Director of the Special Education Policy Branch released a memo noting that "the broad categories of exceptionalities set out in subsection 1(1) of the Act (Behaviour, Communication, Intellectual, Physical and Multiple) are designed to address the wide range of conditions that may affect a student's ability to learn, and do not exclude any medical condition, whether diagnosed or not, that can lead to particular types of learning difficulties."

Appendix II
Some Assessment Instruments Popular in Ontario

Titles below appear in alphabetical order and include the familiar name in brackets. Each summary is brief. For in-depth reviews and information on test construction, refer to the Buros Mental Measurement website (**www.unl.edu/buros**).

Please note: It is extremely important to be aware of the age of both the content and norms of any testing instrument. Results based on content and norms established decades ago may produce misleading or irrelevant information that could affect appropriate programming.

Achenbach Child Behavior Checklist 6-18 (CBCL/6-18)

This assessment instrument aims to obtain, in a standardized format, caregivers' reports of the competencies and behaviour of children (ages six to eighteen). It permits the examiner to get a measure of internal and external problems. Internal problems include social withdrawal, somatic complaints, and anxious/depression. External problems include rule-breaking behaviour, attention problems, and aggressive behaviour. The checklist takes approximately twenty-five to thirty minutes to complete.

Adaptive Behavior Evaluation Scale, Revised (ABERS-R2)

This instrument assesses the adaptive behaviour of students ages four to twelve with intellectual and developmental disabilities. It is individually administered. There is both a school and home version and either version takes approximately twenty minutes to complete. The following ten adaptive skills are assessed: communication, self-care, social, community use, self-direction, health, safety, functional academics, leisure, and work. There are separate norms for males and females, and the school version includes individualized program goals, objectives, and interventions for the 104 assessed items.

Adaptive Behavior Scale, School Edition, 2nd Edition (The ABS-2)

This individually completed scale is used principally to aid in classification, placement, and general programming decisions for individuals ages three to eighteen years eleven months, with developmental delay, by assessing their adaptive functioning. Some evidence suggests that this scale may also be helpful in assessing the adaptive functioning of students with autism spectrum disorders. The ABS-2 is divided into two parts. The first focuses on personal independence, and the second assesses social adaptation. The rater (test completer) can be a parent, teacher, social worker, etc. The scale takes approximately thirty minutes to complete. (Note: The American Association on Intellectual and Developmental Disabilities was scheduled to release a new version of this test in 2012. It was not available when this book went to press.) The ABS-2 enjoys popularity with educators and health professionals who emphasize adaptive behaviour in assessing mental handicap. It is used most frequently to assess an individual's ability to thrive in a particular placement (independent, group home, etc.).

Asperger Syndrome Diagnostic Scale (ASDS)

This easy-to-use rating scale helps determine whether a child has Asperger syndrome. It takes ten to fifteen minutes to complete by parents, teachers, or anyone else who knows the child well. It is designed to assess individuals ages five to eighteen, giving them an AS Quotient.

Beck Youth Inventories, 2nd Edition, for Children and Adolescents (BYI-11)

These inventories, designed for students seven through eighteen years of age, assess symptoms of depression, anxiety, anger disruptive behaviour, and self-concept. They can be administered either individually or in groups. Each inventory takes approximately five to ten minutes to complete.

Beery-Buktenica Developmental Test of Visual Motor-Integration, 6th Edition (Beery VMI)

This screening test helps detect visual motor deficits in students two to eighteen years old. It can be administered to individuals or groups and takes ten to fifteen minutes to complete. It measures gross motor, fine motor, and visual and fine motor development. It is a culture-free test useful in the case of students from diverse cultural and linguistic backgrounds.

The Behavior Evaluation Scale, 3rd Edition (BES-3)

The BES is a scale for evaluating behaviour in students K to 12. It is filled out by the teacher or another adult and covers areas such as learning problems, interpersonal difficulties, unhappiness, and depression. It takes about fifteen minutes to complete and is useful for comparison purposes when completed by several significant adults in the subject's life. However, this or any evaluation scale should never be used as a sole determinant for identification or placement.

Boehm Test of Basic Concepts, 3rd Edition (2000) (The Boehm-3): The Psychological Corporation

A standardized individual or group screening test of comprehension, quantity, and time concepts designed to assess knowledge basic to early academic success. If used to assess school readiness, it may help identify students at risk for learning difficulties. The grade range is K to 2; it takes thirty to forty minutes to administer and produces a percentile score.

Behavior Rating Inventory of Executive Function (BRIEF)

This rating scale is used by parents, teachers, and day-care providers to rate a child's executive functions (e.g., working memory, ability to plan/organize, emotional control). It is designed to assess children and adolescents between the ages of five and eighteen with developmental and acquired neurological conditions such as learning disabilities, AD/HD, traumatic brain injury, Tourette's, and autism, and takes about ten to fifteen minutes to complete.

Brigance Comprehensive Inventory of Basic Skills-II (CIBS-II)

An individually administered instrument that assesses pre-academic, academic, and vocational skills so teachers can define objectives and plan individual programs with greater ease. The grade range is preschool to 9; it takes fifteen to ninety minutes to administer and in some sub-tests produces a grade or age level score. Sub-tests consist of readiness, speech, listening, research and study skills, reading, spelling, writing, and math. (Several other similar instruments by Brigance are available.) This edition contains both criterion-referenced and standardized assessment data.

The Canadian Achievement Test, 4th Edition (The CAT-4)

A standardized, norm-referenced, and criterion-referenced group test to assess achievement. Grade range is 1 to 12; time to administer is flexible (depending on the number and combination of sub-tests). Produces percentile, stanine, scaled, and grade equivalent scores. The major content areas are reading, spelling, language, and mathematics. The test is reasonably easy to administer. All norms are based on a representative sample of students across Canada in grades 1 to 12, and the test produces a detailed Student Diagnostic Profile (SDP) that can be very useful if personnel take the time to interpret the results.

Canadian Cognitive Abilities Test (CCAT)

This standardized, norm-referenced group test measures verbal, quantitative, and non-verbal cognitive abilities. The grade range is K to 12 (primary battery for K to 2 and Levels A to H for grades 3 through 12); it takes ninety minutes over three sessions to administer and produces standard, percentile, and stanine scores for age groups, and percentile and stanine scores for grade groups.

The CCAT has high validity and reliability estimates, and reviewers praise it for careful norming and standardization. Supporters say it has better predictive value than IQ tests; critics argue that cognitive ability by itself is not a straightforward entity to assess.

The Canadian Test of Basic Skills (CTBS)

A Canadianization of the Iowa Test of Basic Skills, very popular in Ontario, the CTBS is a standardized, norm-referenced, and group-administered achievement test for K to 12 that produces mounds of data. The Primary Battery Form K is used for grades K to 3.5; Elementary Form K for grades 3 to 8; and High School Form K for grades 9 to 12. Also available is a Survey Battery (grades 3 to 8, Form L), which assesses reading, mathematics, and language but does not include science. It can be hand-scored, although a computerized scoring system is also available. Scores range from percentile to scale to grade equivalent. Intra-class data as well as other, extensive comparative data can be made available. The test examines seven areas: vocabulary, reading, language, sources of information, mathematics, maps and diagrams, and science. The CTBS can be extremely time-consuming to administer, but many educators say it is worth the effort. Validity and reliability data are generally good, and the test is well received by reviewers.

Childhood Autism Rating Scale, 2nd Edition (CARS2)

This scale, appropriate for children over two, helps clinicians and teachers identify and classify children with autism spectrum disorders (including Asperger syndrome). The scale is composed of fifteen items and results in a total score that can assist in the determination of autism spectrum disorders and the category (mild to moderate or severe) in which the child may be placed.

Children's Memory Scale (CMS)

Assesses students between ages five and sixteen for their memory abilities (attention and working memory, verbal and visual memory, short- and long-delay memory, recall, and recognition). It takes thirty minutes to complete. The authors suggest that it is a good screening instrument to determine the presence of possible learning disabilities and attention deficit disorders.

Comprehensive Test of Phonological Processing (CTOPP)

This test, appropriate for ages five through twenty-four eleven months, takes thirty minutes to complete and is designed to assess phonological awareness, phonological memory, and rapid naming. There are two versions, one for children ages five and six and one for individuals ages seven to twenty-four. Test results can help identify individuals who are significantly below their age-appropriate phonological ability.

Coopersmith Self-Esteem Inventory (CSEI)

This inventory measures attitudes toward self. It is composed of a brief self-report questionnaire, with a school form appropriate for students ages eight through fifteen and an adult form for those sixteen and older. It takes approximately fifteen minutes to complete and is hand-scored.

Detroit Tests of Learning Aptitude, 4th Edition (The Detroit-4)

This is an individually administered test designed to measure general intelligence and discrete ability areas. It is appropriately used for those in the age range of six through seventeen, and takes about forty minutes to two hours to administer. It produces percentile scores, standard scores, and age equivalents. The test purports to provide a thorough investigation of a person's cognitive functions.

Gates-MacGinitie Reading Tests, 2nd Canadian Edition (The Gates-MacGinitie)

A standardized, norm-referenced, group test designed to measure silent reading skills. Grade range is K to 12. It takes fifty to sixty minutes to administer and produces grade, standard, and percentile scores. The Gates-MacGinitie is offered at nine levels and gives two basic measures: vocabulary and comprehension. These tests are pen-and-paper tests completed by the subject(s), usually in groups. They can be useful for making broad comparisons and are often used for test-retest procedures because alternate forms are available.

Kaufman Assessment Battery for Children, 2nd Edition (The K-ABC-II)

A standardized, individual, norm-referenced test of intelligence and achievement for ages three to eighteen. It takes thirty to seventy minutes to administer and produces age level, standard, and percentile scores. Five scales – Simultaneous, Sequential, Planning, Learning, and Knowledge – are assessed in twenty sub-tests. The K-ABC-II is a complex and involved instrument requiring expertise, time, and patience in the examiner. A major claim made for the test is that it is an excellent instrument for assessing children of different backgrounds and with diverse problems. Draws heavily on neuropsychology and cerebral specialization theory; whether a test based on these elements can be educationally useful is still uncertain.

Keymath 3 Diagnostic Assessment (Keymath 3)

This is the most recent version of a standardized, individually administered test designed to assess mathematics skills. Age range is four years six months to twenty-one years eleven months. The complete assessment takes thirty to ninety minutes to administer, but individual sub-tests can be administered if appropriate, shortening the administration time. Results produce grade level and age equivalents, percentile ranks, and stanines. The test measures mathematical knowledge of numeration, rational numbers, geometry, addition, subtraction, multiplication, division, mental computation, measurement, time and money, estimation, data analysis, probability, and problem solving. Keymath is easy to administer; it is diverse, colourful, and widely applicable.

Kovacs Children's Depression Inventory 2 (CDI 2)

The test helps counsellors and clinicians to detect symptoms of major depressive disorder in children and adolescents ages seven to seventeen. It contains twenty-eight items that ask the student to respond to statements that best describe his or her feelings within the previous two weeks. It takes only five to ten minutes to complete and can be administered individually or in a group setting.

Leiter International Performance Scale, Revised (The Leiter-R)

A non-verbal test of intelligence and cognitive abilities measured by assessing areas such as reasoning, memory, and attention. It includes twenty sub-tests that measure both general intelligence and discrete ability areas. Scores are provided for the sub-tests as well as a composite IQ score. Often used for non-English speakers and individuals with hearing and language difficulties or severe disabilities such as autism spectrum disorders or traumatic brain injury. Directions are pantomimed and gestured. Age range is two years to twenty years eleven months. There are no time constraints, and the scoring is objective. Subjects usually enjoy the test process. There is no leeway for partial scoring, which seems contradictory given that there is no guarantee that the subjects have fully understood the tasks or are fully capable of responding. The Leiter-R is heavy and awkward to use and store but is a popular and potentially useful instrument for certain subjects.

McCarthy Scales of Children's Abilities (The McCarthy Scales)

A standardized, individual, norm-referenced test of general intellectual ability frequently offered as an instrument to identify children with possible learning disabilities. Age range is two and a half to eight and a half years; it takes an hour to administer and produces mental age, standard, and percentile scores. The McCarthy Scales include several verbal tasks appropriate for children with suspected learning disabilities and have good reliability support. Ironically, no children classified as exceptional were included in the norming sample!

Multidimensional Anxiety Scale for Children (MASC)

For use with individuals eight to nineteen, this scale assesses the major dimensions of anxiety in young persons. It is composed of thirty-nine items and takes approximately fifteen minutes to complete. It uses the following measures: Physical Symptom, Social Anxiety, Harm Avoidance, Separation/Panic, Anxiety Disorders, Total Anxiety Index, and Inconsistency Index.

Peabody Individual Achievement Test, Revised, Normative Update (The PIAT-R/NU)

An individual, norm-referenced, standardized test designed to give a wide measure of general achievement, with particular emphasis on reading, spelling, and arithmetic achievement. The grade range is K to 12, ages five to twenty-two years eleven months; it takes fifty to seventy minutes to administer and produces age-level, grade-level, standard, and percentile scores. The PIAT-R uses a multiple-choice answer format. It requires recognition of correct spelling and tests sentence comprehension as well as mathematical problem-solving skills. Provides a quick, overall, preliminary view, but should not be regarded as the last word.

Peabody Picture Vocabulary Test, 4th Edition (PPVT-4)

A standardized, individual test of single-word receptive vocabulary of standard (American)

English. The age range is two years six months to ninety years. It takes ten to twenty minutes to administer and produces age- and grade-based standard scores and percentile and stanine scores. The PPVT-R format presents pictures to elicit a response to a word; it is non-threatening. A good first test in a battery that is well designed and well normed. But not too much should be made of the results of a test of single-word vocabulary.

Raven's Progressive Matrices (The Raven's)

This test assesses a person's intellectual and reasoning ability by his or her completion of progressively more complicated visual analogies. It is entirely non-verbal, suitable for all ages from six to adult, and is available in standard and advanced levels. There is a coloured version for younger children. The Raven's can be used very effectively for a test-teach-test approach. Because it is non-verbal, it may reveal some cognitive strengths in poor readers.

Slingerland Screening Tests for Identifying Children with Specific Language Disability, Revised (The Slingerland)

Revised in 2005, this test is a non-standardized, informal group test of visual, auditory, and kinesthetic skills related to reading and spelling. It is designed to identify students with a specific language disability. The age range is six to twelve; it takes sixty to ninety minutes to administer. It produces no scores but has guidelines for evaluating test performance. The tests are strictly informal and permit a great deal of subjectivity. Some students become very frustrated during administration because extensive writing is required.

Stanford-Binet Intelligence Scale, 5th Edition (SB5)

Designed to assess intelligence and cognitive abilities for individuals two to eighty-five years of age, this edition retains many features of previous editions with significant improvement in psychometric design. Its authors claim that this edition, like the previous one, is designed to help differentiate between mental handicap and learning disability, to identify giftedness, and to understand why a student is having learning problems; the authors also say that the scale's ability to measure ability is improved because the difficulty of items is tailored to the cognitive functioning of the individual completing the test. The test measures five factors of cognitive ability: fluid reasoning, knowledge, quantitative processing, visual-spatial processing, and working memory.

Test of Reading Comprehension, 4th Edition (TORC-4)

A standardized, norm-referenced test for individual or group that is designed to give a normed measure of silent reading comprehension independent of specific curriculum via five sub-tests: Paragraph Construction, Relational Vocabulary, Sentence Completion, Text Comprehension, and Contextual Fluency. Appropriate for students seven years to seventeen years eleven months (grades 2 to 12). It takes forty-five minutes to administer and produces a Reading Comprehension Index helpful in determining which students may need improved reading proficiency.

Vineland Adaptive Behavior Scales, 2nd Edition (Vineland-II)

This assessment tool is designed to assist in the identification of children and adults (up to twenty-one years eleven months) with developmental disabilities, autism spectrum disorders, and Asperger syndrome. It is composed of a survey interview and parent/caretaker-rating form and teacher-rating form that take about twenty to sixty minutes to complete. The scales identify abilities in personal and social skills needed for everyday living.

Wechsler Individual Achievement Test, 2nd Edition (WIAT-II)

This "achievement battery" is designed for students from age four to adult. The WIAT-II assesses achievement in reading, spelling, mathematics, and listening and can help obtain an understanding of discrepancy between academic achievement and intellectual ability.

The Wechsler Intelligence Scale for Children, 4th Edition (WISC-IV)

This is an individual, standardized, and norm-referenced test designed to offer an ability score (IQ) and to offer information about a subject's skills in a variety of areas. This version of the WISC is a significant departure from previous editions. Test results now give four individual index scores: Verbal Comprehension Index (VCI), Perceptual Reasoning Index (PRI), Working Memory Index (WMI), and Processing Speed Index (PSI), rather than the two (Verbal and Performance) provided in early editions. The Verbal Comprehension Index is composed of five sub-tests: similarities, vocabulary, comprehension, information, and word processing. The Perceptual Reasoning Index is composed of block design, picture concepts, matrix reasoning, and picture completion. The Processing Speed Index is composed of coding, symbol search, and cancellation, and the Word Memory Index is composed of digit span, letter-number sequencing, and arithmetic. The Full Scale Intelligence Quotient (FSIQ) score is derived from the four composite scores. Classroom teachers usually do not administer a WISC, but they do (or should) receive results. Ideally, teachers will be given the sub-test results as well as the Full Scale and Composite Scores, for these may contain diagnostic information on which a plan of remediation can be based. The WISC-IV, like its predecessors, has wide acceptance as a clinical and diagnostic tool. Although the manual for the test states that the instrument is intended for use with people ages six to sixteen years eleven months, it is not uncommon for the test to be used with students older or younger. (Theoretically, adult and older students should be tested on the WAIS-III, the Wechsler Adult Intelligence Scale, and younger children on the WPPSI-III, the Wechsler Pre-Primer Scale of Intelligence.) Reliability and validity coefficients are high; the WISC-IV is particularly well standardized and can produce some useful diagnostic information. Takes approximately ninety minutes to two hours to complete.

Wide Range Achievement Test-4 (WRAT-4)

Based on the previous three editions, the WRAT-4 is an individual, norm-referenced, standardized test designed to assess skills in reading (word recognition and sentence completion), written spelling, and arithmetic computation. Age range is five to adult; it takes fifteen to forty-five minutes to administer (depending on the age of the person being tested); and it produces grade level, standard, percentile, and stanine scores. This test is easy and fast to administer and score and can be a fairly efficient first step in an assessment. It should never be used as the sole element in any evaluation, assessment, or admission procedure (but often is!). The arithmetic computation sub-test tests what the subject's curriculum offered rather than his or her ability.

Woodcock-Johnson Psycho-Educational Battery, Revised (The Woodcock or the WJ-R)

An individual, standardized, norm-referenced test designed to measure cognitive ability, academic achievement, and interests over a wide range. The age range is three to adult; it takes ninety minutes to two hours to administer and produces grade level, age level, percentile, and standard scores, along with scores the authors call "functional level" and "relative performance index." This is a busy and involved instrument with a large number of sub-tests. Areas covered consist of measures of "cognitive ability" (e.g., analysis-synthesis, memory for sentences, etc.) as well as an achievement battery (e.g., calculation, dictation, proofing). The WJ-R provides a large amount of information, but is difficult and time-consuming to administer.

Woodcock-Johnson III Tests of Achievement, Normative Update

An individually administered, standardized test designed to assess cognitive ability, academic achievement, and scholastic interest. It is divided into two batteries, achievement and extended, and takes about fifty-five to sixty-five minutes to complete. This test is appropriately used with anyone between the ages of two and ninety. It assesses the following: letter-word identification, reading fluency, story recall, understanding directions, passage comprehension, calculation, applied problems, math fluency, writing samples, writing fluency, and spelling. The extended battery provides additional information helpful in diagnosing specific academic strengths and weaknesses.

Woodcock Reading Mastery Tests, Revised, Normative Update (The Woodcock Reading or WRMT-R/NU)

This is an individual, standardized, criterion- and norm-referenced test designed to measure a wide range of reading skills. The grade range is K to 12. It takes thirty to forty-five minutes to administer and produces a wide set of scores, including grade level, percentile, relative mastery, achievement index, and reading range. This test offers six sub-tests covering letters, words, and passages. The word-comprehension sub-test uses analogy, and the passage comprehension makes use of cloze procedures (in which words are deliberately left out of a passage and the reader must use context to fill them in), both of which are highly regarded techniques. The concept of "relative mastery" provides a useful indication of what can be expected of a student. Also useful is this test's concept of instructional range in which an indication can be made of where a student can be expected to perform. Reliability and validity data are very good.

Some General Terms Used in Testing (see chapter 7 above for more)

Age Norm (Age Score) A score indicating average performance for students classified according to chronological age.

Base Level The level at which all items of a test are passed, just preceding the level where the first failure occurs. All items below the base level are assumed correct. Contrast with "ceiling level."

Battery A group of selected tests administered to a student.

Ceiling Level The highest item of a sequence in which a certain number of items has been failed. All items above the ceiling item are assumed incorrect.

Chronological Age (CA) Age from birth expressed in years and months; e.g., seven years six months.

Correlation Coefficient (r) A statistical index that measures the degree of relationship between any two variables.

Diagnostic Testing An intensive, in-depth evaluation process using formal, standardized tests and informal tests designed to determine the nature and severity of specific learning problems.

Intelligence Quotient (IQ) An index of mental capacity, expressing a student's ability to perform on an intelligence test.

Mean (M) The sum of a set of scores divided by the number of scores.

Median (MD) The middle point in a set of ranked scores.

Mental Age (MA) A measure of a student's level of mental development, based on performance on a test of mental ability and determined by the level of difficulty of the test items passed.

Mode (MO) The score that occurs most frequently in a distribution. In the distribution 18, 14, 12, 11, 10, 10, 7, the mode is 10.

Percentile Rank A type of converted score that expresses a student's score relative to his or her group in percentile points. Indicates the percentage of students tested who achieved scores equal to or lower than the specified score.

Projective Technique A test situation in which the student responds to ambiguous stimulus materials, such as pictures, ink blots, or incomplete sentences, thereby supposedly projecting personality characteristics. **Protocol** The original record of the test results.

Rank Ordering The arrangement of scores from highest to lowest.

Raw Score The score initially obtained by scoring a test according to directions in the manual.

Reliability The degree to which a student would obtain the same score if the test were re-administered assuming no further learning, practice effects, or other changes.

Scaled Score A score used to measure the deviation between the student's score and the mean or average score.

Standard Deviation (SD) The most commonly used measure of variation. A statistic used to express the extent of the distribution's deviations from the mean.

Standard Score Derived score that transforms a raw score so it has the same mean and the same standard deviation.

Standardization This refers, in test construction, to the process of trying the test out on a group of students to determine uniform or standard scoring procedures and methods of interpretation.

Standardized Test Contains empirically selected materials, with specific directions for administration, scoring, and interpretation. Provides data on validity and reliability and has adequately derived norms.

Stanine A weighted scale divided into nine equal units representing nine levels of performance on any particular test. The stanine is a standard score.

Validity The extent to which a test measures what it is designated to measure. A test valid for one use may have negligible validity for another.

Appendix III

Ontario Legislation and Policies Affecting Special Education

The *Education Act*

Usually referred to as "The Act"; governs the operation of schools and school boards in the province. The requirement mandating special education is now found in paragraph 170 (1) 7. Section 1(1) defines exceptional pupil, special education program, and special education services (see Definitions and Categories in appendix I, above). Other sections deal with various elements. For example, subsections 57(3), (4), and (5) deal with the Tribunal stage in appealing an IPRC decision. The obligations most immediately affecting day-to-day issues are covered for the most part in Regulations and Policy/Program Memoranda.

Key Regulations Affecting Special Education

296 Ontario Schools for the Blind and the Deaf.

298 Operation of Schools – General: Subsection 3(3) permits a reduction in the length of the instructional program for pupils with exceptionalities below the required five hours per day. Section 14 sets out qualifications teachers must hold to be placed in charge of or to teach in a special education program. Section 26 sets out the relationship between principals and professional support staff, including psychiatrists, psychologists, and social workers. Section 30 provides for special education programs for preschool children who are deaf or hard of hearing. Section 31 sets out maximum enrolment for special classes.

181/98 Identification and Placement of Exceptional Pupils. (See chapter 6 above.)

306 Special Education Programs and Services requires each school board to maintain a special education plan for the delivery of special education programs and services.

464/97 Special Education Advisory Committees (SEACs) governs the appointment to and operations of these committees.

Policy/Program Memoranda*

Policy/Program Memoranda (PPMs) are statements on Ministry policy and often include information about the *Education Act* and regulations made under the act. The PPMs listed here contain information about the education of pupils with exceptionalities.

PPM 1 Ontario Schools for the Blind and Deaf as Resource Centres

PPM 8 Learning Disabilities

PPM 11 Early Identification of Children's Learning Needs

PPM 59 Psychological Testing and Assessment of Pupils

PPM 76C Alternative Educational Programs and Services for Deaf, Blind, and Deaf-Blind Exceptional Pupils

PPM 81 Provision of Health Support Services in School Settings

PPM 85 Educational Programs for Pupils in Government-Approved Care and/or Treatment Facilities

PPM 89 The Residential Demonstration Schools for Students with Learning Disabilities

PPM 127 Provincial Secondary School Literacy Test in English-Language Secondary Schools – Accommodations, Deferrals

PPM 140 Incorporating Methods of Applied Behaviour Analysis (ABA) into programs with Autism Spectrum Disorders (ASD)

PPM 144 Bullying Prevention and Intervention

PPM 145 Progressive Discipline and Promoting Positive Student Behaviour

---

* Details and information with regard to all PPMs can be found at **http://www.edu.gov.on.ca/extra/eng/ppm/ppm.html**

Appendix IV
Technology in the Classroom

Recent advancements in the use of technology in Ontario's classrooms offer students both the promise and reality of a type of learning that looks and feels very different from what traditionally has been thought of as "schooling." Within special education, the line between technologies "for special education" and "education" is blurry indeed. As technologies emerge, both practicing educators and faculties of education are overdue to realize that we are playing catch-up with a technological wave that seems to be moving faster than anyone thought possible.*

> *"My grade 3/4 class is a very active, child-centred learning community. Language activities often include traditional learning centres infused with technology to create modern learning stations. For example, at our weekly spelling stations, the students can choose to work with tablets, gaming systems, interactive whiteboard activities, and interactive tabletops and laptops, in addition to several other types of educational manipulatives. Modelling clay, alphabet stamps, magnetic letters, magazines, and waxed string provide optional media for spelling practice. Child-created games are also encouraged, such as concentration and bingo. The creation of modern learning stations not only engages the students in meaningful learning opportunities but also offers multiple means of representation and expression to ensure that all students experience successful academic and social participation."*
>
> – Heather Snider, classroom teacher

---

* This appendix was prepared by Alexandra Dunn, Speech Language Pathologist, Tania Mason, Student Engagement Teacher, and Heather Snider, Classroom Teacher, of the Upper Canada District School Board. All three of these individuals are currently working in the field. The authors of this book thank them for their valuable contribution.

It is important to note that while assistive devices for students with special needs are relatively common within the educational vernacular, technology need not be specific to special education students and should be considered within a whole-class context. Technology can allow for more positive inclusive opportunities and indeed more flexibility in curriculum delivery, especially when it applies to all of the students in a classroom, not as something extra for some.

Keep in mind that technology seems to change daily.

As more traditional instructional approaches to teaching, learning, and technology use are enhanced by approaches in line with twenty-first-century knowledge-building and skill, *new* digital technologies are becoming more readily available. Students have increased opportunities to learn new technologies that are deemed important for future economic productivity. Teachers need to evaluate how and when to use new technologies within the activities of the classroom. The active application of subject knowledge for solving real world problems within more collaborative, project-based learning environments demands the introduction of digital technologies that link the classroom with the world beyond the classroom walls. Activities that emphasize knowledge creation and innovation require the introduction of yet other technologies in the classroom. (See ICT Competency Standards for Teachers, 2008.)

Depending on the needs of the students and the makeup of the class, technology can be used in many effective and appropriate ways. Following are some examples of different types of currently available technologies as well as suggestions on how they can be used in classrooms. These technologies include interactive whiteboards (e.g., SMART Boards, ActivBoard), gaming systems, tablets, interactive tabletops, document cameras, and student response systems.

Interactive Whiteboard (IWB) Stations

Visual/Auditory Supports

- Large interactive interfaces promote a wide variety of software use. These programs allow for the development of multiple visual supports, such as pre-made visual schedules that provide students with a more visual representation of their school day or what a particular activity will look like.
- A larger work surface makes information easier to see.
- IWBs allow for planned and on-demand use of visuals to support the sharing of auditory information.
- IWBs allow for integrated use of video, demonstrating and augmenting oral information.
- Tools help to target focus of attention on material at the IWB, which increases attention and increases comprehension.

Physical/Mobility Supports

- When paired with an adjustable stand, the IWB can be lowered or raised depending on student need.
- Some IWBs are multi-touch, allowing multiple points of contact; therefore, students with mobility issues who need to steady themselves with one hand can do so and interact with the IWB with the other.
- External keyboards and/or onscreen keyboards allow students who have difficulty writing to enter information into a wide variety of applications.

Social/Communication Supports

- IWBs allow for customization of information by introducing text, graphics (including bringing in symbol support), audio, links to websites, video clips to activities. This flexibility of introducing linguistic and non-linguistic representations provides enhanced opportunities for instruction, often resulting in improved understanding.
- A large interactive work surface lends itself to whole-group and small-group instruction, helping students to work naturally together toward a common goal.
- IWBs encourage reluctant participants to engage, which creates greater participation for *all* students.
- The IWB encourages students to participate longer with one another in the whole group or small groups, allowing more opportunities to model and share other social behaviours, e.g., turn-taking, initiating conversation, sharing ideas within a motivating group activity around a meaningful curricular goal.
- Projections of theme displays on the IWB and/or pictures can be imported into the operating software of some IWBs. This enables modelling and use during instruction for students who require symbol support for language learning and literacy supports.
- Lessons with annotation may be shared with students who may have missed instruction or who may need to see the information multiple times, thanks to the recording features built into many IBWs and accompanying software.
- The recorder feature allows group interaction to be recorded so the teacher can watch and provide feedback and/or use the interaction to inform instruction.
- The interactive surface allows more opportunities for manipulation of curricular content for kinesthetic learners.

Gaming Systems

Visual/Auditory Supports

- Most gaming systems have highly developed built-in graphics and visual representations, including 3D and supportive audio. With appropriate software, these types of interactive games can support a broad range of learners and improve curriculum understanding.

Physical/Mobility

- Most systems are highly mobile or can be activated remotely. Additions such as toggle switches can be easily adapted to existing systems.

Social/Communication

- Depending on the software, interactive activities and games can allow for students to communicate actually and virtually.
- Using a system that is known to or belongs to the child or that is considered socially desirable provides a comfort level, confidence, and engagement; these, in turn, can promote collaboration with peers through peer instruction and co-operation.
- Gaming systems can enable accessibility to curricular activities; creativity is the only limit. Requires thinking "as if there were no box" to bring curricular content into the ever-changing media available.

Tablets

Visual/Auditory Supports

- Curricular content can be augmented with the use of photos, videos, charts, and graphs.
- Content can be easily enlarged by student on-demand.
- Accessibility settings on some systems allow for a Zoom-to-Large and White-on-Black view for higher contrast.
- VoiceOver and Speech Selection are accessibility features that provide screen reading options and navigation.
- Volume can be independently controlled and set to an acceptable noise level so hearing can be facilitated and/or to prevent noise-induced hearing loss.
- Earphones can be utilized when appropriate (single /multiple).

Physical/Mobility

- Portable and can be used at multiple workstations.
- Screen size and ability to enlarge view allow for better accuracy for those who have fine motor issues.
- Some tablets allow individual gestures to be customized to meet individual student needs.
- Some tablets allow students who cannot access the surface directly to interact with the content from their wheelchair, stander, or alternative location using a switch (a form of indirect selection using a button communicating with the tablet directly or via Bluetooth, which can be activated using a finger, fist, chin, knee, head).

Social/Communication

- Headphone splitters can be used to allow for multiple students to interact with one tablet, thereby encouraging collaboration, problem solving, and other social skills such as taking turns.
- VGA or HDMI cable adapters can be used with projectors or videomirroring can be used to showcase or share content from the tablet with the whole group.

Learning and Literacy

- Many apps provide skills practice in engaging, game-based play and allow teachers to customize content.

Interactive Tabletops

General Supports

- These offer multiple formats (auditory, visual, and kinesthetic), which can be adapted for individual student learning needs.
- Allow for the customization of information by introducing text, graphics (including bringing in symbol support), and audio and video clips on the table surface that can be manipulated by students and teachers.

Visual/Auditory Supports

- Design software available that allows the changing of background and font colour in order to reduce visual glare and to customize to students' visual profiles.
- Pictures can be customized along with font sizing to accommodate visual needs of students.
- Lessons can be programmed in multiple quadrants. Stimuli such as pictures/fonts don't have to be the same for everyone and therefore can be manipulated through lesson design, based on need.

- For students with auditory difficulties, some activities can be completed without the need for verbal instruction.
- Students, including those with low vision or who struggle with reading, can hear the instructions presented orally. In some cases, the instructions can be repeated as needed.

Physical/Mobility Supports

- Enable students who may not be able to hold a pencil or complete paper pencil tasks efficiently an alternate way of completing curriculum-based work.
- Most interactive tabletops come equipped with USB ports that allow students to access the device through alternate means such as a joystick or trackball.

Social/Communication supports

- Students with different access methods (e.g., joystick, keyboard) can work together to complete one activity.
- Picture communication symbols can be imported and used as a viable response mechanism.

Document Camera

General Supports

- The document camera makes every book a big book, enlarging font size for those who need it, and increases students' opportunities for collaboration and learning.

- Can be used to magnify actual items in the child's environment that can be photographed and seamlessly added to the lesson to make language visual across the curriculum.
- Many Document Camera offers 3D content, enabling teachers to enhance lessons by providing additional detail/activities such as virtual tours.
- Allows students to share their work products with the class.

Student Response Systems

General Supports

- Student Response Systems (SRS) can provide an alternate means of expression for students for whom speech alone and/or writing would not be functional in a traditional classroom.
- When used as a voting tool, SRS can increase student engagement during whole or small group discussion and debate. If they have voted and left their mark, they have more of a vested interest in the outcome.
- Some Student Response Systems present students with large, colourful buttons with simple symbols, which decreases visual clutter, and raised texture, making it easy for students to answer with touch.
- SRS give students the chance to communicate their understanding of the material without feeling that they will be stigmatized for not getting the "right" answer.

Readings and Resources

Berkeley, S., & Lindstrom, J. H. (2011). Technology for the struggling reader: Free and easily accessible resources. *Teaching Exceptional Children, 43*(4), 48–55.

Caferio, J. (2008). Technology supports for individuals with autism spectrum disorder. *Technology in Action, 3*(3).

Clinker, M. & Moore, B. (2008). Smartboards, literacy, and differentiated communication: Out of the box integration. Presentation at the Bridges to Learning Conference, Toronto, ON, May 2008.

Dunn, A., & Brusse, T. (2011). Designing classroom technology to meet the needs of ALL. Paper presented at Computer-Human Interaction, Vancouver, BC.

Dunn, A., & Inglis, A. (2010/2011). Smart inclusion for the 21st century classroom: Integrating SMART boards and assistive technology. *Closing the Gap Solutions, 29*(5), 6–11. Minneapolis, MN.

Dunn, A., & Farrall, J. (April 2012). "A" is for access! Switch accessibility and the iPad. *EasySpeak Magazine* (spring), an online publication. Retrieved at: http://easyspeakenterprises.com/page/magazine

Dunn, A., Snider, H. & Mason, T. (2012) *Smart Inclusion: Breaking News* (April/May), 10–12. Closing the Gap Solutions. Minneapolis, MN.

Goossens, C. (2000). Aided language stimulation for the cognitively young (2nd ed.) Paper presented at the meeting of Augmentative and Alternative Communication in the Desert, Phoenix, AZ.

Goossens, C., Crain, S. & Elder, P. (1992) *Engineering the preschool environment for interactive, symbolic communication*. Birmingham, AL: Southeast Augmentative Communication Conference Publications.

ICT competency standards for teachers. (2008). United Nations Educational, Scientific and Cultural Organization. Retrieved at: http://cst.unesco-ci.org/sites/projects/cst/default.aspx

Kintsch, A. & DePaula, R. (2002). A framework for the adoption of assistive technology. *CiteSeerX – Scientific Literature Digital Library and Search Engine (United States)*. Retrieved at: http://l3d.cs.colorado.edu/clever/assets/pdf/ak-swaaac02.pdf download http://citeseerx.ist.psu.edu/viewdoc/summary?doi=?doi=10.1.1.124.3726

McClaskey, K. & Welch, R. (2009) Whiteboards engage autistic students. *Learning and Leading with Technology* (Feb.), 30–31.

Mason, T., Roy, P., & Snider, H. (2011). Smart inclusion adventures in the classroom. Closing the Gap Solutions, Minneapolis, MN.

Narkon, D. E. Wells, J. C., & Segal, L. S. (2011). E-word wall: An interactive vocabulary instruction tool for students with learning disabilities and autism spectrum disorders. *Teaching Exceptional Children, 43*(4), 38–45.

Parette, H. P. (2011). Using animation in Microsoft PowerPoint to enhance engagement and learning in young learners with developmental delay. *Teaching Exceptional Children, 43*(4), 58–67.

Ray, L. (2004). The Web and special education. *Computers in the Schools, 21*(3–4), 53–67.

Xin, J. F., & Sutman, F. X. (2011). Using the smart board in teaching social stories to students with autism. *Teaching Exceptional Children, 3*(4), 18–24.

Links:

A wikispace that offers a range of tools to help educators implement Universal Design for Learning **http://udltechtoolkit.wikispaces.com/**

Apps for AAC by Jane Farrall **http://www.spectronicsinoz.com/article/iphoneipad-apps-for-aac**

Apps for Children with Special Needs **http://a4cwsn.com/**

Apps for Literacy Support by Greg O'Connor **http://www.spectronicsinoz.com/article/apps-for-literacy-support http://www.apple.com/education/special-education/**

Apps lists, accessibility tutorials for students with special needs, by Luis F. Perez **http://mobilelearning4specialneeds.wikispaces.com/**

Barb Fernandez's Understanding the iLiteracy Model for Teaching ALL **http://www.scribd.com/doc/60587862/iLiteracy-Model-for-Teaching-All-using-the-iPad**

Center for Applied Special Technology **http://cast.org**

iDevice Apps for Special Education, Eric Sailers (SLP Sharing) **http://slpsharing.com/2011/10/07/iphone-and-ipod-touch-apps-for-special-education/**

Learning in Hand is a resource for educational technology by Tony Vincent. From netbooks and Web applications to iPods, iPads, and podcasting, Tony has put together practical information for educators. **http://learninginhand.com/**

Resource sharing site for Classroom Suite 4 **http://aex.intellitools.com/**

Resource sharing site for SMART solutions **http://exchange.smarttech.com/index.html?lang=en_CA#tab=0**

setBC is an organization that assists British Columbia school districts in supporting students whose access to the curriculum is restricted **http://www.setbc.org/**

Sharing site for information and resources around Smart Inclusion discussed here **http://smartinclusion. wikispaces.com**

SMART Table Virtual User Group **http://exchange.smarttech.com/details. html?id=dd96c998-1d7a-46f2-8c8c-556cb540549c**

    http://smarttech.com

    http://www.prometheanplanet.com

SNOW **http://snow.idrc.ocad.ca/node/195**

Teachers Love Smart Boards: Notebook Lessons, Tips and Tricks **http://smartboards.typepad.com/**

Technology and Media Division Council for Exceptional Children **cec.org**

Tom Barrett's Interesting Ways series **http://edte.ch/blog/interesting-ways**

Subject/Context Index

astigmatism, 223

attention deficit/hyperactivity disorder (AD/HD), 24,
    33, 107, 121, 130–38, 195
  causes, 131
  classroom behaviour, and, 131
  prevalence, 130
  "demonstration" schools, 46
  symptoms, 130

auditory training, 212

augmentative and alternative communication (AAC),
    237–38

Augmentative Communication Services Clinic, 237

autism
  resource guide for, 15
  standards for, 15

Autism Behavior Checklist (ABC), 181

Autism Diagnostic Interview, Revised (ADI-R), 181

Autism Diagnostic Observation Schedule (ADOS), 181

Autism Ontario, 188

Autism Society of Canada, 178, 180, 183, 185

Autism Speaks, 183

autism spectrum disorder (ASD), 21, 22, 24, 177–89
  Applied Behavior Analysis (ABA), and, 183, 184
  characteristics of, 179
  definition of, 177
  diagnosis of, 181–82
  Effective Educational Practices for Students with
    Autism Spectrum Disorders, 15, 185
  genetics, and, 180, 181
  Intensive Behavioural Intervention (IBI), and, 184
  issues, 186–87
  misconceptions about, 177
  pervasive developmental disorders, and, 178
  prevalence, increase in, 35, 37, 179–81
  red flags for, 181
  resource guide for, 15
  standards for, 15
  strategies for, 187–89
  tests, and, 245, 246, 248
  transitions, and, 179
  treatment of, 183–86

autistic disorder, 178

Autonomous Learner Model, 155

B

Barbier, Charles, 228

bands of confidence, 86

bandwagon effect, 186

base level, 249

battery, 250

Beck Youth Inventories, 2nd Edition, for Children and
    Adolescents (BYI-11), 243

Beery VMI, *see* Beery-Buktenica Developmental Test
    of Visual Motor-Integration, 6th Edition, 244

Beery-Buktenica Developmental Test of Visual

Motor-Integration, 6th Edition (Beery VMI), 244

behavioural disorders
  assessment of, 121
  bullying, and, 114, 115
  categories of special needs, 31
  causes of, 117, 118–20
  childhood depression, and, 120
  conceptual models of, 125–26
  conduct disorder, and, 123
  co-occurring disabilities, and, 107
  decrease in, 118
  defining, 122
  identifying signs of, 117, 118
  intervention, and, 127–28
  IQ, and, 115
  issues of, 122–24
  media, and, 118
  misconceptions about, 114–15
  oppositional defiant disorder, and, 124
  reactive attachment disorder, and, 121
  services, and, 114
  strategies for, 133–38
  teachers' perceptions of, 117–18
  terminology, 116
  video games, and, 126–27

Behavior Evaluation Scale, 3rd Edition, The (BES-3),
    244

Behavior Rating Inventory of Executive Function
    (BRIEF), 244

behaviour modification, 127–28, 133, 170, 183, 184,
    236

behavioural intervention, 183, 184

BES-3, *see* Behavior Evaluation Scale, 3rd Edition, The

bilateral hearing loss, 209

Bill 4, 14

Bill 82 (*Education Amendment Act*), 1, 6, 7, 171
  categories of exceptionalities, and, 14, 24, 32–33
  continuing issues in, 10, 19–28
  elements of, 8
  implementation of, 8–9
  Identification, Placement, and Review Committees,
    and, 13, 48–50
  special education and, 251

biophysical approach, 126

Bleuler, Eugen, 179

blind
  schools for, 3, 45
  Talmud, and, 2

blindisms, 230

blindness
  assistive technology, and, 228
  causes of, 222–23
  classifications of, 222
  definitions of, 222

educational implications of, 226–27
issues, 225
misconceptions about, 221
mobility assists, and, 228
placement, and, 228–29
prevalence of, 222
resource teacher, 224
strategies for, 229–30
technological innovations, 225, 253–55
vision problems, classroom checklist, 223
visual disabilities, 116
Bloorview MacMillan Children's Rehabilitation Centre, 4
Boehm Test of Basic Concepts, 83, 244
Bonaparte, Napoleon, 2, 228
Braille, 221, 224, 225, 228
Braille, Louis, 2, 228
BrailleNote, 228
BRIEF, *see* Behavior Rating Inventory of Executive Function
Brigance Comprehensive Inventory of Basic Skills-II (CIBS-II), 83, 244
bullying, 114, 115
Buros Mental Measurement, 243
BYI-11, *see* Beck Youth Inventories, 2nd Edition, for Children and Adolescents

C
CADDRA, *see* Canadian Attention Deficit Hyperactivity Disorder Resource Alliance
Canadian Achievement Test, 4th Edition (CAT-4), 244
Canadian Association of the Deaf, 207, 211
Canadian Attention Deficit Hyperactivity Disorder Resource Alliance, 131
Canadian Charter of Rights and Freedoms, 12, 184
Canadian Cognitive Abilities Test (CCAT), 83, 244
Canadian Council of Ministers of Education, 33
Canadian Hearing Society, 203, 213
Canadian National Committee on Mental Hygiene, 4
Canadian National Institute for the Blind, 203
Canadian Test of Basic Skills (CTBS), 245
cancer, 200
CAPD, *see* central auditory processing disorder
care-based facilities, 6
CARS2, *see* Childhood Autism Rating Scale, 2nd Edition
cascade model, 47–48
cataracts, 223, 225
CAT-4, *see* Canadian Achievement Test, 4th Edition
categories
behaviour disorders, 31, 114–38
communication disorders, 31
autism spectrum disorders, 177–89
learning disabilities, 93–111
speech and language disorders, 232–39

exceptionalities, and, 32, 241–42
intellectual and developmental differences, 31
giftedness, 142–56
intellectual and developmental disorders, 159–74
physical and health difficulties, 31
neurological disabilities, 192–204
sensory disabilities, 31
blindness, 221–30
deafness, 206–18
CBCL, *see* Child Behaviour Checklist
CCAT, *see* Canadian Cognitive Abilities Test Form
CDI2, *see* Kovacs Children's Depression Inventory 2
ceiling level, 249, 250
central auditory processing disorder (CAPD), 99, 235–36
central nervous system disorder (CNS disorder), 96
central nervous system dysfunction, 98
Centre Jules-Leger, 46, 211
cerebral palsy (CP), 192, 193–94, 233, 246
Challenge Program, 10
Child Behavior Checklist (CBCL), 84, 121, 243
Childhood Autism Rating Scale, 2nd Edition (CARS2), 245
childhood depression, 120
childhood disintegrative disorder, 178 , 182
children with exceptionalities
parents' role in education, 9
Children's Memory Scale (CMS), 245
chromosomal abnormality, 166
chronic health conditions, 130, 192, 193, 199, 200
CIBS-II, *see* Brigance Comprehensive Inventory of Basic Skills-II
civil rights movement, 6
classroom strategies
autism spectrum disorders, and, 187–89
behavioural disorders, and, 133–38
deafness, and, 217–18
giftedness, and, 156
intellectual and developmental disabilities, and, 172–73
learning disabilities, and, 109–11
neurological disabilities, and, 203
speech and language disorders, and, 238–39
visual impairment, and, 229–30
CMS, *see* Children's Memory Scale
CNS disorder, *see* central nervous system disorder
cocaine, 166
cochlear implant, 210
cognitive ability, 83, 245, 248, 249
colour blindness, 223
colour deficiency, 223
college connections, 51
Communication Assessment and Support Team, Niagara Peninsula Children's Centre, 119

communication
  autism spectrum disorders, and, 179
  deaf, and, 209–10
  Student Response Systems, and, 255
Community Health Centres, 129
Comprehensive Test of Phonological Processing
  (CTOPP), 245
Computerized Test of Information Processing (CTIP),
  88
computers, 68, 98, 100, 110, 161, 163, 189, 197, 198,
  203, 218, 225, 228, 229, 245
conduct disorder, 123–24
conductive hearing loss, 24, 207
congenital disorders, 207
  facial diplegia, 199
  hearing loss, 208
  heart defects, 167
  malformations, 200
  vision loss, 222
content-area assessment, 85
Continuum Model, 47–48
co-occurring disabilities, 36–37, 107, 108, 199–200
Co-ordinated Services Unit, 15
Coopersmith Self-Esteem Inventory (CSEI), 84, 245
coprolalia, 192, 197
Cornett, Orin, 213
correctional facility, 47
correlation coefficient (r), 250
Council for Children with Behavioral Disorders,
  122–23
Council for Exceptional Children, 56
Council of Directors of Education, 27
CP, *see* cerebral palsy
credit recovery, 51
CSEI, *see* Coopersmith Self-Esteem Inventory
CTBS, *see* Canadian Test of Basic Skills
CTIP, *see* Computerized Test of Information
  Processing
cued speech method, 213
cultural anomalies
  assessment procedures, and, 24
curriculum, adaptations in, 19
curriculum-based assessment, 78
cystic fibrosis, 200

D
DCD, *see* developmental coordination disorder
deaf
  Ponce de Leon, and, 2
  schools for, 45–46
  Talmud, in, 2
deafness, 207
  classifications of, 208
  cochlear implant, and, 210
  communication style, and, 209–10, 212–14

  degrees of, 209
  educational implications, and, 214–16
  hearing aid technology, and, 206, 214
  hearing loss problems, 116, 130
  hearing loss types, and, 207
  indications of, 208
  misconceptions about, 206–7
  placement, and, 211
  prevalence of, 211
  resources for, 44
  strategies for, 217–18
decibel ratings, 209
Detroit Tests of Learning Aptitude, 4th Edition (The
  Detroit-4), 245
development coordination disorder, 195
developmental delay, 94, 194, 199, 203
developmental disabilities, *see* intellectual and
  developmental disabilities
developmentally disabled, school for, 3
DI, *see* Differentiated Instruction
diabetes, 200
diagnosis (and labels), 24
Diagnostic and Statistical Manual of Mental Disorders
  (DSM), 114, 116, 177, 178
diagnostic testing, 250
Differentiated Instruction (DI), 15, 16, 26, 65, 68, 109,
  145, 149
diplegia, 194
diplopia, 223
direct support, 44
dopamine deficiency, 131
Down syndrome, 166, 167, 168
Drewett, Bruce, 64
dropouts, 4
drug therapy, *see* medication
Drury (Ernest C.) School, 45, 211
DSM, *see* *Diagnostic and Statistical Manual of Mental
  Disorders*
Duchenne muscular dystrophy, 195
dyslexia, 96, 98, 102
dyspedagogia, 93

E
EAs, *see* educational assistants
Eaton v. Brant County Board of Education, 12–13
echolalia, 179
ecological view, 7
Education Amendment Act, see Bill 82
*Education for All: The Report of the Expert Panel on
  Literacy and Numeracy Instruction for Students
  with Special Education Needs, Kindergarten to
  Grade 6*, 15, 26, 164
Education for All Handicapped Children Act, Public
  Law 94-142, 6, 8, 116
education plans, *see* Individual Education Plan

education programs for teachers, 9

Educational Programs in Government-Approved Facilities for Care, Treatment and Custodial or Correctional Purposes (Section 23s), 47

Education Quality and Accountability Office (EQAO) tests, 38

educational assistants (EAs), 9, 11, 44, 55–56, 106, 170, 188, 200, 202, 203, 238

  qualifications, 56

  role of, 55–56

Effective Educational Practices for Students with Autism Spectrum Disorders, 15, 185

elective mutism, 235

emotional disorders, *see* behavioural disorders

emotional intelligence, 148

emotionally disturbed, 116, 179

empathy, 109

employment and vocational training, 165

enrichment programs, 155

Enrichment Triad Model, 144–45, 154, 155

environmental approach, 126

epilepsy

  absence seizures, 195, 196, 203

  ancient Greece, and, 2

  dealing with seizures, 196

  fetal alcohol syndrome, and, 168

  tonic-clonic seizures, 195

Epilepsy Association, 196, 203

Epi-pens, 200

epiloia, 166

EQAO, *see* Education Quality and Accountability Office

eugenics, 4, 5

"evidence–based" research, 27

exceptional students

  defining, 31–33, 241

  percentage of school-age population, as, 33–35

  numbers by type, 37–38

exceptionalities

  categories of, 241–42

eye infections, 24

F

facilitated communication (FC), 185

FAE, *see* fetal alcohol effects

FAS, *see* fetal alcohol syndrome

FASD, *see* fetal alcohol spectrum disorder

FC, *see* facilitated communication

feeble-minded, 2, 4, 160

fetal alcohol effects (FAE), 118, 168

fetal alcohol spectrum disorder (FASD), 168

fetal alcohol syndrome (FAS), 118, 130, 166

fingerspelling, 213, 214

fluency disorder, 234

Focus Adolescent Services, 123

formal tests, 83, 87–90

Frames of Mind (Gardner), 147

French Sign Language (FSL), 213

funding, 19, 22–23, 34

  in non-school settings, 47

G

Gallagher, James, 154

Gardner, Howard, 147, 151

Gates-MacGinitie Reading Tests, 2nd Canadian Edition, 246

gender

  behavioural disorders, and, 114, 118

  bullying, and, 115

  colour deficiency/blindness, and, 223

  conduct disorder, and, 123

  intellectual and developmental difficulties, and, 159

  Duchenne muscular dystrophy, and, 195

  Rett's disorder, and, 178

  stuttering, and, 232

  video games, and, 127

genetic research, 119, 169

  see also heredity

giftedness, 142

  characteristics of, 144

  defined, 143–45

  enrichment programs, and, 155

  Enrichment Triad Model, and, 145

  issues of, 148–49

  misconceptions about, 142

  nomination process, and, 151–52

  organizational models, and, 153–55

  Pentagonal Implicit Theory of Giftedness, and, 146

  strategies for, 156

  Triarchic Theory of Intellectual Giftedness, and, 146

  underachievers, and, 152

glaucoma, 223

Globe and Mail, 131

glossary of testing terms, 249–50

Goddard, H. H., 160

Goethe, Johann Wolfgang von, 2

Goleman, Daniel, 148

GPS tracking devices, 225, 228

grand mal seizures, *see* tonic-clonic seizures

Gray, Carol, 185

Gray Centre for Social Learning and Understanding, 185

Grey's Anatomy, 187

guide dogs, 221, 228

H

hard-to-serve, 7, 14

hearing aids, 206, 214

hearing impaired

  resources for, 44

hearing loss problems, *see under* deafness
hemiplegia, 194
heredity, 93
  see also genetic research
Hincks Delcrest Children's Centre, 117
Hippocrates, 2
Hoffman, Dustin, 187
Hoffman, Heinrich, 131
Hope Commission, 5
hospital schools, 38
House Rules, 187
Human Rights Commission, Ontario, 5
hydrocephalus, 194
hygiene, 44, 170, 202
hyperactivity, 94, 118, 128, 130, 131, 133, 168, 185, 195, 197
  see also attention deficit/hyperactivity disorder
hyperkinesis, 131
hyperopia, 224

I

iatrogenic disorder, 123
IBI, *see* Intensive Behavioural Intervention
ICT Competency Standards for Teachers 2008, 252
Identification, Placement, and Review Committees (IPRCs), 8, 13, 15, 21, 34, 48–50, 121, 171
  appeal process, 8, 11, 76–77
  concerns, 24
  Eaton Case, and, 12
  establishment of, 10
  Individual Education Plan, and, 60
  not always necessary, 10, 34, 49
  parental role in, 10, 11
  section 23 placement, and, 47
  steps in, 75–77
IEP, *see* Individual Education Plan
immigrant families, 24–25
improved access, 26
inclusion, *see* integration
Individual Education Plan (IEP), ix, 6, 9, 10, 13, 15, 19, 34, 41, 50–51, 58–73, 200
  case studies, and, 91
  chronic health needs, and, 200
  contents of form, 20, 65
  definition of, 59–60
  development of, 21, 64–66
  Differentiated Instruction, and, 109
  direction setting, and, 62–64
  educational assistants, and, 55
  Identification, Placement, and Review Committee, and, 43, 59, 60
  implementation of, 66
  information gathering, and, 61–62
  parental involvement, and, 67
  policy requirements for, 59

preparation of, 60–61
process of, 41–43, 61–64
purpose of, 41
re-examination, and, 43
Regulation 181/98, and, 59
referral, and, 40
resource document, 10, 11
responsibility for, 67
review of, 66
school teams, and, 42, 68–73
Individuals with Disabilities Education Act (IDEA), 122, 130
Informal tests, 82
Institute of Biomaterials and Biomedical Engineering, 194
integration, 12, 13, 20, 47, 164
  prerequisites for success, 165
intellectual and developmental disabilities
  assessment and placement, and, 170–71
  causes, concern for, 166–67
  definitions, 160–62
  inclusion, and, 20, 164–65
  instructional implications, and, 167
  IQ test scores and, 161
  issues of, 163–67
  mental retardation, and, 160, 171, 179
  misconceptions about, 159
  strategies for, 172–73
intelligence quotient (IQ), 83, 145, 159, 248, 250
Intensive Behavioural Intervention (IBI), 184, 186
Interactive Whiteboard (IWB) stations, 253
Internet, 199
Intervention-focused assessment, 80
Iowa Test of Basic Skills, 245
IPRCs, *see* Identification, Placement, and Review Committees
itinerant teachers, 203, 211, 224
IQ, *see* intelligence quotient
IQ tests, 83, 96
  behavioural disorders, and, 115
  Canadian Cognitive Abilities Test Form, vs., 245
  cerebral palsy, and, 194
  deaf students, and, 212
  gifted students, and, 142, 146, 151, 152
  inadequacy of, 147
  intellectual and developmental disabilities, and, 159, 160, 161, 166, 169
  learning disabilities, and, 94
Itard, Jean Marc, 2
IWB, *see* Interactive Whiteboard Stations

J

Jones, Reginald, 23
Journal of Adolescence, 127

K

K-ABC-II, *see* Kaufman Assessment Battery for
    Children, 2nd Edition
Kanner, Leo, 179
Kaufman Assessment Battery for Children, 2nd
    Edition (K-ABC-II), 246
Keymath 3 Diagnostic Assessment, 246
Kirk, Samuel, 21, 95
Klinefelter syndrome, 166
Kovacs Children's Depression Inventory 2 (CDI 2), 246

L

labels, 23, 24, 178
Lancet, 177
language disorders, *see* speech and language disorders
language milestones, 234–35
Langue de Signes Québécoise (LSQ), 213
learned helplessness, 167, 170, 173
learning disabilities
    assessment of, 106–8
    characteristics of, 98–105
    definitions of, 94–97
    dyslexia, vs., 102
    identification of, 21, 106–8
    issues of, 107–8
    misconceptions about, 93
    school problems, and, 105
    special schools for, 46
    strategies for, 109–11
    term creation, 4, 95
Learning Disabilities Association of Ontario, 7, 96
Learning for All, K–12, 15, 26, 28, 35, 164
least restrictive environment, 12
legal blindness, 222
Leiter International Performance Scale, Revised, 246
l'Épée, Charles Michel de, 213
Levin, Ben, 49
linguistic difficulties, 24
lip reading, 207
    see also speech reading, 207
Locke, John, 2
LSQ, *see* Langue de Signes Québécoise

M

Macdonald (W. Ross) School, 45, 211
macular degeneration, 224
mainstreaming, *see* integration
major depressive disorder, 246
malleable intelligence, 167
manualism, *see* sign language
MASC, *see* Multidimensional Anxiety Scale for
    Children
maturation lag, 96
MD, *see* muscular dystrophy
McCann, John Barrett, 3

McCarthy Scales of Children's Abilities, 247
Mcdonald, Ronald, 3
measles, 207
media, 21, 28, 130, 187
mediation, 13, 14
medical information, 193
medical model, 7
medication, 120, 125, 126, 128
meningitis, 207
meningocele, 194
mental retardation, *see under* intellectual and
    developmental disabilities, 160
Merrick, John, 3
metacognition, 103
MHS, *see* Multihealth Systems Publishing Company
mild intellectual disability, 166
minimal brain dysfunction, 131
minimally brain-injured, 96
Minister of Education, 13
Ministry of Health and Long Term Care, 237
minorities, 24
mnemonics, 111
Mobius syndrome, 199
modifications and accommodations, 41, 43, 52, 64, 229
monocular vision, 224
moral deficit, 131
motor disorders, 194
Mountbatten Brailler, 228
Mozart, Wolfgang Amadeus, 185
MRI technology, 96
Multidimensional Anxiety Scale for Children (MASC),
    247
Multihealth Systems Publishing Company (MHS), 88
multiple disabilities, 199–200
multiple exceptionalities, 36–37
multiple intelligences, 147
multiple menu model, 154
mumps, 207
muscular dystrophy (MD), 192, 195
mutism, 169, 206, 235
myopia, 224

N

National Advisory Committee of Handicapped
    Children, 95
National Association for the Deaf, 211
National Autism Center, 185
National Joint Committee on Learning Disabilities
    (USA), 98
National Standards Report, 185
NBC (broadcasting), 187
Neuro Trauma Foundation of Ontario, 32
neurological disabilities
    advocacy groups, and, 203
    classroom implications of, 202–3

SRS, *see* Student Response Systems
standard error of measurement (SEM), 90
Stanford-Binet Intelligence Scale, 5th Edition (SB5), 247–48
Sternberg, Robert, 143, 146, 149, 151
Still, George, 131
strabismus, 224, 225
strategies, *see* classroom strategies
Student Diagnostic Profile (SDP), 244
Student Response Systems (SRS), 255
Student Support Leadership Initiative, 129
stuttering, 232, 234
sub-average intellectual functioning, 160
supervised alternative learning for excused pupils programs (SALEP), 52
Supreme Court of Canada, 11, 12–13, 184, 186
surgical implantation surgery, 210
sympathetic ophthalmia, 223
syntax, 101, 111, 210, 214, 235
syphilis, 166

T
tabula rasa, 2
Talmud, 2
task analysis, 174
TBI, *see* traumatic brain injury
TEACCH program, *see* Treatment and Education of Autistic and related Communication Handicapped Children
Teacher Education Programs, 9, 107
teacher training, 28, 46, 65
Teaching Students Who Are Gifted and Talented: Programming for Children with Special Needs, 143
teams, *see* school teams
technology, use of, 98, 173, 252
Temple Grandin, 187
Terman, Lewis, 151
Test of Reading Comprehension, 4th Edition (TORC-4), 248
tests, 61–62, 82–83, 87–90
    see also assessment
therapy, 183, 192, 193
three-ring model, 145
time to learn, 165
time management, 104
Tomatis method, 185
Tomlinson, Carol Ann, 26
tonic-clonic seizures, 195
TORC-4, *see* Test of Reading Comprehension, 4th Edition
Total Communication Method, 213, 214, 216
Tourette syndrome (TS), 121, 131, 192, 193, 197, 202
Tourette Syndrome Foundation, 203
trait plasticity, 167

transition plan, 41, 52, 66, 77, 170
traumatic brain injury (TBI), *see* acquired brain injury
Treatment and Education of Autistic and related Communiocation Handicapped Children (TEACCH), 185
Treves, Frederick, 3
Triad Model, *see* Enrichment Triad Model
Triarchic Theory of Intellectual Giftedness, 146
tribunals, 13
Trillium School, 46
TS, *see* Tourette syndrome
tuberous sclerosis, 166, 199
tunnel vision, 224
twice-exceptional learners, 154
types of exceptionalities, *see under* categories

U
UDL, *see* Universal Design for Learning
underachievers, gifted, 151
United States Congress, 6
United States National Institute of Mental Health, 181
Universal Design for Learning (UDL), 15, 16, 26, 65, 68, 149, 164
University of Toronto, 194
U.S. Centers for Disease Control and Prevention, 180
U.S. Public Law 94-142, *see Education for All Handicapped Children Act*

V
vaccination, 177
video games, 126–27, 253
Vineland Adaptive Behavior Scales, 171, 248
violence, 114, 126, 127
visual impairment, 116, 221–30
    cerebral palsy, and, 199
    checklist for, 223
    see also blindness
visual stimulation, 227
voice disorders, 234
voice recognition, 173
voice-activated cell phones, 225
Voltaire, 2

W
Wechsler Individual Achievement Test, 2nd Edition (WIAT-II), 83, 248
Wechsler Intelligence Scale for Children, 4th Edition (WISC-IV), 83, 151, 170, 248–49
Whitney (Sir James) School, 45, 211
WIAT-II, *see* Wechsler Individual Achievement Test, 2nd Edition
Wide Range Achievement Test-4 (WRAT-4), 249
Williams syndrome, 169
WISC-IV, *see* Wechsler Intelligence Scale for Children, 4th Edition

WJ-R, *see* Woodcock-Johnson Psycho-Educational Battery, Revised

Wolfensberger, Wolf, 6

Woodcock Diagnostic Reading Battery, 83

Woodcock Reading Mastery Tests, Revised, Normative Update (WRMT-R/NU), 249

Woodcock-Johnson Psycho-Educational Battery, Revised (WJ-R), 249

Woodcock-Johnson III Tests of Achievement, Normative Update, 249

Working Table on Special Education, report of, 65

WRAT-4, *see* Wide Range Achievement Test

WRMT-R/NU, *see* Woodcock Reading Mastery Tests, Revised, Normative Update

Z

zero tolerance, 118

Author Index

(As included in the *Readings and Resources* sections at the end of chapters.)